ITALY AND THE WEST

COMPARATIVE ISSUES IN ROMANIZATION

ITALY AND THE WEST

COMPARATIVE ISSUES IN ROMANIZATION

Edited by
Simon Keay and Nicola Terrenato

Oxbow Books

Published by
Oxbow Books, Park End Place, Oxford OX1 1HN

© Oxbow Books, 2001

ISBN 1 84217 042 2

A CIP record for this book is available from the British Library

This book is available direct from
Oxbow Books, Park End Place, Oxford OX1 1HN
(Phone: 01865-241249; Fax: 01865-794449)

and

The David Brown Book Company
PO Box 511, Oakville, CT06779
(Phone: 860-945-9329; Fax: 860-945-9468)

and

via our website
www.oxbowbooks.com

Cover: Porta di Giove, Falerii Novi, Italy

Printed in Great Britain by
The Short Run Press
Exeter

Contents

List of Contributors

SUSAN ALCOCK
Department of Classical Studies
University of Michigan
2160 Angell Hall 435 S. State St.
Ann Arbor, MI 48109-1003
USA

JEAN ANDREAU
École des Hautes Études en Sciences Sociales
54, Boulevard Raspail
75006 Paris
France

ELENA ANTONACCI
Museo Civico di Foggia
Piazza Nigri 1
71100 Foggia
Italy

ENRICO BENELLI
Soprintendenza Archeologica per le Marche
Via Birarelli 18
60121 Ancona
Italy

MARCELO CASTRO LOPEZ
Centro Andaluz de Arqueologia Iberica
Universidad de Jaen
Paraje de Lagunillas s/n
Edif. B. 1
23071 Jaen
Spain

EMMANUELE CURTI
Department of History
Birkbeck College
Malet St.
London
WC1E 7EX
UK

SERGIO FONTANA
Via Clementina 11
Roma 00184
Italy

MARIA PAOLA GUIDOBALDI
Soprintendenza Archeologica di Pompei
Via Villa dei Misteri 2
80045 Pompeii
Italy

LUIS GUTIERREZ SOLER
Centro Andaluz de Arqueologia Iberica
Universidad de Jaen
Paraje de Lagunillas s/n
Edif. B. 1
23071 Jaen
Spain

SIMON JAMES
School of Archaeological Studies
University of Leicester
Leicester
LE1 7RH
UK

SIMON KEAY
Department of Archaeology
University of Southampton
Southampton
SO17 1BJ
UK

ANTHONY KING
King Alfred's College
Winchester
SO22 4NR
UK

MASSIMILIANO MUNZI
Via Primo Acciaresi 4
Rome 00157
Italy

NICOLA TERRENATO
Assistant Professor of Classical Archaeology
Department of Classics
University of North Carolina-Chapel Hill
North Carolina
USA

JEAN-PIERRE VALLET
UFR LSHS
Université Paris 13
Avenue Jean-Baptiste Clément
93430 Villetaneuse
France

PETER VAN DOMMELEN
Department of Archaeology
University of Glasgow
Glasgow
G1 8QQ
UK

JONATHAN WILLIAMS
The British Museum
London
WC1B 3DG
UK

GREGORY WOOLF
School of Greek, Latin and Ancient History
University of St Andrews
St Andrews
Fife
KY16 9AL
UK

The debate on Romanization has been active for many decades now, but recently its intensity has been increasing and its scope expanding. The range of approaches and ideas which have been discussed in recent years is extremely wide and it has included very strong criticism of the very use of the term (e.g. Barrett 1997; Van Dommelen, this volume: 72). For this reason, it is appropriate to begin this book with a few words justifying the use of the word Romanization. Even if they do not necessarily assign the same meaning to it, most of the contributors to this volume obviously still believe that is a useful tool that designates a field of research. At the same time, there is no denying that when Romanization was first introduced, it was an extremely value-laden term, which was entirely appropriate to a contemporary nationalist and colonialist ideology. As always happens, however, old concepts can be redefined to serve radically different agendas: stripped of their 'baggage', they can take on a new lease on life, if they are not devalued by largely fruitless semantic debate. In the current context, Romanization can be used in a weak sense and still prove very useful to our debate. In other words, it can be used simply as a convenient label that refers loosely to events involved in the creation of a new and unified political entity, although it should be not be used to describe the occurrence or direction of acculturation between Romans and non-Romans. There is no doubt that this process brought about the creation of a new cultural universe. However, it should be remembered that this entity called itself "Roman", rather than Romano-African, Hispano-Roman, Romano-British or Gallo-Roman (Woolf 1997), even though it had begun to lose its ethnic connotations as far back as the early Iron Age and was to become little more than a denomination.

We have to face the apparent paradox that at least two very different cultural groupings have shared this denomination "Roman". There was the original culture of the city-state of Rome, which was rooted in the Latin Iron Age, and the late Republican and Imperial culture, which resulted from a cross-fertilization of the Hellenistic mentality with a variety of central and western Mediterranean and European perspectives. The latter constellation of cultures came to be known as "Roman", even if, from our point of view, it had at least as good a claim to be called "Greek" or "Native". This apparently confusing situation is illustrated by the fact that the cultural transformations that took place in Rome itself between the fourth and the second centuries BC can be described as the Romanization of Rome. In this process, the traditional culture of the city, to the disbelief of many old-timers, such as Cato the Censor, was heavily transformed by external influences to become something very different. Its name may have remained the same, but its structure was different and it had lost its homogeneity.

In our parlance, therefore, the term "Romanization" can be retained to designate the formation of this 'second' and composite Roman culture with all of its complex implications, ranging from the diffusion of new ideas and straight acculturation all the way to cultural resistance, conservation and the bricolage of old concepts. This transition played a key role in the cultural and political trajectories of most of the communities bordering the Mediterranean, including Rome itself, and there are many elements that can be profitably compared in different contexts. Even if "Romanization" displays a very marked variability at local level, as most of the contributions in this volume argue, common themes and cross-currents still occur, sometimes unexpectedly, and even in radically different situations. Indeed, the use of the term "Romanization" as an umbrella term, as in the title of this book, has made it much easier to characterize the arena of the contributors' discourse.

Notwithstanding the recent massive scholarly output on "Romanization", there are still connections and avenues that have remained comparatively unexplored. Perhaps the most striking, at least from our point of view, is the very limited dialogue on the subject between scholars investigating Italy and the provinces, particularly those in the west. In most works dealing with the Romanization of the provinces, for example, the cultural uniformity of Italy is taken for granted, and the adjective "Italian" is simply used as a synonym to avoid repeating "Roman" too many times. Alternatively, the on-going debate about the Romanization of Italy has largely ignored contemporary developments in the western provinces, with the implicit belief that as the Italian situation was unique, it has needed to be addressed in isolation.

In a sense there has long been an underlying dialogue between academics investigating the historic, artistic, architectural, epigraphic or economic relationships between Italy and its Mediterranean neighbours, although this has rarely been explicit, heavily empircist and usually discussed in terms of influences flowing from Rome outwards. However, when it has come to the analysis of the phenomenon of cultural change, or Romanization, in general, the interests of those researching Italy and the provinces have seldom coincided, with the exception of a handful of scholars. Consequently, the dynamics of one of the most fundamental cultural relationships in the western Empire, that which existed between Rome, Italy and the western provinces, remain largely unstudied. Moreover, the potential synergies between contrasting north and south European academic traditions have never been tapped. The more traditional and historical approaches current in Italy (for example, Torelli 1999), Spain (for example Blázquez and Alvar 1996) and, to a degree, France (for example, David 1997) still stand in isolation to the theoretically aware studies of Romanization and cultural change in Britain, the United States and the low countries (for example Millett 1990, Blagg and Millett 1990, Metzler *et alii* 1995; Webster and Cooper 1996).

This polarized situation is somewhat unsatisfactory. Italian-centred research into the subject is still influenced by a strict philological and historicist approach, which justifies itself by the exceptional abundance of documentary information. This approach has generated rich narratives dealing with the process of expansion and its material correlates. They have taken the singularity of Italian events for granted, and have implicitly assumed that they could only be interpreted on their own terms. Similar perspectives continue to dominate research in Spain, Portugal and, in some quarters, France. By contrast, recent debates about the emergence of the north-western provinces of the Roman Empire have developed intriguing new theoretical approaches, which have brought the issue of 'Romanization' close to the broader themes of other social sciences and thus enhanced the value of their interpretative models. They have been influenced by the work of regional archaeological traditions, or "schools", which have in common a relative abundance of high quality archaeological data and a scarcity of epigraphic and historical sources. They have approached the debate by breaking down the rigid barriers of classicism, and experimenting with social reconstructions that depart radically from the text-dependant traditional narratives.

This polarization of approaches in the study of "Romanization" has come about through a surprising lack of communication, which has impeded attempts to draw comparisons between Rome and Italy, and the provinces. At times it has degenerated into a mutual disregard that, although rarely openly expressed, can be clearly read between the lines. Studies of Italy, for example, were implicitly regarded as little more than narrow-minded and parochial historicism, while those of the western provinces were naive and banale reductionism at its worst. While it is all too easy to bemoan this impasse, a careful review of the literature suggests that there is an alternative approach that it is the intention of this book to broach. It is our contention that a cross-fertilization of ideas from both traditions could produce important new results by taking a fresh look at comparative issues and comparable elements. The success of this hinges upon a recognition of the detailed specialist skills of the Italian and broader Mediterranean tradition as well as the achievements of the broader and more stimulating theoretical work of Roman provincial archaeology. In a post-modern perspective, nobody can afford to forego the wealth of contextual information that characterizes Italy or the stimulating new insights of the provincial work. The Romanization of the peninsula provides an almost complete repertory of well-documented individual situations, while the western provinces offer us the opportunity to test elaborate models and to explicitly illustrate the variables at work.

This book represents a first attempt to bridge this divide and to develop a common language for looking at cultural change in the western Roman Empire, and to evaluate some received ideas about Romanization. It is hoped that at the very least, it will provide a starting point for future discussions about the archaeological evidence for the relationship between Italy and the western provinces.

It was originally conceived as a session at the Third Annual Meeting of the *European Association of Archaeologists* at Ravenna in 1997, with the intention that its results should be published. The speakers for Italy were Emmanuele Curti, Elena Antonacci, Rick Jones, Peter Van Dommelen, Massimiliano Munzi, Maria Paola Guidobaldi, Nicola Terrenato, Jonathan Williams, Enrico Benelli and Jean-Pierre Vallat. The original list of speakers for the western provinces session consisted of Simon Keay, Marcelo Castro López, Luis María Gutiérrez, Greg Woolf, Thierry Odiot and Jean-Luc Fiches, Sergio Fontana, Anthony King and Gonzalo Ruiz Zapatero. This publication involved the inclusion of most of the above papers, together with commissioning two others (Simon James and Sue Alcock) to broaden the coverage.

The structure of the book is straightforward. It begins with a series of Italian case-studies, that are followed by a reflective discussion (Vallat). The second part of the book comprises six provincial studies from the western provinces, followed by a discussion from a specialist in the early Roman archaeology of the eastern Mediterranean (Alcock). The aim has been, therefore, to establish a dialogue between Italy and the western provinces and to contextualize it within broader discussions. The chronological scope of the Italian section essentially concerns the Republican period, a critical moment in the emergence of 'Roman' Italy. That of the provinces is contingent upon the key moments of contact and integration into the Roman empire, ranging from the later Republic (the Hispaniae) down to the mid 1st century AD (Britain). This does not mean to say that 'Romanization' is an issue that only concerns the period between the late Republic and the early years of the Empire. The development and 'Romanization' (in the senses defined in this book) of provincial communities was an ongoing process that was integral to the changing character of the Roman Empire that continued throughout the first two centuries AD. However, this is a horizon that raises a range of different and complex issues, such as belonging within and 'experiencing' the Roman empire, which are best left for another forum of discussion. It will also be noticed that, with one exception, the role of the army has been excluded from exlicit discussion in the volume. This can be partially explained by the chronological horizon chosen for discussion; the mobility of the Roman army for much of the Republic makes this less susceptible for study than the imperial period, when the permanent presence of the army in frontier provinces made it a powerful catalyst for social, economic and cultural change. At the same time, the focus of attention away from military issues in the volume could also be seen as a reaction against the privileged position that military studies have hitherto occupied in the discussion of Romanization in the north-western provinces of the Roman empire.

Following the completion of all the contributions to the book, the editors were invited by the *École des Hautes Études en Sciences Sociales* (Jean Andreau, Claudia Moatti and Jean-Pierre Vallat) to a pre-publication presentation of the book in Paris in June 2000. This generated a range of very positive reactions and comments that are summarised at the end of the book in the form of a short closing commentary by Jean Andreau. This, together, with the range of the contributions themselves, and the two discussion papers by Vallat and Alcock, has ensured that the book has a truly international perspective on a crucial issue in Roman archaeology.

The editors would like to thank all the speakers and the authors for their contributions to the Session and the book. They are also particularly grateful to Maurizio Tosi and the organizers of the original conference, as well as to the Universities of North Carolina at Chapel Hill and Southampton for their help and support. Translations of papers into English were drafted by Kathryn McDonnell and Hugh Cayliss, and revised by the editors.

References

Blagg, T. and Millett, M. (eds.) 1990. *The Early Roman Empire in the West*. Oxbow: Oxford.

Barrett, J. 1997. Romanization: a critical comment. In D. J. Mattingly (ed.) *Dialogues in Roman Imperialism*. JRA: Portsmouth, pp. 51–64.

Blázquez, J. M. and Alvar, J. (eds.) 1996. *La romanización en occidente*. Actas: Madrid.

David, J. M. 1997. *The Roman Conquest of Italy*. Blackwell: Oxford.

Metzler, J., Millett, M., Roymans, N. and Slofstra, J. (eds.). *Integration in the Early Roman West. The role of Culture and Ideology*. Dossiers D'Archéologie du Musée National D'Histoire et D'Art IV: Luxembourg.

Millett, M. 1990. *The Romanization of Britain*. CUP: Cambridge.

Torelli, M. 1995. *Studies in the Romanization of Italy*. University of Alberta: Edmonton.

Woolf, G. 1997. Beyond Romans and Natives. *World Archaeology* 28: 339–350.

Webster, J. and Cooper, N. 1996. *Roman Imperialism: post colonial perspectives*. School of Archaeological Studies: Leicester.

PART 1
ITALY

Chapter 1

Introduction

Nicola Terrenato

The scholarship on the Romanization of Italy displays some very specific traits that may be worth mentioning briefly, by way of introduction to the series of papers dealing with various geographical contexts of the peninsula. Perhaps the main new trend that can be discerned in the studies collected here, as well as in the recent literature, is a wide-ranging reassessment of established models. Indeed, archaeological research in the last decade or so has begun to pose a strong challenge to some key issues constituting the received wisdom about the Romanization of Italy. As a parallel development, there have been also successful attempts at deconstructing the very roots of the traditional views, which have reviewed the formation of ideas on this issue, especially as far as the Italian and German tradition are concerned (Linderski 1984; Frézouls 1983). In brief, their crucial insight is the critique of the basic perception of Romanization as the triumph of a superior and more advanced culture over primitive communities, and one that was brought about by military expansion and which resulted in the creation of a very uniform political and cultural entity. This view, clearly articulated for the first time by nineteenth century German and Italian scholars, seems to be overly influenced by the modern Romantic concept of nation-state. The Roman Empire is indeed treated as if it were a contemporary nation, marking a very sharp break with much of the Renaissance and Enlightenment thought on the subject (Desideri 1991). Significantly, the foundations of our historiography on Roman expansion in Italy were laid down in an age that witnesses the suppression of local identities in Germany and Italy, with the essentially failed hope of forging a modern nation-state out of many smaller regional entities.

The idealism prevailing in the first half of our century and the Marxism that took over after the second world war, although for radically different reasons, did little to modify the belief in Italy as a solid cultural block, cementing together pervasively acculturated communities (Terrenato 1998). Throughout this line of scholarship, what really went unquestioned was the cultural outcome of Romanization. Politically, it may have been defined a federation, a confederation or an empire, but there was no doubt that all Italians had become a solid block by the end of the Social War (Munzi, this volume). It is only our generation that is beginning to appreciate the variety of responses that Romanization elicited among the various ethnic groups, social classes, genders, spheres and even within the same person in different conjunctures of his or her life. In this new approach, the nature and the impact of Romanization can begin to be assessed in a realistic way. No new orthodoxy should be sought, but rather, in a framework of explicit dialectics, a wider arena to accommodate debate and different reconstructions should be created.

It is clear that this new perspective has had deep implications for our perception of Roman imperialism. It is not surprising thus to see that a lively exchange of opinions has recently taken place on the topic (eg Woolf 1993; 1997; Mattingly 1997). Not enough attention, however, in the excitement of trying out new global interpretations, has been so far paid to the issue of early Roman expansion in Italy. The formative phase that enables Rome to transcend a mere regional role may hold a decisive clue to understand the nature of the resulting entity: the Roman Empire. In particular, there is an essential component that seems to have been underestimated in most mainstream historical reconstructions of the conquest, which treat it as a one-way process: we have ample evidence of the bi-directional negotiation between the Italian communities and Rome. Whatever explanation is called into question for expansion, from the quest for economic exploitation, to simple defensive reactions, or the militaristic structure of Roman society, the possible *motivations* for the Italian peoples to become part of the new political entity are seldom taken into account (e.g. Harris 1979). Although there is significant evidence that entire communities or smaller groups had been not unwilling to become part of a larger entity, why they did so is a question that has seldom been asked. Answering it is crucial if we are to understand how Roman Italy was kept together for more than half a millennium.

Some observations on the archaeology of early Roman expansion

In the current analyses of the process of expansion two main interpretative lines are generally followed: one based on military and political factors and the other on economic ones (a very clear synthesis in Woolf 1993). In rough terms, they are respectively the product of primitivist and modernist approaches to ancient societies. The former, still dominant in Anglo-American scholarship and elsewhere, sees expansion as a reflex generated by the peculiar social and political structure characterizing Rome. In the latter, more widespread in Italy and France, territorial expansion is seen as an essential ingredient for the proto-capitalist revolution of the late Roman Republic.

Let us consider what archaeology has been recently contributing to this debate. A main role has been undoubtedly played by rural areas. Field surveys, for instance, are showing a wide variety of different situations; so much so that some historians understandably seem to be despairing of ever obtaining a clear picture (eg Patterson 1987). Some common trends, however, seem to be discernible in this strong variability. Perhaps the most striking one is the massive increase in the density of rural habitation that takes place between the fourth and the second centuries BC. This is a complex phenomenon that cannot be simply taken at face value in terms of demographic expansion. It is possible that some of the rural population only becomes archaeologically visible in this period, possibly as a result of the increasingly diagnostic ceramic productions or improved standards of living for the lower classes. Whatever its precise nature, this discontinuity is the sharpest in the rural history of many Italian regions. It is an indicator that had been already been picked up decades ago by projects such as the South Etruria Survey (Potter 1979), the Ager Cosanus (Attolini *et al.* 1991) or other work in Campania

(Arthur 1991). The problem, however, is that in these regions the process broadly coincides with the period of the conquest. Thus, it is not surprising that both elements were seen to be linked or that this 'boom' in the number of farms was understood to have been a direct consequence of Roman expansion and, specifically, the confiscation and redistribution of land. In recent years, this interpretative framework, favoured especially by those believing in an economic explanation for Roman imperialism, has begun to be tested in other regions of Italy. The results of this work seem to contradict the simple equation that saw rural expansion as an immediate consequence of Romanization. Survey in areas such as the Biferno (Barker 1995) or the Cecina Valleys (Terrenato and Saggin 1994), have recorded similar settlement intensification during the Hellenistic phase, although here it preceded the Roman conquest. This raises doubts about the causal link between incorporation within the Roman state and the appearance of new sites in the countryside. The appearance of farms in most of Italy probably needs a radically different interpretation, which has yet to be debated. At the present time, however, what could be provocatively said is that we cannot exclude the opposite conclusion: namely, that the diffusion of this settlement type may be part of a phenomenon that makes the unification of Italy feasible. But this suggestion would take us beyond the scope of this paper.

When reviewed closely in the light of the above, economic expansionism seems to become increasingly weak as an argument: the intensification of agriculture cannot be taken as a direct consequence of the historical process. A few more words need to be said about villas. These sites are often seen as having a second massive impact on the countryside after the spread of farms and as having played a key role in the complete revolution of the Italian economy. However, this interpretation needs to be reassessed with updated information. It is now clear that villas appear in a variety of cultural, geographic and chronological contexts with completely different functions. They range from country residences for local elites with architectonic tastes influenced by Rome, to establishments involved in the capital-intensive exploitation of the most diverse neighbouring resources (Terrenato 1998a:113). Their appearance sometimes brings about a transformation in modes of production. However, this appears to have been a limited phenomenon and certainly cannot be taken as the main driving force behind the expansion of villa settlement as a whole. It is sufficient to point out that villas are found in areas where the pre-Roman economic equilibrium remains vastly unchanged with the conquest.

The closest parallel for Romanization in Italy is perhaps Hellenization, in the sense that it was a process that reduced differences across a range of disparate phenomena such as elite taste, the organization of land or political systems, across a peninsula where local and ethnic peculiarities always played the strongest role (Curti *et al.* 1996). This shift in the dialectic between localism and globalism produces a new entity, a new cultural habitat, in which the previously shocking prospect of unification becomes suddenly acceptable. This alternative explanation for the creation of Roman Italy places a far greater emphasis on the elements of convergence and spontaneity than ever before. Furthermore, it suggests that the new federation existed only because the majority (although by no means the totality) of Italians were in favour or neutral about it. If we accept this perspective, it is clearly the negotiation between elites that is materially responsible for the making things happen. It must be recalled that the forces that drew Italian aristocracies together had been at work since the archaic period. Horizontal mobility between elites was always a very strong component, expressing itself in many ways, from intermarriage between neighbouring elites, and the resettlement of entire clans, to the coups and countercoups that were endemic in the period and are epitomized by the bloody scenes depicted in the François tomb. Notwithstanding all this strong interaction, centrifugal forces always prevailed right up to the Hellenistic age. From the fourth/third century BC onwards, the balance is inclined in favour of those social and cultural groups which, in Roman and non-Roman communities, saw stronger integration as a positive development. Precisely who these people are, why they favour integration and what exactly happens at the material and ideological level are three basic questions that in my opinion should rank very high in the research agenda on the Romanization of Italy. Some relevant data and interpretation is beginning to emerge in the contributions collected here. It appears clearly, to give only one example, that the ruling elites of many urbanized communities played a major role in the process of expansion, while their equivalents in less structured or non-sedentary ethnic groups put up fierce resistance. Integration probably also appealed to the former social groups as a way of maintaining control over their dependent classes. With the creation of an overarching structure and of a federal army, the aristocratic order of the individual city-states was much better guaranteed. The role of Rome in cases of civic unrest, even in situations outside its own territory, is very significant. Many further observations in the same vein should be added to this, if we are to fully understand the factors that brought about such a radical change in Italian equilibria.

Having discussed economic explanations for Roman expansion, there is still the opposite interpretation: namely, that of seeing the Roman Empire as the result of unplanned militarism and the product of a self-feeding machine blindly engulfing as many peoples and as much land as possible. In this primitivist view (that is being consciously exasperated here) new conquests and acquisitions are simply the fuel needed by the internal dynamic of Roman power. A massive shortcoming of this approach should be evident in the light of what has just been said: only a very passive role is left for the conquered peoples, ignoring the complex interaction between Roman and Italic elites. Moreover, it completely fails to account for the long life of the resultant Empire. It may have been created by military power, but what kept it together once the legions had moved on to frontier areas? An interpretation based solely on army, taxation and coinage seems to leave out some of the really powerful movers behind the process.

From a completely different standpoint, much post-colonial research has been emphasizing the role of oppression in ancient imperialism. A stress on violence, class and ethnic struggle, resistance and exploitation characterizes much of the recent literature, in which negotiation is often assigned a modest role. It would be indeed naive to imagine an Empire simply as a spontaneous federation of ethnic groups. Conflict, even harsh conflict, certainly existed. The question is whether we see it as the prime mover, or even the main tool for the historical process that we are trying to understand. It can reasonably be argued, as we will see in this volume, that war, repression and struggle are not necessarily to be seen as the default context in which Romanization takes place. Some of this warfare is literally diplomacy carried on with other means; it is often the expedient to which pro-Roman aristocracies resort to defeat internal opposition to integration. Those episodes where destruction takes place on a massive scale are comparatively rare and can usually be explained by contingent conditions. Even some examples that are often taken as paradigmatic cases of Rome's iron fist, such as its treatment of the Faliscans after 241 BC, are less straightforward than they appear to be. Some ethnic groups, such as the Samnites or the Ligurians, were certainly reluctant to be annexed; cities that were obvious rivals of Rome either in terms of their location, such as Veii, or ambitions, such as Carthage, clearly had radically different strategies. Many military confrontations that took place after the conquest appear to have been struggles over administrative balances, such as the Social War, or conflicts between aristocratic factions, rather than determined attempts to break away from the Empire.

However it is interpreted, it is clear that Romanization was a highly complex process that produced a new entity, whose character is not easily simplified. Throughout the centuries of the Empire, Italy remained very heterogeneous, as the following papers will show. It has elsewhere been argued that sharp differences run across Roman Italy along geographic, ethnic, social or gender boundaries (Terrenato 1998b). In the light of what has been said above, an explanation for this lack of uniformity lies in front of our eyes. The majority of pre-Roman communities (or rather their elites) agreed to become part of the Empire precisely because they were offered, they bargained, and they struggled for the privilege of retaining the core of their cultural and social structure, their autonomy and their prerogatives.

References

Arthur, P. 1991. *Romans in northern Campania: settlement and land-use around the Massico and the Garigliano Basin*. British School at Rome: London.

Attolini, I., Cambi, F., Castagna, M., Celuzza, M. G., Fentress, E., Perkins, P. and Regoli, E. 1991. Political geography and productive geography between the valley of the Albegna and the Fiora in northern Etruria. In G. W. W. Barker and J. Lloyd (eds.) *Roman Landscapes*. British School at Rome: London, pp. 142–152.

Barker, G. W. W. (ed.) 1995. *A Mediterranean Valley*. Leicester University Press: London.

Curti, E., Dench, E. and Patterson, J. 1996. The Archaeology of Central and Southern Roman Italy: recent trends and approaches. *Journal of Roman Studies* 86: 170–189.

Desideri, P. 1991. La romanizzazione dell'impero. In *Storia di Roma*. Einaudi: Torino, II.2, pp. 577–626.

Frézouls, E. 1983. Sur l'historiographie de l'impérialisme romain. *Ktema* 8: 141–162.

Harris, W. V. 1979. *War and Imperialism in Republican Rome, 327–70 B.C.* Oxford University Press: Oxford.

Linderski, J. 1984. Si vis pacem, para bellum: Concepts of Defensive Imperialism. In W. V. Harris (ed.) *The Imperialism of Mid-Republican Rome*. American Academy: Rome.

Mattingly, D. J. (ed.) 1997. *Dialogues in Roman Imperialism*. JRA: Portsmouth.

Patterson, J. R. 1987. Crisis? What Crisis? Rural change and urban development in Imperial Appennine Italy. *Papers of the British School at Rome* 55: 115–146.

Potter, T. W. 1979. *The Changing Landscape of South Etruria*. Elek: London.

Terrenato, N. and Saggin, A. 1994. Ricognizioni archeologiche nel territorio di Volterra. *Archeologia Classica* 46: 465–482.

Terrenato, N. 1998a. Tam firmum municipium. The Romanization of Volaterrae and its cultural implications. *Journal of Roman Studies* 88: 94–114.

Terrenato, N. 1998b. The Romanization of Italy: global acculturation or cultural bricolage? In C. Forcey, J. Hawthorne and R. Witcher (eds.) *TRAC 97*. Oxbow: Oxford, pp. 20–27.

Woolf, G. 1993. European social development and Roman imperialism. In P. Brun, S. van der Leeuw and C. R. Whittaker (eds.) *Frontières d'empire*. Nature et signification des frontières romaines. Association pour la Promotion de la récherche archéologique en Ile de France: Nemours. pp. 13–20.

Woolf, G. 1997. Beyond Romans and natives. *World Archaeology* 28: 339–350.

Chapter 2

The Romanization of Italy through the epigraphic record

Enrico Benelli

Introduction

Romanization is an ambiguous concept, referring to a complex phenomenon that involves different structures in transition within a society. Political Romanization, which takes place mostly in the realm of the *histoire evénementielle*, is apparently more readily definable. However, even the adoption of Roman institutions requires a certain degree of arbitrariness in fixing a starting point, given the great variability of the forms of integration in the Roman state. Interactions between strongly unbalanced states normally result in changes, influences and *de facto* limitations of the sovereignty of the weaker, even without obvious institutional transformations. In this sense, there can be a Romanization of politics without political Romanization, in which direct interventions are limited to particular crises or to the establishment of patronage relationships. Thus, if political Romanization is fraught with interpretative ambiguities, even more ineffable are the complex processes responsible for cultural change (Woolf 1998: 7–16). The present paper will deal with some of the crucial aspects of the latter within the Italic world (for a recent review of the concept of the Romanization of Italy, see Terrenato 1998).

Cultural Romanization is a process that we can observe by comparing pre-Roman Italic cultures with the culture of Roman Italy. The latter displays a local and regional variability that it is not easy to chart, mostly because many of the common elements that we can archaeologically detect have only a functional value. We can interpret the changed functional needs leading to the adoption of new elements in the material culture as a result of Romanization. But the true, deep historical and cultural meaning of these transitions escapes us almost entirely. The peoples of Italy shared the same historical context long before Roman expansion, as Pallottino (1984) clearly pointed out. When Rome hegemonizes first central Italy and then the entire peninsula, she rules over peoples that had had strong mutual relationships ever since the beginning of the first millennium BC. There were no major technological gaps, or radical economic and social differences between these ethnic groups. On the contrary, common elements in their material culture are clearly discernible, so much so that these peoples may appear simply to possess variants of the same culture. Roman expansion thus takes place within a fairly unified context, in terms of culture, in which local peculiarities stand out as indicators of diversity (Pallottino 1984: 153–180; also Vallat 1995: 201–204).

Pre-Roman epigraphy is one of the main characterizing traits of these Italic groups, both in terms of the language used and in the role of inscriptions in their material culture. The generalized adoption of Roman epigraphy in this context has a strong cultural value, precisely because pre-Roman inscriptions were one of those manifestations where local variability was more pronounced. This is particularly clear in the context of rituals, and above all, those in the funerary sphere. The transition from pre-Roman languages to Latin is only *one* particularly striking aspect of this cultural change, as language is only *one* of the choices that whoever commissions the inscription has to make. It is important to realize that it does not necessarily reflect everyday spoken language. The issue of Greek-speaking areas will not be treated here, given the unique status of Greek. Unlike Italic languages, in fact, it went on being used in inscriptions during the Empire for a variety of reasons. In these regions one cannot really speak of a transition from pre-Roman to Roman epigraphy, as elsewhere in Italy.

The transition from pre-Roman to Roman epigraphy

The transition from pre-Roman to Roman epigraphy can be approached in different ways: the earlier Latin inscriptions can easily be listed from Volume I and supplements of the *Corpus Inscriptionum Latinarum*. This would only produce very limited results, since every area and almost every text requires a contextual and historical analysis of its own. For instance, the use of Latin clearly has a different meaning in colonies, where a Latin-speaking component was physically present, and in inscriptions on movable objects, that can have travelled and even be referred to allogenous elements. Traces of the intense mobility of Rome's allies within Italy are attested in many ways (Campanile 1991), and not only by Latin inscriptions. It is enough to recall the Etruscan inscription from the Temple of *Magna Mater* on the Palatine. This is a third century BC dedication, in northern Etruscan writing, with a name typical of Clusium (Chiusi) and with typically Etruscan formula (Colonna 1989–90: 876–877) on an object produced in Rome (Cristofani 1993). Or, in another context, one may cite the first century BC Venetic dedication found in the region of the Marsi (La Regina 1989: 429–430; also Prosdocimi 1990: 183–184).

The presence of individual inscriptions in Latin tells us very little in general about local cultures. In the context of public epigraphy, it is enough to mention only a few well known instances, such as the inscription of Genucius Clusinus at Caere (Cerveteri), probably to be dated to 273 BC (Cristofani and Gregori 1987: 4), or the boundary decrees of Roman magistrates in Veneto, dating to the second half of the second century BC (Sartori 1981: 106–110). These are all Roman texts in Latin that, however, do not mark any discontinuity within local material or epigraphic cultures.

A somewhat stronger historical and cultural significance could be assigned to the transition to Latin in public inscriptions erected by local authorities. However, this kind of evidence is scarce and ambiguous, so that it is dangerous to generalize from a few isolated cases. In the central Apennine region, with the exception of the Paelignians (Sironen 1995), the adoption of Latin goes back to the third century BC. This produces an interesting and peculiar local epigraphy, in which pre-Roman languages are replaced by a Latin with many dialectal influxes (e.g. Marinetti 1984–85; for the Vestini, Mattiocco and Tuteri 1991). Public inscriptions in Umbria are in Latin from the mid-second century BC onwards (Coarelli 1996: 249), even if Umbrian is not entirely abandoned. From then on, however, it is normally written in Latin characters, as in the famous example of the second version of the *tabulae Iguvinae*. Oscan, on other hand, seems to survive until at least the first decades of the first century BC. Here, the use of the Latin alphabet seems to be more related to geography than to chronology (a survey in Tagliamonte 1996: 221–234). In any case, it must not be forgotten that these inscriptions are the product of political choices, and thus reflect the political identity of each community. Local contingencies and events influence this sphere, so that these texts are attestations of little more than a single moment in a complex local history that has escaped us almost completely. The number of such public inscriptions is not large enough to distinguish between the norm and the exception.

To investigate the transition from the pre-Roman world to the full unification at the very beginning of the Empire, we thus need to turn to the much more common private inscriptions and in particular the funerary texts. These reflect a set of choices made by whoever commissioned the monument, and which are undoubtedly influenced by local culture as well as individual and familial considerations. At the same time, they are the result of a conscious interaction between the individual and his or her cultural makeup. In contrast to public inscriptions, they are not simply a set of isolated cases, but allow us to attempt an organic reconstruction of each milieu in its reality and evolution.

The frequency of such records in the various regions of Italy is very uneven. What we normally have is a fairly sharp break between pre-Roman epigraphy (usually linked to a given type of monument) and Roman inscriptions (with completely different monuments). The chronology is often uncertain and the terms of the transition remain conjectural. Throughout the whole of the Oscan-speaking district, Oscan inscriptions were only found in association with Latin texts bearing Oscan names at the necropolis of Orto Ceraso (Teano). These attest to the continuity of burial customs and to the use of the new common language as the principal means of self-representation for the deceased (Miele 1995).

We have some evidence for Puglia, but not enough to reconstruct the forms and chronology of the transition. It is not known when pre-Roman languages were last used, since the latest texts are only dated on the basis of their palaeography. Little help is gained from the only partially published sanctuary-caves, visited in antiquity by individuals of disparate provenances. In one of the pre-Roman cemeteries of Lecce there are two Latin inscriptions, written on the inside of the slabs constituting the tomb according to local custom. At least one of them, that of Visellius, is probably dated to the second century BC (Giardino 1994: 183 n. 139). What remains uncertain is whether these are immigrants adapting to local customs or Messapians latinizing their name, perhaps after an individual grant of citizenship. The conclusions to be drawn from either possibility are naturally very different, illustrating the problems of data scarcity for any historical reconstruction. Another isolated Apulian case shows the preservation of local names and name structure translated into Latin. It is a Latin inscription from the tomb Lagrasta I at Canosa, with a consular date of 67 BC (CIL I (2), 748; Cassano 1992: 215). The meaning of this coexistence between conservatism and innovation can only be understood by looking at the richer evidence provided by other regions. It is thus clear how the stages of the transition from pre-Roman to Roman epigraphy can only be followed in some privileged contexts. Isolated documents, even if interesting, have only a very limited use, with the ethnic and cultural provenance of the individuals involved remaining unknown.

Etruria

The richest region for our present purposes is undoubtedly Etruria, and in particular the cities of Clusium and Perusia (Perugia). Together, they have yielded 4000 Etruscan funerary inscriptions datable to the post-Hannibalic period: Rome itself only provides 1100 Republican inscriptions (Panciera 1995: 320). Even if most of the texts from the two cities date to the second century BC, there are still about 1000 inscriptions – between Etruscan and Latin ones – that document the stages of the transition from Etruscan to Roman epigraphy. This abundance is not even paralleled in other fairly rich Etruscan contexts, such as Tarquinii, where the texts pertaining to the transition period number in the tens. In these poorer contexts only exceptionally significant elements can be reconstructed. For instance, the *Tomba delle Iscrizioni* at Caere illustrates a lineage that straddles the moment of Latinization, thus providing a guide for the interpretation of other documents (Cristofani 1965). The first generation to use Latin can be dated to the first decades of the first century BC, the moment when Caere received full Roman citizenship. The transition is sudden, without uncertainties, and similar to what happens with the *cippi* from the same city. The latter carry only purely Etruscan or Latin inscriptions, with no intermediate forms, except some echoes in Latin names. This clearly indicates that this transition value was a cultural choice, preceded, however, by an exclusively local stage. During the third century BC, the typical south Etruscan name structure is gradually replaced by a formula with *praenomen*, *gentilicium* and patronymic, with the abbreviation *c* for *clan* (son) and s for *sekh* (daughter). This formula is rarely attested elsewhere in Etruria and the abbreviations are exclusive to Caere, and only paralleled in Roman epigraphy. This transition must be connected with the concession of the *civitas sine suffragio* to the town between 390 and 273 BC (Sordi 1961: 107–134; Harris 1971: 45–47; Humbert 1972; Humbert 1978: 403–416), as first suggested by Kaimio (1975: 195). Thus, at the beginning of the first century BC, the Caerites had long been accustomed to using a name structure clearly influenced by Rome, although this did not deflect them from also using Etruscan. The identification of the deceased in one form or another is thus clearly the result of what are eminently cultural choices.

Clusium and Perusia

Clusium and Perusia, as we have seen, are the contexts where the transition from Etruscan to Latin is better documented, thanks to a rich corpus, also including some 'mixed' texts, or Etrusco-Latin, as they were called in the nineteenth century. It is a record fraught with interpretative issues that cannot be discussed here and that have little relevance for a broader historical reconstruction (for a full discussion, see Benelli, forthcoming). The crisis point in pre-Roman funerary epigraphy in these two cities, as elsewhere, is naturally 90 BC. This is when having Roman citizenship meant having an acceptable name enrolled in the tribes and in the census (Galsterer 1976: 187–204 for the historical context and meaning of the *lex Iulia*). This also marks the beginning of a period in which official Roman names coexist with unofficial Etruscan ones. The difference between the two systems is essentially in the *praenomina*, but epigraphy shows much more pronounced changes being caused by the diversity of epigraphic traditions than by name structure alone. While funerary inscriptions in the Roman world almost always contain the complete official name of the deceased from the end of the second century BC onwards, there is a much greater freedom at Clusium and Perusia. The Etruscan usage of names seldom has patronymics, more frequently metronymics (the two are often mutually exclusive). The mention of the *cognomen* often excludes the *gentilicium* and there are a wide variety of contractions and abbreviations. These must be regarded as epigraphic customs rather than as official formulas, since there are a considerable number of cases (several dozens at Perusia, almost 200 at Clusium) in which the same deceased person has two inscriptions on different media.

The latest attestation of an unofficial Etruscan name in conjunction with a Roman one (as well as the last epigraphic record of Etruscan) is a bilingual inscription from Arretium (Arezzo), datable to AD 15–20 (ET Ar 1.8; Benelli 1994: 15–16). The latest non-bilingual inscriptions are to be found on three urns from the tumulus of the *hepni* at Asciano, dated by coins to the last decade BC. (ET AS 1.74+75, 1.85, 1.88; Mangani 1983: 61 n. 211, 64–65 nn. 223–224). Thus, the two name systems co-exist for almost a century. With the exception of Asciano, which is located in an Arretine backwater and cannot be considered as representative, the transition from Etruscan to Latin at Clusium and Perusia is well dated to the mid-first century BC. For about a generation after the *lex Iulia*, funerary inscriptions continue to be written in Etruscan, but in the second half of the century the use of Latin spreads rapidly, leading to the emergence of the so-called Etrusco-Latin inscriptions. The language used in these is a rather correct Latin, as already noted by Kaimio (1975: 185–189), who published the best study of these texts. Those with Etruscan linguistic elements account for less than 5% of the total. The Etruscan content of these Etrusco-Latin inscriptions is best defined as a cultural persistence, and is evident in the urns, which are connected with the local burial customs that survive until AD 10–20, and in the composition of the text. The naming hardly ever includes the full official name of the deceased. Patronymics are often omitted or an Etruscan *praenomen* may appear, derived from the unofficial name. Similarly, female *praenomina*, metronymics and gamonymics also occur.

The stages of this transition witness an ongoing combination of traditional and Roman elements. The first examples of Latin writing go back to the first half of the first century BC. At this time, even if the inhabitants of Clusium and Perusia were Roman citizens and thus provided with a Roman name, they still wrote most of their funerary texts in Etruscan. After the transition to Latin, both burial and epigraphic customs survive, creating an epigraphy that is linguistically Latin but culturally not Roman. It is only in the Augustan period that there is a generalized adoption of purely Roman forms (for a full discussion, see Benelli, forthcoming). The process leading the citizens of the two cities to identify themselves as Romans took about three generations, at least as far as the funerary evidence is concerned. Each of the transitional stages displays a combination of innovation and conservation, suggesting a stepwise acculturation, and one not pressured by norm or ideology.

Veneto

Some very interesting analogies can be drawn between the situation at Clusium and

Perusia and that of the Veneto. This was a region that was culturally very different from Etruria, but has produced a considerable epigraphic record of the transition to Latin, especially from Este. Recent work (Benelli 1999) suggests that similar stages of development can be found among the Veneti, notwithstanding the political and institutional differences. This ethnic group was at first granted only Latin citizenship. This also necessitated the adoption of a Roman name, but the need was less pressing, since there was no immediate enrolment in the Roman voting tribes; full citizenship only came about in 49 BC. Here also, the use of Venetic remains widespread in funerary inscriptions until the mid-first century BC. In the second half of the century, there are both Venetic texts in Latin script and 'Veneto-Latin' inscriptions, perfectly paralleling Etrusco-Latin ones. Here too, Latin is used for inscriptions that in any case retain a local character, expressed by the choice of monuments and freedom in the choice of names and naming formulae.

Again, the progressive self-identification of the Veneti as Romans follows stages that suggest a very similar interpretation. In the Veneto-Latin inscriptions, the use of female *praenomina* is even more striking and, paradoxically, are almost always Roman rather than Venetic. In any case, the use of female first names for funerary texts is a major step away from Roman epigraphic culture. At the same time, the use of *Latin* female *praenomina* (that could not be part of the official Roman name) militates against a complete rejection of Roman culture. The transition from Venetic to Latin, as in Etruria, takes place at a time when the local language was certainly still used: the latest Venetic inscriptions are datable to the middle Augustan period.

One of the most significant indications of the review so far is the perfect parallelism in the transition process for women and men. This is in contrast with what happens in the provinces, where Roman citizenship was mostly emphasized for its political value and was, thus, more connected to the male sphere. The names of women, on the other hand, even if they belonged to Roman citizens, tended to be expressed in the indigenous form (Fontana, this volume). This confirms the idea that for Italians there was cultural meaning in self-identification as Romans. It also brings us back to our starting hypothesis that the transition from pre-Roman languages to Latin is best seen as one of the final stages in a process of cultural homogenization that spanned many centuries.

Further reflections

Returning to the interior of northern Etruria, the exceptional richness of the documentation allows us to deepen our analysis and to shed light on some specific phenomena involved in the transition. A group of Latin inscriptions from Clusium, for instance, datable to the first decades of the first century BC, can be attributed to immigrants on the basis of their names (Benelli, forthcoming). These individuals cannot be Sullan colonists, since there is no real evidence for a *deductio* (Pack and Paolucci 1987). Clusium does not become a colony until the Julio-Claudian period, perhaps during the reign of Claudius, as was the case for Perusia (Solin 1991: 153–154; Eck 1995). Individual grants – hypothesized from the mention of *Clusini novi* in Pliny – can also be excluded as a consequence of the dispelling of the myth of the so-called double communities (Gehrke 1983). The immigrants must be explained, therefore, by individual mobility. Interestingly enough, they appear to be perfectly integrated into the local funerary customs and to have been often related to local families. One such lineage can be reconstructed for the first half of the first century BC, strongly emphasizing the strength and continuity of local traditions (Giacomelli 1970).

Another very interesting phenomenon in this area is the appearance of bilingual funerary inscriptions, which can be easily subdivided into two groups (Benelli 1994: 56–57). The main one, datable to the Augustan period, is characterized by the juxtaposition of two absolutely typical name formulae (Etruscan for the Etruscan part, Roman for the Latin one). The only possible exception is the presence of the metronymic in the Latin part, which is a sort of cultivated element. At Clusium, all the bilingual inscriptions of this kind are associated with a narrow circle of interrelated families, who became the municipal elite in the Imperial period (Benelli 1994: 64–65, ET AS 1.325; Cl 1.2430; Cl 1.858; Cl 1.356; Cl 1.320; Cl 1.1221; Cl 1.1449; Cl 1.957; Cl 1.1181; Cl 1.354). The only example from Perusia is also clearly connected with the ruling classes (ET Pe 1.313): this is the famous bilingual of the Volumnii, placed in the family tomb that had been closed for more than 150 years. It is not by chance that the two phases in the use of this tomb coincide with two crises in the relationships between Rome and Perusia: the Hannibalic war (Diana 1989; Sordi 1989–90) and the Augustan period. The Perusian Volumnii are, thus, highly likely to be identified with the Roman senatorial family (Benelli 1994: 65–66). In both cases, the bilingual inscription represents a conscious attempt by the emerging municipal elites to draw a connection with the local past, in an age in which the use of Latin for funerary inscriptions is widespread.

A similar example of what might be termed an antiquarian reference, is found in the boundary stones with Etruscan inscriptions found in Africa. These correspond to individual land grants of Augustan date in the countryside of Thuburbo Maius (ET Af 8.1–8; for the chronology, Benelli, forthcoming). The magistrate in charge of the land division has a family name, *unata*, probably originating from Clusium. Here, among the texts mentioning this family, there is one belonging to the second group of bilinguals (ET Cl 1.2632; Benelli 1994: 25). Now the latter, in contrast with the bilinguals already mentioned, is characterized by non-Roman elements in the Latin part – an arrangement similar to that on Etrusco-Latin inscriptions. The datable pieces in this group point roughly to the second quarter of the first century BC. The bilingual of the *unata* is inscribed on a travertine sarcophagus, which is remarkable in itself. Sarcophagi at Clusium are rather unusual, and always associated with the most prominent families. Perhaps the very ritual of inhumation was an indication of status in this context (Colonna 1993). The most striking element is the Latin *gentilicium* of *arnth unata*, Otacilius. This is very far from its Etruscan equivalent and cannot be one of the many attested forms of Latinization (Rix 1956). The key to understand this transformation lies probably in the Latin *praenomen* of this character, Manius; it was unusual and linked to the tradition of specific families, particularly the Otacilii. In the first half of the first century BC, they are part of the Sullan faction and have Celtiberian clients (Criniti 1970: 173–176, 189–192). Now, if a member of the elites of Clusium chose his Roman name out of respect to the Otacilii, there must have been a strong political implication, and it might even explain the curious behaviour in 82 BC of Celtiberian horsemen near Clusium.

The case of Otacilius/*unata* is obviously a specific and striking case. Normally, however, the Latinization of *gentilicia* follows a completely different path. Drawing on indigenous names, *gentilicia* with a Roman appearance are created, some of which are identical to known Roman equivalents. This was made easier by the diffusion of onomastic roots common to the entire Italic world and identified by glottological analyses (for the Latinization of *gentilicia*, Rix 1956). What is interesting is that similar processes occurred in those parts of Italy that did not have a stable system of *gentilicia* prior to the *lex Iulia* (for the case of Veneto, Benelli 1999).

Conclusions

In the first place, the heterogeneity of the evidence for the transition from Italic to Roman epigraphy must be emphasized. Some regions have practically nothing to contribute to the issue, and the present review remains necessarily geographically limited in scope, thereby reducing the significance of the possible conclusions. The process that led Italians to identify themselves as Romans apparently assumes different forms from one region to another, and even from one city to another. Where there was little or no local funerary epigraphic tradition before the advent of Roman practice, as among the Samnites, the transition is impossible to follow. A particular case worthy of more attention in this context is that of the Paelignians.

Where instead such traditions were strong and well-rooted, different trajectories can be charted and were dependent upon the local cultural choices. In Etruria itself, the best known region, significant differences between individual cities can be detected and are to be explained by their histories. If there is one feature in common, it is that the mid-first century BC seems to have been an important watershed almost everywhere, with the exception of cases like that of Caere, which were integrated into the Roman state at an early date. Even where there was no local tradition, the appearance of Roman forms is not usually datable before this time. In all likelihood, this is when the generations who had been adults at the time of the Social War and the *lex Iulia* were extinguished. Antiquarian references normally belong to the highest social classes.

Finally, the process in question seems to be the final act in the progressive unification of Italian cultures. This was a world that had witnessed two centuries of political, economic and cultural homogenization, with a dizzy acceleration after the Hannibalic war; this was a society with no programmed schooling, thus slowing down the spread of forms of linguistic self-representation. The strong variability even among centres of the same cultural milieu shows clearly that the Romans had no systematic *Sprachpolitik*. It was rather a transition that was guided in its forms and timing by internal cultural evolutions.

References

Benelli, E. 1994. *Le iscrizioni bilingui etrusco-latine*. Olschki: Firenze.
Benelli, E. forthcoming. Le iscrizioni funerarie chiusine di età ellenistica. *Studi Etruschi* 64.
Benelli, E. 1999. La romanizzazione attraverso l'epigrafia: il Veneto e il modello etrusco. In *Protostoria e storia del Venetorum angulus. Atti del XX Convegno di Studi Etruschi e Italici*. Istituti Editoriali Poligrafici Internazionali Pisa: Roma.
Campanile, E. 1991. La mobilità personale nell'Italia antica. In E. Campanile (ed.) *Rapporti linguistici e culturali tra i popoli dell'Italia antica*. Giardini: Pisa, pp. 11–21.

Cassano, R. 1992. Ipogei Lagrasta. In R. Cassano (ed.) *Principi imperatori vescovi. Duemila anni di storia a Canosa.* Marsilio: Venezia, pp. 203–224.

Coarelli, F. 1996. Da Assisi a Roma. Architettura pubblica e promozione sociale in una città dell'Umbria. In G. Bonamente, F. Coarelli (eds.) *Assisi e gli Umbri nell'antichità. Atti del Convegno Assisi 1991*, Società editrice Minerva: Assisi, pp. 245–258.

Colonna, G. 1989–90. Le iscrizioni votive etrusche. *Scienze dell'Antichità* 3–4: 875–903.

Colonna, G. 1993. I sarcofagi chiusini di età ellenistica. In *La civiltà di Chiusi e del suo territorio. Atti del XVII Convegno di Studi Etrusci e Italici.* Olschki: Firenze, pp. 337–374.

Criniti, N. 1970. *L'epigrafe di Ausculum di Gn. Pompeo Strabone.* Vita e Pensiero: Milano.

Cristofani, M. 1965. *La Tomba delle Iscrizioni a Cerveteri.* Sansoni: Firenze.

Cristofani, M. 1993. L'iscrizione etrusca. In *Archeologia Laziale XI. Undicesimo incontro di studio del comitato per l'archeologia laziale.* CNR: Roma, pp. 37–38.

Cristofani, M. and Gregori, G.L. 1987. Di un complesso sotterraneo scoperto nell'area urbana di Caere. *Prospettiva* 49: 2–14.

Diana, B. 1989. L'atteggiamento degli Etruschi nella guerra annibalica. *Rivista di Storia Antica* 19: 94–106.

Eck, W. 1995. Augustus und Claudius in Perusia. *Athenaeum* 83: 83–90.

ET   Rix, H. (ed.) 1991. *Etruskische Texte. Editio minor.* Narr: Tübingen.

Galsterer, H. 1976. *Herrschaft und Verwaltung im republikanischen Italien*, Beck: München.

Gehrke, H. -J. 1983. Zur Gemeindeverfassung von Pompeji. *Hermes* 111: 471–490.

Giacomelli, G. 1970. Iscrizioni tardo-etrusche e fonologia latina. *Archivio glottologico italiano* 55: 87–93.

Giardino, L. 1994. Per una definizione delle trasformazioni urbanistiche di un centro antico attraverso lo studio delle necropoli: il caso di *Lupiae. Studi di Antichità* 7: 137–203.

Harris, W. V. 1971. *Rome in Etruria and Umbria.* Oxford University Press: Oxford.

Humbert, M. 1972. L'incorporation de Caere dans la *civitas Romana. Mélanges de l'École Française de Rome. Antiquité* 84: 231–268.

Humbert, M. 1978. *Municipium et civitas sine suffragio.* École Française: Rome.

Kaimio, J. 1975. The Ousting of Etruscan by Latin in Etruria. *Acta Instituti Romani Finlandiae* 5: 85–245.

La Regina, A. 1989. I Sanniti. In *Italia omnium terrarum parens.* Scheiwiller: Milano, pp. 299–432.

Mangani, E. 1983. *Museo civico di Asciano. I materiali da Poggio Pinci.* Vision Viella: Siena.

Marinetti, A. 1984–85. L'iscrizione ILLRP 303 e la varietà del latino dei Marsi. *Atti dell'istituto veneto di scienze, lettere ed arti* 143: 65–89.

Mattiocco, E. and Tuteri, R. 1991. Due iscrizioni vestine. *Bollettino di Archeologia* 9: 79–88.

Miele, F. 1995. Le stele. In *Da Sidicini a Romani. La necropoli di Orto Ceraso a Teano*, Napoli, pp. 12–14.

Pallottino, M. 1984. *Storia della prima Italia.* Milano: Rusconi.

Panciera, S. 1995. La produzione epigrafica di Roma in età repubblicana. Le officine lapidarie. In H. Solin, O. Salomies, U. -M. Liertz (eds.) *Acta colloquii epigraphici Latini.* Societas Scientiarum Fennica: Helsinki, pp. 319–342.

Pack, E. and Paolucci, G. 1987. Tituli clusini. *Zeitschrift für Papyrologie und Epigraphik* 68: 164–173.

Prosdocimi, A. L. 1990. Appunti per una discussione non avvenuta. In G. Zampieri (ed.) *Padova per Antenore.* Editoriale Programma: Padova, pp. 179–188.

Rix, H. 1956. Die Personennamen auf den etruskisch-lateinischen Bilinguen. *Beiträge zur Namenforschung* 7: 147–172.

Sartori, F. 1981. Padova nello stato romano dal sec. III a.C. all'età dioclezianea. In L. Bosio (ed.) *Padova antica. Da comunità paleoveneta a città romano-cristiana.* Sarmeola di Rubano, pp. 97–189.

Sironen, T. 1995. La cultura epigrafica dei Peligni. In H. Solin, O. Salomies, U. -M. Liertz (eds.) *Acta colloquii epigraphici Latini*. Societas Scientiarum Fennica: Helsinki, pp. 343–346.

Solin, H. 1991. Analecta epigraphica. *Arctos* 25: 139–156.

Sordi, M. 1961. *I rapporti romano-ceriti e l'origine della civitas sine suffragio*, Bretschneider: Roma.

Sordi, M. 1989–90. Laris Felsnas e la resistenza di Casilino. *Studi Etruschi* 56: 123–125.

Tagliamonte, G. 1996. *I Sanniti*, Longanesi: Milano.

Terrenato, N. 1998. The Romanization of Italy: global acculturation or cultural bricolage? In C. Forcey, J. Hawthorne, R. Witcher (eds.) *TRAC 97*. Oxbow: Oxford, pp. 20–27.

Vallat, J. P. 1995. *L'Italie et Rome 218–31 av. J. -C.* Colin: Paris.

Woolf, G. 1998. *Becoming Roman. The Origins of Provincial Civilization in Gaul*. Cambridge University Press: Cambridge.

Chapter 3

Toynbee's Legacy: discussing aspects of the Romanization of Italy

Emmanuele Curti

"At the time of writing in AD 1962, the marks of *dirus Hannibal*'s presence in South-East Italy during the fifteen years 217–203 BC were still discernible" (Toynbee 1965, 2: 35)

Introduction

The opening quote by Toynbee was written more than thirty-five years ago, and is familiar to all scholars interested in the Romanization of Italy. His volumes on Hannibal's expedition to Italy represent the first major analysis of the south of the peninsula in the period immediately after the Roman conquest. Toynbee discussed the crucial effects of Hannibal's invasion on south Italy and its later administration by Rome, but had little interest in the period which preceded the Punic invasion. He felt that the impact was so devastating that profound "marks" were still visible at the time of his visit. Since the publication of his work, however, there has been much research in this field, and this contribution is an attempt to review this and to assess how far our understanding of the Roman presence in south Italy has changed. Furthermore, given my position as an Italian scholar working in Britain, I will contrast Italian and British attitudes in this debate.

The third century BC

When we consider the standard works on the Romanization of Italy, there is a perceptible general tendency to focus upon the period following the final defeat of Hannibal, as if the presence of Rome could only be clearly recognized after the complete surrender of Italy to Rome. There seems to be difficulty in accepting the fact that Rome had already conquered and subdued a large part of Italy from the end of the fourth century BC onwards. As suggested in a recent synthesis (Curti *et al.* 1996: 188), there are two possible explanations for such situation:

1) We, as ancient historians, are very conscious of the gap for most of the third century BC in Livy's otherwise crucial account. Once his surviving narrative resumes with the war against Hannibal, it is no coincidence that events become clearer and enhance our understanding of the period.

2) As archaeologists, we are usually divided in two groups. On the one hand, there are those of us who study the pre-Roman peoples, while others focus upon the Romans. Such specialization can create problems of definition, since the indigenous cultures tend

to become less evident by the beginning of the third century BC, and Roman material culture is not readily identifiable before the second century BC.

Therefore, the third century is perceived as a period of uncertainty in which hardly any change can be detected. Clearly, however, this interpretation is an artefact borne out of the silence of the sources and should not lead us to underestimate the importance of the impact of Rome upon the peninsula during this period. Furthermore, there is another major problem in our general approach to this matter. The Romanization of Italy is only understood to have taken place once a clearer image of Italy becomes apparent, or when it becomes a meaningful geopolitical term. While this is clearly true for the second century BC, we cannot overlook those developments that had already taken place in the course of the previous century.

It is clear that ever since the war against Hannibal the Roman senate had definite plans to intervene and reorganize in the peninsula, with an eye to prevent new rebellions by Italici of the kind that had taken place during the Punic interlude in Italy. However, we should also consider exactly how Italia was perceived in the third century BC, when the largest part of the peninsula was under Roman control. Did the Romans already have a clear sense of peninsular unity? There is still a perception that the early Roman campaigns against the populations of the rest of Italy were a series of inevitable conquests (Keay, this volume for similar views about Hispania). Once the Campanians, Samnites and Daunians had been defeated, Rome then had to protect herself from a range of peoples, such as the Iapigians, Messapians, Bruttians and the Greek colonies in the south, and the Etruscans, Umbrians, Piceni and Gauls in the north. Subsequent expansion is seen as the result of a patchwork of operations, in which the Romans only subdued native peoples in order to prevent possible attacks or as part of a mission to share the benefits of conquest with their future allies.

> "Rome's eventual neutralization of the Gallic invaders was also important, but the crucial factor is to be found in the generosity and flexibility of the ways in which she gradually bound the rest of Italy to herself and the manpower upon which she could call as a result. It is thereafter the success with which Rome expanded and her willingness to share the fruits of expansion which explain the strength built upon consensus both of the Roman political system and of the Italian confederacy from the late fourth to the early second century." (Crawford 1982: 42)

This concept of a Roman or Italian confederacy seems to have conditioned our perception of Italia as a coherent political entity. I wonder how much this interpretation is the result of a modern perspective, which tends to confuse Italia with modern Italy: interestingly enough, Italic is sometimes translated in English as "Italian", with a clear sense of ambiguity. Italia originally denoted a geographical space, the definition of which has a long and intricate history (Prontera 1994); its conversion into a political entity is a Roman invention. It is, thus, crucial to define the genesis of this idea. While this dates to the period after the Hannibalic war in its developed form, we should also consider its formative stages during the earlier conquest.

Did the Romans recognize the Italian peninsula as a privileged area, or as a natural extension of the Roman state? It would be difficult to impose this retrospectively as far back as the end of the fourth century BC. However, we do have to accept that during the third century BC, Rome must have devised a strategy to forge a political unit out of these disparate territories. This was a process which led to the foundation of colonies at Placentia and Cremona in 218 BC, following the conquest of the rest of the peninsula and adjacent islands. However, the great range of ethnic difference across Italy ensured that this was no easy task. Consequently, our goal must be to examine the nature of pre-Roman and Roman culture prior to the second century BC, overcoming the problems inherent in the interpretation of the literary and archaeological evidence.

By comparing maps of Italy for the fourth and the end of the third centuries BC, we can observe a striking transformation. In the first instance, there is a proliferation of new roads and cities (Wiseman 1987; Coarelli 1988). It is evident that, in some ways, certain areas benefited from this new system, by being brought closer to Rome, while others were excluded – even if they had been under Roman control for a long time (for example the heart of Samnium). Roman roads are often interpreted as having a largely military purpose. However, it is clear that soon they became a new and privileged means of communication between different areas of the peninsula. They radically transformed the existing market system, and generated new routes to serve Roman interests. The nodes of this network were formed by the new Roman and Latin colonies. Together, the roads and cities played a major role in the emergence of a new political identity. This two-pronged colonial presence, together with a scattered presence of Roman and Latin citizens, progressively shaped Roman Italy (Gabba 1988; Coarelli 1992; Cornell 1995: 362–367). They are also symptomatic of the development of a revolutionary *Roman* urban system which stands in contrast to the character of indigenous settlements (but see Keay, this volume for a provincial contrast).

Political debate in the fourth-century Greek world had deeply transformed the sense of a political community and consequently, the planning of inhabited space. Greek colonies in Magna Graecia and Sicily had been affected by social reforms, which ended archaic views of society (Gabba 1998; Curti 2000). Symptoms of this change were the spread of democratic values, the issue of land-distribution, passing laws on the abolition of debt-bondage, and constructing new public buildings that reinforced a sense of community (for example, the *bouleuteria*). Rome was clearly influenced by this, and the colonies embodied a new way of imagining the city (Curti; forthcoming). These new developments soon had an impact upon the Italian peninsula, giving rise to changes in local economies and in ways of structuring local communities; this obviously had repercussions at regional and 'national' levels. Differences in the character of colonial policies between the third and second centuries BC has rarely been noticed. Literary and archaeological sources suggest that Latin colonies vastly outnumber Roman ones in the third century, while the reverse is true in the subsequent century. This clearly illustrates the contrast between Roman-Italian policies before and after the Hannibalic experience. In other words, if there had been an attempt at using the Latin colonies to create a lower citizenship status within the occupied peninsula, the dramatic experience of the war had persuaded Rome to reorganize her presence. The complex variety of political entities – Roman, Latin and Allied – was no longer functioning as a system. While the success of Latin colonies in the third century was based upon them administering large territories, the demand for Roman citizenship by the second century BC forced Rome to reduce the number of new Latin foundations. New needs were obviously disrupting a pre-existing situation based on local communities (and reinvented local identities), in favour of movement towards a 'national' status.

These brief reflections inevitably prompt us to discuss the economic implications of the Roman conquest. Were economic interests the driving force behind the expansion? This was the subject of a well-known *table ronde* held in Rome, and involving Erich Gruen, Emilio Gabba and Filippo Coarelli (Harris 1984, 83–87). While it is dangerous to over-emphasize this, it is nevertheless difficult to believe that the Romans were not taking economic gain into account – at least as a by-product of conquest – given that the conquest and the subsequent re-organization were very costly. The control of such a huge area inevitably meant that the Roman Senate (and Senators) were brought into contact with a new economic reality. They now had to defend their interests both in Italy and in the wider Mediterranean. On the one hand, treaties (*foedera*) between Rome and the Italic peoples allowed the latter to continue trading with their traditional partners, as well as with new ones made available as a consequence of Roman expansion; the well-documented *negotiatores italici* are a good example of this. On the other hand, Rome gained a dominant role in controlling and creating markets.

Another issue fundamental to understanding Romanization is land exploitation and its role in the transformation of the ancient Italian economy. For Rome, this was an important means of harnessing the Italian landscape. Many studies have focused upon Roman centuriation, particularly in connection with the foundation of Latin colonies, whose mission included the reshaping of their own territories. Less has been written about the *ager publicus* during the pre-Hannibalic period, owing to the reticence of the literary sources. Here again we see the internal structure of these operations from the Roman point of view. We know about their techniques of land division and distribution, since examples have been claimed from many parts of Italy. But little is known about the earlier practices. Few scholars have attempted to write a history of land exploitation by Italic peoples (Yntema 1993; Barker 1995), because of inherent difficulties in interpreting the archaeological evidence for pre-Roman landscapes. The written sources tell us nothing about agricultural techniques or local economies, and there is not anything that could be interpreted as possible land divisions. We still are still in ignorance about the specific relationship between indigenous cities or settlements and their lands. These kinds of question need to be addressed and can only be answered through careful and systematic recording of the archaeological evidence. The impact of Rome will only be adequately gauged when we have a clear understanding of the pre-Roman context.

The broader context

There is little doubt that Rome precipitated a major transformation of Italy during the third century BC. Less clear is the broader reaction to this across the Mediterranean, given the tendency to lose sight of the Hellenistic perspective in favour of a Roman-centred reading of these historical events. The external world is only invoked in the case of Pyrrhus' expedition, the later campaign against the Illyrian pirates or, less frequently, Roman diplomatic activity around the Mediterranean (Clemente 1976). We seem unable to consider Rome as a part of Hellenistic history, perhaps because Rome was never Greek or directly affected by Alexander the Great. By the end of the century, her role became evident both through direct action and through participation in Mediterranean power-politics, such as Rome's alignment with Pergamon and Ptolemaic Egypt against the Macedonians, Seleucids and Carthaginians. However, this had been a gradual process in international image-building. It involved the development of an international vocabulary, in order to participate as an equal in the on-going dialogue between other leading powers.

This leads us to the issue of the Hellenization of Rome (Feeny 1998: 57–70; Curti *et al.* 1996: 181–88; Woolf, this volume). There is little doubt that the development of a Greek identity at a political level was key to the achievement of her international recognition. Mythical traditions had been current in Rome and the rest of Italy since the end of the fourth century BC, and had already contributed towards the creation of a new identity. In the third century, however, the Romans took this one stage further and started to transform their traditions by thinking in historical terms. The work of the contemporary historian Fabius Pictor is emblematic of the way that the Romans began to reorganize their past and, therefore, their identities. Since it was written in Greek, it drew the Romans into the broader Mediterranean community of those who had re-defined their past within the context of a Greek historical framework.

Prior to the third century BC, the Romans had been the subject of works by Greek historians. From now on, however, they were able to define their own historical context. For most of the Italic peoples, however, the 'invention' of history will arrive too late. It became one of the instruments of Romanization, and could be used to depict a new discourse in which native peoples became merely episodes in a narrative of conquest. This is clearly exemplified by Cato's *Origines*, focused on the *poleis* as centres of action. It celebrates the key role of Rome in an imagined state, by opening with her history, and then continuing with that of the other Italic communities.

Another aspect of the same process is the blurring of original ethnic identities. This begins with the Latins, whose denomination becomes an empty concept in ethnic terms, and which was only used in a consciously antiquarian form. Consequently, 'Latin' is transformed into a political status, with 'Latin' colonists being drawn from Rome and other Italic communities. At the same time, other indigenous peoples appear to have undergone some kind of transformation. An important archaeological feature in this respect, is the disappearance of red-figure pottery production in south and central Italy. Its iconographic repertoire and use in funerary contexts had been diverse and regionally specific. Its disappearance is not only symptomatic of the impact of the Roman presence, but is also indicative of the loss of aspects of their identities and the need to reinvent a new vocabulary to express them.

Historiographical issues

An historiographical perspective is key to a new understanding of Italic culture. Until a few decades ago, mid-Republican Italy was seen through the paradigm of Roman historical tradition. Moreover, there has been a substantial increase in the archaeological evidence in recent years, not least as a result of the work of the Soprintendenze. At the same time, Italian universities have started to research into the Italic cultures. Since the early nineteenth century, this had been a sub-discipline of Etruscology, the discipline that had competed with Greek and Roman archaeology in Italian universities (Barbanera 1998: 121–24). This was reflected in the activity of scholars, such as Massimo Pallottino who created the *Istituto di etruscologia e antichità italiche* at the University of Rome, and the inclusion of Italic studies within the key journal *Studi Etruschi*. Since Etruscology and Classics followed divergent paths, Italic studies were sundered from Roman archaeology. It has only been recently that research into Italic culture has developed as a subject in its own right and taught as such in a university environment.

This academic schism is not peculiar to Italy. It is to be explained, in part, as a product of the European infatuation for the mysterious Etruscans that has its roots in the eighteenth century (Barocchi and Gallo 1985). The study of this people has had a long and honourable history. Nowadays, however, there are very few scholars left working on Etruscology in a country such as Great Britain. One of the more recent publications on the subject is *Etruscan Italy* by Spivey and Stoddart (1990). This is particularly interesting since even from the title, one is led to believe in the existence of an Etruscan Italy as a political entity. This can only be a modern perspective, and one which, by creating an opposition between Etruscan and Roman Italy, is meant to be provocative. The introduction to the book helps us to understand this position:

> "We can no more expect a fair account of Etruscan history from the Romans than we could have expected a fair account of Czechoslovakian history from a Soviet academician" (Spivey and Stoddart 1990: 11).

The authors claim that they are writing a history of the Etruscans without using any Roman written sources, in an attempt to discover an Etruscan perspective. If this were taken to the extreme, we would learn little that was new about Etruscan culture in historical terms. It should be remembered that our reconstruction of Etruscan history depends upon Greek and Roman historical accounts. It is perfectly legitimate to distance oneself from Romanocentric views: however, ignoring valuable sources is not a solution. This is equally true for modern historians: the study of modern Czechoslovakian history presumably needs to take the Soviet perspective into account. The Etruscans epitomize perfectly the current divide between British archaeologists and ancient historians and classicists. On the one side, there are archaeologists who have an uncomfortable relationship with the written sources, which are seen as the domain of Oxbridge-dominated classicists. On the other, there is the deep-rooted view that texts are eminently more appropriate than material culture for writing about the classical past (Cornell 1995: 26–30; on Classicists versus Archaeologists, see Halsall 1997; Beard 1999). Consequently, in Britain, the academic divide lies between archaeologists and ancient historians. This stands in contrast to the Italian situation, where the difference is to be found amongst the archaeologists themselves and, in particular, between Etruscologists and those specializing in the study of other Italic peoples. However, here there are signs of improvement and of genuine collaboration between the specialists in different fields.

The study of Italic peoples in Britain is still not very widespread and is in some way perceived as a sub-branch of Classical archaeology. Even the Greek colonies of south Italy have not received the attention that has been traditionally lavished upon the Greek mainland; Boardman's study (1980) remains the most important contribution to the subject. The exception is the British passion for the Samnites. Ever since the publication of Salmon's famous study (1967), a number of scholars have dedicated their attention to this central Apennine people, combining, for once, both the historical and archaeological perspectives. One reason for this British 'obsession' for Samnites could be sought in the richness of Livy's account of the Samnite wars, one of the few surviving account of a non-Roman people by a Roman historian. At the same time, it is worth considering other possible explanations, such as a liking for Samnites because they put up such staunch and sustained resistance to Rome. As Emma Dench pointed out:

> "Salmon is inclined to see the destructive force of Rome at hand everywhere, hell-bent on the elimination of these admirable simple peasants" (Dench 1995: 5).

This fascination for Samnites persists down to the present-day, and can be illustrated by Oakley's study (1995). Here, a commentator on Livy's description of the Samnite wars (Oakley, forthcoming), uses the Samnitic material culture simply as a means of illustrating the text. There has been a lively archaeological interest in the same area, best exemplified by the multi-period Biferno valley project (Barker 1995). While this archaeological analysis is internally consistent, it fails to address the broader historical issues.

Emma Dench (forthcoming), analyzing Dyson's (1991) definition of the divide between Romanists who know little anthropology and prehistorians who don't know Roman history, senses "the hints of a political war" between the two groups. Dyson would depict Romanists as right wing extremists who always promote a Romanocentric imperialistic discourse. It is worth noting, however, that if Roman historians had never been interested in Samnium, prehistorians might never have worked in the region. The present stalemate can only be broken by developing new inter-disciplinary initiatives and moving on to new areas in Italy. The absence of such 'fierce' competition in Italian academia seems to be connected to a stronger interdisciplinary activity: it is also worth remembering the substantial contribution made by linguists (a discipline that barely exists in Britain) to the understanding of Italic inscriptions. Besides investigating languages and identities, they have begun to take an interest both in the texts and the objects on which they were inscribed, thus providing a link between historians and archaeologists.

Conclusions

It is clear that Toynbee's perspective still colours our interpretation of southern Italy in the third century BC. The Roman intervention in the region is seen as having been so violent and vigorous (Torelli 1993: XVIII), that its impact it can still be seen today. There is still a sense that in southern Italy, time has been suspended for the centuries between the Roman occupation and the present day. This image of Roman devastation has been reinforced by an approach that has only been to detect the Roman presence – or its absence. Although we may understand what the Romans did in southern Italy, we still know very little about the pre-existing situation. Much remains to be done before we can properly understand the transfomation of its landscape. One important avenue of research is clearly represented by large-scale systematic field-walking and remote-sensing. These techniques have the potential to reveal traces of ancient agricultural activity, even if they cannot be properly dated (Gabba 1985).

Contemporary historians dealing with modern southern Italy, on the other hand, never blame the Roman occupation for the state of the region. Ever since Gramsci's *La questione meridionale* (southern question) other causes have been invoked (for recent bibliography, see Lumley and Morris 1997). However, this does not necessarily mean that modern historians are right. It is indeed possible that Roman occupation may have

left behind deep "marks". In a recent study on Roman landscapes (Barker 1991), Barker
subscribes to Toynbee's view without actually mentioning him and quoting instead Carlo
Levi's book *Christ Stopped at Eboli* "history has swept over [the local peasants] without
effect". Barker admits that this statement is exaggerated but at the same time concludes
that:

> "But in essence, too, Levi touched on the truth of what life has been like for most ordinary
> people for millennia, and particularly since Romanization crystallized the division between
> the two Italies" (Barker 1991: 54).

While some aspects of this interpretation of the *questione meridionale* may well be true, in
general terms it is an oversimplification. The struggle against a sense of ineluctability is
a major problem that South Italian culture has had down to the present day. It is a
mistake to attribute the cultural and economic atrophy of southern Italy to the Romans
and perhaps better to realize that it may have been the result of more recent political
policies.

By way of conclusion, we still need to consider the broader question of Romanization.
The contributions to this make book it clear that this is still an open question that is
generating much debate. At a time when overspecialization has made this more difficult,
we need to adopt an inter-disciplinary approach to this and define our own theoretical
standpoints. It is curious to note that Italian scholarship has tended to avoid this issue,
with the possible exception of Marxist academics, such as Lepore, Coarelli and Torelli.
Since Italians have mostly paid attention to factual and substantive issues (see also
Terrenato, this volume: 54ff), they must begin to engage in the theoretical dialogue or
they will be excluded from the on-going debates on Romanization.

British scholars on the other hand are much keener to debate these issues. The
Theoretical Roman Archaeology Conferences (TRAC) are a good example of this. There is a
danger, however, that this tendency deflects the focus of discussion away from the
proper historical contexts towards theory for theory's sake. It is as if this intellectual
debate is more interested in thinking about ways to 'unlock doors', than in what lies
behind them. For example, we could break down 'Romanization' into constituent issues,
such as acculturation and resistance (Millett 1990; Mattingly 1997), in the vain hope of
finding a perfect balance between the different factors involved.

It must be understood that definitions of Romanization are a product of the social,
cultural and political context of the time in which they developed. Thus, Haverfield's
understanding was very much a product of early twentieth century imperial Britain
(Freeman 1997). Most recent approaches to Romanization instead seem to emphasize
aspects of negotiation, debate and cultural interaction (Woolf 1997). If this were
appropriate to describe the relationship between a ruling country and its dominions, then
it could also be applied to modern colonial situations. However, it would be interesting
to see if modern colonized peoples would accept the term 'debate' as a description of
their relationship with colonial powers such as Britain, France, Germany, Spain, Italy and
so on. What about the often very violent imposition of order, social norms and new
cultural practices? Were these the 'terms' of the 'debate'? Consequently, one cannot help
but suspect that these more recent theoretical approaches are effectively sanitizing, for
the sake of political correctness, as it were, our perception of the Roman Empire (see

James, this volume). From a personal standpoint, I do not believe that the Romans were simply involved in sustained negotiation with the Italic peoples during the conquest period. Romanization is a value-laden term but does still captures the essence of a simple truth: the imposition of political rule by one people over others.

References

Barbanera, M. 1998. *L'archeologia degli italiani: storia, metodi e orientamenti dell'archeologia classica in Italia*. Editori Riuniti: Roma.

Barker, G. 1991. Two Italies, one valley: an Annaliste perspective. In J. Bintliff (ed.) *The Annales School and Archaeology*. Leicester University Press: London.

Barker, G. (ed.) 1995. *A Mediterranean valley*. Leicester University Press: London.

Barocchi, P. and Gallo, D. (eds.) 1985. *L'Accademia etrusca*. Electa: Milano.

Beard, M. 1999. What might have happened upstairs. *London Review of Books* (September): 7–8.

Boardman, J. 1980. *The Greeks overseas: their early colonies and trade*. Thames and Hudson: New York.

Clemente, G. 1976. Esperti, ambasciatori del Senato e la formazione della politica estera romana tra il III e il II secolo a.C. *Athenaeum* 54: 319–352.

Coarelli, F. 1988. Colonizzazione romana e viabilità. *Dialoghi di Archeologia* 6: 35–48.

Coarelli, F. 1992. Colonizzazione e municipalizzazione. *Dialoghi di Archeologia* 10: 21–30.

Cornell, T. 1995. *The Beginnings of Rome*. Routledge: London.

Crawford, M. 1982. *The Roman Republic*. Harvard University Press: Boston.

Curti, E. 2000. From Concordia to the Quirinal: notes on religion and politics in Mid-Republican/ Hellenistic Rome. In E. Bispham and C. Smith (eds.) *Religion in Archaic and Republican Rome and Italy*. Edinburgh University Press: Edinburgh, pp. 77–81.

Curti, E. forthcoming a. Planning colonies: Roman and Greek experience in fourth- century Italy. In J. Wilson and G. Bradley (eds.), *Parallels and contrasts in Greek and Roman Colonization*.

Curti, E. Dench, E. and Patterson, J. 1996. The Archaeology of Central and Southern Roman Italy: recent trends and approaches. *Journal of Roman Studies* 86: 170–189.

Dench, E. 1995. *From Barbarians to New Men*. Clarendon Press: Oxford.

Dench, E. forthcoming, Samnites in English: the Legacy of E. Togo Salmon in the English Speaking World. In M. Ierardi and H. Jones (eds.) *Samnium, Culture and Settlement*.

Dyson, S. 1991. The Romanization of the Countryside. In G. Barker and J. Lloyd (eds.) *Roman Landscapes*. British School at Rome: London, pp. 27–28.

Feeney, D. 1998. *Literature and Roman Religion*. Cambridge University Press: Cambridge.

Freeman, P. W. M. Mommsen through Haverfield: the origins of Romanization studies in late 19th-c. Britain. In D. J. Mattingly (ed.) *Dialogues in Roman Imperialism*. Journal of Roman Archaeology: Ann Arbor, pp. 27–50.

Gabba, E. 1985. Per un'interpretazione storica della centuriazione Romana. *Athenaeum* 63: 265–84.

Gabba, E. 1988. La colonizzazione Romana tra la guerra latina e la guerra annibalica. Aspetti militari e agrari. *Dialoghi di Archeologia* 6: 21–28.

Gabba, E. 1998. L'invenzione greca della costituzione Romana. In S. Settis (ed.) *I Greci*. Einaudi: Torino 2.3, pp. 855–867.

Harris, W. V. (ed.) 1984. *The Imperialism of Mid-Republican Rome*. American Academy in Rome: Rome.

Halsall, G. 1997. Archaeology and Historiography. In M. Bentley (ed.) *Companion to Historiography*. Routledge: London, pp. 805–827.

Lumley, R. and Morris, J. (eds.) *The New History of the Italian South. The Mezzogiorno Revisited.* University of Exeter Press: Exeter.

Mattingly, D. J. 1997. Dialogues of power and experience in the Roman Empire. In D. J. Mattingly (ed.) *Dialogues in Roman Imperialism.* Journal of Roman Archaeology: Ann Arbor, pp. 7–26.

Millett, M. 1990. *The Romanization of Britain.* Cambridge University Press: Cambridge.

Oakley, S. 1995. *The hill-forts of the Samnites.* British School at Rome: London.

Oakley, S. forthcoming. *A commentary on Livy, Books VI-X.* Clarendon Press: Oxford.

Prontera, F. 1994. Die Grenzen von "Italia" bei Antiochos von Syrakus. In E. Olshausen and H. Sonnabend (eds.) *Stuttgarter Kolloquium zur historischen Geographie des Altertums.* Hakkert: Amsterdam, 4, pp. 423–430.

Salmon, E. T. 1967. *Samnium and the Samnites.* Cambridge University Press: Cambridge.

Spivey, N. and Stoddart, S. 1990. *Etruscan Italy.* Batsford: London.

Torelli, M. 1993. Introduzione. In L. De Lachenal (ed.) *Da Leukania a Lucania.* Istituto Poligrafico dello Stato: Roma, pp. XIII-XXVIII.

Torelli, M. 1995. *Studies in the Romanization of Italy.* University of Alberta Press: Edmonton.

Torelli, M. 1998. *Tota Italia: essays in the cultural formation of Roman Italy.* Clarendon Press: Oxford.

Toynbee, A. 1965. *Hannibal's legacy: the Hannibalic War's effects on Roman life.* Oxford University Press: London.

Wiseman, T. P. 1987. *Roman Republican Road-Building.* In T. P. Wiseman, *Roman Studies.* Cairns: Liverpool , pp. 144–153 (=1970. *Papers of the British School at Rome* 38: 122–152).

Woolf, G. 1997. Beyond Romans and natives. *World Archaeology*, 28 (3): 339–350.

Yntema, D. G. 1993. *In search of an ancient countryside: the Amsterdam Free University field survey at Oria, province of Brindisi, South Italy (1981–1983).* Thesis Publishers: Amsterdam.

Chapter 4

Landscape changes: Romanization and new settlement patterns at Tiati

Elena Antonacci Sanpaolo

Introduction

At the end of the second Samnite war, the Roman presence in Daunia was regulated by the treaties of 318 BC with Tiati (later Teanum Apulum, near the modern town of San Paolo di Civitate), Arpi and Canusium (Canosa) (fig. 4.1). The creation of the Latin colony of Luceria (Lucera) ensured Samnitic control over the Tavoliere. The historical sources for the conflict between the Romans and the Samnites, show that the landscape of Tiati was characterized by an ethnic-tribal identity. At the outset of Romanization in the late fourth century BC, the settlement patterns were very similar to those of the sixth century BC, with the distinctive trait of burials inside the settlements. This view is confirmed by recent fieldwork and the discovery of a settlement pattern organized into *pagi* and *vici* (Quilici and Antonacci Sanpaolo 1994; Antonacci Sanpaolo *et al.* 1995; Antonacci Sanpaolo and Quilici 1995; Antonacci Sanpaolo 1995a; 1995b; forthcoming a; forthcoming b; forthcoming c; forthcoming d; forthcoming e; forthcoming f; forthcoming g). In this ethnic world, political entities developed rapidly. This process was accelerated by the conflict between the Romans and Samnites and assisted by the need for external political mediators. By placing Tiati among the *civitates foederatae*, Rome showed that it was fully able to evaluate the economic and military potential of such territory. In 318 BC, the aristocracy began to take political power, since they controlled a central political authority. This situation depended upon whether the *Teates* were able to ensure peace in their territory, after their *deditio*.

Whether or not Tiati sided with Hannibal is a difficult question. We only definitely know that other centres in Daunia, such as Arpi, Aecae (Troia), Vibinum (Bovino) and Herdonia (Ordona), defected to Rome. One shred of evidence, however, is the use that the city makes of an uncial system for its coinage after 217 BC. This system is generally associated with the payment of the Roman army stationed in this area (Marchetti 1975: 478), which would suggest that Tiati remained with Rome, at least for a time. However, in the absence of a precise chronology for the coins, the question must remain open.

As far as settlement patterns are concerned, the territory is transformed in the third century BC, with the population gradually concentrating around settlements in strategic locations and an organizational structure for the control of the territory government beginning to emerge. During the third and the second centuries BC, the prosperous area around Coppa Mengoni, Chiesa di Civitate and Pezze della Chiesa became densely

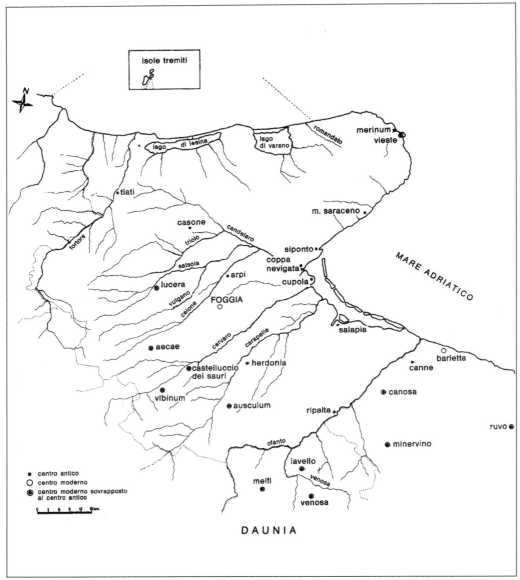

Figure 4.1: The most important settlements of Daunia

populated (Antonacci Sanpaolo forthcoming e). This was a naturally defended area, with access to the main route of communication to the east, the Tratturo, and a good supply of water and clay. There is also clear evidence for the emergence of central places with political and administrative functions, which would have entailed a reorganization of the landscape (fig. 4.2). Thus, major steps toward the urbanization of the region were taken,

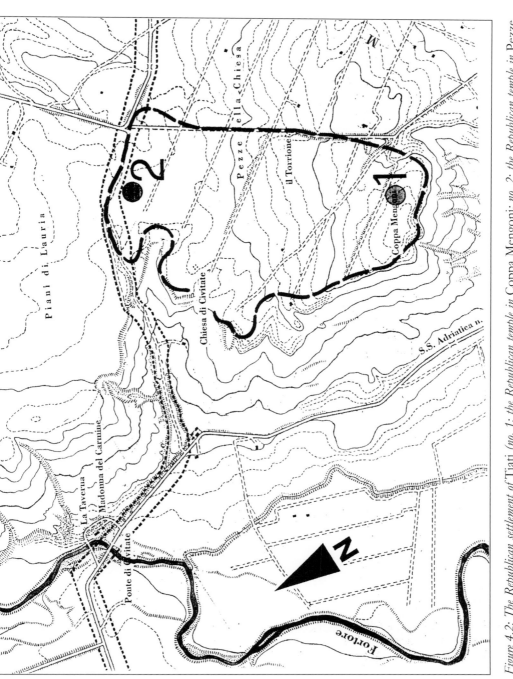

Figure 4.2: The Republican settlement of Tiati (no. 1: the Republican temple in Coppa Mengoni; no. 2: the Republican temple in Pezze della Chiesa)

although the process was only completed with the creation of the _municipium_. The earliest villas in the area, such as those at Monsignore and Ricci, near San Severo, date to the end of the second century BC. Otherwise, many farms appeared throughout the territory during the second century BC and, in general, remained in use down until at least the early Empire. Indeed, most were occupied for even longer and were sometimes incorporated into larger villa estates. The organization of the landscape thus appears to have been dynamic right through until the late Roman period (Antonacci Sanpaolo 1998).

The Via Litoranea was the main road in the area, which connected Larinum (Larino) with Sipontum (Siponto), and crossed Tiati. This same road used by the armies of Hannibal, the consul Claudius Nero, Caesar (Polyb. 3.88; Livy 27.43; Caes. _BCiv._ 1.23) and probably by the Roman expedition to Luceria (Lucera) during the Samnitic wars (Livy 9.2.6). During the Aragonese period a section of it became part of the Tratturo Regio.

Cult-places

During the fifth and fourth centuries BC, many cult places were created across the vast territory of Tiati (Antonacci Sanpaolo forthcoming a). They were used as meeting places by dispersed rural communities and may also have had some administrative functions, such as focuses for the social, economic and political activities of scattered villages and farms. From the beginning of the third century BC, Roman religious influence is perceptible in the votive deposits which yield 'Latial' type anatomical _ex-votos_ (fig. 4.3). An important role in this process is played by nearby Luceria (Lucera), a Latin colony of

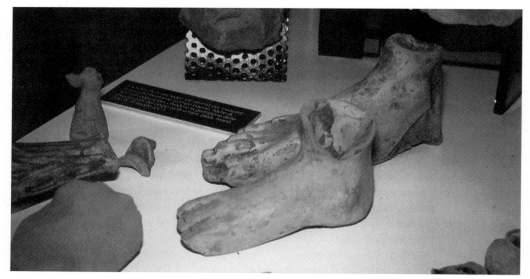

Figure 4.3: Anatomical ex-voto

314 BC, whose votive deposits contain Etruscan, Campanian and Latial artefacts that were presumably associated with the colonists (D'Ercole 1990). The association is suggested by typological similarities, and by the fact that the moulds for votive offerings found at Tiati and at the Belvedere sanctuary of Luceria (Antonacci Sanpaolo 1999) were the same.

The urbanization of Tiati was a gradual process. The limits of the town were defined by geographical features and by the Tratturo to the east: it was apparently undefended. Temples were a key feature in its topography, being located at opposite ends of the inhabited area during the third century BC, expressing the power of its ruling aristocracy and symbolizing the dominance of Tiati over its hinterland. The Republican temple no.1 (fig. 4.2) at Coppa Mengoni is situated on one of the highest locations in the area. Its rectangular plan is visible on air photographs, while large stone blocks, fragments of columns in limestone and bases of columns in terracotta have been found at the site. Its votive deposit yielded over 150 fragments of black glazed *paterae* of Morel type 1312 (Morel 1981) which dated to the third and second centuries. Other finds included two sherds incised with graffiti, miniature vessels, *thymiateria* and loom weights, two of which with inscriptions in the Oscan language. The architectural decoration of the temple included fragments of *antepagmenta*, with a double round fillet surmounted by palmettes with seven petals and traces of dark red paint. Parallels for the palmettes are to be found in the Rankengöttin motif on the lowest cornice of the temple at Pietrabbondante (*Sannio. Pentri e Frentani* 1984: 169, 50.5, inv. no. 451; Capini and Di Niro 1991: 155-156, d10, tab. 2d). It also resembles the palmettes of the *antepagmenta* found at several sites in central Italy (Andrèn 1939-40; Richardson 1960).

The revetment plaques of the Coppa Mengoni Republican temple invite comparison with examples from Belvedere in Luceria and Fregellae (D'Ercole 1990: 277, P9–P11; Coarelli 1986: 52, tab. XXVII-XXVIII). The production of this kind of *antepagmenta* dates to between the second half of the second and the beginning of the first centuries BC (Capini and Di Niro 1991: 156). The cult worshipped at the Coppa Mengoni temple was quite distinctive; the discovery of several loom weights in the votive deposit suggest that it was a female deity who was in some way associated with all-important wool production and sheep farming. The gender of the divinity is further indicated by the discovery of the representation of a female dedicator (Antonacci Sanpaolo and Quilici 1995: 96, fig. 9) and by the Oscan female name on another one. In the latter case, the initials of a woman's three names reveal a composite onomastic form, reminding us of the contacts between Oscan-Samnites and Apulo-Messapians (Poccetti 1980; Antonacci Sanpaolo 1995b: 90, fig. 8; Poccetti forthcoming, n. 3). These connections are further illustrated by another loom weight from the same site, of second century BC date, which bears the first four letters of the Oscan alphabet (fig. 4.4a–d; Antonacci Sanpaolo 1995a: 41; Antonacci Sanpaolo 1995b: 90. fig. 9; Antonacci Sanpaolo and Quilici 1995: 96; Poccetti forthcoming: n. 2). A further loom weight sheds light on the complex relationships between the various terracotta workshops in the area; it bears the Greek letters P and I (Antonacci Sanpaolo and Quilici 1995: 96, fig. 9). The same initials also appear on a veiled head, two fragments of a terracotta hand from the Belvedere of Luceria and on some matrixes from Tarentum (Taranto). This is clearly a potter's mark, suggesting the possible existence of specialized Tarentine craftsmen at Luceria manufacturing for its

Figure 4.4a–d: Loom weight from the Coppa Mengoni *votive deposit. It is inscribed with the first letters of the oscan alphabet and dates from the second century BC*

elites. The presence of the same trade-mark on a loom-weight at Tiati seems to indicate complex mutual relationships between different workshops, involving the circulation of moulds and craftsmen (Antonacci Sanpaolo 1999b).

The other temple at Tiati lies to the east of the Chiesa di Civitate (fig. 4.2 no.2). Its excavations yielded a considerable number of structural elements, such as tufa blocks, mud-bricks, fragments of concrete, tiles, pantiles, as well as votive material. Its position under the lee of the Tratturo suggests that it had some connection with transhumance routes along the Tratturo. This would suggest that it was part of an *emporium*, which provided the necessary legal assistance for the transactions. The two temples at Tiati went out of use in the middle first century BC and had an important function in providing a central focus for the area and in marking the limits of the unwalled settlement. They were presumably connected to elite local families, reinforcing their control over the urban community and exploitation of the surrounding territory.

Elites, centralization and production

There are two other sources of evidence which hint at the emergence of centralized authority at Tiati during the third century BC; the local issue of coins and the presence of elite burials. The Oscan coin legends bear the abbreviated forms *Tiati* and *Ti* of the genitive plural form of the ethnic denomination *Tiiatium* (fig. 4.5). This reflects the establishment of local autonomous governmental institutions, while the use of the ethnonym is compatible with the structure of *pagi* and *vici*. At this time, consequently, the civic entity (*touta*) and the ethnic-tribal unity (*nomen*) become identified with each other. The weight of the Tiati coins was high, being only equalled only by those of Arpi, suggesting that the reason for issue is to be found in local economic prosperity and fuelled by a wish to participate in the economic system that emerged after the Roman conquest. The coins were minted on the Campanian weight standard, a common choice for Rome's allies. One issue, now lost, provides us with a glimpse of the ruling aristocracies by bearing the Oscan words *bidai iakiai*: they refer to a member of the Vedeii, a *gens* attested at Puteoli (Pozzuoli) and Nola (Siciliano and Stazio forthcoming).

Figure 4.5: Coin of Tiati

Figure 4.6: Objects from a sumptuous monumental burial, the Tomba degli Ori, *containing two dead persons in supine position*

The consolidation of a landed aristocracy, which would have dominated the community and played an important role in the urbanization of Tiati, is illustrated by the existence of monumental burials. Perhaps the best example is the Tomba degli Ori (fig. 4.6), which contains two inhumations in the supine position, rather than being crouched as is typical in Daunia. It dates to the late third century BC and fronts the key route of the Via Litoranea at south-eastern edge of the settlement. Such prestigious monumental burials belie Toynbee's thesis that Daunia was in deep crisis after the second Punic war (Toynbee 1983; see Curti, this volume).

The gradual transformation of the territory in this period involves a decline in the *vici*, as is the case of Piana di Lauria, Mezzana and Marana della Difensola. At the latter site, for instance, sporadic surface finds suggest that the pottery kilns cease production at the beginning of the third century BC. Kilns closer to Tiati, however, continue to function throughout the century, as do those at the Coppa Mengoni and Pezze della Chiesa within the growing urban centre (Antonacci Sanpaolo forthcoming f). The former site was located at the western edge of the settlement, not far from its political focus. At Marana della Difensola, occasional finds of surface pottery of late third and second century BC date are similar to pieces in the museum at San Paolo Civitate, including stamps in Oscan on black and red glazed dishes (Antonacci Sanpaolo *et al.* 1995; Antonacci Sanpaolo).

Also of relevance to the romanization of the countryside is a villa site located on the Tratturo. The site yielded fragments of black-glazed *patera* with the stamps Oscan *GL* (or *Igl*) dating to the second century BC (Poccetti forthcoming:n. 6), as well as a handle from a Lamboglia 2 amphora with the stamp *P. Atr* ( ) *T* (—) (fig. 8a; Antonacci Sanpaolo and Quilici 1995: 87; Antonacci Sanpaolo forthcoming d; Chelotti forthcoming). The presence in abbreviated form of all three elements of a Roman name is very unusual. The same initials *P*( ) *At*( ) were found on a fragment of black-glaze pottery from Pezze della Chiesa, datable on palaeographic grounds to the second century BC (fig. 4.8g; Antonacci Sanpaolo and Quilici 1995:97; Poccetti forthcoming: n. 5). The recurrence of the same initials written in different languages on two pieces of almost contemporary pottery hints

Figure 4.7a: Flat handle of an amphora of Lamboglia 2 type and with a seal P. Atr ( ) T ( )

Figure 4.7b: A fragment of a black glazed pottery. On it there is a seal with the Oscan letters P( ) At( )

at Oscan-Latin bilingualism. This would support the presence of Latin-speaking people at this time (generally, see Benelli in this volume).

Land and political transformation

Another important feature of the local economic and cultural system may have been a reorganization of the territory of Tiati under Gracchus. This was attested by the *Liber Coloniarum* (I, 210, 14; 2.261.16-19 Lachmann) and has now been confirmed by recent fieldwork. The *Liber Coloniarum* mentions that the ager Teanensis was divided into *centuriae* of 20 iugera each, as at Herdonia, Ausculum (Ascoli Satriano), Arpi, Collatia, Sipontum and Salapia. The preliminary results of our research represent a considerable departure from the earlier reconstructions of the layout (Jones 1980: 89, fig. 1; Jones 1990: 112, no. 224 Masseria Scoppa; Toynbee 1983: 700; Volpe 1990: 214, fig. 218 after B. Jones). These had attributed *centuriae* with sides of 16 *actus* to Ergitium, a *statio* on the Via Litoranea, which is known from the *Tabula Peutingeriana* and from the *Itinerarium Ravennate*, and has been identified as Torre di Casone. This land division has been dated to 318 BC (Torelli 1984: 328), although other scholars attribute it to the period of Gracchus (Pani 1994: 167), Sulla or Augustus (Volpe 1990: 214). Some see the assignations recorded in the *Liber Coloniarum* as part of a territorial re-organization following the hypothetical defection of Tiati during the Hannibalic war (Pani 1992:602; Grelle 1993: 30-31; Pani 1994: 167; Silvestrini 1994: 235).

The new data are drawn from an accurate analysis of air-photographs, one of which shows clear traces of centuriation to the north of Masseria Scoppa near San Severo (RAF n. 10490/1943, F. IGM 156- Aerofototeca of Rome). Each *centuria* measures 20 x 20 *actus*, and all are oriented southwest to northeast with respect to the *decumanus* (fig. 4.8). During field-survey, fragments of black glazed and Arretine pottery were found in the vicinity of two farms which, on the basis of the air photograph, should be part of this land division. These sites date to between the first century BC and the first century AD (Antonacci Sanpaolo forthcoming g). The pattern of *limites intercisivi* suggest that olive and wine production dominated over cereals, a crop which is traditionally considered to have been the most important in the economy of Republican Daunia.

It is possible that the submission of Tiati to the Romans had involved the confiscation of a part of the territory. Its *foedus* with Rome in 318 BC was certainly *iniquus* (Livy 9.20.7) and from this perspective, the traces of centuriation found at Casone may suggest the reduction of this area to *ager publicus* at this time (Russi 1976:7; De Juliis 1996: 8). However, this would not have entailed an immediate agrarian reorganization, as suggested by the chronology of our discoveries. Local farmers could have remained in place, perhaps being subject to a payment of rent to the censors.

Conclusions

This review of the evidence suggests that the landscape of Tiati was gradually transformed from a dispersed settlement pattern characterized by *vici* with a common ethnic-tribal identity at the end of the fourth century BC, to one that was more concentrated and led to the creation of a proto-urban centre. This transition took place within the context of

Figure 4.8: Air photograph of the R.A.F. (no. 10490/1943, F. IGM 156- Aerofototeca of Rome) showing clear traces of the division of the territory into centuriae *on the north of* Mass. Scoppa *(near the modern town of San Severo, a part of the old* Ager Teanensis*). Each* centuria *measures x20* actus *with an orientation on the southwest and northeast* decumanus

negotiations with Rome, that would have been led by local élite families who acted as intermediaries with the Romans. This social class was composed of people involved in land control, pottery production, textile manufacture and, in a broad sense, in the management of the transhumant livestock. The economic power of these people underwrote their political and administrative activities. They also sponsored religious buildings, gathering places and instruments of political control over the territory.

If there is a change in the settlement pattern, both in towns and in rural areas, this co-existed with a continuation of Italic cultural traditions. These include the typology of the votive offerings (anatomical *ex-voto* and loom-weights associated with the traditional pastoral world), and the use of the Oscan language. Gradually, however, urbanization brought about the decline of the old *vici*, and the Republican cult-centres at Coppa Mengoni and Pezze della Chiesa died out.

Acknowledgements

The work presented here was carried out by the Cattedra di Topografia dell'Italia Antica at University of Bologna, under the supervision of Prof. Lorenzo Quilici, and the field direction of the author.

References

Andrèn, A. 1939–40. *Architectural Terracottas from Etrusco-Italic Temples*. Gleerup: Lund.

Antonacci Sanpaolo, E., 1995a. *Dalla terra ai nostri occhi. Tiati, Teanum Apulum, Civitate-Topografia storica e archeologia del territorio*. Foggia.

Antonacci Sanpaolo, E. 1995b. Ricerche archeoambientali nella Daunia antica. Paesaggio vegetale e allevamento tra documentazione archeologico-letteraria ed analisi dei reperti naturalistici. In L. Quilici, S. Quilici Gigli (eds.) *Agricoltura e commerci nell'Italia antica*. Bretschneider: Roma, pp. 73–102.

Antonacci Sanpaolo, E. 1998. San Severo (Fg) – Ricognizioni di superficie. *Taras* 18: 30–33.

Antonacci Sanpaolo, E. 1999a. Il progetto Carta Archeologica della provincia di Foggia: metodo, risultati ricognitivi e committenza. I casi di Ascoli Satriano, San Paolo di Civitate e San Severo. In B. Amendolea (ed.) *Carta archeologica e pianificazione territoriale: un problema politico e metodologico*. Roma.

Antonacci Sanpaolo, E. 1999b. L'archeologia del culto tra Tiati e Luceria: le forme del simbolismo nella stipe del Belvedere. In E. Antonacci Sanpaolo (ed.) *Lucera. Topografia storica, Archeologia, Arte*. Bari.

Antonacci Sanpaolo, E. forthcoming a. Cults and transhumance in the Ancient Daunia. The example of *Tiati*. In F. Bertemes, P. F. Bihel (eds.) *Archaeology of Cult*.

Antonacci Sanpaolo, E. forthcoming b. Survey, pianificazione e ricerca: la "Carta Archeologica della Provincia di Foggia". In *Archeologia senza scavo. Nuovi metodi di indagine per la conoscenza del territorio antico*. Udine.

Antonacci Sanpaolo, E. forthcoming c. Tiati-Teanum Apulum. Città e territorio tra II e I secolo a.C. In *Dai Gracchi alla fine della Repubblica*.

Antonacci Sanpaolo, E. forthcoming d. Le forme insediative preromane nel territorio di *Tiati* tra pastorizia transumante e scambi commerciali. In *Teanum Apulum. Dall'identità etnica alla città*. Roma.

Antonacci Sanpaolo, E. forthcoming e. *Tiati* tra età medioRepubblicana e guerra sociale: dall'identità etnica al processo di poleogenesi. In *Teanum Apulum. Dall'identità etnica alla città*. Roma.

Antonacci Sanpaolo, E. forthcoming f. Urbanistica di *Teanum Apulum* dalla nascita del municipium alla tardoantichità. In *Teanum Apulum. Dall'identità etnica alla città*. Roma.

Antonacci Sanpaolo, E. forthcoming g. Suburbio e territorio di *Teanum Apulum* fra proprietà imperiali e fattorie: le strutture del paesaggio agrario. In *Teanum Apulum. Dall'identità etnica alla città*. Roma.

Antonacci Sanpaolo, E. and Quilici, L. 1995. *Tiati-Teanum Apulum*-Civitate: topografia storica del territorio. In *Tiati-Teanum Apulum-Civitate ed il suo territorio*. San Severo, pp. 81–99.

Antonacci Sanpaolo, E., De Juliis, E. M. and Sfrecola, S. 1995. Daunian Geometric Pottery: a new workshop at *Tiati* (San Paolo di Civitate, Foggia, Italy). An Archaeometrich Approach. In B. Fabbri (ed.) *The Ceramic Cultural Heritage*. Gruppo Editoriale: Faenza, pp. 401–405.

Capini, S. and Di Niro, A. (eds.) 1991. *Samnium. Archeologia del Molise*. Quasar: Roma.

Chelotti, M. forthcoming. Nuovi contributi alla conoscenza dell'epigrafia romana di *Teanum Apulum*. In *Teanum Apulum. Dall'identità etnica alla città*. Roma.

De Juliis, E. M. (ed.) 1996. *San Severo: la necropoli di Masseria Casone*. Edipuglia: Bari.

D'Ercole, M. C. 1990. *La stipe votiva del Belvedere a Lucera*. Bretschneider: Roma.

Grelle, F. 1993. *Canosa romana*. Bretschneider: Roma.

Jones, G. D. B. 1980. Il Tavoliere romano. L'agricoltura romana attraverso l'aerofotografia e lo scavo. *Archeologia Classica* 32: 85–100.

Marchetti, P. 1975. *Histoire economique et monetarie de la deuxième guerre punique*. Académie royale de Belgique: Bruxelles.

Morel, J. P. 1981.*Céramique campanienne : les formes*. EFR: Rome.

Pani, M. 1990. La tradizione letteraria. In *Le epigrafi romane di Canosa*. Edipuglia: Bari, pp. 170–173.

Pani, M. 1992. Le città apule dall'indipendenza all'assetto municipale. In *Principi, imperatori, vescovi. Duemila anni di storia a Canosa*. Marsilio: Venezia, pp. 599–604.

Pani, M. 1994. La colonia. In M. Mazzei (ed.) *Bovino. Studi per la storia della città antica*. La Colomba: Taranto, pp. 167–169.

Poccetti, P. 1980. Piramidetta con iscrizione osca dalla Daunia. *Annali Istituto Orientale di Napoli. Sezione linguistica* 2: 67–76.

Poccetti, P. forthcoming. Per un dossier linguistico preromano relativo a *Teanum Apulum*. In *Teanum Apulum. Dall'identità etnica alla città*. Roma.

Quilici, L. and Antonacci Sanpaolo, E., 1994. San Paolo di Civitate (Foggia). Ricognizione topografica. *Taras* 14: 57–61.

Russi, A. 1976. *Teanum Apulum. Le iscrizioni e la storia del municipio*. Roma.

Sannio: Pentri e Frentani. 1984. *Sannio. Pentri e Frentani dal VI al I sec. a. C.* Enne: Campobasso.

Siciliano, A. and Stazio, A. forthcoming. *Teanum Apulum*: la monetazione. In *Teanum Apulum. Dall'identità etnica alla città*. Roma.

Silvestrini, M. 1994. Dalla civitas daunia al municipio romano: un profilo storico. In J. Mertens (ed.) *Herdonia. Scoperta di una città*. Edipuglia: Bari, pp. 235–244.

Toynbee, A. J. 1983. *L'eredità di Annibale. Le conseguenze della guerra annibalica nella vita romana*. Einaudi: Torino.

Torelli, M. 1984. Aspetti storico-archeologici della romanizzazione della Daunia. In *La civiltà dei Dauni nel quadro del mondo italico*. Olschki: Firenze, pp. 325–336.

Volpe, G. 1990. *La Daunia nell'età della romanizzazione. Paesaggio agrario, produzione, scambi*. Edipuglia: Bari.

Chapter 5

Strategies and forms of political Romanization in central-southern Etruria (third century BC)

Massimiliano Munzi

"Address the Roman procurator as Hegemon. Do not use other words. Stand at attention."
M. A. Bulgakov, *The Master and Margarita*

Roman expansion between federalism and imperialism

Rome had embarked upon the process of domination in Etruria by the time of the Hellenistic period. Her involvement had taken the form of a long and complex series of wars alternating with political alliances, which preceded any kind of acculturation. These early contacts, as Pallottino clearly recognized (1984: 244), did not significantly affect the socio-cultural structure of Etruscan communities. As in other parts of the peninsula, the Roman conquest of central and southern Etruria entailed a reshaping of political and territorial organization, as well as of administrative structures. A review focussed upon the process of political Romanization thus seems particularly appropriate for an analysis of how Rome developed from a city-state into a larger entity during the third century BC. The Rome of the middle Republic was no longer a city-state, but not yet the capital of an empire, and even less the capital of a proto-nation-state. It rather appeared to be the hegemonic centre of an articulated territorial system, sometimes described as a heterogeneous federal aggregate, but which can perhaps be more properly defined as a hegemonized space, a kind of embryonic empire.

Before analysis of Roman strategies on the basis of the archaeological data currently available, it is appropriate to briefly review the historiographic debate on the topic. This aims at sketching out the main long term trends in the subject. Observations on the extreme variability of the system of asymmetrical alliances created by Rome dates back to Montesquieu (1734: chap. 6), who summarized it thus:

> "Ils (the Romans) avaient plusieurs sortes d'alliés. Les uns leur étaient unis par des privilèges et une partecipation de leur grandeur, comme les Latins et les Herniques; d'autres par l'établissement même, comme leurs colonies; quelques-uns par les bienfaits, comme furent Massinisse, Euménès et Attalus, qui tenaient d'eux leur royaume ou leur agrandissement; d'autres par des traités libres, et ceux-là devenaient sujets par un long usage de l'alliance, comme les rois d'Égypte, de Bithynie, de Cappadoce, et la plupart des villes grecques; plusieurs enfin par les traités forcés et par la loi de leur sujétion, comme Philippe et Antiochus"

The French philosopher clearly characterized the hegemonic nature of the international treaties stipulated by the Roman Senate ("le titre de leur allié fût une espèce de servitude, il était néanmoins très recherché").

Over a hundred years later, we find the classic evaluation of the Roman-Italic system provided by historiography at around the turn of the century. In the works of Julius Beloch, the understanding of the realities of Italy in the middle Republic had already taken major strides forward. The very title of his seminal essay on the topic epitomizes well the modernity of his approach – *Der Italienischen Bund unter Roms Hegemonie* (Beloch 1880). Still useful today is his integrated use of the concepts of *Bund* (which in German means both league and treaty), and *Hegemonie*, in describing a state system implicitly paralleled by Bismark's Reich. In this work, Beloch analyzes in detail the component elements of the *Bund* (the hegemonic centre of Rome with the *ager Romanus*, the colonies *civium Romanorum* and the *praefecturae*, the Latin colonies and the *civitates foederatae*) as well as the tools used (the *foedera aequa* and *iniqua*). A map shows the political subdivisions of Italy in the third century BC.

Gaetano De Sanctis provides the most balanced account of the Roman conquest of Italy, using terms and concepts predominantly derived from the history of medieval and modern Italy. *Il Comune e lo Stato nell'Italia unita* is the title of the chapter of his *Storia dei Romani* dealing with the expansion (De Sanctis 1907: 430–464). In it, the *comuni* are the allied cities and the *municipia* incorporated within the Roman state. From this perspective, Rome would have achieved a sort of Italian unification *ante litteram* akin to the "Eingung Italiens" (Mommsen 1854), even if De Sanctis qualified this united Italy as a confederation. Notwithstanding the terms that seem today out of place, the analysis of the variability of political structures and of the *foedera* binding them was particularly insightful. De Sanctis fully grasps the importance of the system of bilateral treaties in the peculiar confederation brought together by particular Rome:

> "Ma la federazione che si raccoglie intorno a Roma ha questa nota caratteristica, che i singoli alleati non sono stretti da alcun legame federale tra loro: il solo legame che li unisce è il patto di alleanza che ciascuno di essi ha con Roma. Tra l'uno e l'altro di tali patti corre molto divario secondo che i contraenti si sono alleati spontaneamente a Roma o vi sono stati costretti per forza d'armi" (De Sanctis 1907: 451)

The Italian historian then goes on to emphasize how the system was based on an alliance between Roman and local elites, and reinforced by the economic advantages that the allies obtained, in terms of war booty.

In the wake of Beloch, the more common terms used to explain the particular political makeup of third century BC Italy are federation (literally 'a system of *foedera*') and confederation, which implicitly recall contemporary federal formations, such as the German Reich and the United States of America. Tenney Frank for one assimilates the Roman-Italic system to a federation, using "The Roman Federation" as the title for his essay in *The Cambridge Ancient History* (Frank 1928). He emphasizes the coexistence within the federation of allies with different legal *status*, depending on the circumstances that led to the stipulations of the treaties. The same terms are used in his book on Roman imperialism (Frank 1929), in which he opposes the economic explanation of Roman expansion expounded by De Sanctis. He favours instead a liberal and justificationist view, which would be demonstrated by the ample concessions of citizenship to subject states (Frank 1929: 63–69; the theory of accidental, or defensive, imperialism has had a large following, e.g. Badian 1968). In the same years Ettore Pais, in his *Storia di Roma* (Pais 1907), used the term *confederazione italica*, defining it as follows:

> "Era un intreccio di piccoli stati accanto ad unità maggiori di città sostanzialmente libere, vincolate solo rispetto alla politica esterna, a fianco di distretti e communi che riconoscevano la piena dominazione e in altri casi la supremazia romana" (Pais 1928: 434).

Pais was describing a decentralized organization, unlike that of modern France or unified Italy, but rather based on a system of multiple alliances, with highly variable characters. However, they all recognized Roman dominance, to whom the conduct of foreign policy was conceded. For Pais, the concession of Roman citizenship was the expression of a tendency on Rome's part to clemency and to the benign assimilation of the conquered, even if he had to admit that in some cases citizenship had to be obtained by force. In contrast to the cruelty of Punic and Hellenistic states, "il reggimento romano rivelava una indiscutibile superiorità". The myth of *Romanitas* is clearly in full bloom at this point (on the concept of empire in Italian history during Fascism, Cagnetta 1979).

After the Second World War, A. Toynbee (1965, I: 84–266, in the chapter "The Roman Commonwealth in Peninsular Italy in 266 BC") made use of the terms "commonwealth", clearly derived from an implicit parallel with the British Empire. He preferred it to speaking of a Roman federation because this would involve equal participation of all the member states to the decision-making process, whereas foreign affairs were conducted solely by Rome. Toynbee goes on to identify the causes of Rome's success, in contrast to other imperial systems in antiquity, with its policy of inclusiveness towards her allies, as shown above all by two crucial measures: not imposing any tribute on her satellite communities and extending generously the privilege of Roman citizenship to subject peoples. W. V. Harris (1971: 85–201) paid particular attention to the system of *foedera*, interpreting them, however, as part of a strategy of alliances with Etruscan elites. According to him, the principal tools used by Rome in Etruria and Umbria were interference in the internal politics of the allied states, colonization, the road system, the diffusion of Latin and individual grants of citizenship prior to the Social War. Harris dealt again with Roman imperialism in the Middle Republic, underscoring the importance of the economic advantages of Roman expansion, as De Sanctis had already done (Harris 1979: 58–67). More recently E.S. Staveley (1989; also Cornell 1989), in the new edition of *The Cambridge Ancient History*, goes back to Toynbee's Commonwealth, preferring it to Frank's federation. He emphasizes the appropriateness of the term to design a system in which Rome controlled foreign policies but left almost complete autonomy to the allied states in their internal affairs.

In the last two decades Roman imperialism has become, in the perceptions of the historians, increasingly more aggressive and intentional. In this perspective, Roman warfare takes on the nature of a structural component of society, with its annual rhythm regulated by the need for booty, slaves and land, but also by the military ideology of Victory. The concession of citizenship becomes an instrument of Roman aggression, requiring men and land rather than tribute (Oakley 1993; for imperial expansion in Britain, Hanson 1997). Thus, incorporation is seen as a political and military imposition, accompanied by a cultural self-Romanization brought about by the aristocratic solidarity, based upon their common economic interests, between the Roman and Italic nobilities. But even in the cultural sphere, a deliberate Roman policy of assimilation has been suggested (Hanson 1997; Whittaker 1997). In any case, as the cases of Capua, Volsinii (Orvieto), Falerii and later the Social War show, imperial expansion in Italy was not a one-way process (Vallat 1995: 6–8).

The new political geography of the third century BC

Having reviewed the debate over the interpretation of the Roman hegemonic system in the third century BC, the aim of this contribution is now twofold. On the one hand, to analyze the changes that Roman intervention imposed on pre-existing conditions in central Etruria; on the other, it interprets these processes, synthesizing them and rephrasing the concepts of confederation and hegemony, that are central to any reconsideration of Roman imperialism. What were the stages leading to the creation of the Roman confederation (to use this not entirely appropriate but still evocative term) in central Etruria? In this respect, let us consider the Etruscan states of Vulci and Volsinii.

Vulci loses its autonomy in 280 BC at the hands of the consul Ti. Coruncanius. This entails the confiscation of a considerable portion of its territory (fig. 5.1). What is the sound evidence behind this assertion? The coastal zone between Albegna and Tafone is

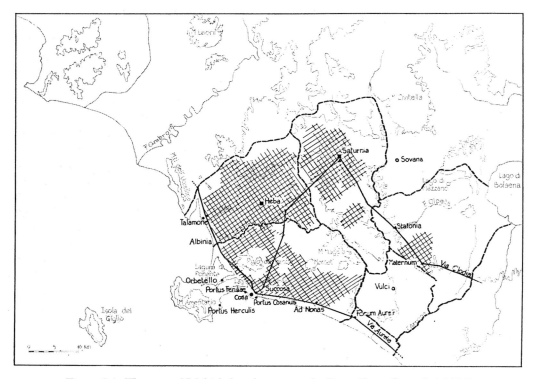

Figure 5.1: The state of Vulci before the conquest by Rome (from Carandini 1985)

certainly appropriated and reorganized as the *territorium* of the newly-founded (273 BC) colony of Cosa (Brown 1980: 6; Scott 1988). The high valleys of Albegna and Fiora also gain independance from their old administrative centre. Here, Rome founded the Roman colony of Saturnia in 183 BC, but the *praefectura Saturniensis*, mentioned by Festus (p. 262 L), probably preceded this event. The area was thus placed under the jurisdiction of a *praefectus*, who had a seat in the Etruscan settlement of the Urinii, now renamed Saturnia. The existing settlements in the prefecture retained their administrative prerogatives and they had the grant of the *civitas sine suffragio*. The reorganized territory probably reached the coast, following the Albegna and incorporating the area later to be administered by the colony of Heba (Humbert 1978: fig. 3,5).

East of the upper Fiora valley is the territory of Sovana. This city probably had long-standing anti-Vulci alliances with Rome, such as may perhaps be read into certain depictions of archaic date in the François Tomb at Vulci. Controlled by Vulci during the Hellenistic era, Sovana now acquires or recovers its autonomy, probably as a result of a new *foedus* with Rome (Colonna 1974: 272 ff.; Maggiani 1985: 84–87; Mansuelli 1988: 52; Michelucci 1995).

Much more problematic is the interpretation of the district between Tafone, Arrone, and the lake of Bolsena, in the aftermath of Roman victory. This is the traditional location of Statonia and the prefecture it controlled. Accordingly, it was maintained that all these lands had been confiscated by the conquerors and attributed to the *praefectura Statoniensis*, with the exception of a small strip around Vulci. In this light, the impact of Romanization on Vulci's territory was seen in dramatic terms, with the ancient Etruscan *polis* almost completely sundered from its lands (Torelli 1981: 261–262; fig. 5.2). This reconstruction should now be completely reconsidered on the basis of the revised placement of Statonia in the Bomarzo area, since it was based exclusively on a very dubious location of the prefecture and its lake (figs. 5.3–4). This new hypothesis finds support in the recent discovery of an inscription naming a Statonian *quattuorvir* (fig. 5.5) in the Malano woods and in the consequent reconsideration of the literary sources mentioning the *lacus Statoniensis* (Stanco 1994; Munzi 1995; 1998; Berrendonner and Munzi 1998). It seems now clear that Vulci, despite having lost once and for all its role as an autonomous regional power, was not completely humiliated by the Romans. The Roman senate instead probably allowed her to retain a limited form of autonomy, regulated by the imposition of a *foedus iniquum*. The same *foedus* would have ensured that the city retained control of a portion of its former territory. The conquerors do not seem to have annexed the district between Fiora and Arrone, since they did not establish the structures needed to administer justice among *cives sine suffragio*, such as the prefecture (fig. 5.6).

The possibility cannot be excluded, however, that part of this territory, and in particular the district of Visentium (Bisenzio), was otherwise subtracted by Rome from the former control of Vulci. Visentium might have been made autonomous by a *foedus* with Rome, similar to that enjoyed nearby Sovana. In this reconstruction, the via Clodia, possibly dating back to the third century BC, would have been drawn on a stretch of *ager Romanus* and represent the boundary between Vulci and Visentium (Regoli 1985: 50–51; according to Harris the road was completed in 183 BC, 1971: 161, 166–167; Attolini 1985: 139). The *Aurelia vetus*, which was laid out in 241 BC between Rome and Pisae, certainly crossed the *ager Romanus* (De Rossi 1968; Tortorici 1985; Coarelli 1988: 42–48; *contra*

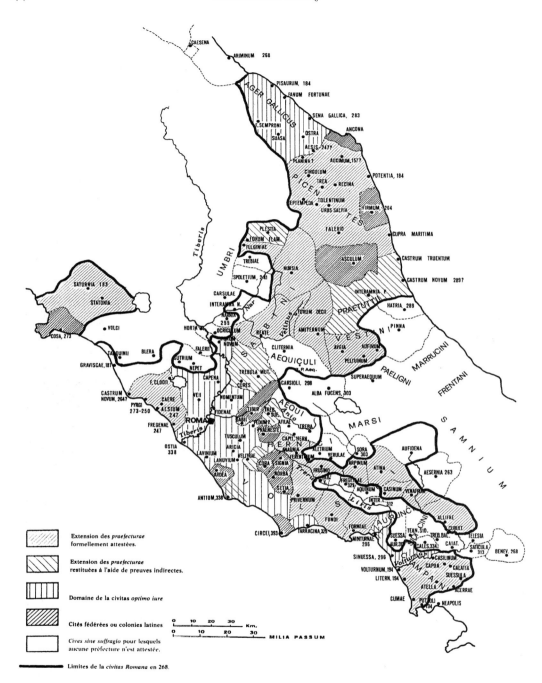

Figure 5.2: The territory of Vulci after the Roman conquest, according to the old hypothesis for the location of Statonia (from Humbert 1978)

Figure 5.3: Proposed location of Statonia near Bomarzo (IGM 137 I SO – II NO); the arrow indicates the location of the funerary monument of the quattuorvir of Statonia

Figure 5.4: The funerary inscription of the quattuorvir of Statonia (photo M. Munzi)

Harris 1971: 163–165). Crossing the territory of federated Vulci, the *via publica* had to use a strip of land confiscated on purpose: this was where Forum Aurelii was located, a *vicus* in which justice was administered and markets held.

The enclave of *cives sine suffragio* administered by the prefecture of Statonia, as we have seen, must be placed in the Etruscan side of the Tiber valley. Prior to Roman conquest, both Volsinii and Tarquinii extended their influence in the area, so that it is impossible to attribute it with certainty to the territory of either. The evidence seems to weigh more in favour of Tarquinii, whose closest outposts towards the Tiber were Horta (Orte) and Ferentium (Ferento; Torelli 1981: 218). The same princely clan of the *Urinate*, owner of the famous "Grotta Dipinta" tomb at Piammiano (Bomarzo), had relatives at Tarquinii and Axia, in Tarquinian territory (today Castel d'Asso; Berrendonner and Munzi 1998). However, the cultural and political, influence of nearby Volsinii is also present (Baglione 1976: 69–70; Torelli 1980: 215 sees in the area a combination of influxes from Orvieto, Tarquinii, and Falerii).

Parallels for this policy of limited annexation can be found in the treatment received by Caere (Cerveteri), Falerii, and presumably Tarquinii (Tarquinia; Torelli 1981: 256–258). It should also be recalled that when Caere's territory was halved by Rome in 273 BC (Dion. Hal. 33), the city itself was administered by a prefect (Cristofani 1989). The creation of the *praefectura* at Statonia was probably a consequence of the defeat suffered by the Etruscans in 281 BC (Munzi 1995: 291–292). The defeated Etruscans were probably Tarquinians, as the sequence of military events suggests. The triumph *de Etrusceis* awarded to Q. Marcius Philippus in 281 BC is preceded by operations around the Vadimone lake, which we now believe to be the *lacus Statoniensis*. The actual battle at the lake with the Boii

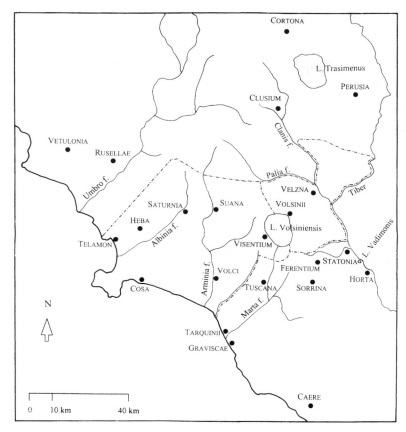

Figure 5.5: The territories of Vulci and Volsinii before the Roman conquest (drawing by M. Munzi – L. De Michelis)

in 283 BC was won by P. Cornelius Dolabella. The following year, Q. Aemilius Papus fought against Etruscan troops (Dion. Hal. 19.13.2) that Frontinus places (Str. 1.2.7) near an *oppidum* whose name, corrupted in the codices, is in fact identifiable as [Stat]onia.

A passage by Macrobius may also contain information about military events concerning Statonia (Munzi 1997). Dealing with the capture of Carthage in 146 BC, he provides a list of Italian cities taken through *devotio* by Rome and whose gods had been evoked: *In antiquitatibus autem haec oppida inveni devota: +Stonios+, Fregellas, Gavios, Veios, Fidenas; haec intra Italiam.* Four of the five cities are known along with the military clashes to which Macrobius implicitly refers: Fregellae captured by L. Opimius (Livy 27.9.3, 27.7.6); Gabii occupied by Tarquinius Superbus (Livy 1.53–54); Veii captured by M. Furius Camillus in 396 BC, with the consequent transfer of the cult of Juno Regina to Rome; and finally, Fidenae captured in 426 BC. The first city in the list is not identifiable in its attested form. The city's name is given in the accusative case as *Stonios* in the oldest of the

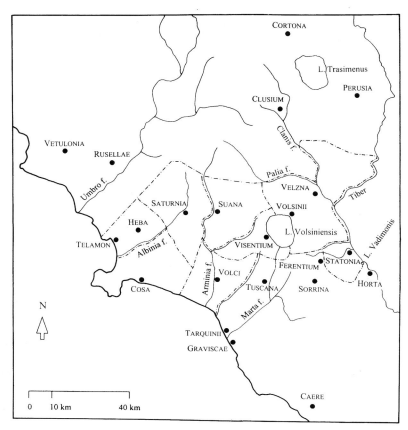

Figure 5.6: The territories of Vulci and Volsinii after the Roman conquest: new hypothesis for their territorial reorganization (drawing by M. Munzi – L. De Michelis)

manuscripts (Neapolitanus VB10, dated to the beginning of the ninth century) and in all of the other manuscripts except for one which instead has *Tonios*. The name of the city was probably corrupted in the MS tradition and the form *Stonios* should be considered the closest and most faithful to the original name (Willis 1994: 186; *contra* Marinone 1967: 72, 404–405). In it we could now see Statonia, given also that the list is limited to cities in Latium, in Volscan territory, and in Etruria. If this hypothesis is correct, the *devotio* of Statonia would have to be understood in connection with the events of 283–282 BC, or with the period of the wars waged by Rome against Volsinii or Tarquinii, also to be dated to the first half of the third century BC. The clashes in Statonian territory, now traceable in the literary evidence with perhaps greater frequency than previously believed, are probably an integral part of comprehensive military aggression against Tarquinii. The operations around Statonia aimed at controlling of the middle course of the Tiber, a main concern of Roman expansionist policies (Pallottino 1984: 245).

A century-old struggle had pitted Rome against Volsinii, the Etruscan *velzna*. Battles were fought in the years 392, 308, 294 and 280 BC. The defeats suffered by the Etruscan city at the beginning of the third century BC effectively reduced its actual autonomy. In 280 BC, with the triumph of Ti. Coruncanius over the Volsinians and the Vulcentes, the latter were deprived, as we have seen, of a good part of their territory and their political independence. A similar policy was probably followed against *velzna*, also resulting in the stipulation of a *foedus*. This much can be gathered from the account of Zonaras (8.7.4–6), according to whom the Volsinians had long submitted to Rome by 280 BC. For this reason, the local aristocracy would have lost interest in political activity leaving it in the hands of men of humble origins (Laffi 1983: 65–66; Harris 1985: 153) or perhaps trusted men of servile origins (Benelli 1996). The city, however, must have maintained a certain degree of autonomy, since the so-called slaves would also have conducted military expeditions, indicating the persistence of some kind of foreign policy.

Faced with *servi* (freed or not) who in a few years reached the top of Etruscan institutions and took possession of the local senate, Rome felt it her duty to intervene at Volsinii. Her action was in all likelihood prompted by a concern that the city might change its foreign policy and encourage others to follow (Benelli 1996). It also found legal justification in the assistance requested by the expelled *domini* and, above all, in the still valid *foedus* of 280 BC. The war of 265–264 BC against Volsinii thus takes on the appearance of a punitive expedition by Rome against a rebelling *civitas foederata*. Its epilogue is the destruction of the old city and the terrible reprisals taken against its defenders. A new location was imposed on the surviving Volsinians. Even if the sources are silent on this point, we can assume that the new city remained *foederata* (Harris 1971: 35–143; 1985: 156; Gros 1981: 21–22) rather than being transformed into a Roman colony (Pailler 1987).

This is a rather early instance of political interference and military intervention by Rome in the sovereignty of an allied state. These actions were to become increasingly common as Rome consolidated her dominance in Italy. They were exhibited on a grand scale with the repression of Bacchanalia voted by the Senate in 186 BC (Laffi 1990: 287–291), and which primarily affected the new Volsinii (Pailler 1988). The measure was extended throughout all Roman territory, and to all the Latin and Italic communities (*per totam Italiam*; Livy 39.14.7–8; 39.18.2; 39.18.7–8).

What happened to the vast expanse of land that once belonged to Volsinii? If there were confiscations we have no record of them. Moderate reductions of the city's territory are very likely, in view of the treatment meted out to Vulci in the same years. The areas which may have been confiscted from Volsinii should perhaps be sought near the Tiber, as a northerly extension of the Statonian enclave, and along the Via Cassia. A concession of *civitas sine suffragio* under the prefect of Statonia is not unlikely.

A little more than two decades after the destruction and relocation of *velzna*, an analogous fate befell Falerii. If the war of 241 BC was begun by the Faliscans, they chose a suprisingly bad time, just after the end of the First Punic war. The cause of the conflict has been identified already by De Sanctis as the refusal by Falerii to adhere to one of the clauses of the *foedus* in force. The supply of troops or the refusal to renew the alliance are more likely explanations than an open revolt against Rome (De Sanctis 1916: 279; Flower 1998). The result was obviously a Roman victory and the displacement of the city to

Falerii Novi, the punitive purpose of which is now debated (Keay *et al.* 2000). Once again, we owe the tale of the destruction and relocation of an antagonist of Rome to Zonaras alone (8.18). He shows a particular, perhaps suspect, fondness for accounts of massacred urban populations, sacks, and the destruction of cities (Myttistratos in 258 BC, Lipara in 252 BC, and Ilurgeia in 206 BC; respectively Zonar. 8.11.10; 8.14.7; 9.1.7; in general Ziolkowski 1993). With the episode of Falerii, the military conquest and political reorganization of central-southern Etruria is concluded.

The confederation as a hegemonized space and the political Romanization of central-southern Etruria

In the course of the third century BC, the organization of Italy develops beyond the city-state model. Rome takes its place alongside other territorial states in the western Mediterranean, such as Carthage (Fantar 1993: 2, 7–76) and, in a certain sense, Syracuse (Consolo Lagher 1997: 231–238; 1998). Military engagements and political treaties had enabled these cities to become more broad-based and more articulated, if distinct, statal entities. The Carthaginians ruled a geographically discontinuous and thalassocratic empire, whose mercantile foundations were exaggerated out of all bounds by Italian and German scholars in the 1930s for political reasons (Ciaceri 1935: 28–32; Levi 1936: 60–61; Pais 1938: 430, 435; De Sanctis 1964: 75; discussion in Cagnetta 1979: 89–95). Syracuse was continually oscillating between despotism and unity and had thalassocratic aspirations over Italy and expansionist aims in Magna Graecia. All these states were now opposed by a strong Roman state, which emerged from internal central Italian struggles as a powerful hegemonic leader of a political aggregation that planned to continue its territorial expansion.

The relationship between Etruscans and Romans in the fourth and third centuries BC can thus be interpreted as a struggle for hegemony over central Italy. It is in this light that the political evolution of central-southern Etruria can be read. During the fourth century BC, Etruria had seen the hegemony of Tarquinii over a growing federation. This was supported by its punitive expeditions and by the internal policing of the federation, as is recorded by the *Elogia* of the *Spurinnae* (Torelli 1975). Rome's expansion in central Etruria tilts this delicate balance. A clear struggle for hegemony first pits Rome against Tarquinii (Sordi 1987), and then against Vulci and Volsinii, which had become leaders of the anti-Roman faction.

During the conflict and even more at its conclusion, Rome actively reorganized the large domain now firmly under its political control. This was composed by states administered in different ways: the *civitates foederatae*, whose theoretical autonomy was in practice heavily limited by the terms of the *foedus*; the *coloniae latinae*; the Roman State and its dominions. The latter were organized in prefectures for the *cives sine suffragio*, and, beginning in the first half of the second century BC, in *coloniae romanae* for *cives optimo iure*. Each of the formally autonomous states was allied directly with Rome, and it was precisely this system of bilateral pacts that guaranteed Roman superiority. The *foedera* can all be formally *aequa*, but were in reality mostly *iniqua* (Harris 1971: 101–113; Ferrary 1990: 217–218; Lazenby 1996: 11). However, inequality presents itself in different ways. Some *civitates foederatae* such as Clusium and Perusia had never been defeated, but also indeed

Suana (Sovana). They must have enjoyed a presumably friendly treatment, combining *munera* with honours, or in other words, domination and freedom (Grelle 1990: 253–254), a far better form than that which befell the defeated Vulci and Volsinii.

Similar arrangements later prevailed between Rome and the Hellenistic kingdoms. Some of these, such as Pergamon, Rhodes or Egypt, were incorporated not because they were defeated militarily, but as a result of diplomatic agreements in many ways comparable to real *foedera aequa*. These served mutual interests and prevented open conflict, while recognizing Roman hegemony. More generally in Greece, Roman dominance had been asserted through warfare but also through Greek diplomatic devices, such as *philia*. Roman expansion there, co-existed with formal Greek freedom and, for decades, had not involved ony territorial annexations. It was an asymmetrical political balance, managed by a unanimously recognized superpower (Gabba 1990: 201–205, 215–233).

Some states remain completely outside this emerging new order, such as Carthage and Pyrrhus' Epirus. The former was an African and Mediterranean power, the latter, a Balkan and Adriatic one. Rome and Carthage had a treaty, renewed in 306 BC (Filinus' treaty) and again in 279–278 BC (the third treaty of Polybius). This was the result of a long diplomatic history which began at the end of the sixth century BC, and possibly earlier (Polyb. 3.21–27). It decreed mutual non-intervention in their respective spheres of influence, as well as commercial agreements and possible military co-operation against Agathocles in the first case and against Pyrrhus in the second (Scardigli 1991; Lazenby 1996: 31–33; Palmer 1997: 15–16, 20, 25). This international equilibrium remained in place until the Romano-Punic conflict, which rendered the treaty obsolete and escalated the struggle to a Mediterranean scale. Perspectives of global supremacy were then opened up to Rome. They brought about the formation of a fully-fledged imperial community, and created an icon which lives on in twentieth century imperialist ideology.

Acknowledgments

This paper summarizes and updates the conclusions of my PhD thesis (Munzi 1997), defended at University of Rome I under the direction of Prof. Andrea Carandini, who is thanked here. New stimuli came from discussions with Nicola Terrenato.

References

Attolini, I. 1985. Saturnia e il suo territorio. La centuriazione, la viabilità e gli insediamenti. In Carandini 1985, pp. 139–141.
Badian, E. 1968. *Roman imperialism in the Late Republic*. Oxford.
Baglione, M. P. 1976. *Il territorio di Bomarzo*. CNR: Roma.
Beloch, J. 1880. *Der italischen Bund unter Roms Hegemonie*. Leipzig.
Benelli, E. 1996. Sui cosiddetti penesti etruschi. *La Parola del Passato* 51: 335–344.
Berrendonner, C. and Munzi M. 1998. La *gens urinate*. *Mélanges de l'École Française de Rome. Antiquité* 110.2: 647–662.
Brown, F. E. 1980. *Cosa. The Making of a Roman Town*. University of Michigan: Ann Arbor.
Cagnetta, M. 1979, *Antichisti e impero fascista*. Dedalo: Bari.
Carandini, A. (ed.) 1985. *La romanizzazione dell'Etruria: il territorio di Vulci*. Electa: Milano.

Ciaceri, E. 1935. La conquista romana dell'Africa. In *Africa Romana*. Milano, pp. 27–48.

Coarelli, F. 1988. Colonizzazione romana e viabilità. *Dialoghi di Archeologia* 6.2: 35–48.

Colonna, G. 1974. La cultura dell'Etruria meridionale interna con particolare riferimento alle necropoli rupestri. In *Aspetti dell'Etruria interna*. Olschki: Firenze, pp. 253–.

Consolo Langher, S. N. 1997. *Un imperialismo tra democrazia e tirannide. Siracusa nei secoli V e IV a.C.* Bretschneider: Roma.

Consolo Langher, S. N. 1998. Cirene, Egitto e Sicilia nell'età di Agatocle. In *La Cirenaica in età antica (Atti del Convegno Internazionale di Studi, Macerata 12-20 maggio 1995)*. Macerata, pp. 145–160.

Cornell, T. J. 1989. The Conquest of Italy. In F. W. Walbank, A. E. Astin, M. W. Frederiksen, R. M. Ogilvie (eds.) *The Ancient Cambridge History*. 2nd ed. VII.2. *The Rise of Rome to 220 B.C.* Cambridge, pp. 351–419.

Cristofani, M. 1989. C. Genucius Clevsina pretore a Caere. In *Atti del Secondo Congresso Internazionale Etrusco*. Bretschneider: Roma, I, pp. 167–170.

De Rossi, G. 1968. La via Aurelia dal Marta al Fiora. In *La via Aurelia da Roma a Forum Aurelii*. De Luca: Roma, pp. 121–155.

De Sanctis, G. 1907. *Storia dei Romani*. II. *La conquista del primato in Italia*. Milano-Torino-Roma.

De Sanctis, G. 1916. *Storia dei Romani*. III.1. *L'età delle guerre puniche*. Milano-Torino-Roma.

De Sanctis, G. 1964. *Storia dei Romani*. IV.3. Firenze.

Fantar, M. H. 1993. *Carthage. Approche d'une civilisation*. Alif: Tunis.

Ferrary, J. -L. 1990. Traités et domination romaine dans le monde hellénique. In L. Canfora, M. Liverani, C. Zaccagnini (eds.) *I trattati nel mondo antico. Forma, ideologia, funzione*. Bretschneider: Roma, pp. 217–235.

Flower, H. 1998. The significance of an inscribed breastplace captured at Falerii in 241 B.C. *Journal of Roman Archaeology* 11: 224–232.

Frank, T. 1928. Pyrrhus. In S. A. Cook, F. E. Adcock, M. P. Charlesworth (eds.) *The Cambridge Ancient History*. VII. *The Hellenistic Monarchies and the Rise of Rome*. Cambridge, pp. 638–664.

Frank, T. 1929. *Roman Imperialism*. New York.

Gabba, E. 1990. L'imperialismo romano. In *Storia di Roma. 2.I.*. Einaudi: Torino, pp. 189–233.

Grelle, F. 1990. Città e trattati nel sistema imperiale romano. In L. Canfora, M. Liverani, C. Zaccagnini (eds.) *I trattati nel mondo antico. Forma, ideologia, funzione*. Bretschneider: Roma, pp. 237–256.

Gros, P. 1981. *Bolsena. Guida degli scavi*. EFR: Roma.

Hanson, W. S. 1997. Forces of change and methods of control. In D. J. Mattingly (ed.) *Dialogues in Roman Imperialism*. Portsmouth-Rhode Island, pp. 67–80.

Harris, W. V. 1971. *Rome in Etruria and Umbria*. Clarendon Press: Oxford.

Harris, W. V. 1979. *War and Imperialism in Republican Rome 327-70 B.C.* Oxford.

Harris, W. V. 1985. Volsinii and Rome, 400–100 B.C. *Annali della Fondazione "C. Faina"* 2: 143–156.

Humbert, M. 1978. *Municipium et civitas sine suffragio. L'organisation de la conquête jusq'à la guerre sociale*. EFR: Roma.

Keay, S., Millett, M., Poppy, S., Robinson, J., Taylor, J. and Terrenato, N. 2000. *Falerii Nova: a New Survey of the Walled Area*, PBSR 68, 1–93.

Laffi, U. 1983. I senati locali nell'Italia repubblicana. In *Les "bourgeoises" municipales italiennes aux IIe et Ier siècles av. J. -C.* CNRS: Paris-Napoli, pp. 59–74.

Laffi, U. 1990. Il sistema di allenze italico. In *Storia di Roma, 2.I.* Einaudi: Torino, pp. 285–304.

Lazenby, J. F. 1996. *The First Punic War*. UCL Press: London.

Levi, M. A. 1936. *La politica imperiale di Roma*. Torino.

Maggiani, A. 1985. Sovana. In Carandini 1985, pp. 84–88.

Mansuelli, G. A. 1988. *L'ultima Etruria. Aspetti della romanizzazione del paese etrusco. Gli aspetti culturali e sacrali*. Patron: Bologna.

Marinone, N. 1967. *I Saturnali di Macrobio Teodosio*. Torino.

Michelucci, M. 1995. Dall'età del ferro alla romanizzazione; Sovana: topografia e storia. In M. Quagliuolo (ed.) *Comune di Pitigliano. Museo civico archeologico*. Grifo: Montepulciano-Roma, pp. 123–129; 141–145.

Mommsen, T. 1854, *Römische Geschichte*. I. *Bis zur Schlacht von Pydna*. Berlin.

Montesquieu, Ch. -L. de Secondat de 1734. *Considérations sur les causes de la grandeur des Romains et de leur decadence*. Paris.

Munzi, M. 1995. La nuova Statonia. *Ostraka* 4.2: 285–299.

Munzi, M. 1997. *Le città dell'Etruria centrale in età romana. Storia urbana, edilizia, evergetismo e rapporto con i territori*. Dottorato di Ricerca in Archeologia Classica – Università di Roma La Sapienza.

Munzi, M. 1998. I praedia Statoniensia dei Sestii: rinvenimenti epigrafici a Piammiano (Bomarzo). *Ostraka* 7.1-2: 85-92.

Oakley, S. 1993. The Roman Conquest of Italy. In J. Rich, G. Shipley (eds.) *War and Society in the Roman World*. London, pp. 9-37.

Pailler, J. -M. 1987. Enceinte, Métrologie et politique. *Mélanges de l'École Française de Rome, Antiquité* 99: 529–534.

Pailler, J. -M. 1988. *Bacchanalia. La répression de 186 av. J. -C. à Rome et en Italie*. EFR: Roma.

Pais, E. 1928. *Storia di Roma dalle origini all'inizio delle guerre puniche*. V. *Dalla resa di Napoli all'intervento di Pirro. Roma alla testa della confederazione italica*. Roma.

Pais, E. 1938. *Roma dall'antico al nuovo impero*. Hoepli: Milano.

Pallottino, M. 1984. *Etruscologia*. Hoepli: Milano (7th ed.).

Palmer, R. E. A. 1997. *Rome and Carthage at Peace*. Steiner: Stuttgart.

Regoli, E. 1985. La romanizzazione del territorio di Vulci. In Carandini 1985, pp. 48–52.

Scardigli, B. 1991. *I trattati romano-cartaginesi*. Pisa.

Scott, R. T. 1988. The Latin Colony of Cosa. *Dialoghi di Archeologia* 6.2: 73–77.

Sordi, M. 1987. Tarquinia e Roma. In M. Bonghi Jovino, C. Chiaramonte Treré (eds.), *Tarquinia: ricerche, scavi e prospettive*. ET: Milano, pp. 159–169.

Stanco, E. A. 1994. La localizzazione di Statonia: nuove considerazioni in base alle antiche fonti. *Mélanges de l'École Française de Rome, Antiquité* 106: 247–258.

Staveley, E. S. 1989. The Roman Commonwealth. In F. W. Walbank, A. E. Astin, M. W. Frederiksen, R. M. Ogilvie (eds.) *The Ancient Cambridge History*. 2nd ed. VII.2. *The Rise of Rome to 220 B.C.* Cambridge, pp. 421–455.

Torelli, M. 1975. *Elogia Tarquiniensia*. Sansoni: Firenze.

Torelli, M. 1980. *Etruria*. Laterza: Roma-Bari.

Torelli, M. 1981. *Storia degli Etruschi*. Laterza: Roma-Bari.

Tortorici, E. 1985. La via Aurelia vetus e la via Aurelia nova. In Carandini 1985, pp. 56.

Toynbee, A. 1965. *Hannibal's Legacy*. I-II. London.

Vallat, J -P. 1995. *L'Italie et Rome 218-31 av. J. -C.* Paris.

Whittaker, C. R. 1997. Imperialism and culture: the Roman initiative. In D. J. Mattingly (ed.) *Dialogues in Roman Imperialism*. Portsmouth-Rhode Island, pp. 143–163.

Willis, I. 1994. *Ambrosii Theodosii Macrobii Saturnalia*. Stuttgart-Lipsia.

Ziolkowski, A. 1993. Urbs direpta, or how the Romans sacked cities. In J. Rich, G. Shipley (eds.) *War and Society in the Roman World*. London, pp. 69–91.

Chapter 6

A tale of three cities: the Romanization of northern coastal Etruria

Nicola Terrenato

Introduction

The aim of this paper is to analyze and compare the relevant evidence for the Romanization of three cities in northern Coastal Etruria, Luna (Luni), Pisae (Pisa) and Volaterrae (Volterra). The purpose of this review is not so much to provide a detailed account of the historical processes involved in the incorporation of these communities, but rather to use the present case study to develop some theoretical and methodological points concerning the Romanization of Italy. In particular, the aim is to show how the reconstruction of a complex and multifaceted transition, such as the one in question, can be strongly influenced by the type of data taken into consideration. Moreover, the observed phenomenon can appear in a radically different light when seen from the contrasting theoretical standpoints that have dominated scholarship in successive waves, such as nationalism, idealism, historicism or Marxism. The present paper approaches this multi-layered and complex historiographic discourse by separately dealing with the each of the various different classes of evidence that pertains to the case-study in question. This is because each of these themes appears to have been of particular relevance for one of the main trends that have characterized past scholarship. Thus, high art and public architecture have played a particular role in idealistic reconstructions, epigraphy and antiquarian observations in historicist ones, and settlement and pottery studies in Marxist ones. Looking at each data-set in its own terms can illustrate the strengths and limitations of different interpretative stances.

Such an approach necessarily results in a degree of simplification, given the constraints of space and the need to deal with the substantive issues related to the three cities in question. Obviously, the historiographic schools reviewed in this way, and the Marxist one in particular, did not ignore other data altogether. They simply tended to read all the other indicators in the light of those conclusions that a particular class of evidence suggested would have been diagnostic. Also, the picture of Romanization emerging from each class of evidence has consciously been exaggerated in order to highlight the contrasts in the conclusions that can be reached in a less-than-holistic perspective. This is especially true for the paragraph on art and architecture, which, however, should not be seen in any way as an attempt at undermining the absolute value of the studies there reviewed. It is rather a reaction to the excessive, indeed sometimes almost exclusive, role that these indicators have had in an entire branch of the literature. More than in the individual case-studies, this dominance was particularly obvious in some of the broader syntheses, in which the acculturation of many non-Roman communities was summarily assumed to have happened on the basis of a few artefacts or monuments. In this respect, as in several others, there has been a surprising amount of overlap between the reconstructions put forward by even the apparently most disparate historiographic schools (Terrenato 1998b).

Moving on to the three cities of the title, it is worth pointing out that the critique carried out in this paper is not specifically levelled at the works dealing with coastal northern Etruria. If anything, Luna, Pisae and Volaterrae have been treated in a far more balanced way than most other Italian communities. They have been chosen simply because of the light thrown on them by a series of recent archaeological studies (syntheses in Rossignani 1985a; Pasquinucci and Menchelli 1999; Terrenato 1998a). They also represent a fairly compact geographical context: their territories extend from north to south along the Tyrrhenian coast in a band of about 100 km in length, and expanded inland by up to 50 km in the south. However, while Pisae and Luna were located rather near the coastline, which in Roman times ran several km further to the east of where it lies today, Volaterrae was built on a high and naturally fortified plateau some 35 km inland. A low and fertile coastal plain extends in the central and southern part of the region, while further north the landscape becomes hillier, as the Apennines veer west to join the Alps. These hills are intersected by the very wide valley of the Arno, characterized by vast fluvial terraces, frequently offering good sources of pottery clay. Pisae lies close to the estuary, taking advantage of its location as a natural fluvial harbour. The other two main rivers running from east to west, the Magra and the Cecina, provide only a limited amount of arable land. As one moves upland, into the Alps-Apennines from Luna, or towards the Colline Metallifere south of the Arno, the hilly and occasionally rocky landscape is largely suitable for pasture alone. This is, however, compensated for by considerable mineral resources. White marble was (and still is) quarried on a massive scale from the Apuane, stone was quarried from the Monte Pisano, while alabaster, salt, copper and sulphur were extracted in the hinterland of Volaterrae.

Art and architecture

In many syntheses on the Romanization of Italy, a dominant place has been given to artistic production and public monuments. There are several elements underpinning this approach. In the first place, these were considered the noblest and most distinctive manifestations of the human spirit, in the idealist tradition that permeated classical studies in Italy and Germany. Moreover, the priorities implemented by archaeologists in the field, ensured that most of the available evidence was represented by high art and architecture. Classical archaeology began in Italy as a hunt for works of art, in order to cater for private and public collectionism (Barbanera 1998: 3–48). It then drew in the investigation of those public monuments where these artefacts were more likely to be found, or whose massive remains were threatened by modern development. A mixture of ideological and cultural resource management considerations has, thus, given a long-unchallenged prominence to a specific class of evidence. Such an approach to archaeology went hand in hand with historical reconstructions almost based exclusively on ancient literary sources (see Keay, this volume for a fuller discussion). Material culture would be mostly seen as supplementing some details and as background for the kind of political and military narrative that could be derived from extant texts. It is not surprising that this usually resulted in one-sided perceptions of the process. Rome's expansion would be archaeologically illustrated by her magnificent built monuments, providing material proof of the positivity of the process, in terms of high culture, organization and prosperity. Our case-study can easily provide good examples of this kind of approach.

Our knowledge of the urban centres of Luna, Pisae and Volaterrae is rather uneven, due to the differing nature of the archaeological record at the three cities and to the circumstances of its recovery. Luna was an abandoned site and was obviously much easier to investigate on a large scale. Occasional excavations have explored a considerable area ever since the nineteenth century. Major systematic campaigns were carried out at the site during the 1950s and 60s, resulting in the exposure of a sizeable portion of the city, and centering on the forum square which is still visible today (Frova 1973). The buildings identified to date include a theatre and an amphitheatre, the Capitolium and probably another temple, as well as some elite *domus*. Most of these can be easily paralleled with standard types in Roman architecture (even if the public building on the south side of the Forum square still awaits a convincing interpretation and reconstruction). On the whole, however, what has been uncovered appears to be in perfect resonance with the few scraps of information provided by the literary sources: the colony was given Roman right and founded in 177 BC, and only thrived until the Middle Imperial period (Rossignani 1985a: 12–16). In tune with this, its public archaeology can be constructed as a miniature Rome, which was planted in a previously non-urbanized area, and into which Roman colonists introduce urbanism, literacy, law, as well as higher art and more harmonious architecture. In this perspective, Romanization appears as a process of penetration and diffusion, in which the indigenous Ligurians are simply pushed back to make room for the light-bearing conquerors. They leave hardly any evidence for their acculturation, since they were hardly "visible" archaeologically, either before or after the conquest (with the exception of a few tombs at nearby Ameglia; Durante 1982).

We are far worse informed about Pisa, as a result of the continued of occupation of the city and its very high water-table, which makes urban excavations particularly challenging. Pre-Roman remains are so rarely recorded, that one can say little more than that the city existed (Pasquinucci 1994). Even Roman structures are very scarce. The only surviving standing structure (the so-called Neronian Baths; Pasquinucci and Menchelli 1989) belongs to an early Imperial bath complex, while the stratified remains of houses have been uncovered at the Piazza del Duomo and in its vicinity, as well as at a few other sites (Pasquinucci 1995). Excavations in progress at the moment are revealing an exceptional group of shipwrecks connected with the city's harbour. What is missing in terms of monumental evidence, however, is partially compensated for by the written and epigraphic sources, especially for the early Roman period. They mention temples (including an *Augusteum*), a theatre and an amphitheatre, several bath complexes, and perhaps even an honorary arch (Storti 1989). Thus Pisa, which was an allied city ever since the first Punic war and obtained colonial status under Augustus, also seems also to fit into the received pattern of incorporation: in other words, it was a half-breed Etruscan town which was transformed into a thriving port city by the Romans. Again, the pre-Roman phase is hardly visible and the emphasis naturally falls on the massive programme of public architecture that was contingent upon Romanization. Monumentality, prosperity and homogeneization are the most visible elements of the archaeological record.

The case of Volaterrae has been dealt at some length in a previous paper (Terrenato 1998a). It basically conforms to a very similar pattern, except that this time the Etruscan city—a major settlement since the Early Iron Age (Cateni and Maggiani 1997)—has left considerable remains, in the form of fortifications and a temple complex on the Acropolis, both of which are datable to the Hellenistic period (Galluccio forthcoming). Romanization is illustrated by the addition of large structures such as cisterns, but above all the theatre and *porticus* complex, which was excavated in the 1950s and '60s, and has been dated to the Augustan and Tiberian period (Munzi and Terrenato 2000). There is also mention of a *forum*. Volaterrae was an ally of Rome by the late third century BC, becoming a *municipium* in 90 BC and receiving colonial status by the Julio-Claudian period (Harris 1971: 264; Munzi and Terrenato 1994). Here, for a change, the indigenous Etruscans are visible, both through their architectonic achievements and even more in their cinerary urns, which have been accumulating in the civic Museum ever since the 1700s (Cristofani 1977). Nevertheless, even this proud Etruscan metropolis was frequently assumed to have become an average Roman city by the time of Augustus. And, yet again, the presence of monumental, if patchy, urbanism following the standardized Roman canon can be taken to diagnose a radical political, economic and cultural change. In this perspective, all three cities, which differed in terms of their pre-Roman ethnic and social composition, urban history, location and economy, still turn out to share common characteristics by the time of the Augustan period. If one was to confine oneself to this evidence alone, the inevitable conclusion would be that such spectacular homogeneity in these key cultural fields could only be explained by the spread of a superior culture.

Another perspective sometimes adopted in analysing Roman urbanism is to look at city layouts. This characterizes a branch of archaeology known as ancient topography in the Italian and German traditions. From this perspective, the three cities in question show considerable differences. Luna was built according to a strict orthogonal plan, divided into four main strips (each of four *actus* in width) along a northeast/southwest axis constrained by the coastline (Sommella 1988: 219). Pisae probably had already a somewhat regular plan flanking the northern bank of the Arno in a pre-Roman phase, perhaps dating back to the time of the Hellenistic expansion and which was modified with the conquest (Tolaini 1992: 11–15). Volaterrae, on the other hand, always seems to have had a very irregular plan which was unaffected even by the addition of Roman monuments (Cateni and Maggiani 1997; Fiumi 1976: 7–10). These strongly differing patterns are obviously explained with reference to common sense observations, rather than linked with differences in the process of Romanization. Luna was a new foundation and Pisae lies on a flat alluvial plain. Volaterrae instead was tightly constrained by the morphology of the jagged sandstone plateau on which it sits. Even if these considerations carry some weight, a fuller reconstruction could be attempted. This approach, combined with others, would have the potential to make an important contribution to a better understanding of Romanization. The tendency, however, has been to adhere to an eminently descriptive and empirical approach. The potential of analyzing urban layouts, together with the complex urban vicissitudes underlying them, has not been fully exploited, particularly when compared to the inflated value assigned to the discovery of classical architectural types.

The other class of evidence that has been competing with architectural studies to monopolize the attention of archaeologists is, of course, artistic production. In this respect, there are again marked differences between the towns in the pre-Roman situation. Volaterrae had a strong tradition of stone sculpture and carving in local alabaster (as well as painted pottery), which began in the late archaic period and peaked in the Hellenistic period (Maggiani 1985). Pisae had a much more limited production of grave markers and other prevalently small pieces (Settis 1984: 63–67), while in the Luna area Ligurian art is virtually non-existent. With the advent of the Augustan period, however, the sculpture from all three cities displays a striking degree of uniformity. The portraits of the imperial family put on display in the theatre at Volaterrae or the theatre and basilica in Luna—a city also heavily involved in the extraction of marble from the nearby Alpi Apuane—are practically indistinguishable in their style (Fiumi 1976: 85–86; Rossignani 1985a: 60, 72, 113). The same is true for Pisae, even if the provenance of the pieces now in the Camposanto is much less clear (Settis 1984: 133–141). What emerges clearly from this evidence is that communities with remarkably different tastes, traditions and experiences are all drawn to a new universal artistic language, apparently as a result of Romanization. Volaterrae may have been adhering to its cinerary urns a little longer, while Luna was quicker to adopt the new imagery. This can be illustrated by the second century BC terracottas from the Great Temple, which exhibit neo-Attic influences and which were probably commissioned by a Roman aristocrat involved in the establishment of the colony (Coarelli 1970: 87; Rossignani 1985b). In the end, however, the result is the same: a style characterized as Roman becomes the standard form of figurative expression, in the same way that Latin styles become dominant in high literature (well exemplified by the first century AD Volaterran poet A. Persius).

It is thus obvious that when preference is accorded to evidence of this kind, the Romanization of Luna, Pisae and Volaterrae appears as a process that revolutionizes the existing situation and results in the adoption of an entirely different cultural system. This transformation seemingly implies a new form of urbanism as well as new kinds of artistic and literary expression, in turn made possible by an intensified cultural interaction and increased prosperity. In this reconstruction, the dissolution of local ethnic identities allows the pervasive diffusion of new cultural models, creating an unprecedented uniformity. What is even more important, is that the transition is seen as having a strong positive value, since it involves the introduction of higher artistic and architectonic styles, closer to the ideals of Greek perfection and adequately representing the more evolved entity brought together by Rome. In this idealistic framework, artistic expression, the highest form of human expression, is clearly seen as the clearest embodiment of Rome's civilizing mission. This self-consistent approach has explicitly or implicitly pervaded much of the work done on the Romanization of the whole empire till the 1950s and still haunts current views of Romanization (for a classic example, Ward-Perkins 1981: 213–4). Even when the composite nature of Roman imperial culture is appreciated, as in some recent work, its diffusion is still perceived as a major positive development. The natives may have had an important role in it, but it is still seen as a process that refines the western barbarians and arrests the decadence of the eastern Greeks (Woolf 1995). This framework clearly needs to be carefully deconstructed before moving on to new theories.

The idealist perspective on Romanization can be criticized in different ways from many points of view; thus, only some general points will be made here. Quite apart from assigning art the value of being a reflection of culture in the wider anthropological sense, the causal relationship of these transformations to the Roman conquest can be questioned. In the first instance, the chronological sequence of these events causes some problems. The annexation of the Italian communities by Rome took place over a period of about three centuries. In our case study, it extends between the first half of the third century BC (Pisae was a Roman base in the first Punic war), through until the early first century BC (Volaterrae was sieged and taken by Sulla only in 80 BC). The adoption of styles in art and architecture, however, does not immediately follow the conquest, as the logic of direct causality might suggest. Instead, it happens in the Augustan period, which was a long time after the events which supposedly prompted the change. Indeed, the perfect synchronism in the spread of neo-classic style amongst communities annexed at different times, strongly suggests a different explanation. It seems much more appropriate to interpret this in terms of the diffusion of a fashion, rather than as a consequence of events which took place one or two centuries before. The flourishing of public art and architecture under Augustus should be seen instead as a consequence of the spread of the propaganda needed to support the political order that emerged after the civil wars (see, for instance, Zanker 1987). This is an Empire-wide trend that appears to be absolutely independent of the conquest. Indeed, the spread of this new style in some regions of the west has been long seen as an indicator of instant acculturation (for a critique, see Keay, this volume).

In retrospect, it is also clear that this was not the first wave of stylistic change to affect settled communities in the Mediterranean. The spread of eastern styles and artefacts in Italy between the eighth and the sixth centuries BC, for instance, had nothing to do with an Asian hegemony over Italian peoples. This Orientalizing period may have been different in character but it does provide us with an early example of the independance of artistic styles (Rathje 1979). Hellenism was another Mediterranean-wide stylistic change. Here, Greek models become widespread over a relatively short period of time and in completely different ethnic contexts (Zanker 1976). The paradoxical success of Greek art and literature in a period marked by the annexation by Rome of most of the Hellenic world surprised the Romans themselves. Later still, the dominant culture of the early Empire recycles and develops many of these Greek elements, resulting in the creation of something very different to Roman traditions.

In broader terms, these considerations call into question the real relevance of manifestations of high art as indicators of power balances. The diffusionist (and implicitly colonialist) concept that superior cultures tend to replace inferior ones seems to fit very badly with the evidence as it has been reviewed here. The fluctuations, not to say vagaries, of taste in Italy seem instead to be strongly influenced by their own internal dynamics and biased by the effects of propaganda, iconography and self-representation; their links to politics and society are complex and deceptive. Even in the more recent sociological approach to the subject introduced by Marxist art-historians in the 1960s is still very one-sided when taken in isolation, and one heavily biased in favour of the literate upper classes, their public behaviours and their more volatile manifestations. High art in the Hellenistic period and under Augustus progressively lost its direct relationship with the core culture of the society expressing it, and became instead a statement directed to a restricted audience with its own distinctive and autonomous discourse. Alternatively, there is the provocative argument that monumental architecture and high art played a key role in cultural interaction within the whole community and that this remained essentially unchanged from the Archaic period. Tumuli and theatres, brooches and bas-reliefs were all meant to forcefully assert the status, prestige and wealth of the aristocrats paying for them vis-à-vis the subordinate commoners. Their crucial role in reinforcing élite power and in signalling conspicuous consumption affected their external appearances, but hardly touched their structural function.

Historical and antiquarian approaches

Romanization has also been approached from the mainstream historical standpoint, where interpretations are based upon the literary sources and epigraphic evidence. Over the last two centuries, this approach has had its own internal intellectual trajectory which cannot be reviewed in detail here (but see Desideri 1991). In its form, this line of research tended to reach similar conclusions to those reviewed in the previous paragraph. Thus, at a basic level, all pre-Roman communities were conquered and, more importantly, all acquired Roman institutions, adopted Latin as a language and were subject to Roman law. Only recently has the full complexity of these processes begun to be analyzed, and this suggests that their cultural meaning is much less clear-cut than had been previously thought (Benelli, this volume).

This branch of research has traditionally relied upon written sources of direct historical relevance. However, from the 1970s, it has been progressively integrated with prosopography, onomastics and the study of cults and funerary practices, approaches that had originally characterized antiquarian research (Barbanera 1998: 182–183). In this way, a much wider range of indicators was brought to bear on the issue of Romanization. Even if this still embodied a bias against lower classes, illiterates and marginal members of society at least; real families and individuals were introduced as actors in the complex processes involved in the transition from pre-Roman to Roman. This was an undeniable improvement from focusing entirely on the artistic fancies of a faceless aristocracy. One example suffices to make the point. The degree of continuity displayed by pre-Roman elite lineages after the conquest has supplied crucial information about the actual implications of the incorporation for some prominent members of the native communities into the Roman Empire (Panciera 1982). The survival of native landed clans, and the land tenure systems on which their power was based, can be a fundamental element of continuity in social organization. Moreover, funerary inscriptions can also reveal the presence of exogenous elements in the local community, such as veterans, or inform us about specific social roles, such as freedmen, while the evolution of local cults can provide important indicators of the ideological makeup of the community, to mention only a few examples. Properly combined, these elements can begin to unveil some of the cultural complexities involved in the process of Romanization.

When observed from this vantage point, our three cities, whose public art and architecture had appeared so similar, begin to exhibit marked differences. Volaterrae is characterized by an exceptionally strong degree of continuity in its Etruscan aristocracy. Its members are senators who have been attested throughout the Empire, but who still controlled large areas of the city's territory (Torelli 1982: 290). By contrast, the funerary stelae which often denote external elements, are all but absent. An almost complementary pattern is displayed by the colony at Luna. Here, the Ligurian elite is almost invisible, while there is a massive and early appearance of foreign elements, which should undoubtedly be linked with the creation of the colony (Angeli Bertinelli 1983). Pisae occupies an intermediate position: there are only traces of the survival of Etruscan clans (Torelli 1969: 288–289), but fewer attestations of veterans and freedmen than at Luna (Ciampoltrini 1982).

Even this oversimplified picture can help us to begin to contrast the different contexts in which the annexation of each community took place. At Volaterrae, it is clear that aristocratic native clans, such as the *Caecinae*, negotiated the terms of their incorporation with Rome, and successfully protected their own interests in subsequent centuries, promoting stability in key areas such as land tenure patterns, social order and the dominant ideological system (Terrenato 1998a: 106–109). They were so successful that some elements of Etruscan rural feudal culture apparently continued with few changes into Late Roman and Early Medieval Tuscia (Mazzarino 1957; Motta 1997). Pisan elites proved to be less effective. The successive capturing and re-taking of this strategically located city by Etruscans, Ligurians and Romans made the preservation of the traditional structure much more problematic. Moreover, the growing commercial significance of Pisa's port probably stimulated social change, as is attested by the emergence of new families involved in manufacture and trade (Pasquinucci 1995: 313). This is consonant with the emergence of new sociological groups, such as freedmen, army veterans and others. These were much less constrained by established norms of behaviour and obligation towards the élites, resulting in a far-reaching transformation of the traditional social structures. Luna appears to have yet another aspect to its character: the role of the colony was inextricably linked with the difficult relationships that the Ligurians had with Rome. This ethnic group, together with the Samnites, put up the staunchest and most obstinate resistance to annexation by Rome (Harris 1989: 114–118). Luna was consequently created with the clear purpose of interposing a buffer zone between them and the Etrusco-Romans to the south, as well as controlling a vital naval base for the fleet in the northern Tyrrhenian sea. In the light of this, it is not surprising to find that the colonial élite was mostly of external origin and that it bore little relationship to the pre-Roman situation (Angeli Bertinelli 1983). These straightforward observations reveal the potential of integrating historical and antiquarian approaches, and the possibility of achieving much more articulate and context-sensitive interpretations of Romanization.

Settlement systems and material culture

The approach described above was further developed during the late 70s and 80s, and subsequently enriched by the formation of a vital and active group of Marxist archaeologists interested in the Romanization of Italy (Barbanera 1988: 181–183). This new trend led to a massive expansion of the database and to the inclusion in analyses of classes of evidence that had been hitherto rather neglected, such as rural settlements, pottery and other artefacts of everyday use. A new phase of field surveys and excavations was consequently spurred by the realization that too little was known about the countryside, where most of the means of production were located (for a review, Terrenato 1996). The emphasis, however, was again mostly on global trends, i.e. those that seemed to characterize all contexts. The Marxian framework called for the definition of general models, such as the slave mode of production, that would explain the entire Roman socio-economic system (see the contributions in Giardina and Schiavone 1981).

The spread of some settlement types was now seen as an univocal indicator for the major economic transformation brought about by Romanization. Villas were located and excavated in many Italian regions and in southern Etruria in particular, leading to the reconstruction of a productive system based on slaves and specialized agriculture (Carandini 1988). In parallel, the study of widely circulated amphora types produced in Italy seemed to point to the existence of a large-scale manufacturing and commercial network that functioned in a quasi-capitalist way (*Amphores* 1989). Our area, however, was not at the core of this major reconsideration of central Italy in the Roman period. Surveys and rural excavations in the territories of the three cities lagged behind in comparison to other areas closer to Rome. As a result, there was a tendency to assume that in northern Etruria the situation was similar to that encountered in the south (Luchi 1981). Early intensive survey work carried out on a limited scale around Luna could do little to contradict the dominant orthodoxy. Even if only two villas were located and local variability was rightfully stressed, the rise and fall of agriculture around the town was seen entirely in a global Roman perspective (Ward-Perkins *et al.* 1986). Later on, other areas confirmed that, at least in inland zones, the impact of the villa system was much less immediately recognizable. Much of northern Etruria was consequently characterized as a sort of backwater where "residual modes of production" still prevailed (Torelli 1981: 426) and where villas were "peripheral" in their nature (Carandini 1994). While this innovative and influential approach marked a major advance in out understanding of the phenomenon, it involved a tendency to underestimate the importance of local diversity. Roman Italy was seen as a strongly integrated and interdependent entity, in which market laws were regulating most transactions, and, as a consequence, those communities that had no major role in this were characterized as marginal. As a result, the Marxist views underplayed heterogeneity in a way that was not dissimilar to the idealist perspective, although for completely different reasons.

Recent research in Italy in general, and in northern Etruria in particular, is revealing a far more articulate picture, which requires a more context-sensitive explanatory framework. Villas, for example, only appear in some districts at different periods and were occupied for different lengths of time and in different cultural contexts. In the territory controlled by Volaterrae they are very rare, and concentrate on its periphery along north-south lines of communication (the Via Aurelia, along the coast, and the valley of the river Elsa). However, the bulk of the territory, by contrast, seems to be completely devoid of villas. Moreover, they do not replace small farms, go on being occupied till the Late Roman period and appear to have been owned by descendants of the local Etruscan aristocracy (Terrenato 1998a: 99–102). Volaterran villas, on the whole, show very little evidence of heralding the advent of a new economic age. Instead they seem to be new status symbols for the local gentry, displaying conspicuous consumption and marking control over the landscape in much the same way as the archaic Etruscan tumulus tombs in same area (Carafa 1994).

At Luna, not surprisingly, villas exhibit different traits. They seem to have been involved in the specialized production of wine and oil, which rapidly declined after the first century AD, as also happened in southern coastal Etruria (Ward-Perkins *et al.* 1986), even if the villas themselves had a much longer life (Rossignani 1985a: 138–140). Only a few villa sites are known from the territory of Pisa, and their appearance seems to date to the Augustan period. The only known owner comes from a family – the *Venuleii* – of possible Etruscan origin (Torelli 1969: 288–289). Traces of centuriation connected with the Augustan *deductio* of a colony at Pisae have also been identified, suggesting that there was a general reorganization of the landscape. However, this does not involve a complete transition to a slave economy, even if there is massive evidence for manufacturing and commercial activities (Pasquinucci and Menchelli 1999: 130–134). The pattern thus seems to differ from that of southern Etruria, especially in view of the absence of a Middle Empire crisis in this district.

In short, the presence of villas now appears to be an indicator that in itself has no universal meaning, but must instead be interpreted within the context of each community. Villas are not necessarily associated with an economic or social revolution, nor with the arrival of new exogenous elites. As a matter of fact, the earliest villas date to the second century BC, thus about a hundred years before the actual annexation of northern Etruria. Their diffusion has long been assumed to be a direct consequence of the conquest, but it now rather appears to have been a cultural trend with dynamics of its own.

Similar conclusions can be reached for the other main settlement type in Roman Italy – the small farm. Improvements in the intensity of landscape coverage and in local coarse ware typologies, has meant that a much larger number of small and less recognizable sites has been located through survey work in recent years than ever before. This suggests that farmsteads were extremely common and that they probably always represented the majority of sites in most Italian landscapes. Moreover, refinements in the dating of the artefacts also shows that the main period of their spread took place between the late fourth and the second centuries BC. This is verified in the territories of the three cities in question and is, remarkably, the only archaeological trait that the three landscapes really have in common. As a matter of fact, it is becoming more and more clear that the massive expansion of these small sites in the Hellenistic period is a trend that affects most of peninsular Italy. As argued in the introduction to this volume, this phenomenon has a very good chance to be associated with the unification of Italy, but not as a direct consequence of it as has sometimes been assumed.

The trajectory of this new settlement system, and its role within society as a whole, again exhibit a degree of heterogeneity. At Volaterrae the farms co-exist down to late Roman times, with villages and a few villas largely owned by Etruscan aristocrats, suggesting a long-lived survival of the traditional forms of social dependency (Terrenato 1998a: 109–112). At Pisae, continuity is much less marked, with the creation of many new sites around the change of era. This must be probably seen in connection with the new colonial status of the city, as well as with the strong expansion of the productive settlements that characterize this area. Now that the troubles with the Ligurians were finally over, the territory of Pisae becomes one of those pockets of intense manufacturing expansion that emerged between the late Republic and the early Empire in several districts of central Italy. Kiln and harbour sites concentrate particularly along the Pisan coastline, but they peter out rather rapidly once the boundary with Volaterrae is crossed (Pasquinucci and Menchelli 1999). At Luna, on the other hand, the spread of farms is in all likelihood a result of assignations to colonists coming from outside. These appear not to have had a particularly long life and seem to have been abandoned in the Middle Empire (Ward-Perkins *et al.* 1986). They may have been replaced by large estates controlled by the owners of the surviving villas. This kind of rural community was not reinforced by shared cultural structures, and was probably very prone to development into large latifundia, as is attested by other Italian examples.

Conclusions

This tale of three cities had the purpose of exemplifying the variability that can be encountered, even within just a small fraction of the rich cultural mosaic that Roman Italy represents. Romanization can truly be seen as having been "the best of times, the worst of times" (as in the Dickensian two cities paraphrased in the title), depending on place, class, individual and perception. Even more importantly, our discussion attempted to show how diametrically opposed historical reconstructions could be generated as a result of the evidence used. These observations seem to go some way in exploring the nature of the variability that Romanization can display in terms of processes involved, Roman strategies and native responses. This diversity can be defined as ranging along at least two dimensions. On the one hand it works across geographical space, since even neighbouring ethnic communities can follow widely divergant trajectories; on the other, it also works across societies, since different social groups within the same community respond in very different ways. It is the latter dimension that is responsible for the apparent contradictions in the material remains. The public behaviour of the elites in towns is radically different from that of the rural population and so it is not surprising that their public architecture and settlement patterns point in opposite historical directions.

The realization that we are dealing with a complex and multi-dimensional process, rather than a unilinear one, however, does not imply a paralyzing relativism, which seems to be hampering some of the pioneering works on variability (e.g. Patterson 1987). The Romanization of Italy can still be construed as a coherent narrative, with a clear direction and an internal logic, even having accepted the views expounded in this paper and in the introduction to this section. However, new historical tools are needed to generate syntheses, without losing sight of the inherent complexity of the issues.

It is perhaps appropriate to make a few observations at this point. Variability does not seem to be infinite and boundless; indeed recurrences, trends and ranges can be identified in attempting to define Romanization. Also, when the indicators of cultural change are properly placed in their social context, rather than taken at face value, many local processes can be reconstructed with a reasonable degree of confidence. At the same time, drafting evidence from one context to "fill the gap" in another should be avoided. There is little doubt that this is an understandable reaction in the face of fragmented and incomplete evidence; it is also quite a common technique, being originally derived from philology and based on an unquestioned belief in a fundamentally homogeneous classical world. However, in the light of what has been said in the present paper, it would be unwise to use any of the workings of Luna to understand those of Pisae or Volaterrae, except the least relevant ones. Consequently, reconstructions should be holistically based on the whole range of the evidence, taking all useful elements into account, but not indiscriminately combining decontextualized evidence.

This approach runs the risk of an even greater danger when syntheses of the whole of Italy are considered: that of generating case-studies that simply reflect the preconceptions of the scholars attempting them. By only selecting and combining those elements which are considered to be 'typical', the final reconstruction is simply a circular argument that confirms the prevailing ideological biases. Indeed, much of the current wisdom about the Romanization of Italy is generally based on patchworks of a limited range of overplayed pieces of evidence. The urban reorganization and the centuriation of the Po plain, the foundation of the colony at Cosa, the repression of Falerii, the confiscations in the territory of Vulci, the dominance of slave-run villas in the Ager Veientanus, the manufactures at Arretium (Arezzo) are all examples of these canonical pieces of evidence. By treating them as highly paradigmatic, one arrives at the common view of Roman Italy as a homogeneous entity brought together and entirely reshaped by the Romans. This conventional picture is in reality much weaker than is conventionally assumed and, in terms of interpretative value, ends up by being less than the sum of its constituent parts. Moreover, once the case-studies are fully contextualized, they can be thoroughly deconstructed and shown to be exceptions rather than the rule.

Local reconstructions, such as those presented here, not only exhibit marked differences between themselves, but do not fit into the conventional picture of the structural and long-term outcome of Romanization. Consequently, the events surrounding the conquest of each city or ethnic group can be reconsidered with fresh interest. They are not simply fragments of *histoire evénementielle*, but may instead contain important clues as to the character of each community. They also provide an instructive cross-section, cutting across the whole range of variability of responses to Romanization. We could say that Volaterrae appears to be a case of mostly negotiated incorporation that leaves the basic social and cultural structure intact. Luna, at the other extreme, appears as a new city planted by Rome within a community not previously urbanized, populated by elites brought in from outside, and with a completely new organization. Pisae appears as an Etruscan centre, whose economy undergoes substantial transforma-tions as the result of internal dynamics and on account of its favourable position in relation to trading networks. In this tale of three cities, it is only Luna that largely conforms to to the standard model of Romanization that is criticized in the introduction to this volume. Exceptional cases such as Luna, however, seem to have been overplayed in many attempted reconstructions of the development of Roman Italy. It is perhaps time to develop a new understanding that is based upon a wider range of archaeological data of improved quality.

Acknowledgements

The present paper is largely based on my PhD dissertation, completed at University of Pisa in 1994 under the supervision of Andrea Carandini. The ideas contained in it were further developed during a stay at University of Durham, made possible by a Leverhulme Visiting Fellowship, which is gratefully acknowledged. The comments offered during the discussion at Ravenna stimulated improvements in this paper.

References

Amphores 1989. *Amphores romaines et histoire économique: dix ans de recherches.* École Française: Rome.

Angeli Bertinelli, M. G. 1983. *Ordo populusque Lunensium. Quaderni del Centro Studi Lunensi* 8: 39–52.

Barbanera, M. 1988. *L'archeologia degli Italiani.* Editori Riuniti: Rome.

Carafa, P. 1994. Organizzazione territoriale e sfruttamento delle risorse economiche nell'agro volterrano tra l'Orientalizzante e l'età ellenistica. *Studi Etruschi* 59: 109–121.

Carandini, A. 1988. *Schiavi in Italia.* NIS: Rome.

Carandini, A. 1994. I paesaggi agrari dell'Italia romana visti a partire dall'Etruria. In *L'Italie d'Auguste à Dioclétien.* École Française: Rome, pp. 167–174.

Cateni, G. and Maggiani, A. 1997. Volterra dalla prima età del Ferro al V secolo a. C.. In *Atti del XIX convegno di studi etruschi ed italici.* Olschki: Firenze, pp. 43–92.

Ciampoltrini, G. 1982. Le stele funerarie d'età imperiale dell'Etruria settentrionale. *Prospettiva* 30: 2–12.

Coarelli, F. 1970. Polycles. *Studi Miscellanei* 15: 75–89.

Cristofani, M. (ed.) 1977. *Urne volterrane. 2, Il Museo Guarnacci.* Centro Di: Firenze.

Desideri, P. 1991. La romanizzazione dell'impero. In *Storia di Roma.* Einaudi: Torino, II.2, pp. 577–626.

Durante, A. 1982. La necropoli di Ameglia. *Quaderni del Centro Studi Lunensi* 6–7: 25–46.

Fiumi, E. 1976. *Volterra etrusca e romana.* Pacini: Pisa.

Frova, A. (ed.) 1973. *Scavi di Luni.* Bretschneider: Rome.

Galluccio, F. forthcoming. Volterra etrusca alla luce delle recenti scoperte. *Opuscula Romana.*

Giardina, A. and Schiavone, A. (eds.) 1981. *Società romana e produzione schiavistica.* Laterza: Rome, Bari.

Harris, W. V. 1971. *Rome in Etruria and Umbria.* Clarendon Press: Oxford.

Harris, W. V. 1989. Roman Expansion in the West. In *Cambridge Ancient History.* Cambridge University Press: Cambridge, 8, pp. 107–162.

Luchi, O. 1981. I territori di Volterra e di Chiusi. In A. Giardina and A. Schiavone (eds.) *Società romana e produzione schiavistica.* Laterza: Rome, Bari, pp. 311–317.

Maggiani, A. (ed.) 1985. *Artigianato artistico: l'Etruria settentrionale interna in età ellenistica.* Electa: Milano.

Mazzarino, S. 1957. Sociologia del mondo etrusco e problemi della tarda etruscità. *Historia* 6: 98–122.

Motta, L. 1997. I paesaggi di Volterra nel tardoantico. *Archeologia Medievale* 24: 245–267.

Munzi, M. and Terrenato, N. 1994. La colonia di Volterra. *Ostraka* 3(1): 31–42.

Munzi, M. and Terrenato, N. (eds.) 2000. *Il complesso monumentale di Vallebuona a Volterra.* Insegna del Giglio: Florence.

Panciera, S. (ed.) 1982. *Epigrafia e ordine senatorio.* Edizioni di storia e letteratura: Rome.

Pasquinucci, M. and Menchelli, S. 1989. *Pisa: le terme di Nerone.* Bandecchi e Vivaldi: Pontedera.

Pasquinucci, M. and Menchelli, S. 1999. Landscape and economy of the territories of Pisae and Volaterrae (coastal North Etruria). *Journal of Roman Archaeology* 12: 123–142.

Pasquinucci, M. 1994. Il popolamento dall'età del Ferro al Tardo Antico. In R. Mazzanti (ed.) *La pianura di Pisa e i rilievi contermini.* Società Geografica Italiana: Rome, pp. 183–204.

Pasquinucci, M. 1995. Colonia Opsequens Julia Pisana. *Annali della Scuola Normale Superiore di Pisa* 25: 311–317.

Patterson, J. R. 1987. Crisis? What Crisis? Rural change and urban development in Imperial Appennine Italy. *Papers of the British School at Rome* 55: 115–146.

Rathje, A. 1979. Oriental imports in Etruria. In D. Ridgway and F. R. Serra Ridgway (eds.) *Italy before the Romans: the Iron Age, Orientalizing, and Etruscan periods.* Academic Press: London, New York, pp. 145–183.

Rossignani, M. P. (ed.) 1985a. *Luni guida archeologica.* Zappa: Sarzana.

Rossignani, M. P. 1985b. Gli Aemilii e l'Italia del Nord. In G. Cavalieri Manasse and E. Roffia (eds.) *Splendida Civitas Nostra. Studi Archeologici in onore di Antonio Frova.* Quasar: Rome, pp. 61–76.

Settis, S. (ed.) 1984. *Camposanto Monumentale di Pisa. Le Antichità II.* Panini: Modena.

Sommella, P. 1988. *L'urbanistica romana.* Jouvence: Rome.

Storti, S. 1989. Pisa: rinvenimenti in ambito urbano. In M. Pasquinucci and S. Storti (eds.) *Pisa Antica. Scavi nel giardino dell'arcivescovado.* Bandecchi e Vivaldi: Pontedera, pp. 93–97.

Terrenato, N. 1996. Field survey methods in Central Italy (Etruria and Umbria). *Archaeological Dialogues* 3: 216–230.

Terrenato, N. 1998a. *Tam firmum municipium.* The Romanization of Volaterrae and its cultural implications. *Journal of Roman Studies* 88: 94–114.

Terrenato, N. 1998b. The Romanization of Italy: global acculturation or cultural bricolage? In C. Forcey, J. Hawthorne and R. Witcher (eds.) *TRAC 97.* Oxbow: Oxford, pp. 20–27.

Tolaini, E. 1992. *Pisa.* Laterza: Rome, Bari.

Torelli, M. 1969. Senatori etruschi della tarda repubblica e dell'impero. *Dialoghi di Archeologia* 3: 285–363.

Torelli, M. 1981. Osservazioni conclusive su Lazio, Umbria ed Etruria. In A. Giardina and A. Schiavone (eds.) *Società romana e produzione schiavistica.* Laterza: Rome, Bari, 1.

Torelli, M. 1982. Ascesa al Senato e rapporti con i territori d'origine. Italia: Regio VII (Etruria). In S. Panciera (ed.) *Epigrafia e ordine senatorio.* Edizioni di storia e letteratura: Rome, 4–5, pp. 275–299.

Ward-Perkins, B., Mills, N., Gadd, D. and Delano Smith, C. 1986. Luni and the Ager Lunensis: The Rise and Fall of a Roman Town and its Territory. *Papers of the British School at Rome* 54: 81–146.

Ward-Perkins, J. B. 1981. *Roman Imperial Architecture.* Pelican: London.

Woolf, G. 1995. The formation of Roman provincial cultures. In J. Metzler, M. Millett, N. Roymans and J. Slofstra (eds.) *Integration in the early Roman West.* Musée National d'Histoire et d'Art: Luxembourg, pp. 9–18.

Zanker, P. (ed.) 1976. *Hellenismus in Mittelitalien.* Vandenhoeck und Ruprecht: Göttingen.

Zanker, P. 1987. *Augustus und die Macht der Bilder.* Beck: Munchen.

Chapter 7

Cultural imaginings. Punic tradition and local identity in Roman Republican Sardinia

Peter van Dommelen

In 237 BC, Roman troops landed in Sardinia, marking the beginning of nearly seven hundred years of Roman rule which was to profoundly transform the lives and traditions of its inhabitants. Most of these changes, which are conventionally described by the term "Romanization", took place in the Imperial period, when the major cities were reorganised along Roman lines, villas were built in the countryside and an extensive road system was laid out across the island (Meloni 1987c). The apparent implication that Romanization was primarily a phenomenon of the Imperial period, however, begs the question of what happened to Sardinia in the preceding centuries of the Roman Republic. Since the island was formally incorporated into the Roman state as early as 227 BC, when the *provincia Sardiniae et Corsicae* was created, and because it was directly administered by the Roman consuls or their representatives, it seems difficult to believe that two centuries of Republican rule had no effect on the island.

The course of events in Sardinia during the third and second centuries BC is relatively well documented by a variety of historical and other literary sources. However, the aim of this paper is to analyze the archaeological evidence in an attempt to look beyond the conventional historical representation and to examine some structural aspects of the social situation of Republican Sardinia. My primary goal is not so much that of providing an alternative general synthesis, but rather to nuance the conventional one and to highlight the complexities, ambiguities and inconsistencies of the situation at grass-roots level. Furthermore, I want to use the Sardinian evidence as a means to explore the notion of Romanization. In order to do so, I shall focus specifically on the region of west central Sardinia, where excavations and intensive field survey have been yielding a wealth of new information (Van Dommelen 1998a: 177–195).

Occupation and resistance

Within the context of the Romanization of the Italian peninsula and the western Mediterranean, the Sardinian case is particularly interesting, because the island constituted the first substantial expansion of the Roman Republic outside the Italian peninsula; the *provincia* established in 227 BC was in fact an innovation created to administer these new territories. The Sardinian situation was therefore substantially different to that of the Italic *civitates* and Italiote city-states of the Italian mainland which had been brought under Roman control through a variety of treaties and other arrangements (see Munzi:

this volume). In contrast to these independent communities, moreover, Sardinia had already seen several centuries of foreign domination, as the southern half of the island had become an integral part of the Carthaginian state in the fourth century BC. Consequently, Sardinia's closest ties were with North Africa rather than with the Italian peninsula. Yet, the integration of the island within the expanding Roman state made it part of the same historical developments and conditions that united the regions of the Italian mainland. Precisely because of this combination of profoundly different roots and a shared historical trajectory, Roman Republican Sardinia seems to offer a particularly interesting case which may contribute to a more general understanding of Romanization processes in the Republican period.

The Roman take-over of Sardinia in 237 BC took place in the aftermath of the First Punic War, which had ended in 241 BC with the Carthaginian withdrawal from Sicily. While Sardinia had hardly played any role in the war with Rome, it became involved in the ensuing Mercenary War, when the Carthaginian forces in Sardinia joined the rebellion in 240 BC and eliminated their officers. When the rebels in North Africa were defeated in 238 BC and Carthage was about to restore its authority in Sardinia, Rome intervened. Ostensibly they responded to an appeal from the rebels on the island, but even an historian as pro-Roman as Polybius conceded (3.28.1–4) that the Romans simply took advantage of the weakened condition of Carthage. Unable to resist, Carthage had to renounce its claim to Sardinia is an additional clause to the peace treaty of 241 BC. Under the command of the consul Ti. Sempronius Gracchus, Roman troops took possession of the island in 237 BC. Roman rule was formalised in 227 BC with the inauguration of the new province and the annual appointment of a *praetor*. At the same time, a fiscal policy was imposed which was geared to the export of large supplies of grain from the agricultural areas of southern Sardinia. The efficiency of this system combined with the fertility of the soil to make Sardinia in Cicero's words (*Leg. Man.* 12.34) one of the "three grain-producing foundations of the state" (*tria frumentaria subsidia rei publicae*: see Meloni 1987a: 219–225).

Unlike Carthage, however, the Sardinians faced the Roman occupation with fierce and enduring resistance: the indigenous 'Nuragic' tribesmen of the northern part of the island in particular, who had previously warded off Carthaginian rule, rebelled repeatedly. No less than 25 triumphs *de Sardeis* or *de Iliensibus et Balaris* are recorded for the 140 years following 238 BC (Van Dommelen 1998a: 168–172). This clearly shows that Roman authority in the mountains of central and northern Sardinia was contested for a long time (fig. 7.1). Although the cities and plains of the south are conventionally regarded as having been firmly under Roman control from the very beginning (Meloni 1987a: 218), the Punic inhabitants of the south resented Roman rule no less than their northern fellow-islanders, with whom they joined forces in 215 BC for a massive armed revolt (Livy 23.32.5–12; see Meloni 1990: 57–64). Given the context of the Second Punic War between Carthage and Rome (219–201 BC), it is not surprising that Carthage did not keep aloof from this event – but its naval and military forces sent in support of the uprising arrived only after the Romans had defeated the rebels.

Such resistance to Roman domination is variously explained. Amongst the 'barbaric' tribes of the mountains, the occurrence of 'native revolts' is usually taken for granted, as if it were a natural phenomenon for them to resist 'civilization' as represented by Roman

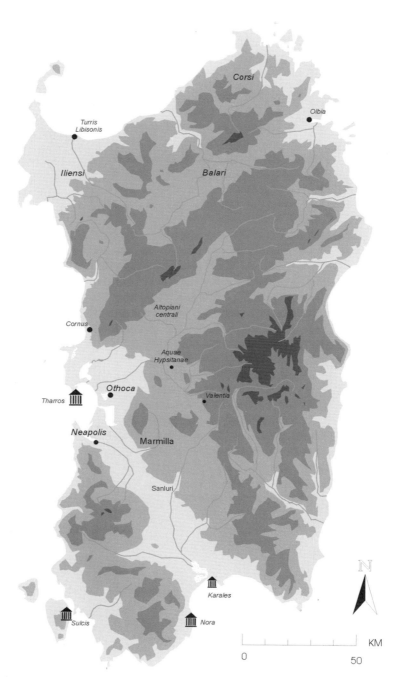

Figure 7.1: Map of Sardinia, showing the major Roman settlements and the approximate location of the areas inhabited by the Iron Age tribal groups

rule (Dyson 1985: 251–253). Punic resistance in the south is similarly seen as straightforward because of the Roman-Carthaginian antagonism of the Punic Wars and the exploitation of Sardinia by Rome as their granary (Mastino 1995: 35–36). The archaeological evidence, however, suggests that the situation was rather more complex. The archaeological record for the Republican period in southern Sardinia in particular is characterized by a predominantly *Punic* appearance, which not only demonstrates a substantial cultural continuity between the Punic and Republican periods but which has also been shown to have been remarkably vital and innovative. Both the cities and the countryside of southern Sardinia upheld their Punic traditions and remained in touch with the Punic world outside the island (Bondì 1987). Moreover, when the archaeological and historical evidence have been considered together, it has been possible to identify several instances in which Roman products from the Italian mainland were consciously avoided in favour of Carthaginian imports. It is at least in these cases, as I have argued elsewhere (Van Dommelen 1998b), that the explicit association of Sardinians with the Punic world at large, and Carthage in particular, can be interpreted as 'silent' or 'cultural' resistance to Roman rule.

Romanization and cultural change

This rapid sketch of Roman Republican Sardinia suggests that any consideration of Romanization processes on the island must start by tackling the role of Punic culture in the Republican context rather than by compiling distribution maps of Roman products. This latter approach has been quite common and has led to the exclusion of Roman Republican Sardinia from discussions, because it is based on the assumption that such 'typically Roman' products as mosaics and bath-houses constitute an effective 'yard-stick' for measuring 'an advanced degree of Romanization' (Rowland 1977: 460). The relative absence of Roman material culture of Republican date means that this kind of approach has inevitably led to the conclusion that Republican Sardinia was by and large a failed case of Romanization (Sirago 1992). As is shown by the failure of Meloni's study to mention anything of Republican date in a chapter dealing with "the Romanization of Sardinia" (Meloni 1987b), the common assumption is that Sardinia only became Romanized from the Augustan period onwards, when Punic culture gave way to Roman civilization. In this view of Romanization, which was originally constructed by Haverfield and Mommsen at the beginning of this century, the adoption of Roman material culture is the critical element of change. In evident contrast to this view, however, Romanization has more recently been defined as a socio-economic process, "in which material culture was used actively to construct, define, redefine and maintain social identities and relationships" (Metzler *et al.* 1995: 2). In the case of Sardinia, such a revised notion of Romanization entails a shift in focus from Roman to Punic (material) culture for assessing 'Romanization' and it requires a radical rethinking of the meaning of material culture in the Sardinian context of the Republican period.

The prominent place now commonly accorded to local indigenous elites in accounts of Romanization in northwestern Europe has moreover tended to stress the indigenous contribution and to offset it against the impact of the Roman occupation (Slofstra 1983; Millett 1990; Roymans 1996). As a result, continuities of indigenous features into the Roman period have been emphasized and the degree of Roman restructuring of local and regional situations has been downplayed (e.g. Roymans 1996). At the same time, Romanization processes have increasingly been represented in binary or dualist terms: the indigenous role *versus* Roman influence. While this is a powerful and to a large extent a necessary correction to earlier one-sided pro-Roman perspectives, such a dualist representation of Romanization has considerable implications and shortcomings which should not be overlooked. Perhaps because of its differences from the northwestern European situation, the Sardinian case provides an ideal occasion for exploring the more general and theoretical aspects of these issues, as it immediately lays bare the *crux* of a dualist representation: who is to be regarded as indigenous in Republican Sardinia? One obvious answer points of course to the fierce 'Nuragic' Sardinians of the mountains as the 'true' bearers of Sardinian identity, but where does this leave the inhabitants of the plains and coastal areas of the south with their Punic traditions? Considering them to be on the Roman side and thus implicitly labelling them as colonial, which has been the conventional approach, cannot stand up to scrutiny, since these people resisted Roman occupation no less than their fellow-islanders in the north. Since similar questions have been posed to the notion of 'Roman' in northwestern Europe, which would fail to appreciate the distinctive appearance of the Roman provinces (Woolf 1995), there seems to be ample cause for dismantling these clear-cut dichotomies and blurring the distinctions between them.

From a theoretical point of view, part of the problem arises from a reluctance to use the concept of agency and a tendency to see culture as a coherent and unambiguously defined entity. A shift in attention from 'cultures' to socio-economic groups of people in a specific regional context readily reveals the inherent ambiguities and uncertainties of Romanization processes. 'Cultural identity' rather than 'culture' then becomes the pivotal concept for considering the socio-economic developments taking place, because it is directly related to people's actions, experiences and perceptions (Friedman 1990; also Barrett 1996). By drawing on the substantial literature on the role of material culture in the definition and representation of identities (e.g. Miller 1994), one can consider 'Romanization' in terms of cultural identity, and regard material culture as a differential and regionally varied process; this would enable comparisons to be drawn between rather different situations. At the same time, it may also help us to understand the apparent 'failure' of Romanization in Sardinia and to understand those developments that did take place.

Punic culture and indigenous identities in Republican Sardinia

Roman Republican settlement in the Cabras and Arborèa coastal lowlands surrounding the shallow Gulf of Oristano, and the adjoining wide Campidano plain (fig. 7.2), closely followed the patterns that had emerged in previous times, as is true of other parts of southern Sardinia. Urban settlements included Tharros in west central Sardinia, the only major city of the region, and the two minor towns of Othoca and Neapolis. They were all based on earlier Phoenician or – in the case of Neapolis – Carthaginian foundations, that had been established between the eighth and the sixth centuries BC. Likewise, small-scale rural settlements invariably had Punic antecedents, even though they were much more recent and did not become widespread before the mid-fourth century BC. Throughout the third and second centuries BC, urban and rural settlement continued to

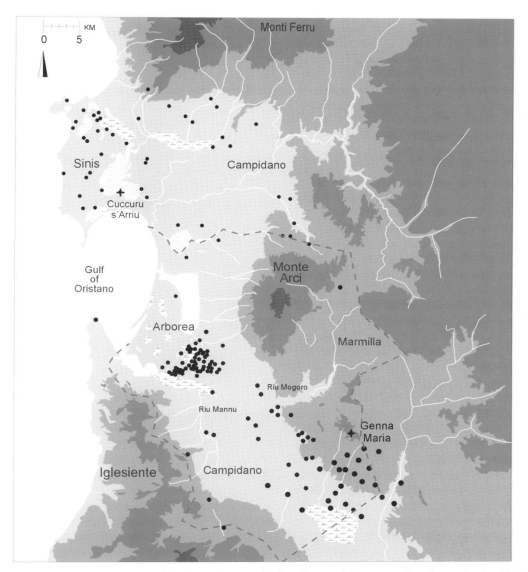

Figure 7.2: Map of west central Sardinia, showing the distribution of known rural settlement in the third and second centuries BC

have a thoroughly Punic appearance in terms of architecture and everyday material culture. The same holds for the cemeteries, regardless of whether they were urban or rural, in which Punic burial rites and the use of Punic material culture as grave goods remained the norm down to the second century BC. With regard to the major cities of Republican Sardinia, it should moreover be noted that their Punic features were not just preserved because of a lack of Roman restructuring – for instance because the first Roman *forum* was not constructed before the Augustan period or because Italian house types did not replace the Punic ones until well into the first century BC (Bejor 1994). On the contrary, the Punic appearance of the cities was not just an archaic survival, but rather more an end that was actively pursued by their inhabitants, as is made evident by the many so-called 'neo-Punic' innovations adopted in south Sardinia. 'Neo-Punic' architectural elements, pottery types and a revised version of the Punic alphabet, emerged in Punic North Africa *after* the Second Punic War and it is therefore significant that they still found their way to the cities of Republican Sardinia. In Tharros, the construction of a small temple at the perimeter of the settlement area in the late second century BC vividly demonstrates the vitality of Punic culture in Republican Sardinia. Its groundplan and decoration closely match contemporary examples of neo-Punic temple architecture, such as the well-preserved chapel from Thuburbo Maius near Carthage, while nothing remotely comparable can be found elsewhere in Sardinia or on the Italian mainland (Acquaro 1983). The close ties and apparently intensive contacts between southern Sardinia and North Africa throughout the Republican period also extended beyond the cities to their rural hinterland, where North African imports were not uncommon (Van Dommelen 1998b: 39–40).

The deep roots of Punic settlement in the regional history of southern Sardinia could easily be defined as 'native', if only in a literal sense of the word. Such a classification, however, would be challenged by the evident contrast, in terms of both appearance and distribution, that separates these forms of urban and rural settlement from the earlier prehistoric nuraghi. Unlike the towns and farms of the Punic and Roman periods, which conform to general 'classical' traditions of settlement and land-use encountered throughout the Mediterranean, nuraghi (fig. 7.3) are not only widespread and characteristic of Sardinia

Figure 7.3: A typical nuraghe (photo P. van de Velde)

– more than 7,000 of them have been recorded – but they also go back for over a millennium to the Middle Bronze Age. At least from a modern point of view, there seems to be no doubt that Nuragic settlement and material culture represent the authentic indigenous culture of Sardinia. Yet, in west central Sardinia, Nuragic Iron Age settlement had started to withdraw from the areas around the Gulf of Oristano in the first half of the seventh century BC and had virtually completely disappeared from the region by the end of the sixth century BC. Only in the Marmilla hills of the interior as well as in the mountains further inland did the nuraghi remain inhabited (Van Dommelen 1998a: 87– 103). In the end, a profound division between southern Sardinia and the central and northern parts of the island emerged, which roughly coincided with the fertile plain and hills on the one hand and the rugged mountains on the other. In the conventional representation, any sense of Nuragic identity was lost in those areas which had come under Carthaginian authority and where Punic culture had replaced indigenous traditions. The latter were only retained in the central and northern highlands, which came to constitute a true 'reservation' for Nuragic culture, and where the indigenous 'spirit' of independence and resistance survived (Lilliu 1988: 481). In this view, the fierce resistance mounted against the Roman authorities by precisely these people makes perfect sense. The inhabitants of the plains and hills of southern Sardinia, by contrast, are represented as having irredeemably lost their indigenous culture and with it any claim to a 'true' Sardinian identity (Lilliu 1988: 471–474).

Indigenous constructs: the case of Cuccuru s'Arriu

In this context, the site of Cuccuru s'Arriu stands out, because it sits uncomfortably with the picture outlined above. It is located to the north of the Gulf of Oristano in the marshy Cabras lowlands (fig. 7.2), lying roughly halfway between the Sinis and northern Campidano. This area was densely occupied in the Bronze Age, but relatively free of Iron Age Nuragic settlement, given that most had been abandoned as early as the ninth century BC (Sebis 1987). Besides a group of Neolithic burials, the most prominent feature of the site is a Nuragic well-sanctuary (fig. 7.4). It consists of a round well, whose rim is nearly one metre below ground level, and which was covered by a classic Nuragic bee-hive shaped dome made of an irregular drystone wall. Its base had a diameter of c. 5 m. Access to the well is provided by a flight of stairs which reaches from the perimeter of the covering down to the well at its centre. There may have been other structures outside the entrance, as at other well-sanctuaries, but later restructuring of this area has obliterated any traces. In comparison to the major well-sanctuaries elsewhere in Sardinia, such as S. Vittoria of Serri or S. Anastasia in Sardara, the one at Cuccuru s'Arriu is rather small and is likely to have been of local rather than regional significance. As such, it is comparable to other minor well-sanctuaries, such as Sa Testa near Olbia (see overview in Lilliu 1988: 521–542). The prehistoric finds consist almost exclusively of pottery (mainly cups and bowls of common domestic types) and certainly attest to occupation of the building during the ninth and eighth century BC (Sebis 1982).

After a long period of abandonment, the site was reused as a Punic shrine. In this phase, a building of 9.70 x 4.50m was added to the Nuragic domed well in line with the stairway. It consisted of a wall of upright ashlars and was presumably unroofed. As the installation of a small altar and a substantial concentration of finds at the furthest end of

Peter van Dommelen

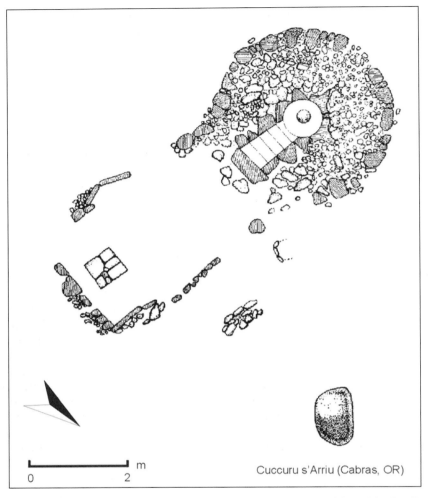

Figure 7.4: Plan of the well-sanctuary of Cuccuru s'Arriu (after Sebis 1982:fig. 8)

this enclosure show, this area constituted the focal point of the site in the Punic phase. The well-sanctuary itself was presumably still accessible, since the collapse of the dome and the consequent blocking of the stairs seem to have occurred at a later stage. The rubble that had filled in the stairway and the central chamber included four Punic stelae and a *cippus* that may have originally stood inside the structure. It is worth noting that the strict division between these finds and the Punic phase of reuse, as proposed in the excavation report (Giorgetti 1982), is highly artificial, being exclusively based on a perceived chronological separation, which in turn depends entirely on the stylistic dating of the stelae (Siddu 1982). Since a later date cannot be excluded (Moscati 1991; Tore 1992), it is assumed here that the stelae belong to the phase of reuse. Just outside the Punic building, a small votive pit was found, containing finds similar to those encountered near the altar. The presence of a conspicuous number of incense burners, including several of the *kernophoros* type (i.e. representing a female head carrying a ritual basket or *kernos*), suggests that the shrine at Cuccuru s'Arriu was probably used for the performance of rural fertility rites of a type widely celebrated in the countryside of Sardinia. The finds include various types of pottery ranging from transport amphorae to imported fine wares, including several oil-lamps, as well as more explicitly ritual objects such as incense burners and anatomical *ex votos*. Particularly notable is a ceramic slab carrying a relief portrait of a female head in a common Hellenistic style. Near the altar, a substantial quantity of burnt animal bones (mainly birds) was found. The pottery indicates that the cult was not inaugurated before the very end of the third century BC, by which time Sardinia had been taken over by the Roman Republic. The shrine fell into disuse in the middle first century BC (Giorgetti 1982).

While none of the elements attested at Cuccuru s'Arriu is unparalleled, it is the very combination of these features which deserves detailed consideration and above all further clarification. The phase of Punic reuse certainly stands out because of its late chronology, which effectively spans the Republican period. At the same time, there can be little doubt about the Punic character of both the material culture used and the rituals performed at the site. This was a type of fertilty cult that was loosely associated with the Greek goddess Demeter, who may indeed be represented by the statuettes and the ceramic head found at the site. However, its appearance in Sardinia from the later fourth century onwards was closely related to the official inauguration of the Demeter cult in Carthage in 396 BC. It is also clear that this was shaped by North African Punic forms and traditions, both most tangibly represented by the incense burners (Barreca 1986: 170–171). The Punic connotations of the cult are, thus, unmistakable. This, together with its chronology, the ongoing contacts between Tharros and its hinterland and North Africa, and the armed revolt of 215 BC (in which this region played a critical role), means that Cuccuru s'Arriu could easily be interpreted as yet another example of the way in which people adhered to their Punic cultural background and mounted a cultural resistance to Roman domination.

This interpretation appears to be sufficiently well founded to counter the aforementioned claims that the Sardinians of the plains and of the hills were incapable of resistance. Nevertheless, both views share a basic assumption about these people: that the Punic material culture used and their Punic customs indicate that they were primarily oriented towards, and loyal to, Carthage. Their resistance against Roman Republican rule and their difference from the mountain tribes are thus both paradoxically grounded in one and the same association of the Punic culture of south Sardinia with that of Carthage. This observation effectively throws us back on what now clearly emerges as the fundamental issue at stake: what does 'Punic' mean in Roman Republican Sardinia? Since neither the disappearance of Nuragic material culture from southern Sardinia nor the Carthaginian connections of the Punic Sardinians can be denied, it would seem that both views have brought to the fore different aspects of an issue which is rather more complex. Because the shrine of Cuccuru s'Arriu appears to embody all these contradictions and inconsistencies at once, it seems a good place to reconsider the meanings and associations of Punic (material) culture.

Constructing identities in Roman Republican Sardinia

A quick glance at a recent overview of Punic ritual sites in Sardinia (Pirredda 1994) immediately reveals that the reuse of Nuragic sites is anything but unusual in the Sardinian context. While there is no shortage of sanctuaries built in a conventional Punic architectural style, such as the temple at Tharros cited above, with quite a few buildings actually meeting Hellenistic standards, there is also a substantial number of Punic ritual sites occupying abandoned Nuragic monuments. These are normally nuraghi in which the central courtyard or one of the towers is reused. Even in this respect, the shrine of Cuccuru s'Arriu is not really exceptional. There are several other instances of reused well-sanctuaries (e.g. at Camposanto of Olmedo) and in the case of nuraghe Su Mulinu of Villanovafranca it was precisely the Iron Age shrine in one of the towers which was reused for ritual purposes in later times (Pirredda 1994: 833). Moreover, the reuse of Nuragic monuments was not restricted to ritual purposes: nuraghi in particular were frequently reused for settlement, either through actual reoccupation of the structure or by adding a new building to the existing monument. Nuragic megalithic tombs were also reused in various ways: in some cases new burials were actually deposited in the chamber (as at Bruncu Espis of Arbus) but in others a house was built in the immediate vicinity of the tomb. Given the eminent visibility of the Nuragic constructions, there can be no doubt that the association with the monuments was deliberate. While a burial monument could offer a good settlement location and a residential tower could be reused as a shrine, the original function of the Nuragic monument in the Bronze or Iron Age does not however seem to have mattered much to the occupants in later times – even if they were aware of it (see Blake 1998: 63–64). At Cuccuru s'Arriu, the shift in ritual focus from the well itself to the area in front similarly suggests that it was not direct functional continuity that underpinned Punic reuse of Nuragic buildings. The principal attraction for the reuse would therefore have been the generic association between these monuments and their prominent positions in the landscape. The very fact that these monuments were selected for such specific reasons indicates that they were perceived as meaningful places, and it is likely that some sort of link with the past, whether distant or not, would have been imagined.

Equally pertinent is the observation that practically all shrines installed in Nuragic monuments are related to the same set of rituals involving incense burners and votive gifts, which are loosely associated with the so-called 'Demeter cult' (Barreca 1986: 170–171; Lilliu 1993: 19). This suggests that the claim about the thoroughly Punic nature of this fertility cult in Sardinia must at least be nuanced, if not significantly revised. Indeed, the choice of a location with particular connotations clearly sets it apart from other Demeter sanctuaries in Sicily, North Africa or Spain (Lilliu 1993: 15–19). While the preference for nuraghi or similar monuments is a uniquely Sardinian phenomenon, the sense of place involved in such a choice is even more significant because it embeds the rituals within a local context, while simultaneously alienating them from their original background.

Other indications that the 'Demeter cult' was perceived as much less Punic than usually assumed come from the excavation of the shrine installed in the courtyard of nuraghe Genna Maria of Villanovaforru, situated in the Marmilla hills of west central

Sardinia (fig. 7.2). In this case, the rituals performed included the offering of oil-lamps which several centuries earlier had already been a feature of the Iron Age cult celebrated in the nearby nuraghe Su Mulinu of Villanovafranca (Van Dommelen 1998a: 153). Similar quantities of oil-lamps have been found at nuraghe Lugherras of Paulilatino, situated on the highlands to the east of the northern Campidano plain: the context of the reported finds strongly resembles that of Genna Maria (Lilliu 1990: 433–437). Although there is at least one other instance of a large number of oil-lamps found in what may be a Punic shrine at nuraghe s'Aneri of Pauli Arborea (Lilliu 1993: 29), offering oil-lamps does not seem to have been a widely shared characteristic of the fertility rituals performed in nuraghi and its absence at Cuccuru s'Arriu, therefore, need not cause concern. Given the concentration of this particular custom in the Marmilla and Monte Arci area (west central Sardinia), it might perhaps be regarded as a local peculiarity. Although the dearth of systematically excavated Punic sanctuaries (see Pirredda 1994) does not allow any assessment of the representativeness of the Genna Maria and Lugherras evidence, it nevertheless shows that the Punic fertilty rituals could be combined with local customs. There is therefore much to be said for the suggestion that the 'Demeter cult' in Sardinia can be considered as a local invention which creatively combined North African Punic rituals with local Sardinian features, such as the abandoned Nuragic monuments and at least occasionally some older customs (Van Dommelen 1997: 318–320).

This view has significant implications for the interpretation of the phase of reuse at Cuccuru s'Arriu, because it suggests that the Punic material culture and rituals need not be, and are indeed unlikely to have been, perceived as Carthaginian or North African by the people who used them, namely the inhabitants of south Sardinia. This does not exclude the maintenance of contacts with Carthage, as has been demonstrated; Sardinia and North Africa had indeed much in common because of their shared past and cultural background. At the same time, it rather emphasizes the local dimension that the so-called Punic culture had acquired in Sardinia over several centuries.

Such an interpretation can be further substantiated by two more observations about the 'Punic' finds from Cuccuru s'Arriu. First, the four stelae found in the stairway are of a type usually erected in an urban *tophet* sanctuary and are consequently out of place in the context of a rural fertility ritual. The *tophet* of Tharros in fact offers close parallels to the four examples of Cuccuru s'Arriu and it is not unlikely that the stelae were produced in Tharros itself. The unusual context of the rural shrine suggests that these objects had been appropriated by the inhabitants of the Cabras plain and adapted to their specific local needs – if not physically, then at least conceptually. While one may assume that these people knew Tharros and its *tophet*, they were apparently equally capable of reusing these stelae in a different context in a similar way to how they reused the Nuragic monuments. At the same time, the differences should not be exaggerated either, since the rituals performed in the rural sanctuary also carried Punic connotations. Moreover, the adoption of stelae for slightly different purposes from the original ones would have been facilitated by the appearance in the third century BC of a new type of stela, used as a grave marker in some rural cemeteries in this part of Sardinia. This process of adaptation has been shown to represent a specifically regional development of west central Sardinia, in which Punic standards for the production and use of these objects were gradually reworked (Moscati 1991).

The other observation concerns some *kernophoros*-shaped incense burners found in various Punic ritual contexts, which never seem to have been actually used for the burning of any substance. These objects should therefore rather be regarded as portraits or partial statuettes (Campus 1997: 169). Such a development makes all the more sense because in later Roman times the 'Punic' fertility rituals seem to have been replaced, at least in the north of Sardinia, by a cult of the Roman goddess *Ceres* in which sculpted female heads were the primary cult objects (Vismara 1980: 79–81). Together, these two elements not only demonstrate how a change in perception can eventually lead to a physical change of the object involved, but they also emphasize the point that identical objects can be perceived and used in quite different ways. While the actual use of the incense burners at Cuccuru s'Arriu remains unverified, it is of course interesting to note that there was one female portrait present in the shrine. This does not exclude the possibility that the *kernophoros* incense burners were actually put to practical use, but it nevertheless shows that the potential for different perceptions of the objects was present.

All this amounts to the conclusion that 'Punic' in Roman Republican Sardinia – or at least in the western region – cannot be equated with Carthaginian nor glossed as 'colonial'. The contradiction between Carthaginian connections and pan-Sardinian coalitions as noted in the previous section similarly dissolves in the light of the foregoing, because a primarily local identity of the inhabitants of southern or west central Sardinia is not inconsistent with either of these relationships. This identity does not somehow comprise two separate 'cultures' but should rather be regarded as a distinct sense of self-awareness created by people with a specific 'hybrid' background which itself rooted in a particular set of historical conditions (see Van Dommelen 1997).

Conclusions: material culture and cultural imagination

The question that remains as yet unanswered is whether the heading of 'Romanization' provides a suitable framework for examining the situation of west central Sardinia in the Republican period. Whilst it is obvious that it is not the case if 'Romanization' is to be equated with the adoption of Roman (material) culture, I contend that the foregoing analysis of Republican Sardinia has shown that the Roman Republican occupation of the island did not remain without consequences, even if these cannot be 'measured' in terms of Roman material culture. The absence of a recognizably Roman presence on Sardinia thus effectively draws attention to the limits of the term 'Romanization', and shows that its inherent focus on uniformization obscures alternative responses to Roman domination. Because of the inherent overtones of assimilation and the implicit colonialist perspective which are fundamentally at odds with an analysis in terms of social agency and cultural identities, I suggest that the notion of 'Romanization' should therefore be abandoned altogether (see Mattingly 1997: 8–11).

Because the Sardinian situation as described above constitutes an instance of precisely such an alternative response to Roman expansion in which Roman material culture plays no part, I suggest that my discussion of Cuccuru s'Arriu provides a suitable starting-point for conceptualizing local responses to Roman expansion in terms of local agency and cultural identity whilst avoiding the pitfalls of the notion of Romanization. I particularly wish to emphasize two points that I see as critical for understanding the Sardinian situation and which may similarly be relevant to other contexts elsewhere. The first one is based on the widespread observation that meanings of material culture are not fixed, but subject to constant reinterpretation. With regard to Roman material culture, this means that Roman expansion need not be accompanied, let alone denoted, by *Roman* material culture, as has repeatedly been observed in other regions, too: the persistent Greek nature of the Roman east provides an obvious parallel (Woolf 1994: 116–118). But whereas Roman material culture did acquire a place in Roman Greece (Woolf 1994: 125–130), it remained much more low-key in Sardinia throughout the Republican period–a phenomenon also noted in the Spanish provinces (Keay 1995: 292–301). In Sardinia in particular, the Roman occupation must first of all be understood in terms of the transformations brought about in the meaning of local material culture, as exemplified by the reuse of the Nuragic buildings and Punic objects at Cuccuru s'Arriu.

The other point hinges on the term 'imagining' as the connection between material culture and cultural identity. I have of course borrowed this notion from Benedict Anderson's apt phrase "imagined communities" which includes first of all the idea of the 'creation' or 'invention' of a distinct identity as a member of a specific community and which at the same time explicitly takes the notion of identity beyond the individual level (Anderson 1983: 14–16). Representing cultural identites as "imaginings" furthermore underscores the active role played by the local community in the construction and reproduction of their identity. Material culture is often an integral part of this process because it adds a tangible dimension to it and because it provides, as it were, 'firm ground' to the images. Material culture, or rather its meaning, thus becomes part and parcel of the cultural imagining (see Miller 1994: 70–71; 77–80).

From this perspective the radical reinterpretation of Punic-style material culture from colonial to local in the Roman Republican period can thus be understood as the response of the inhabitants of at least west central Sardinia to the changed political and economic conditions caused by the Roman occupation and taxation (Van Dommelen 1998b: 40–43). With regard to the Spanish regions occupied by the Roman Republic, it has similarly been argued that "the [Spanish] *provinciae* were being Romanized in the sense that they were being drawn into a closer *economic relationship* with Rome" (Keay 1995: 294). In the case of west central Sardinia, the 'Punic' objects provided the raw material for constructing a distinctive local identity in the new context of the Roman Republic and for imagining a local community that was above all 'not-Roman'. Nor was it Nuragic or Carthaginian, however, despite some obvious affinities. These ties nevertheless provided solid ground for the 'imaginings' of a local identity through the appropriation of both the Nuragic monuments and Punic traditions. In the cultural imagination of the inhabitants of west central Sardinia, the *local* meaning of these monuments and traditions must have been paramount. Cicero's portrayal of the Sardinians as "sons of Africa" *(Pro Scauro* 19.45), however, may at the same time serve as a reminder of the situated nature of meanings attributed to material culture: from a Roman perspective, the Carthaginian connotations of the Punic-style customs in south Sardinia overshadowed the local meanings.

Since all kinds of material culture, including Roman objects, may have been used for imagining local communities, the Sardinian situation is likely to have been less exceptional than it has always been assumed to be. At least in the Republican period, the repeatedly observed persistence of distinct local identities suggests in effect that these were common features in the regions of Italy and the western Mediterranean which were occupied or otherwise dominated by the Roman Republic (see Keay 1995). Although Roman material culture was more prominently involved in the creation of local cultures on the Italian mainland than on Sardinia, there appears to have been a remarkably similar sense of local identity in for instance northern Etruria, where Roman objects, including Roman-style villas, were combined with long-established 'Etruscan' forms of land-use and social organization (Terrenato 1998: 109–112). The common denominator of these cases seems to be that the Republican domination of the region induced local inhabitants to literally 're-think' themselves and their world within the context of the Roman Republic.

Acknowledgements

I wish to thank David Fontijn, Bill Hanson and the editors for their helpful comments on an earlier draft of this paper.

References

Acquaro, E. 1983. Nuove ricerche a Tharros. In *Atti del I congresso internazionale di studi fenici e punici.* CNR: Rome, pp. 624–631.

Anderson, B. 1983. *Imagined communities: reflections on the origin and spread of nationalism.* Verso: London.

Barreca, F. 1986. *La civiltà fenicio-punica in Sardegna.* Delfino: Sassari.

Barrett, J. 1996. Romanization: a critical comment. In D. Mattingly (ed.) *Dialogues in Roman imperialism. Power, discourse, and discrepant experience in the Roman empire.* JRA: Portsmouth, Rhode Island, pp. 51–64.

Bejor, G. 1994. Romanizzazione ed evoluzione dello spazio urbano in una città punica: il caso di Nora. In A. Mastino, P. Ruggeri (eds.) *L'Africa romana X.* Archivio fotografico sardo: Sassari, pp. 843–856.

Blake, E. 1998. Sardinia's nuraghi: four millennia of becoming. *World Archaeology* 30: 59–71.

Bondì, S. 1987. Le sopravvivenze puniche nella Sardegna romana. In M. Guidetti (ed.) *Storia dei Sardi e della Sardegna. (Vol. 1) Dalle origini alle fine dell'età bizantina.* Jaca book: Milan, pp. 205–211.

Campus, A. 1997. Appunti e spunti per un'analisi dei complessi votivi punici in Sardegna. In P. Bernardini, R. D'Oriano, P. G. Spano (eds.) *Phoinikes 'b Shrdn. I Fenici in Sardegna,* La memoria storica: Cagliari, pp. 166–175.

Dyson, S. 1985. *The creation of the Roman frontier.* Princeton University Press: Princeton.

Friedman, J. 1990. Notes on culture and identity in imperial worlds. In P. Bilde, T. Engberg-Pedersen, L. Hannestad, J. Zahle (eds.) *Religion and religious practice in the Seleucid Kingdom.* Aarhus University Press: Aarhus, pp. 14–39.

Giorgetti, S. 1982. Area culturale annessa al tempio a pozzo nuragico. In V. Santoni (ed.) Cabras-Cuccuru S'Arriu. Nota preliminare di scavo (1978, 1979, 1980). *Rivista di studi fenici* 10: 103–127 (Tharros VIII), 113–115.

Keay, S. 1995. Innovation and adaptation. The contribution of Rome to urbanism in Iberia. In B. Cunliffe and S. Keay (eds.) *Social complexity and the development of towns in Iberia. From the Copper Age to the second century AD.* OUP: Oxford, pp. 291–337.

Lilliu, G. 1988. *La civiltà dei Sardi dal Paleolitico all'età dei nuraghi.* ERI: Turin (3rd edition).

Lilliu, G. 1990. Sopravvivenze nuragiche in età romana. In A. Mastino (ed.) *L'Africa romana 7.* Gallizzi: Sassari, pp. 415–446.

Lilliu, G. 1993. Lucerne tardo-ellenistiche e tardo-repubblicane. In *Genna Maria II,1: il deposito votivo del mastio e del cortile.* Cagliari, pp. 43–105.

Mastino, A. C.1995. Le relazioni tra Africa e Sardegna in età romana. *Archivio Storico Sardo* 38: 11–82.

Mattingly, D. 1997. Dialogues of power and experience in the Roman Empire. In D. Mattingly (ed.) *Dialogues in Roman imperialism. Power, discourse, and discrepant experience in the Roman Empire.* JRA: Portsmouth, Rhode Island, pp. 7–24.

Meloni, P. 1987a. La Sardegna e la repubblica romana. In In M. Guidetti (ed.) *Storia dei Sardi e della Sardegna. (Vol. 1) Dalle origini alle fine dell'età bizantina.* Jaca book: Milan, pp. 213–234.

Meloni, P. 1987b. La romanizzazione. In M. Guidetti (ed.) *Storia dei Sardi e della Sardegna. (Vol. 1) Dalle origini alle fine dell'età bizantina.* Jaca book: Milan, pp. 263–295.

Meloni, P. 1987a. L'età imperiale. In M. Guidetti (ed.) *Storia dei Sardi e della Sardegna. (Vol. 1) Dalle origini alle fine dell'età bizantina.* Jaca book: Milan, pp. 235–261.

Meloni, P. 1990. *La Sardegna romana* (2nd edition). Chiarella: Sassari.

Metzler, J., Millett, M., Roymans, N. and Slofstra, J. 1995. Integration, culture and ideology in the early Roman West. In M. Millett, N. Roymans, J. Slofstra (eds.) *Integration in the early Roman West. The role of culture and ideology.* Musée National d'histoire et d'art: Luxembourg, pp. 1–5.

Miller, D. 1994. *Modernity. An ethnographic approach. Dualism and mass consumption in Trinidad.* Berg: Oxford, Providence.

Millett, M. 1990. *The romanization of Britain. An essay in archaeological interpretation.* CUP: Cambridge.

Moscati, S. 1991. Dalle stele votive alle stele funerarie: il 'laboratorio' del Sinis. *Rivista di studi fenici* 19: 145–147.

Pirredda, S. 1994. Per uno studio delle aree sacre di tradizione punica della Sardegna romana. In A. Mastino, P. Ruggeri (eds.) *L'Africa romana XI.* Archivio Fotografico Sardo: Sassari, pp. 831–841.

Rowland, R. 1977. Aspetti di continuità culturale nella Sardegna romana. *Latomus* 36: 460–470.

Roymans, N. 1996. The sword or the plough. Regional dynamics in the romanisation of Belgic Gaul and the Rhineland area. In N. Roymans (ed.) *From the sword to the plough. Three studies on the earliest romanisation of northern Gaul.* Amsterdam University Press: Amsterdam, pp. 9–126.

Sebis, S. 1982. Tempio a pozzo nuragico. In V. Santoni (ed.) Cabras-Cuccuru S'Arriu. Nota preliminare di scavo (1978, 1979, 1980). *Rivista di studi fenici* 10: 103–127 (Tharros VIII), 111–113.

Sebis, S. 1987. Ricerche archeologiche nel Sinis centromeridionale. Nuove acquisizioni di età nuragica. In G. Lilliu, G. Ugas, G. Lai (eds.) *La Sardegna nel Mediterraneo tra il secondo e il primo millennio a.C.* STEF: Cagliari, pp. 107–116.

Siddu, A., 1982. Tempio a pozzo nuragico: le stele puniche. In V. Santoni (ed.) Cabras-Cuccuru S'Arriu. Nota preliminare di scavo (1978, 1979, 1980). *Rivista di studi fenici* 10: 103–127 (Tharros VIII), 115–118.

Sirago, V. 1992. Aspetti coloniali dell'occupazione romana in Sardegna. In *Sardinia antiqua. Studi in onore di Piero Meloni in occasione del suo settantesimo compleanno.* Edizioni della Torre: Cagliari, pp. 239–253.

Slofstra, J. 1983. An anthropological approach to the study of romanization processes. In R. Brandt, J. Slofstra (eds.) *Roman and native in the Low Countries.* Oxford (BAR Int. Ser. 184), pp. 71–104.

Terrenato, N. 1998. *Tam firmum municipium.* The Romanization of Volaterrae and its cultural implications. *Journal of Roman studies* 88: 94–114.

Tore, G. 1992. Cippi, altarini e stele funerarie nella Sardegna fenicio-punica: alcune osservazioni preliminari ad una classificazione tipologica. In *Sardinia antiqua. Studi in onore di Piero Meloni in occasione del suo settantesimo compleanno*, Edizioni della Torre: Cagliari, pp. 177–194.

Van Dommelen, P. 1997. Colonial constructs: colonialism and archaeology in the Mediterranean. *World archaeology* 28: 31–49.

Van Dommelen, P. 1998a. *On colonial grounds. A comparative study of colonialism and rural settlement in first millennium B.C. west central Sardinia.* Leiden University: Leiden .

Van Dommelen, P. 1998b. Punic persistence: colonialism and cultural identity in Roman Sardinia. In J. Berry, R. Laurence (eds.) *Cultural identity in the Roman empire.* Routledge: London, pp. 25–48.

Vismara, C. 1980. *Sarda Ceres. Busti fittili della Sardegna romana.* Dessi: Sassari.

Woolf, G. 1994. Becoming Roman, staying Greek: culture, identity and the civilizing process in the Roman East. *Proceedings of the Cambridge Philological Society* 40: 116–143.

Woolf, G., 1995. 'The formation of Roman provincial cultures'. In J. Metzler, M. Millett, N. Roymans, J. Slofstra (eds.) *Integration in the early Roman West. The role of culture and ideology.* Musée National d'histoire et d'art: Luxembourg, pp. 9–18.

Chapter 8

Transformations and Continuities in a Conquered Territory: the case of the *Ager Praetutianus*

Maria Paola Guidobaldi

The territory described in the Latin sources as the *ager Praetutianus* is now to be identified with the northern part of the Abruzzo, roughly coinciding with the present-day province of Teramo (fig. 8.1). The area was inhabited by the *Praetutii*, one of the peoples that emerged from the fragmentation of the palaeo-Sabellic culture which characterized the Marche, Abruzzo and Sabina between the seventh and the fifth centuries BC. Analysis of this territory before and after the Roman conquest of 290 BC has, on the one hand,

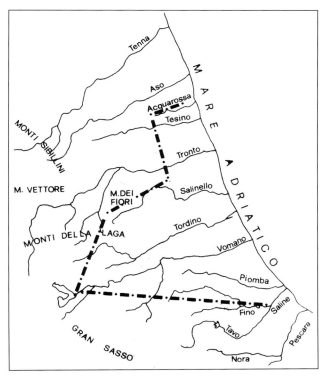

Figure 8.1: Approximate extension of the ager Praetutianus

enabled us to reconstruct the main stages of the formative process leading to the emergence of the *Praetutii*. On the other, it has also permitted transformations and continuities in the territory and in its culture to be evaluated (Guidobaldi 1995).

The first stage in the development of this region is represented by the palaeo-Sabellic cultural *koinè*, that can be illustrated by the rich warrior tombs found at Campovalano, Atri and Basciano. They contain a large quantity of prestige items of Etruscan origin, as well as chariots, and attest to the emergence of aristocratic groups, imitating the luxury of the princely burials of the Tyrrhenian coastal area in more modest terms (fig. 8.2). In the subsequent stage of this formative process, tribal segmentation took place within the Sabellic community. At the Monte Giove shrine, which had been in use since the end of the seventh century BC, stone stele with palaeo-Sabellic inscriptions were erected during the first half of the fifth century. In these texts the community defines itself as *Safina*. The *Safinum nerf* (i.e. the *principes* of the Sabini) seem to be celebrating some heroic figures who were believed to be the guardian spirits of the tribal group (fig. 8.3). At the same time, the paleo-Sabellic inscriptions from the Macerata and Ascoli Piceno districts further to the North attest to the emergence of the ethnic denomination of the *Piceni* (Marinetti 1985: 117–40; 215–23; Guidobaldi 1995: 53–59).

Figure 8.2: Campovalano, cemetery, grave 115. The site of a rich female burial

Evidence for the second half of the fifth and the first half of fourth centuries BC is very scarce, possibly as a result of the growth of main centres such as *Hatria* (Atri) and *Interamnia Praetutiorum* (Teramo). However, the continued occupation of these two cities down to the present, makes it very difficult to investigate this. Another parallel transition, which clearly marks a major cultural discontinuity that cannot yet be fully explained, is the contemporary abandonment of local script on inscriptions. It is also in this period that the ethnic identity of the *Praetutii* is better defined -even if its formative stages largely elude us- leading to the appearance of the fourth and third century BC tombs at Campovalano (fig. 8.4). They seem to imply the existence of a community of limited

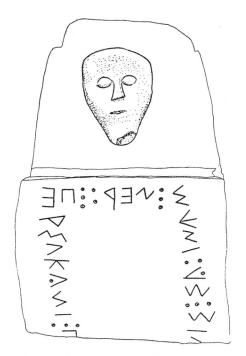

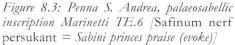

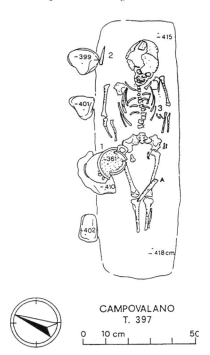

Figure 8.3: Penna S. Andrea, palaeosabellic inscription Marinetti TE.6 [Safinum nerf persukant = Sabini princes praise (evoke)]

Figure 8.4: Campovalano, cemetery. The site of a child's humble grave 397: to the right of the head the saurotēr; and the vase (skyphos) near the right thigh-bone

affluence and with a strongly egalitarian character. It has been also possible to identify a group of Celtic origin living side by side with the *Praetutii*, but maintaining its own ideological traditions, such as the ritual bending of weapons and other iron grave goods (knives, razors and shears).

These are the people that Manius Curius Dentatus conquered at the end of the Samnitic war in 290 BC (Guidobaldi 1995: 61–156). Subsequently, their territory was confiscated, and the title of *civitas sine suffragio* was conferred upon the indigenous peoples. In 241, the Velina tribe was created and the *Praetutii* were attributed to it as *cives optimo iure* (Torelli 1978: 67). The colonies of *Hatria* and of *Castrum Novum* (Giulianova) were founded on confiscated land and lots assigned to Roman citizens. The town of *Interamnia Praetuttiorum* became the site of a *conciliabulum*, where Romans and *Praetutii* lived together and co-operated, and the site of a *praefectura iure dicundo*, whose magistrates were sent out by Rome and had jurisdiction over the entire Praetutian territory. The very name of the city is appropriate to a Roman juridical creation in an area with a palaeo-Sabellic linguistic background. On the other hand, the original constitution of the city, based on a ruling body of eight (*octoviri*), could be related to indigenous traditions. By contrast, inscriptions at the colonies of *Hatria* and *Castrum Novum* record the presence of locally elected senior judges (*praetores*; Humbert 1978: 236–41; Guidobaldi 1995: 183–246).

The creation of the Via Caecilia along a pre-existing route of commuication was part of the same process. This road directly linked Rome with the recently conquered territory and the saltworks of *Hatria*, referred to as *Salinis* on the *Tabula Peutingeriana*. The northern branch of this road led to *Castrum Novum* by way of *Interamnia* and the Tordino Valley, while its southern branch led to *Hatria* and to the coastal saltworks (fig. 8.5). Such a configuration seems perfectly well-suited to the political and administrative organization of Praetutian territory as a Roman province (Guidobaldi 1995: 293–313).

The foundation of *Hatria* and *Castrum Novum* abruptly and unexpectedly introduced urbanism into a world previously characterized by scattered settlements. This, however, did not straightaway revolutionize the existing settlement patterns. The evidence from the *vici* during the second and first centuries BC shows that they were administratively autonomous, and only dependant upon *Interamnia* for the jurisdictional competence of the *praefectura iure dicundo*. Epigraphic and archaeological discoveries have enabled several *vici* to be located, and they are often found associated with shrines built or rebuilt

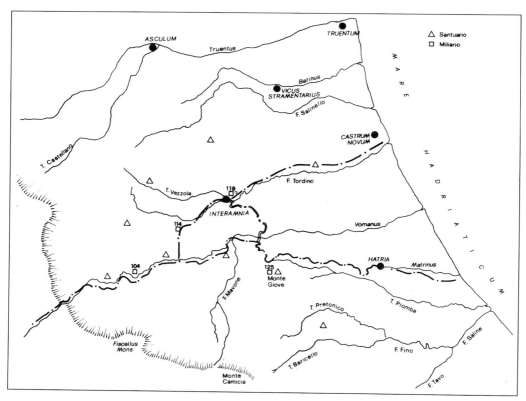

Figure 8.5: Reconstruction of the route of the via Caecilia. *The northern part, moving towards* Interamnia Praetuttiorum *and* Castrum Novum, *passes through the Tordino valley. The southern sector heads towards* Hatria *and the coastal saltworks. A double line and dots marks a probable path that crosses the Forcella and Caprafico and links the northern and southern stretches of the road*

between the second half of the second century and the first half of the first century BC. These cult-places, mostly dedicated to Hercules, were closely integrated into the social and economic context of local indigenous society, thereby attesting to its survival. *Interamnia* itself cannot be considered a real city before becoming a *municipium* after the Social War, or perhaps even until the Sullan colonization. The institutional development of *Interamnia*, from *conciliabulum* to *municipium* and finally *colonia*, corresponds to remarkable changes in its urban layout. For example, the grant of colonial status by Sulla prompted the emergence of a wealthy local aristocracy, who commissioned lavish residences, such as the *domus del Leone*, and realistic portraits, like the well-known clay bust of early first century BC date that is now in the Museo Nazionale Romano.

The distribution of *vici* and shrines (fig. 8.6) among the territories of *Interamnia, Hatria, Castrum Novum* and *Truentum* (as defined by Thyssen polygons) allows several observations to be made (Guidobaldi 1995: 247–77). First, there was a higher concentration of sites in the upland hinterland of *Interamnia*. Secondly, they were rare in the eastern sector of

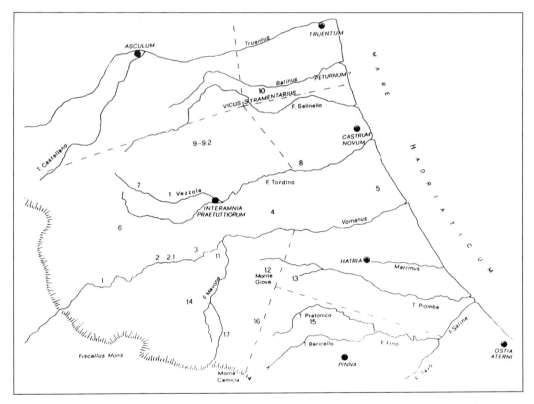

Figure 8.6: Map showing the distribution of the vici *and sanctuaries in the* ager *Praetutianus*

Interamnia's territory between Teramo and the Adriatic coast. Indeed, the only evidence comes in the form of a textual reference to a shrine of Apollo (n. 8), whose cult was introduced by the colonists. This suggests that Roman citizens with individual (*viritim*) land allotments were present. Thirdly, there are very few *vici* (settlements) in the territory of *Hatria*. Whenever the identity of the god worshipped at these shrines, it is always found to be Hercules (as attested by inscriptions found at sites n. 2, 4, 10, 11), which is understandable given the pastoral society of the associated *vici*.

The land assigned to colonists, both individually and upon the creation of *Hatria* and *Castrum Novum*, was intensively cultivated, with vineyards being very common. The wines from *Hatria* and from the *ager Praetutianus* (called *Hatrianum* and *Praetutianum*) are highly commended by several ancient authors. There is also evidence for the existence of Lamboglia 2 amphora kilns at *Hatria* and in the *Castrum Novum* area. This was a wine container that is the Adriatic equivalent of the Dressel 1 amphorae manufactured in Tyrrhenian Italy (Guidobaldi 1995: 206–7). Villas with wine-producing facilities also make their appearance in this area (especially in the Tortoreto district) in the first century BC (Guidobaldi 1995: 288–91).

These stages in the penetration of Latin culture can also be followed in the religious sphere. Soon after the conquest, the Romans take over the indigenous sanctuary at Monte Giove. In the second century BC, religious buildings are created outside city limits and by decree of the *magistri vici*. Architectural terracottas and votive materials for these shrines can be frequently attributed to the workshops of the Latin colony of *Hatria*. This underlines the important role that the colony played in the diffusion of artistic forms that had been defined in Rome and Latium since the first decades of the fourth century BC. Colonization had, thus, spurred the emergence of crafts closely associated with the Latin religiosity that was replacing its indigenous counterpart. The same was true of the production of fine wares. These had been manufactured in *Hatria* since the foundation of the colony, to supply the colonists, and they quickly spread to the countryside, where they ousted local productions.

Acknowledgements

This text represents a very schematic summary of a larger and more articulate study, which I conducted for my PhD dissertation in Greek and Roman Archaeology at University of Perugia, which was later published in book form (Guidobaldi 1995). The reader is referred to it for a fuller discussion on the topics herein outlined, and for a wider bibliography.

References

Humbert, M. 1978. *Municipium et civitas sine suffragio. L'organisation de la conquête jusqu'à la guerre sociale.* EFR: Rome.

Guidobaldi, M. P. 1995. *La romanizzazione dell'* ager Praetutianus *(secoli III-I a.C.).* Università degli Studi di Perugia-Edizioni Scientifiche Italiane: Napoli.

Marinetti, A. 1985. *Le iscrizioni sudpicene. I Testi.* Olschki: Firenze.

Torelli, M. R. 1978. *Rerum Romanarum fontes ab anno CCXCII ad annum CCLXV a. Ch. n.* Giardini: Pisa.

Chapter 9

Roman intentions and Romanization: Republican northern Italy, c. 200–100 BC

J. H. C. Williams

"You should go back to wherever you came from... The Alps are an almost impassable barrier between us" (Roman envoys to invading Gauls, Veneto, 183 BC; Livy 39.54.12)

Republican northern Italy and Romanization Studies

Romanization has been much on everyone's minds over the past few years in the world of Roman studies. Fruitful dialogues have developed between Roman historians, Roman archaeologists and Iron Age prehistorians, and the result has been a lively debate about Romanization, what we mean by it and how we can talk about it. It has perhaps become something of a self-perpetuating meta-discourse with almost as much written about British imperialist attitudes as about Roman ones (e.g. Hingley 1996; Freeman 1996; 1997). Moveover, this is, it must be said, still largely a debate limited to contributors from British and Dutch institutions, for better or worse. The ensuing discussion has, nevertheless, been stimulating if, occasionally, hard to follow (e.g. Jones 1997). Its focus has mostly, though not entirely, been on the northern provinces and the Imperial period at the expense of Italy, the Mediterranean provinces and the Republic (see, e.g., Blagg and Millett 1990a; Millett 1990b; Woolf 1992; Freeman 1993; Hanson 1994; Webster and Cooper 1996; Mattingly 1997; Laurence and Berry 1998; Woolf 1998). This north-western bias reflects the main areas of interest of those archaeologists who initiated this reassessment of the meaning and analytical usefulness of Romanization as a concept.

Republican northern Italy, the subject of this paper, has by contrast not tended to receive much attention within the scope of what we might call the western provinces approach to Romanization. But it has been the subject of considerable thought and writing on the part of mostly Italian and French contributors. How have they approached it? There are, in brief, three main academic groups involved: historians of the Roman conquest and settlement who base their accounts primarily on the literary evidence with occasional sideways glances at the archaeology, of whom the doyen must surely be Emilio Gabba (see, e.g., Dyson 1985: 1–41; Gabba 1984; 1986; 1990; Harris 1989; Oebel 1993); those writing on the Roman archaeology of the region, who tend to concentrate on cities and centuriation patterns (e.g. Tozzi 1972; Chevallier 1980b; 1980c; 1983; Denti 1991) and finally the prehistorians who write about Etruscans, Celts and Ligurians (e.g. Santoro 1978; Peyre 1979; De Marinis 1988; Kruta 1988; Grassi 1991). How do these groups line up around the issue of Romanization? For Romanists of both sorts, the main focus of interest is the spread of Roman artefacts, structures and institutions, the project being to chart the progress of the diffusion of Roman things, practices and people into a previously non-Roman zone. In the Republican period at least, they understandably tend to concentrate on the heavily colonized region south of the Po, where the transition from pre-Roman to Roman in the second century BC seems abrupt and obvious, and pay less attention to Transpadane Italy where direct Roman intervention was less intensive. Prehistorians, no less understandably, have by and large tended to restrict their field of study to the pre-Roman period, and have concentrated on discussing the prehistoric archaeology of northern Italy within the ethnic and chronological framework provided by the various peoples named in the classical texts: Etruscans, Veneti, Ligurians and Celts. The story of Romanization among the pre-Roman peoples of northern Italy as told by prehistorians concentrates largely on the Transpadane region. It is essentially told as a tale of cultural decline, tracing the dissolution of pre-existing ethnic groups and material cultures under the irresistible influence of Roman power. It tends to be narrated as the last chapter in the history of the non-Roman populations of the region, in which there has been a considerable increase in scholarly and popular interest over the last twenty years or so, particularly in the Celts, for a variety of cultural and, more recently, political reasons (Stella 1996: 6, 55, 210–14; Williams 1997: 78 n. 8). The story involves, on the one hand, the erosion of local artefact styles and burial customs and the adoption of Roman ones and, on the other, the continuation and even elaboration of localized pottery styles but "within the context of a society that no longer had its own form of expression but instead yielded to outside cultural influences" (Arslan 1991: 467; see also Arslan 1978). Post-conquest cultural change is thus seen as a tale of indigenous passivity in the face of Roman colonial penetration. However, in an interesting anticipation of later approaches to the question of the Romanization of Britain, nascent urbanization north of the Po and, in particular, the development of Mediolanum (Milan) and Brixia (Brescia) in the second and first centuries BC have been explained as a political strategy driven by local pro-Roman elites and designed to maintain their ascendency in the post-conquest world. This was effected by turning the towns into centres for the control, acquisition and redistribution of imported Roman goods and artefacts, a development that led subsequently to the general Romanization of the population via the widespread circulation of Roman-style goods, and the assimilation of local social structures to the Italian norm through the new and pervasive infuence of the towns as the focus of political and economic power in the region (Arslan 1976–78; 1991; Gabba 1986).

Prehistorians study the peoples and artefacts of the pre-Roman period in northern Italy, Romanists study the Romans and their material culture, but few indeed are those who bridge the divide, at least within the scope of a single work. There have been occasional attempts at the integration of prehistoric and Roman studies – it would be unjust to suggest otherwise (see, e.g., Arslan 1976–78) – but they continue more in parallel than in tandem. There are of course various reasons for this bifurcated conception of the period which arise from the divergent intellectual histories of the two disciplines involved. But there is also a simple lack of good archaeological evidence of the right sort to assist crossover studies. It does seem more difficult to trace the change from pre-Roman to Roman in the archaeology of most of northern Italy than it is, say, in late Iron Age southern Britain where a much broader range of site-types is available. The relevant archaeology of late Iron Age northern Italy is, with the exception of the important site at Monte Bibele, still mostly funerary in nature now as it was 130 years ago when De Mortillet first identifed a group of tombs at Marzabotto as Celtic (see De Mortillet 1870–71; Vitali 1985). There are some interesting new results from Mediolanum relating to emerging urban structures in the second century BC (Ceresa Mori 1995), but there apart there is only so much one can say on the basis of changing burial styles and increasing quantities of such materials as Italian black-glaze ware in late La Tène cemeteries. In many regions of northern Italy, it is extremely difficult to see what was going on in the indigenous communities of the north either side of the Po during and after the Roman conquest in the second and first centuries BC. And it is particularly hard to detect these communities in the new and very Roman-looking landscape and cityscapes which came into being mostly south of the Po in this period. As a result, the post-conquest history of the non-Roman communities, especially those of the Cispadane region, tends to be left out of most accounts by default. This lack, which is certainly one of evidence but also of imagination, makes it much more of a problem to cross the border between Iron Age prehistory and Roman history, both conceptually and chronologically.

The range of approaches to Romanization in post-conquest Republican northern Italy thus broadly divides up as follows: Romanists, particularly text-based historians, look south of the Po first and see Roman colonies and roads as the principal objects of their research and the main themes of their narratives, while prehistoric archaeologists look north of the Po for their material and, for their part, trace the gradual submergence of local traditions of material culture under Roman influence. The interaction between these two worlds of academic discourse seems rather limited, which is the main issue to which I want to draw attention. Why do we write books about the Italian Celts or the Ligurians or, on the other hand, about the Romans south or north of the Po, rather than accounts of northern Italy from, say, 300 BC to AD 100? It is precisely this disciplinary boundary, coupled with a general tendency to focus rather exclusively on the local context, that prohibits the rise of serious comparative approaches to the Romanization of northern Italy.

The limits of the western Provinces Approach to Romanization

It might be objected that the two regions either side of the great river of the north are so clearly different from one another in the manner of their respective Romanizations that even a global treatment of the whole region, let alone a comparative approach taking other areas into account, would be redundant; that the material on offer provokes different approaches because different things happened. This is, in itself, not an unreasonable position to take, and it may well be that *ad hoc* interpretations are better suited to explaining the nuances of local variation than are universalizing theories. Concentration on a single locality may, however, lead one to assume that what is characteristic of a particular region is also typical of the Empire as a whole. So it was, I would argue, for those British archaeologists in the 1980s who, in their path-breaking re-evaluation of the Romanization of the western provinces, observed a lack of evidence, literary and material, for what one might call Roman cultural imperialism, rejected the whole notion as an unwanted inheritance from their imperialist forebears, and instead looked at Romanization as a consequence of locally-driven responses rather than imposition from above (see, for an extended worked example, Millett 1990a). This shift in perspective served the useful purpose of prompting the reassessment of a set of sometimes rather crude assumptions about the relationship between Roman imperial 'policy' and the archaeological evidence for the spread of Roman-style material culture, assumptions which are still very much current in some areas of Roman studies. But it was perhaps wrong to conclude from the British archaeological evidence that Romans never had *any* serious interest in introducing their ways to the natives.

The consequence of the general acceptance of this position by most British archaeologists for the debate on Roman imperialism in the western provinces in the 1980s and early 1990s was that material Romanization of all sorts, from Samian potsherds to monumental town centres, was decoupled from Roman imperialist intentions and, furthermore, the Romans themselves were stripped of any notions that smacked of cultural imperialism. Since then, the debate has moved on considerably and yet we are no closer towards resolving what we mean, or what might be meant, by the term Romanization. As a result, people have become rather tired of the whole business and in most recent years have moved on to talk about other issues such as ethnicity or resistance, in an attempt to find new headings other than Romanization under which usefully to continue discussion of what happened to the people of a region after the Romans conquered it (Webster and Cooper 1996; Mattingly 1997). But the emphasis is still very much on looking at the local and indigenous side of things, their reactions and strategies, with two implicit assumptions: namely, that the views and intentions of Romans are mostly irrelevant to understanding how things worked themselves out on the level of the locality or the individual, at which most archaeological evidence works best and on which archaeologists therefore often tend to concentrate; and that as conquerors the Romans had no coherent idea of imperialist practice anyway, and certainly did not set out to change anything or anyone very much according to a concerted plan or even a more loosely conceived set of cultural attitudes. The first of these assumptions may have some validity, the second, at least as a general conception of the intentions of Romans, is, I would argue, more doubtful, and certainly does not follow from the first, which is how the matter is often presented.

Against this view, it might be objected that there is no indication that there was anything like an official handbook of Roman imperial practice available to generals and governors to tell them how to make natives into Romans, as an argument in favour of the notion that Romans lacked a self-conscious intention to impose their culture upon the conquered. Yet lack of explicit codification need say nothing about solidity of intention on the part of those wielding imperial power. What underpinned the relative consistency of the ways in which, for instance, Britons behaved in and ruled over the British Empire was not a book of rules sent out from the Colonial Office, but the fact that they mostly came from the same sorts of social, religious and educational backgrounds (Judd 1997: 143). This would have been no less true of those Roman aristocrats who were in charge of things in the provinces. They shared a world of values and experiences in common as members of the Roman and Italian upper classes and they therefore tended to think in similar ways and behave more or less consistently in relation to the non-Roman regions and populations under their control. Nicholas Purcell has shown how what else we know of Roman attitudes and habits concerning the organization of geographical space according to inherited religious concepts explains something about the ways in which Cisalpine Gaul was reorientated around towns, roads and centuriated landscapes (Purcell 1990). If this is right, then it must constitute an important element in any explanation of why things, places and people changed as they did in northern Italy the second century BC. If this is true in northern Italy, then it is reasonable to suggest that it may also be the case in other areas as well, though not, of course, necessarily in the same ways or to the same extent.

Between Roman imperialism and local agendas – a third way?

It is proposed here that the obvious misfit between the variability of the archaeological evidence for Romanization within a given region and perhaps dated notions of Roman cultural imperialism says nothing either way about the nature of the Romans' imperialist intentions. The detailed archaeology of a region may indeed suggest that what we call Romanization was an untidy, regional process of negotiated change with variable consequences in the world of material culture, rather than the rigid application and adoption of a single Roman matrix. But this conclusion cannot then be used as proof of the thesis that the Romans were as a rule essentially *laissez-faire* in the way in which they set about dealing with newly conquered areas and their populations. Conversely, to argue that various attitudes held and actions performed by Romans had something to do with the direction taken by post-conquest changes evident in a particular area does not commit us to the view that Roman culture *only* spread as a consequence of paternalistic intervention, or that Roman interventionism explains everything that happened in a region after its conquest.

Take, as an example, the massive changes set in train by the conquest of northern Italy over the early second century BC. Here, if anywhere, it is apparent that a concerted effort was made by a large number of Romans of many different types, from senators to settlers, to transform both land and people over large areas in the first half of the second century BC, from the end of the northern wars in 191 BC up to the construction of the Via Postumia from Genua to Aquileia in 148. It seems clear that centrally-driven imposition is indispensable to any account of the changes which occurred in this region in this period, changes which are evident in both the material and historical records. A consecutive series of decisions was taken over several years by the relevant authorities in the city of Rome to found colonies, build roads, shift local communities from their land-holdings, centuriate huge tracts of land and introduce new populations. The effects of these decisions on both landscape and people were immediately palpable. This is an assertion of extraordinary banality in itself and will come as no surprise to Romanists currently looking at northern Italy, by whom Romanization tends anyway to be seen primarily as a progressive story of colonization and cultural diffusion. But, turning to the rather differently articulated western Provinces approach to Romanization, it does serve to establish the notion that Roman imperialist action was potentially highly interventionist under certain circumstances.

But this, of course, is not the whole story. Even within the context of a region so heavily affected by Roman interventions as the Po Valley, it is clear that there was a lot else going on which does not need to be explained as a consequence or even a by-product of Roman orders and actions, such as the urban development of Mediolanum and Brixia in the second and early first century BC which, as mentioned above, is much more likely to have been locally motivated than a straightforward consequence of Roman imposition. It should of course, but often does not, go without saying that there were still thousands of non-Roman individuals and communities all over northern Italy, north and south of the Po, doing their own thing in a multitude of different ways: interacting with Romans, obeying them, ignoring, resisting them overtly or covertly, even fighting them sometimes, and others who had little or no contact with them at all for much of the time. There are problems of evidence here, as mentioned above. But it also represents a collective failure of the scholarly imagination to postulate, and think about, the continued existence of large indigenous populations after the conquest even in the most transformed areas south of the Po. Some commentators have pointed to the passage of Strabo which claims that the Boii, who inhabited the modern Italian region of Emilia-Romagna, were sent back over the Alps where they had originally come from (Strab. 5.1.6). One might, just as well, cite the passage of Livy where we read that they were deprived only of half their territory after their surrender in 191 BC (Livy 36.39.3). The Gauls may have lost a lot, and perhaps the best, of their lands, but not necessarily everything. Again, the absence of 'Celtic'-style burials (i.e. ones with weapons and wine-drinking gear) from the material record after the third century BC might be taken as evidence for the disappearance or at least dissolution of indigenous ethnic groups in the Cispadane region. Yet, archaeologically visible burials of this sort, of which the corpus from the late pre-Roman Iron Age in northern Italy is anyway not exactly extensive, can only ever have represented a tiny minority of the population, such that their disappearance cannot be used as evidence one way or the other for what happened physically to the remaining majority. The point is that there is plenty of space in both the historical and archaeological records within which sizeable local communities may be allowed to have persisted into the post-conquest Cispadana, even if we cannot see them and have no idea of what happened to them. They simply must have been there, and they must be taken account of in some way or other. The Romans were just not capable of exterminating or expelling whole populations over a region that size (Vitali 1991: 235). What are the options? They may all have joined Roman or Latin colonies as *accolae*. They may alternatively have reconstituted themselves largely on their own initiative into new groups and given rise to some of the *fora* dotted along the Via Aemilia. Even here, in what was perhaps the most heavily redeveloped region in the whole of the Republican Roman Empire, there must have been large areas where Roman power did not reach and where people worked out their own conceptual and material agendas with only a tangential relationship to the new framework.

Where does this lead us? Towards two, complementary observations about the nature of Roman imperial intentions and their explanatory relationship to post-conquest change. First, the example of northern Italy establishes the principles that Romans could, in certain instances at least, have fairly concerted ideas about how they should manage and reshape newly conquered peoples and places; that they were capable of putting them into widespread effect; and that these imported ideas and associated ways of behaviour were capable of inducing substantial changes within local populations after conquest, ranging from their settlement patterns and material culture to their sense of communal identity. To return to the Cispadane region of northern Italy as an example, the admittedly exiguous evidence suggests that the intrusion of Roman institutions and structures effectively suspended expressions of wider ethnic community or social status that were not in some way predicated upon the new urban and rural framework. This is, however, not to say that there were not persistences of identity on the local level among the *fora, vici,* and *conciliabula* of the Po Valley (see the *lex de Gallia Cisalpina, CIL* I² 592, ch. XXI, col. II, ll. 1, 26, 56, for a catalogue of the various types of settlements to be found in Cisalpine Gaul in the late first century BC; for commentary, see Crawford 1996, 1: 461–77). Nevertheless, unlike the Insubres and Cenomani north of the Po, who continued to be recognized by Greek and Roman observers as large-scale ethnic groups in the first century BC, the Cispadane Boii and Senones had by then vanished from their ethnic maps of Italy (Strab. *loc. cit*; Plin. *HN* 3.116). This phenomenon has tended to be interpreted as a consequence either of Roman genocide or of lethal cultural marginalistion. But it might just as well be an indication of the successful integration of indigenous communities into the new world of post-conquest northern Italy. Rather than extirpation, perhaps the willing abandonment of the ethnic identities of the Boii and Senones is worth considering as an option to account for their apparent disappearance. The two main 'Gallic' peoples north of the Po, the Cenomani and Insubres, were by contrast treated quite differently. Their lands were, for a start, not so extensively colonized in the second century BC and treaties were made with them that expressly excluded their members from acquiring Roman citizenship. Their identities survived, then, but perhaps at the cost of exclusion from a status and an identity, that of Roman citizen, which they seem to have come to desire by the time of the Social War (Cic. *Balb.* 32; see also Gabba 1986).

The second point leads on from the observation of considerable variety within the post-conquest history of the Po Valley. To advocate the importance of Roman attitudes and intentions within an account of the post-conquest development of occupied regions does not necessarily entail a conception of them as uniform or immobilized. That is perhaps how they were conceived of by a past generation of scholars who took the now notorious passage of Tacitus' *Agricola* 21 as an exposition a general law of Romanization (so Millett 1990b: 37), and it is still how they are often treated by practicioners of *histoire des mentalités* (e.g. Dupont 1992). The answer to this, however, is not to jettison the notion of Roman imperialist intentions as a whole, but to restructure it by adding the crucial twin ingredients of variability and change, and then rethink its explanatory role (for an example of how this might work, see Metcalfe 1997 for an excellent account of the different, and changing, imperialist ideologies of the British in relation to India). This would, firstly, be a more reasonable position in itself – of course not everybody within a given culture thinks or acts in the same way however much they may have in common, which is, after all, why ideas change through time. It would also counter the archaeologist's objection that historians and 'historical archaeologists' of the old school work with simplistic and monolithic notions of *Romanitas*. Northern Italy again provides a useful illustration of this point. The Latin Right (*ius Latinum*) and then the Roman citizenship were denied to the peoples north of the Po for many decades after these communities had begun to desire them because, I would argue, many Romans could not bring themselves to enfranchise communities of feared and hated *Galli* (Williams; forthcoming:

120–37). These attitudes, at least as they related to the Gallic communities south of the Alps, had changed by the middle of the first century BC and enfranchizement was eventually secured in 49 BC, though not without considerable opposition and hostility. Differences of opinion and changes of mind are inherently human characteristics. They are not specific to Romans and do not add up to a brand of laissez-faire imperialism peculiar to them.

Conclusions

Other papers in this volume address the need for archaeologists to take account of local variables and long-term trends in accounting for post-conquest change in a particular region, in order that we might arrive at a more flexible understanding of what we call Romanization. The moral of this paper is that we should do something similar to our possibly over-generalized conceptions of Roman imperial ideas and intentions too. If different areas of Italy responded differently to the new situation represented by the Roman conquest, as is becoming increasingly evident from new archaeological evidence, then we should also allow the Romans to be a bit more flexible and inconsistent as well, and even to change and develop their ideas and practice through time. Secondly, if we are to introduce the local creative agent into our concepts of Romanization, then we should also revise our understandings of the Romans' post-conquest responses to the several regions they took control of, as being one important way into understanding why Romans did things differently in different parts of the Roman Empire, and how their intentions and actions may have affected the various kinds of cultural change which we call Romanization in each area. Part of the answer to this might be to investigate what sort of preconceptions Romans had about the various lands and peoples they conquered— and in the case of much of northern Italy of course, they were dealing with the despised and loathed Gauls, a point which, I have argued elsewhere, might be thought to be relevant to the question why such drastic measures were implemented over large areas of the Po Valley in the first half of the second century BC (Williams; forthcoming: 207–18).

  Diversity is certainly evident in the post-conquest organization and development of the Po Valley, both in the intentions of Romans motivating it at the highest level and in their consequences for the landscape and people of the north. I am not arguing that the variety we see in the post-conquest development of different regions of the north of Italy is simply, or even primarily, to be explained as a consequence of varying Roman actions and intentions. But, the evidence of Republican northern Italy suggests, neither can the variable development or adoption of Roman-style material culture in all its forms, from walled towns to ceramics, be accounted for solely as a consequence of locally-driven strategies. We need, of course, to examine both Roman and indigenous agendas, without imagining them as readily identifiable and statically opposed cultures or people; and, perhaps just as importantly, without identifying ourselves too exclusively as Romanists or prehistorians.

  The apparent neglect of northern Italy in general, and of Republican northern Italy in particular, in the western Empire debate on the theory and reality of Romanization illustrates how parochial, dare one say provincial, Roman studies in many areas have become, segmented by national, linguistic and disciplinary boundaries. The same is equally true in reverse: the general lack of interest shown in the ideas generated by this debate among those working on other areas of the empire is no less lamentable. There is surely much to be gained from simply putting disparate strands of academic discourse back in contact with one another, with a view to creating new possibilities for dialogue between academic traditions in different parts of Europe, and between different disciplines that live either side of the conceptual watershed separating prehistory from history. Boundaries like these which are so deeply ingrained in scholarship are hard to cross but, as the Romans found on a number of occasions, are like the Alps themselves not completely impassible. Northern Italy might be a good place to try to bring Republic and Empire, Continental Europe and the Mediterranean, archaeology and ancient history back together in a new and productive relationship. While it would be misleading simply to conceive of the region as a transitional region between two worlds north of the Alps and south of the Apennines, it may nevertheless have beneficial consequences for academic interchange to allow this idea to come to the fore for the moment, in order to facilitate the formation of a new kind of academic discourse, broad-minded and open-ended enough to be able to include contributors from fields currently as far apart from one another in character and direction as British Iron Age archaeology and Republican history in Italy, all of whom have important things to say, and much to learn from one another. Perhaps then we might be in a better position to address the important comparative issues in the Romanization of post-conquest northern Italy, and assess its significance within, and contribution too, our continuing discussions of Romanization as a concept.

Acknowledgements

I am grateful to Peter Guest, Andrew Burnett, and the editors of this volume for their comments on this paper.

References

Arslan, E. A. 1976–78. Celti e Romani in Transpadana. *Études Celtiques* 15: 441–481.
Arslan, E. A. 1978. I Celti in Transpadana nel II e I secolo. In Santoro 1978, pp. 81–84.
Blagg, T. F. C. and Millett, M. (eds.) 1990. *The Early Roman Empire in the West*. Oxbow: Oxford.
Blagg, T. F. C. 1991. The Transpadane Celts. In S. Moscati, O. -H. Frey, V. Kruta, B. Raftery, M. Szabó (eds.) *The Celts*. Bompiani: Milan, pp. 460–470.
Ceresa Mori, A. 1995. *Mediolanum* dall'*oppidum* celtico alla città romana. In N. Christie (ed.) *Settlement and Economy in Italy 1500 B.C.-A.D. 1500*. Oxbow: Oxford, pp. 465–476.
Chevallier, R. 1980a. *La Romanisation de la Celtique du Pô. 1 Les Données Géographiques*. Paris.
Chevallier, R. 1980b. *La Romanisation de la Celtique du Pô. 3 Histoire et Administration*. Tours.
Chevallier, R. 1983. *La Romanisation de la Celtique du Pô. 2 Essai d'Histoire Provinciale*. EFR: Rome.
Crawford, M. H. (ed.) 1996. *Roman Statutes*. University of London: London.
De Marinis, R. 1988 Liguri e Celto-Liguri. In G. Pugliese Carratelli (ed.) *Italia, Omnium Terrarum Alumna*. Scheiwiller: Milan, pp. 159–259.
De Mortillet, G, 1870–71. Les Gaulois de Marzabotto dans l'Apennin. *Revue Archeologique* 22: 288–290.
Denti, M. 1991. *I Romani a Nord del Po*. Longanesi: Milan.

Dupont, F. 1992. *Daily Life in Ancient Rome* (trans. C. Woodall). Blackwell: Oxford.

Dyson, S. L. 1985. *The Creation of the Roman Frontier.* Princeton University Press: Princeton.

Freeman, P. W. M. 1993. Review of Millett 1990. *Journal of Roman Archaeology* 6: 438–445.

Freeman, P. W. M. 1996. British Imperialism and Roman Imperialism. In Webster and Cooper 1996, pp. 19–34.

Freeman, P. W. M. 1997. Mommsen through to Haverfield: the origins of Romanization studies in late 19th-c. Britain. In Mattingly 1997, pp. 27–50.

Gabba, E. 1984. Ticinum: dalle origine alla fine del III sec. d.C. In *Storia di Pavia, vol. 1., L'età antica.* Banca del Monte di Pavia: Pavia, pp. 205–247.

Gabba, E. 1986. I Romani nell' Insubria: trasformazione, adeguamento e sopravvivenza delle strutture socio-economiche galliche. In *2° Convegno Archeologico Regionale: Atti.* New Press: Como, pp. 31–41.

Gabba, E. 1990. La conquista della Gallia Cisalpina. *Storia di Roma 2.1.* Einaudi: Turin, pp. 69–77.

Grassi, M. T. 1991. *I Celti in Italia.* Longanesi: Milan.

Hanson, W. S. 1994. Dealing with barbarians: the Romanization of Britain. In B. Vyner (ed.) *Building on the Past. Papers Celebrating 150 Years of the Royal Archaeological Institute.* Royal Archaeological Institute: London, pp. 149–163.

Harris, W. V. 1989. Roman Expansion in the West. In *Cambridge Ancient History 8* (2nd Edn.). CUP: Cambridge, pp. 107–162.

Hingley, R. 1996. The 'legacy' of Rome: the rise, decline and fall of the theory of Romanization. In Webster and Cooper 1996, pp. 35–48.

Jones, S. 1997. *The Archaeology of Ethnicity: Constructing Identities in the Past and Present.* Routledge: London.

Judd, D. 1997. *The British Empire. The British Imperial Experience from 1765 to the Present.* Harper Collins: London.

Kruta, V. 1988. I Celti. In G.Pugliese Carratelli (ed.) *Italia, Omnium Terrarum Alumna: la Civiltà dei Veneti, Reti, Liguri, Celti, Piceni, Umbri, Latini, Campani e Iapigi.* Scheiwiller: Milan, pp. 263–311.

Laurence, R. and Berry, J. 1998. *Cultural Identity in the Roman Empire.* Routledge: London.

Mattingly, D., 1997. *Dialogues in Roman Imperialism. Power, discourse and discrepant experience in the Roman Empire.* JRA: Portsmouth, Rhode Island.

Metcalfe, T. R. 1997. *Ideologies of the Raj.* CUP: Cambridge.

Millett, M. 1990a. *The Romanization of Britain: An Essay in Archaeological Interpretation.* CUP: Cambridge.

Millett, M. 1990b. Romanization: historical issues and archaeological interpretation. In Blagg and Millett 1990, pp. 35–41.

Oebel, L. 1993. *C. Flaminius und die Anfänge der römischen Kolonisation im Ager Gallicus.* Lang: Frankfurt am Main.

Peyre, C. 1979. La Cisalpine Gauloise du ille au ler siècle avant J.-C. Études J'Histoire et Archéologie 1. Presses de l'ecole normale supérieure: Paris.

Purcell, N. 1990. The Creation of Provincial Landscape: the Roman Impact on Cisalpine Gaul. In Blagg and Millett 1990, pp. 7–29.

Santoro, P. (ed.) 1978. *I Galli e l'Italia.* De Luca: Rome.

Stella, G. A. 1996. *Dio Po. Gli Uomini che fecero la Padania.* Baldini & Castoldi: Milan.

Tozzi, P. 1972. *Storia Padana Antica. Il Territorio fra Adda a Mincio.* Ceschina: Milan.

Vitali, D. 1985. *Monte Bibele (Monterenzio) und andere Fundstellen der Keltischen Epoche im Gebiet von Bologna.* Philipps-Universität Marburg: Marburg.

Vitali, D. 1991. The Celts in Italy in S. Moscati, O.-H. Frey, V. Kruta, B. Raftery, M. Szabó (eds.) *The Celts.* Bompiani: Milan, pp. 220–235.

Webster, J. and Cooper, N. (eds.) 1996. *Roman Imperialism: Post-Colonial Perspectives.* Leicester University Press: Leicester.

Williams, J. H. C. 1994. *Rome and the Celts of Northern Italy in the Republic*, unpubl. D.Phil thesis, Univ. of Oxford.

Williams, J. H. C. 1997. Celtic ethnicity in ancient Italy: problems ancient and modern. In T. J. Cornell and K. Lomas (eds.) *Gender and Ethnicity in Ancient Italy.* Accordia Research Institute: London, pp. 69–81.

Williams, J. H. C. forthcoming. *Beyond the Rubicon. Romans and Gauls in Republican Italy.* Oxford.

Woolf, G. D. 1992. The unity and diversity of Romanization, review of Blagg and Millett 1990. *Journal of Roman Archaeology* 5: 349–52.

Woolf, G. D. 1998. *Becoming Roman. The Origins of Provincial Civilization in Gaul.* CUP: Cambridge

Chapter 10

The Romanization of Italy: Conclusions

Jean Pierre Vallat

Nearly all of the contributions to this debate on Romanization insist upon the simplifying and reductive character of the analyses carried out during the last thirty years. The principles and standpoints of the Braudélian school are, however, little by little, making inroads into the perspectives of the Classicists (Bintliff 1991). Taking into account the fact that certain phenomena can evolve at different speeds within a region (the Po plain, Etruria, central Italy), territory (Italy), or a world empire (the Roman Mediterranean), has greatly facilitated the criticism of oversimplifying models that over exaggerate the significance of data drawn from a single example, place, or time, to a whole period, territory, or mode of production. French historiography has recently shown an interest in the process of Romanization, and in the acculturation of Italy and the Roman world from a variety of points of view. One accepted view suggests that the Roman conquest 'brings civilization', or at least introduces Roman colonists, its institutions and culture. It also sees the brutal or gradual elimination of any pre-existing form of indigenous social, economic and political organization or intellectual tradition. Alternative views employed a horizontal perspective, with particular emphasis on lateral relationships, such as those between peoples, creolization, and the acculturation or resistance of the conquered (Beard and Crawford 1993; David 1994; Vallat 1995). On the other hand, issues such as conservatism and innovation, the mutual transformation of those involved in the process of conquest, and the different rates at which they took place, are rarely studied. This is true even though they are very evident in funerary, epigraphic, onomastic and linguistic ritual forms, and, less obviously, in terms of sociability, tastes, or public and private architecture. The homogenization of culture and the self-identification as Roman took several centuries. However, it still needs to be ascertained as to whether the indigenous people of Italy are Romanized, or if it is that Roman culture is so adaptive and tolerant that it changed its character, adapting to local situations and evolving over time (North 1979; 1990).

While I reread the contributions on Romanization given at Ravenna, which are now taking the form of an academic book, I did so by putting them into the context of the work by Carmen Bernand and Serge Gruzinski (1996), which seems to me to have considerable relevance for us as Classicists. Indeed, although their book deals with the conquest of America, which they regard as the "prelude to the westernization of the world", they have in effect completely reworked the pioneering study of Nathan Wachtel

(1971) on a much wider material and conceptual basis. This impressed me as a student, and has prompted a general reflection on the phenomena defined as acculturation. Genocide, witches and stakes, but also marriages, mixed children, food and dressing tastes, weave relationships between the conquerors and the conquered. What is fascinating, however, are the images that different peoples project on to the various protagonists of the conquest. How could the victorious Spaniards do other than draw upon what they knew, and perceive the defeated Indians as Moors or Jews? How could the Indians understand certain treaties or the subtleties of the *Requerimiento*? And furthermore, the Mayas are not the Incas; the Spaniards are not the Portuguese. We should keep this in mind when we seek to understand the Romanization of Etruria, Picenum, Apulia or Cispadane Italy. It is necessary to consider the multiple reactions of the conquered and the conquerors in order to really understand the significance of the *foedus*, the *civitas sine suffragio*, and Latin law. What did Rome want in each case? What did the conquered party understand and what did it wish? How much variability was there from one area to another, and from one period to the next?

Similarly, when some of the contributors to this book point out that British scholars have gone so far as to think of Romanization and conquest as a result of the evolution of indigenous communities as a bottom-up, rather than a top-down phenomenon, it is useful to recall that in this way, British historiography solves the contradiction between the literary sources and the archaeological realities of the indigenous peoples. It also exonerates British imperialism from any blame, by explaining it away as a response to the 'desires' or to the 'evolutionary trajectories' of the indigenous societies that it ruled. This is not to say that these desires or evolutions did not exist; however, we need to understand to what extent they were caused by the conqueror (voluntarily or not), or by the desire of the conquered to please the conqueror, even if only as far as appearances were concerned. The different approaches and the examples of the spread of western power discussed above are not very far removed from the issue of Romanization that this book seeks to explore. Thus, the Romans of the early Republic that conquered Italy are not the same as those that colonized the east 100 years later, or who seized Germany or Arabia under the Empire. The Etruscans are not the Ligurians and did not react to the Roman conquest in the same way as the Greeks had done.

The papers on the Romanization of Italy considered in this volume share this perspective and emphasise the following issues:

- local variables
- long term trends
- conjunctural aspects
- chief characteristics
- heterogeneity of situations in space and time.

We are faced with archaeological and epigraphic material whose volume increases rapidly, while that of the literary sources remains stable. The difficulty of the task that confronts us is, on the one hand, to synthesize the former, while at the same time respecting their diversity and being aware of the degree of interpretation involved, with no illusions as to the objectivity of 'material culture' *per se*. On the other, the latter must be respected, by considering them for what they are (subjective, ideological, and produced by a relatively narrow fringe of society), and remembering not to credit what is essentially the testimony of an elite with being the product of a whole society. Lastly, it is advisable to relate the former and the latter to each other in a complementary and contradictory way. This relationship is difficult because it needs to avoid two pitfalls:

- the evaluation of literary sources can lead us to search the archaeological and epigraphic material for proof and the confirmation of hypotheses born of the literary text. It is clear from the contributions to this book that prosopography, even in the best cases that shows indigenous families continuing to exert dominance in a post-conquest society, cannot mitigate the shortcomings of our broader record for the transition and for Romanization;

- a hyper-critical approach to literary sources can end up as a single-minded quest to use other sources of evidence to invalidate hypotheses generated by the analysis of literary texts. Research into isolated Roman farms and clusters of buildings, such as villages or hamlets, cannot erase the importance of the villa in the economic and social system of Republican Italy or deny the significance of Cato's or Varro's descriptions of the slave-based economy.

Rome did not always and everywhere have the same attitudes towards the vanquished. One cannot, thus, treat Romanization as if it were a single entity, conceived by a single brain, and apply it to any period or situation. The examples of Volaterrae (Volterra), Luna (Luni) and Pisae (Pisa) illustrate realities that were diverse in both time and place, as would studies of Capua, Neapolis (Naples) and Pompeii, or any other part of Italy. The *Agricola* of Tacitus is a handbook on Romanization. It is the product of a certain time and milieu: does it reflect the Roman 'mentality'? Certainly not. Let us summarize the issues in the Italian contributions to this book that have helped contribute to a new understanding of Romanization.

The war and its impact. Colonization and its repercussions

The historians wondered if the colonists had settled and whether or not they had resold their plots of land or not. How strong was native resistance? Was colonization the cause of upheavals, or did it only have marginal influence upon societies, economies and cultures? What was the legal status of the subject cities? How is the *foedus*, the prefecture and *municipium* to be reconsidered? The study of the evolution of northern Italy as a whole (rejecting the division between Cis- and Transpadana) shows that while local communities interacted with Rome, their individual historical circumstances meant that they also resisted, fought, and ignored her. The reactions of each people were dictated by the rules its own society, religion, education and institutions. We should not be led to believe that there was any homogeneous indigenous reality. Even if the subdivision of northern Italy into Cispadane and Transpadane is of little analytical value, we should avoid the falling into the trap of thinking that pre-Roman northern Italy was a single indigenous unit. Alternatively, while Roman governors and generals had no handbook that prescribed how they should deal with native communities, their education and the examples set by their ancestors could lead to stereotyped behaviour. Nevertheless, it is advisable to understand the attitude of the conquerors and their capacity to adapt to the diversity of each situation in local terms and within the specific context of each conquest (Ferrary 1988). Rome did not always and everywhere have the same attitude towards the conquered.

We should also try to understand what lies beneath the concept of transition between indigenous and Roman societies, and which new forms of organization drew upon indigenous and Roman traditions. The Sabellic example discussed in this volume illustrates the importance of investigating how indigenous societies were organized *before* attempting to understand the character of the conquest. Similarly, in the fourth century, when the archaeological record is sparser and writing becomes less frequent, it is essential to study how a modest and egalitarian society is created and co-exists alongside Celtic groups that still retained their customs. How did this situation favour the conquest of Manius Curius Dentatus and its institutional consequences, such as the confiscation of territory, *civitas sine suffragio*, the Velina tribe, the admittance of the Praetutii into full rights, foundation of colonies, *conciliabulum* and prefecture? In contrast to a simplifying vision of the transition between indigenous (characterized its organization into *pagi* and *vici*) and Roman (characterized by its colonies), the new approach proposed here recognizes the importance of the *vici* in the second and first centuries, and sees them as autonomous and subordinate to Interamnia (Teramo) rather than to the colonies.

Society and power

Many studies dealing with pre- and post-conquest societies, the legal status and partitioning of the cities, marriages, alliances and clients, make it possible to investigate ruptures and continuities in the historical sequence. The political aspect of Romanization is visible through the onomastic and linguistic changes that resulted from the social war. Latin is heavily used for the first time in Etruria at around 90 BC, when Caere receives complete citizenship. This change is abrupt. However, an onomastic transition had begun in the third century BC, perhaps as a result of the grant of *civitas sine suffragio* between 390 and 273. The *lex Iulia* of 89 only accelerated the transition to the use of Latin. At Clusium (Chiusi) and Perusia (Perugia) the transition also takes place in the 90s, because an acceptable name is needed for registering in the census and in voting tribes. However, the *Lex Iulia* of 90 and the *civitas optimo iure* do not form clearer barriers in linguistic, onomastic or funerary uses than the laws of Romanization of Cisalpine Gaul in 49, or the transition to the *civitas sine suffragio* in the 300s BC. The evolutions are not linear, as is shown by the study of the municipal elites and their family ties. Thus, in the Augustan period, the Volumnii of Perusia wanted to make reference to their past at a time when the leading municipal classes were emerging, by setting up a bilingual inscription at their tomb, even though it had been closed for 150 years. In periods of crisis, whether they were the Hannibalic wars or the civil wars of the end of the Republic, certain elites felt a double need for legitimation, both with respect to their indigenous roots and their new relationship with the Roman conqueror. But it is not certain that all local aristocracies adopted the same attitude: a comparison with the situation at Pompeii would reveal continuity, with the municipalization of 89/49BC playing a rather limited role (Cebeillac-Gervasoni 1998). It is thus advisable to consider the short and the long term, and the local and the general level. If not all areas evolved in a similar manner during the Romanization process, it is also true that the character of Romanization itself changed from one period to the next, and from one area to another. The indigenous local agents were actors in the process of Romanization, and not merely passive entities submitting to the conqueror. Variety and complexity are not only due to variations in Roman intentions and actions. Attention should also be paid to local strategies of development and the adaptabilities of the conquered.

Culture and cultures in Italy

How did Rome perceive the cultures of Italy and how did the various people perceive Rome? The introduction to this book notes how the documentation for the two faces of this problem is unequal and how historiography has separated the study of the Romanization of Italy from that of the provinces. For the former, historians have *too much* literary documentation, while for the latter, researchers use archaeological evidence *alone*. Was Roman Italy ever a single cultural block, resulting from the acculturation of belated communities? Romanization occurred in a range of guises and elicited a variety of responses from the indigenous groups. Why did some wish to become Romans? Who wanted to do this and who refused? What was the range of choices? What are the political, economic, social, and religious reasons that interacted, dominated here and there, together or separately, in Rome's will to conquer? There is an increasingly precise idea of the languages, institutions, arts, crafts, and industry of the non-Roman peoples of Italy. Our knowledge is best for the Greeks and Etruscans, but is rapidly improving for the Samnites, the Volscians and Oscans, the Venetians, and the Carthaginians of Sardinia and Sicily.

Benelli, taking up an idea espoused by Pallottino, insists on the common character of pre-Roman Italic cultures, such as their economic and social structures, at around 1000 BC. The differences between them may not appear to him to be 'deep', but evidence at the local level is still needed to be establish whether or not they were significant. This is probably the case for the coast and the interior, for the north, centre and south, for the Greeks and Samnites or the Oscans, the Venetians or Ligurians. It may be appropriate to use anthropological or comparative ethnographic approaches to evaluate the significance of both small and substantial differences: clothing, gestures, networks of hospitality and clientele, living conditions and socialization, language and eating habits. Let us not forget that one is often the "barbarian of the other," no matter how refined an individual is or believes himself to be. Take for example the Roman ambassadors sent to Tarentum (Taranto), who arrive if not as conquerors, then at least as dominators. They are surprised to be perceived as barbarians, dressed oddly, and not speaking Greek, or speaking it badly (Dion. Hal. 19.5; Val. Max. 2.2.5; App. *Sam.* 7). The Roman language, the use of Latin to transcribe the indigenous languages rather than the choice of the Greek, often appears to be more linked with individual circumstances rather than with a rational chronological progression. It is often difficult to establish the norm and the exception, to determine what is a local choice at a given time, and what is an underlying tendency. It is important to remember that public and private epigraphy did not evolve at the same rate as broader process of Romanization. Choices could be related to the tastes of the individual, their gender (did men and women Romanize themselves at the same speed?), family or rank within the family (elder, junior). It is fascinating to observe the complexity of situations such as that in Umbria. Latin and Umbrian coexist until the second century, the latter being written sometimes in Latin, sometimes in Greek. The Oscan language survives until the first century BC., and is then still written sometimes in Latin, sometimes in Greek, according to circumstance, rather than to any rational progression. In private inscriptions, especially funerary texts, the cultural phenomena can be well grasped: individual or family choices, and the relationship between the conjunctural and the evenemential level are illustrated by a much richer record than that of public epigraphy.

In Apulia, the transition from pre-Roman languages to Latin cannot be determined on paleographic bases alone. Many cave sanctuaries with inscriptions remain unpublished. The analyses must be careful, as the study of the cemeteries of Lecce shows. In the tomb with the Visellius inscription, which dates to the second century BC., it is impossible to establish whether one is dealing with a migrant who has adapted local funerary habits, with a Messapian who Romanized his name, or with a Messapian who received individual citizenship. It is advisable to consider whole series of inscriptions (the 4000 Etruscan inscriptions of Clusium and of Tarquinia outnumber those of Rome in the same period), but also to pay attention to rare or unique cases. The individual, notable or ordinary citizen who chooses Latin rather than Oscan or Greek to transcribe his name, whether it be native or Romanized, is as significant as using burials at a cemetery as evidence for common customs: individual or family choice of conservatism or innovation, Romans adapting to indigenous uses, Messapians Romanizing themselves, or locals receiving citizenship on a purely personal basis within a context of indigenous culture. It is essential to note that Asciano does not evolve at the same rate as Clusium or Perusia. Here, some persistent Etruscan practices can resist and seem to be "belated," whereas, at the same time, neighbouring areas adopt a completely Romanized and Latinized system, while yet others choose a mixed, bilingual system of double denomination for the deceased. The phenomena are simultaneously slow and fast: three generations are necessary to Romanize the Etruscans of Clusium and Perusia. But their Romanization does not evolve at the same rate in the linguistic, onomastic and cultural spheres (as expressed by funerary practices) and one cannot say if the individuals of this time perceived themselves little by little as Romans or whether they posed as Romans for the conquerors, while retaining a strong sense of Etruscan identity.

Our perception of this kind of phenomenon can only be improved by enhancing our knowledge of indigenous cultures, their continuity and survival under Roman occupation, the perception of the conqueror (admiring or critical) and the feelings of the conquered (superiority, inferiority, culpability vis-à-vis the culture of the conqueror and their own). Such an understanding requires assigning the correct value to the indigenous cultures and to forms of transition from one culture to the other. By virtue of its myths, history, architecture, political (institutions) and social (clientele) practices, Rome knew how to emphasize those facets of the past that it had in common with the other peoples of Italy in order to create a 'presentable face' of conquest. Let us recall the example of Sardinia, where at Cuccuru s'Arriu, there is no continuity between Nuragic and Punic occupation, even if the building is still used because of its location. There is nothing in common with the cult of Demeter in Sicily, Africa or Spain. This is a form of religious expression peculiar to Sardinia, which seems to emerge and later to result in a city that is neither Greek, nor Punic, but quite indigenous. In the same way, dedications to Hercules in the Sabellic district reveal a form of survival by the indigenous culture. Thus, even before the Roman conquest, the local populations profited from a past and a know-how that had led them to a religious *bricolage*. Was this a terrain well-prepared for 'Romanization'? In Rome, the religious repertory also ensured a step-by-step strategy. Aeneas and Romulus, the herôon of the Forum and the *lapis niger*, the altars to Melquart or to Astarte in Rome, Pyrgi, and Veii, the iconography of the battle at Sentinum or the bilingual tablets of this or that city play an important role here. They are as many supporting elements in the Etruscan, Greek, Celtic, Punic, Latin, and Sabine traditions in creating foundation legends, by contrasting 'Trojan' and Punic origins with those of the Greeks, 'culture' with 'barbarity', and Hellenized Romans with the barbaric and plundering Gauls.

Is this an "acculturation without the normative or ideological pressures" of a self-identification with the Romans, as Benelli suggests? It is possible but not certain. The variety of strategies visible at Ateste, chosen according to gender, senior or junior status and the practices of the official and unofficial double name in Etruria, seem to show that there were more pressures on the occupier than have been recognized. These pressures, moreover, could be unconscious or repressed, as the names of the so-called 'second' generation populations in France show today. The conquered need no more than believe that if they do not transform their practices they are denying themselves access to certain public offices and honours, and to practices that are at once political and institutional (the census, the tribe, justice) but also social (hospitality, clients, recognition and acceptance of the other and by the other). Insofar as the absence of programmed and diffuse schooling prevented a rapid diffusion of some practices, the homogenization of the cultures occurred by other modes of transmission: religion, art, architecture, socialization, institutions, the army, migrations, as well as modes of dress and eating practices. Some of these are well-known while others remain broad areas for study.

The Economy and the Connections Between City and Country

The importance of cities in Republican Italy needs to be reassessed in the light of the dynamism of their countrysides. This is a key point in understanding Romanization. Euergetism, the dominant model of the *Urbs* as a model of the *res publica*, perhaps masked the diversity of the *civitates* and the role of *pagi*, *vici* and *fora*, in our views of Romanization, integration and indigenous persistence. Integration in the marketplace and the exchange economy, the role of the road system, and the movement of goods and people, are all issues which concern young researchers. In addition to the villa, wine and peasants of the *vici* at Atri and among the Praetutii presented in this book, one should perhaps add the work of G. Volpe (1990; 1996) on Apulia, in order to have an idea of the development of land cadastration, of cash-crops, and of the economic ruptures and continuities.

In the introduction to this section, Terrenato proposes a revolution, a turnaround in an issue concerning rural economy: field surveys have shown the spread of dispersed settlement between the fourth and second centuries BC, in varied forms, and, we would add, not everywhere at the same time, nor in the same way. But certain populations could become visible at this time because of diagnostic indicators, such as pottery and masonry houses, even though they existed before, but in forms which the archaeologists have not sought or recognized until recently. What do we know of pre-Roman buildings in Italy made of *pisé de terre*, adobe, or timber? How many hut floors and post-holes structures have been excavated? What do we know of the rural settlements of the Samnites, Oscans, Sicilians, Etruscans or even Greeks of Italy? Not much and, as a joke, M. Frederiksen and myself once asked W. Johannowsky whether the Etruscans and Samnites of Capua had lived in tombs, raising the lid from time to time, since so many cemeteries and so few rural and urban settlements were known. Furthermore, it can be debated whether the expansion of dispersed settlement is connected with conquest and Romanization or if it is merely coincidence? The surveys in the Biferno and Cecina valleys show that the same expansion of the 'Hellenistic' period occurs even where Roman conquest is extremely late. Is it possible, then, that the emergence of slave villas and the economic and social unity of Italy were not prompted by conquests, land surveys and colonization ? If so, it is conceivable that it may have been the development of the farms and villas of *vici, pagi* and *conciliabula* that provided the 'Roman' unity to Italy. Land surveys and colonization would then only serve to provide the normative framework to this evolution.

Thus, there takes shape in these pages, a complex and varied Italy, where Romanization is the result of exchanges, acculturation, violence, and negotiation, that did not occur in one direction alone. If in that quest for domination, Rome did not allow herself to be dominated, then she was at least influenced. In other words, the conqueror in Italy was, as in Greece, somewhat overcome by this conquest. Consequently, it is advisable to re-examine the concepts of rupture and continuity, and to accept that there were differences in the rates of change in time and space. Can we perceive Romanization as *not* only "the military expansion of a higher and more advanced culture"? How do we dispose of the romantic idea of nation inherited from the nineteenth century? It is worth observing that, perhaps, neither the Punic Wars nor the crisis of the Gracchi brutally transformed Republican Italy. Much recent work in Italy, France and Spain suggests that the 50s BC mark one of the strongest discontinuities. These years represent the end of the generation that had taken part in the Social War and are marked by the epigraphic rupture between indigenous languages and bilingualism, and the use of Latin. Municipalization played some role in this. The explosion of rural population densities, frantic market integration, and the expansion of the cities are also largely a phenomenon of this time. The "Roman Revolution" of Sir Ronald Syme is undoubtedly integral to all of these phenomena. All this points to the articulation of the long-term and the event, and of conjuncture and structure. We should consider Romanization and acculturation as the replacement of one civilization by another, but also as the survival and resurgence of indigenous forms transformed in order to adapt to the new situation. Art history and the use of neo-classical imagery at various times, must hold a significant place in this analysis.

At a time when the ex Russo-Soviet Empire is dislocated and where centripetal forces override the centrifugal, we have a good example of what can be the final or temporary implication of a conquest. Admittedly, none of the very tempting examples, be they the Russianization of the territories extending from the Baltic to the Pacific in the nineteenth and twentieth centuries, or the Westernization of the world in the sixteenth and seventeenth centuries can be used uncritically as parallels for the problems of

Romanization. But some of the concepts and methods are applicable to what was, at each time, the confrontation between conquerors and conquered. There are cultural, religious and behavioural aspects that endure, or even re-emerge as dominant after being dominated. Take for example the conquest of Tripolitania, where the indigenous tribes came into the *gsour* to benefit from the system and then withdrew (Barker 1996)! Alternatively, there is the prehistorians' view of the transition between pre-Roman and Roman as the ultimate phase of a declining culture or as a civilization in the process of renewal and adaptation. Finally, one might recall the works of those scholars who see the end of the Empire as "the Indian summer" of the Roman world and not as the emergence of late antique or even medieval structures. All these studies show how much the prospects opened by the work gathered in this book call into question the single-minded vision of Romanization as merely Rome's way of imposing itself on its Empire.

References

Barker, G. 1996. *Farming the Desert*. Unesco: Tripoli, London.
Beard, M. and Crawford, M. 1993. *Rome et L'Italie*. Presses Universitaires du Mirail: Toulouse.
Bernand, C. and Gruzinski, S. 1996. *Histoire du nouveau monde*. Fayard: Paris.
Bintliff, J. 1991. *The Annales school and Archaeology*. Leicester University Press: Leicester.
Cebeillac-Gervasoni, M. 1988. *Les élites municipales de l'Italie péninsulaire des Gracques à Néron*. EFR: Rome.
David J. -M. 1994. *La romanisation de l'Italie*. Aubier: Paris.
Ferrary, J. -L. 1988. *Philhéllénisme et impérialisme*. EFR: Rome.
North, J. 1979. Religious toleration in Republican Rome. *Proceedings of the Cambridge Philological Society* 25: 85–103.
North, J. 1990. Religion in Republican Rome. In *Cambridge Ancient History* 7.2.2. CUP: Cambridge, pp. 573–624.
Vallat, J. -P. 1995. *L'Italie et Rome*. Colin: Paris.
Volpe, G. 1990. *La Daunia nell'età della romanizzazione*. Edipuglia: Bari.
Volpe, G. 1996. *Contadini, pastori e mercanti nell'Apulia tardoantica*. Edipuglia: Bari.
Wachtel, N. 1971. *La vision des vaincus. Les Indiens du Pérou devant la conquête espagnole*, Gallimard: Paris.

PART 2
THE PROVINCES

Chapter 11

Introduction

Simon Keay

The papers in the first section of this book call into question earlier 'single-minded' visions of the Romanization of Italy. They reject the view that this was a relatively straightforward matter consisting largely of Rome imposing itself on its Empire. They suggest that the process of conquest and assimilation was a much more complex process which was contingent upon local variables, long-term trends, key moments of conjuncture, the active role of the elites and the heterogeneity of situations in space and time.

It is no longer, thus, possible to implicitly assume that Rome and Italy were the focal points of a pure and unadulterated 'Roman' culture which diffused out to the provinces during the later Republic and early Imperial periods. "Roman" Italy was a far more diverse and fragmented series of cultural realities within which there were a broad range of complex cultural reactions between the Conqueror and the conquered at different points in time. This view clearly has major implications for the ways in which Romanization is seen to occur in the provinces. The aim of the papers in this section of the book is to focus upon the ways in which Roman influence brought about cultural change in different parts of the Roman west and the contrasting forms that it assumed.

The Hispaniae were amongst the earliest provinces in the Roman west and which have long been defined in terms of the intensity of their relationship to Rome and Italy. Keay's paper is a reaction against the more traditional views of culture contact and culture change in the peninsula during the later Republican and early imperial period and attempts to highlight some alternative perspectives about the impact of Rome upon the political, social and cultural lives of its inhabitants. He begins by making the point that this is something that needs explaining rather than simply describing. Recent analyses of the nature of culture contact in the Bronze and Iron ages make it clear that the view of cultural change as a one-way process emanating from a culturally superior Roman Italy is no longer tenable. Keay instead defines his view of 'Romanization' as a symbiotic but unequal process of cultural exchange borne out of unequal relationships between a dominant imperial power and its subject communities. The manifestations of this, in terms of monuments, buildings and inscriptions, were open to a range of different readings. He also sees the elites playing an important role in the adoption of these cultural symbols in the context of strategies of self-empowerment and denial to non-elites. He "tests" this model by applying it to an analysis of cultural change in the Iberian peninsula which runs from the late pre-Roman period through into the early imperial period. The late first century BC onwards was the key moment of cultural change and was brought about by a symbiosis of elite activity at local level and the development of Roman culture as an adjunct of imperial power. Pre-existing cultural variation within the peninsula, however, ensured the development of a range of interlocking Hispano-Roman cultural identities from one region to another.

The paper by Gutiérrez and Castro takes a closer look at the Hispaniae, focusing upon the archaeological evidence for the Romanization of the rich cereal-producing region of the upper Guadalquivir valley. They reject studies which have approached the question of Romanization by concentrating upon the development of towns as Roman cultural symbols in the context of what almost amounts to a biological process of inevitable change. Instead, they suggest that the new Roman political order can only be understood to have existed once the means of production had been transformed. Consequently, they use the two case studies of Giribaile and Atalayuelas to trace the economic development of the landscape from the Iberian through into the early Empire. After the Second Punic War, the former *oppidum* continues in occupation, almost fossilizing the pre-existing territorial order, while the latter is abandoned in a far more radical reorganization of its territory. These differences are explained in terms of contrasting strategies of taxation and destruction, as Rome adapted its strategies of domination and exploitation to the contrasting conditions of the region. A key role in this would have been played by regional aristocrats, made or recognized by Rome. The territorial changes contingent upon the emergent of Roman towns do not occur until the foundation of the colonia at Tucci or the possible concession of municipal status to Atalayuelas in the Augustan and Flavian periods respectively.

In his paper on Roman Gaul, Woolf rejects some of the traditional approaches to Romanization, or "Romanization Theory" as he terms it. He suggests that instead of simply measuring the romanness of individual peoples, or comparing the degree of Romanization from province to another, we should perhaps explore the degree to which provincials were drawn into the "Roman Cultural Revolution". This term was borne out of an analysis of the transformation of cultural life in late Republican and Augustan Rome, which was took place in the context of major political changes and which formed the foundation of High Imperial culture. Woolf argues that this is relevant to provincial contexts, and argues this through in the context of the archaeological evidence from the Gallic provinces. He re-analyses cultural changes that are conventionally understood as a result of the impact of Rome, and sees them instead as a transformation brought about by active provincial participation in a broader cultural revolution centred at Rome. Thus, the development of epic poetry, elite sexuality, the transformation of urban space, the construction of monumental arches and the replacement of earlier ceramics by terra sigillata at Rome are set by the side of the development of religious change, the production of terra sigillata and the spread of bathing in Gaul. He interprets these as being respectively symptomatic of shifts in authority to a new political elite, new ways of eating and perceiving the world, and changes in the perceptions of the body. He also reminds us that the "Roman" Cultural Revolution was also itself a cultural hybrid. Cultural changes at Rome were created out of, and sometimes in reaction to, earlier Hellenistic models, while the provincial contribution through regional "cultural revolutions" played a key role in enabling the development of a distinct Roman culture.

The 'Romanization' of Britain is examined by James. He chooses to respond to some of the ideas put forward by Terrenato in an Italian context. These emphasize elite interaction and negotiation in explaining the mechanics of the entry of communities into the developing Roman Empire and which see the convergence of elite culture and values as central in explaining the longevity of the Roman world. In accepting Terrenato's view, James questions the validity of the current emphasis upon two-way asymmetric interactions between Roman and indigenous elites and, like Woolf, questions whether cultural change is still best conceptualized as a process of 'Romanization' – even if the word comes with a health warning and an explicit definition. In particular, he warns of the dangers of a strict binary opposition between Romans and elites: this tends to exclude the lower sections of society who also had the power to bring about change. After drawing some comparisons between the ways in which archaeologists in Britain and Italy have begun to explore the incorporation and integration of subject communities within the Roman Empire, he moves on to re-examine the 'Romanization' of Britain. In the first instance, he sees the pre-Roman period, with its long tradition of contact with continental Europe, as a precedent and unwitting preparation for incorporation of Britain into the Roman world. Italy, thus, provides a valuable model for understanding the ways in which Senatorial families and members of the Imperial House were becoming locked into the elite networks of northern communities. During the incorporation of Britain into the Roman Empire (55 BC to the second century AD), James suggest that aristocractic regimes in Britain actively sought engagement with Rome. Consequently, much of southern Britain was under Roman hegemony from Caesar's time and the Claudian invasion of AD 43 may have represented the consolidation of long-established hegemonic Roman power than outright military aggression. Moreover it would have helped guarantee the power of key pro-Roman elites, thus fossilizing the pre-existing social order. Key mechanisms in this process, therefore, would have been local elites actively negotiating with Rome in the way the Terrenato proposes for Republican Etruria, as well as carefully targeted Roman violence.

The review of the western provinces concludes with an analysis of cultural change at Leptis Magna, which illustrates some of the processes involved in the integration of Tripolitanian urban communities into the Roman Empire. In this paper, Fontana compares and contrasts the epigraphic evidence from funerary and urban contexts and explores forms of individual and group self-representation. He shows that while public behaviour rapidly conformed to the Roman model with honorary dedications in Latin, some aspects of funerary practice remained untouched by Roman influence. Language and nomenclature record different levels of emulation, and especially different forms of self-representation. These range from the private and oral context of family life, to the group visibility in the funerary sphere, all the way to self-representation as Roman citizens in public life. He suggests that a possible key to conceptualizing these cultural processes is the use of binary oppositions, such as high and low, above and below ground, external and internal, public and private. High is represented by a hinterland with tombs structured in a similar way to many Roman cities, while low is the continuity of hypogea and Punic burial customs. This is the context in which the variability in nomenclature can be understood: men appear oriented towards the public world and a more rapid acculturation, while women remain almost completely outside the sphere of Latin and Romanization. At the same time the preservation of indigenous family systems stands in contrast to the rapid assimilation process that characterizes public life.

By way of conclusion, the final paper by King uses mammal bones from excavations to explore the notion of Romanization in the Western Empire as a whole. It therefore provides a thematic cross section across provincial communities discussed by the other contributors in this section of the book. In this context, King tests the model that 'Romanization' took the form of a dominant diet which would have originated in Rome and which would have been imposed upon, or taken up by, provincial societies. He elaborates this by suggesting that agents of the Roman state, principally the army, also had dietary patterns that were imposed on or copied by the peoples of the provinces. His analyses suggest that in the west, dietary regions appear to roughly correspond to provinces and climatic/topographic zones. While he suggests that climate may have had an influence upon dietary traditions, cultural influence from western-central Italy and the army may also have been important. In terms of diet, therefore, the effect of the Italian core on Rome's distant peripheral provinces was weak. Regional patterns retained their strength, and cultural dietary influences also flowed between provinces. Thus, King concludes that the Romanization of diet was not a uniform cultural process throughout the western provinces, and that their diet is best characterized in terms of regional identities within a loosely drawn Roman koiné.

These contributions have all questioned the notion of 'Romanization' and, from the standpoint of their chosen regions, have explored the nature of their social, cultural and economic relationships with Italy. Naturally enough, this is achieved in the context of an analysis of the archaeological evidence for the incorporation and integration of provincial communities within the Roman Empire. In this context, there are a number of issues where the contributors are in agreement with the Italian contributors, and provide fruitful areas for future research. First, there is the consensus, both implicit and explicit, that the pre-Roman period is vital in providing the proper archaeological context for understanding the range of cultural variation that confronted Rome, both in Italy and across the west. Contingent upon this is the recognition that Rome's perception of conquered peoples and their perception of Rome was very varied, clearly tempering the eventual processes and sequences of incorporation. A second major point of consensus concerns the mechanisms of incorporation. Most papers are in agreement that the elites played a key role, whether in direct negotiation with Rome during the process of integration, as active agents in the creation of new cultural differences, or as more passive secondary players during the administration of the provinces. However, there is also a recognition that there is danger in ceding too much primacy to elites alone, and that there is a risk of ignoring other sectors of society that might have an underlying influence upon cultural change. Finally, a number of papers carefully dissect the notion of "Roman" in cultural terms, and make the point that Roman culture was itself a construct and amalgam, which was being continually re-defined, both at Rome and in the provinces. This makes it very difficult to conceptualize Romanization as a straight binary opposition between Roman and Native. In short, all three of these points deconstruct the simple notion that Rome simply conquered its Empire and made it Roman. They demonstrate that the development of the Roman Empire in the west was a far more complex and nuanced series of interlocking processes and relationships, which are only just beginning to be teased apart.

Chapter 12

Romanization and the Hispaniae

Simon Keay

Introduction

The Hispaniae were amongst Rome's earliest provinces in the west. Their conquest lasted about 200 years, beginning in the late third century BC and being completed in 19 BC. In a conference which looks critically at the Romanization of Italy and its consequences for understanding cultural change in other western provinces, the Hispaniae are ideal as a touchstone for charting the spread of Roman cultural influence from the late third century BC onwards. The historical and archaeological evidence is rich and much new evidence has been published in recent years, particularly in the field of Roman towns and their cultural environments. For example, large-scale urban excavation has begun to radically alter our understanding of a range of Roman towns across the peninsula (see, for example, Trillmich and Zanker 1990). Similarly, systematic epigraphic studies, culminating in the ongoing re-publication of the *Corpus Inscriptionum Latinarum* (Stylow *et al.* 1998 for the most recent volume) have done much to illuminate our understanding of the social and political lives of the provinces. Analysis of architectural decoration and sculptural programmes has also been highly productive. In addition to this, a huge wealth of archaeological data has been published in many journals and regional publications across Spain and Portugal.

It is true to say that all of this information has greatly enriched our perception of the Roman provinces of the Hispaniae during the late Republican and early Imperial periods. However, a scholar unfamiliar with academic traditions in Spain and Portugal might be forgiven for asking why this material is not regularly used to address the broader 'Romanization' debate now flourishing in Britain, the Netherlands and the United States. The reason is quite simply that it is deployed within academic debates in which, in the south European tradition, cultural change, or Romanization, is not perceived as something which needs *explaining* as such. This is because it is seen to be part of a dialectical cultural relationship between Italy and the Hispanic provinces which is already well understood from the literary and epigraphic sources. A counter-argument would be that 'Romanization' only needs explaining in those parts of the Roman Empire away from the Mediterranean region where literary sources are deficient, the epigraphic record is limited and monumental buildings are relatively rare.

It is the contention of this paper, however, that this is not the case and that many of the old certainties about the cultural relationship between Rome, Italy and the Hispanic provinces *are* open to question. One of the great advances in archaeological interpretation in recent years has been to show that there are many alternative readings to the meaning of all kinds of archaeological evidence; the same may also be said of the historical sources. The days when archaeological evidence could be regarded as passive testimony to a known past are long gone and scholars increasingly need to tease apart the layers of academic, political, social influence which unconsciously govern the ways in which we interpret the evidence. This paper begins by looking at some of these and then moves towards defining a new archaeological framework for the study of cultural change in Iberia, by examining a number of key themes.

Previous Approaches to the Romanization of Hispania

There is a deep-seated belief amongst some of the more traditional ancient historians and archaeologists currently studying the Iberian peninsula that Romanization was a self-evident process of change that came to affect all parts of the Iberian peninsula in one way or another. On the one hand, Romans and Italians settled in large numbers and on the other, Iberians, Celtiberians and others took up Roman ways at the expense of their own customs. Since the classical sources only allude to this and do not discuss it as such, there is some difference of opinion as to when this process began and in charting its progression across the peninsula. Generally, however, it is closely identified with the spread of Roman towns and the Roman urban type. In this way, it is understood to have begun shortly after the expulsion of the Carthaginians from southern Spain in 205 BC, to have built up speed during the Republic (particularly from the later second century BC) and to have become widespread under Augustus. In geographical terms, the east coast of Spain and southern Spain were the first to be Romanized, followed by the Ebro valley and eventually by Celtiberia, Lusitania and the communities of north-western Spain and Portugal.

With hindsight, this tide of 'Romanization' is considered to have been an inevitable process of civilization as the non-Roman native communities gradually dropped their own cultural traditions and became "Roman". This is to be explained either by the direct settlement of large numbers of Romans enforcing, or encouraging, the adoption of their own lifestyles as a form of cultural imperialism, or by an implicit belief that Romans were culturally superior, and that it was only natural that native communities should emulate them. New archaeological discoveries are slotted into this picture, reinforcing this model and making it increasingly difficult to question. In this context, material culture –whether it be imported Dressel 1 wine amphorae, Black Gloss Table ware, sculptures or coinage– becomes little more than passive 'baggage' trailing in the wake of relentless Roman settlement.

What is the reason for this? Ultimately, it is because attitudes to the notion of cultural change amongst many scholars studying the Hispaniae are both positivist and traditional. As in other European countries, the agenda for study is still determined by the ancient historians. The inspiration of some is surely to be found in Mommsen's view of the Roman Empire, as a well-oiled imperial machine akin to late 19th century Germany in which individual provinces were akin to modern nation states (Mommsen 1909). They similarly share Mommsen's view that Roman cultural forms, as evidenced by towns and villas etc, are ultimately an integral part of the civilized Roman way of life. Others see the emergence of Roman civilization in the provinces as a by-product of social and economic crises of the Roman Empire, originally outlined by Rostovtseff (1926). In recent years, there has developed a kind of orthodoxy, best exemplified by the monumental *Historia de España* originally edited by Ramón Menéndez Pidal in 1959 (rewritten by Montenegro and Blázquez 1982; Mangas *et al.* 1982) and the volumes written and edited by Blázquez (such as, Blázquez *et al* 1978). The great value of these works as milestones in the history of our understanding of Roman Hispania needs little comment. In more recent years, the sheer volume of new archaeological data has led many of the "certainties" in these kinds of study to be questioned. The newer generation of scholars have tended to analyze the Romanization of Iberia from the regional level and from many different – political, administrative, social, ritual, economic, artistic and architectural – perspectives producing, many valuable articles and books that are too numerous to list here (they include, however, Bendala, 1988; González Román 1981; Salinas de Frías 1986; de Francisco Martín 1989; Le Roux 1995; Blázquez and Alvar 1996; Trillmich and Zanker 1990; Santos Yanguas 1994; Edmonson 1990; Martins 1996; Hidalgo, Pérez and Gervás 1998; Bendala 1998; Mayer, Nolla and Pardo 1998; Pereira Menaut 1988).

In many ways, however, the earlier framework still resists the interpretational challenge of new archaeological discoveries and studies. This is because there is an implicit belief that the historical text, whether written or inscribed, is the prime source for writing history. Its very nature permits an ongoing dialogue between the scholar and his or her data. By contrast, archaeology is still seen as little more than a sub-discipline of history. Archaeological data, with the exception of inscriptions, are understood to be a secondary source of information about the past, with which dialogue is not possible. They are essentially 'passive' products of the historical process whose interpretation is uncomplicated and best left to the historian – a scenario which sees the archaeologist as little more than a technician who collects and collates data. Such a view is far removed from some of the more recent advances in processual and post-processual archaeological theory. The former viewed material culture as a bridge between ancient populations and their environment. Analyses of the patterning of material culture were used to generate models of social systems and ideologies which, in turn, helped to explain cultural variability and change (for example, Binford 1972). More recently, however, some archaeologists have reacted against many of the assumptions underlying this kind of approach and have developed a range of alternative approaches, or post-processual theories, in which material culture is seen to have a crucial symbolic value and that the agency of the individual was important in structuring the archaeological record. One of the most important of these newer approaches has drawn upon structuration theory (Giddens 1984) and sees archaeological objects, such as pottery etc, as symbols that are symptomatic of embedded social meanings, which are susceptible to "reading" and interpretation by archaeologists. The architectural layout of buildings can thus be understood as a reflection of reiterated social practice (Laurence 1994), while individual artefacts can help structure social behaviour (Jundi and Hill 1998). Once the exclusive preserve of prehistorians, these perspectives are being increasingly adopted by classical archaeologists (generally see Dyson 1993).

One by-product of the text-dominated view of cultural change in the Iberian peninsula is that the crucial transitional period of the late third century BC to the late first century AD is studied from a Roman cultural perspective. The history provides the framework and the archaeological data fill in the gaps. This approach is flawed for at least three reasons. In the first instance, our fullest sources are rarely contemporary. The key narratives of writers like Livy and Strabo were composite histories drawn from a range of earlier sources and were written to serve a particular audience in the cultural mileu of Augustan and Tiberian Rome. Secondly, important accounts by such writers as Polybius, Caesar and Pliny, who were contemporary to the events they described and were familiar with the Iberian peninsula, are nonetheless difficult to take at face value. Their narratives have been transmitted to us indirectly (see for example, Richardson 1986: 194–8), were written for particular audiences at Rome and sometimes in a style in which literary conventions take precedence over what we might consider "factual" accuracy (for example, see Mayer 1989). One could suggest, therefore, that to base our understanding of cultural change on these sources would be to fall prey to a range of ethno-centric Graeco-Roman viewpoints and be, thus, one sided. Indeed, it could not be any other way. There are no indigenous texts or commentaries and only a handful of inscribed documents of pre-Roman and Roman Republican date (de Hoz 1995).

Thirdly, one can argue that archaeological data used to illustrate historically-based accounts are also taken out of their cultural context. In order to understand the long-term significance of Iberia's incorporation into the Roman Empire, it is important to remember that this was yet another episode of culture contact and culture change in a long continuum stretching back into the third and second millennia BC (see papers in Díaz Andreu and Keay 1996), although it was clearly exceptional in terms of its extent and depth. Consequently, one needs to understand the genesis and organization of the pre-Roman peoples in order to better appreciate the ways in which their cultural traditions were modified or transformed upon contact with Rome. Despite several attempts to do this from the perspective of those Greek and Roman writers that wrote about the peninsula before the arrival of Rome, it is clear that this can only really be done in conjunction with an analysis and interpretation of the archaeological evidence.

A further by-product of the text-dominated view of the Romanization of the Hispaniae is one that is particularly relevant to this conference. It is the implicit diffusionist assumption that cultural change is to be ascribed to direct Roman influence and that it represents the inevitable triumph of superior Roman civilization over inferior native cultural traditions. The presence of large numbers of Romans and Italians in Iberia is usually seen to be the prime-mover in this process. The army was one source of settlers. Between the later third and earlier first centuries there were nearly always at least two legions present in Citerior and Ulterior (Brunt 1971), some of whom would have inevitably settled in the province. Other sources were the veterans and *hybridae* at such specially created settlements as Italica and Carteia, or the gradual accretion of traders and businessmen who came to form *conventus civium romanorum* at native settlements during the second and first centuries BC (most recently Marín Díaz 1988: 47–112). More questionable, but nonetheless invoked by many historians, are the Italian entrepreneurs that Diodorus (5.35–6) mentions as flocking to the Spanish mines in the late second century BC (see, however, comments by Keay 1995, 326–7, note 22). As is well known, the settlement of Romans and Italians reaches its peak between the middle and later first centuries BC, after the conclusion of the Civil Wars in Iberia and the establishment of colonies by Caesar and Augustus (Brunt 1971).

While nobody doubts the veracity of this as a framework, the danger comes in over-estimating the scale of Italic settlement and, hence, its direct impact on the surrounding populations. Some see it as very large and as responsible for the large-scale import of Italic imports, the increasing use of Roman coinage and the appearance of Roman style houses and buildings at native sites from the second century BC onwards. However, the sources are never explicit about the scale of immigration. In reality, purely Roman or Latin settlements were extremely rare prior to the period of Caesar and Augustus (summarized in Knapp 1977: 105–39), while those Italians and Romans that did settle at native settlements would surely have been numerically inferior to their native hosts. Furthermore, with the passage of time, the binary ethnic opposition of Romans or Italians and natives would have become increasingly blurred with intermarriage. Insofar as there were any "Roman" cultural symbols prior to the later first century BC, there is no evidence that they were ethnically exclusive and that their presence in the archaeological record signals the presence of Italians or Romans. Imported artefacts, like Black Gloss pottery and wine amphorae, and architectural styles could have been chosen by Roman or native alike for a number of reasons, not least fashion, outward expressions of status, loyalty, ethnic identification or emulation.

A final difficulty that bedevils our understanding of the Romanization of the Hispaniae concerns the scale of analysis. The very diverse geography and cultural history of the Iberian peninsula has conditioned the development of a very fragmented political map – in both Spain and Portugal. Consequently, there is a considerable imbalance between those producing valuable broad-brush syntheses and those publishing the data at regional or local level. The former have tended to be ancient historians who work within the framework of modern nation states – Spain and Portugal – and structure the academic debate (see for example, Blázquez 1978 and Alarcão 1995). The reasons for this are, perhaps, implicitly political, and scholars in effect reinforce contemporary claims of Spanish or Portuguese national integrity by reference to a remote Roman past. Analyses based upon the Hispaniae as a group of provinces are rarer. A notable exception is the catalogue to the recent exhibition *Roma en Hispania*, which is a major and important collective work by leading Spanish and Portuguese ancient historians and archaeologists (Almagro Gorbea and Álvarez Martínez 1998) and provides a snapshot of current research in a range of key themes. Otherwise, this tends to be the domain of foreign scholars, who overlook national and regional differences in favour of seeing the Iberian peninsula as a whole and adopted thematic (such as Le Roux 1995), narrative historical (such as Richardson 1996; Curchin 1991) or archaeological (such as Keay 1988) perspectives. Studies of individual provinces, such as Tarraconensis Lusitania and Baetica are even rarer (see however Mayer, Nolla and Pardo 1998; de Francisco Martín 1989; González Román 1981; Keay 1998). There is little doubt that the greatest area of activity is undertaken at the local or regional level, particularly by archaeologists. A plethora of journals and local publications publish large amounts of archaeological data – some of it undigested or simply reproducing the generally accepted picture of Romanization produced in the national syntheses. The amount of data is quite phenomenal and its volume outstrips the abilities of many to synthesize it adequately. For many of the 17 autonomous regions of Spain, the driving force behind the scale of publication is political, in which there is perhaps desire to reinforce regional identity by claiming a share in an exalted common past. For others, such as Catalunya, Galicia and the Basque countries, the degree of Romanness or un-Romanness can be taken as an index of national distinctiveness from other parts of Spain. Consequently, modern regional divisions often provide the framework for archaeological and historical studies (see, for example, the excellent Pons 1994).

Towards a Definition of Romanization

Sir Ronald Syme (1988: 64) described Romanization as a term 'ugly and vulgar, worse than that, anachronistic and misleading'. He understood other people's use of the term to imply the 'execution of a deliberate policy'. Since Romanization is a modern term with no fixed meaning, scholars have developed a range of interpretations to fit their own observations of changes in the historical and archaeological record, sometimes explicitly and at other times implicitly. Amongst English-speaking scholars, debates contingent upon this issue have been particularly fierce in recent years, generating two broad schools of thought. At the risk of gross over-generalization, one might say that the first ultimately accepts the premise that observable changes in material culture reflect provincial societies becoming less native and more Roman as they are absorbed with the Roman Empire. Thus, there are those for whom material culture is essentially a by-product of, and to some extent imposed by, the imperial 'system' (for example, Hanson 1997). Others reject imperial agency in favour of what amounts to 'self-Romanization' by native elites (Millett 1991), in what has been labelled as the "bottom-up" process. A third position stands somewhere between the two and sees some kind of imperial agency working in tandem with the self-Romanization of elites (Woolf 1995; Whittaker 1995). The second school of thought argues that the Romanization of material culture does not reflect native acquiesence in the values of the Roman Empire as much as reactions to that process. This could involve involve the use of artfacts to articulate resistance to Rome (see, for example, papers in Webster and Cooper 1996) or reinforce ethnic identites within provinces (Jones 1997). Alternatively, others understand the Romanization of material culture to reflect personal reactions and choices by individuals to the changing world around them (Barrett 1997; Hill 1997).

There is, thus, no consensus in the definition of Romanization or, more significantly, about those observable processes which scholars are attempting to characterize. Much of the debate has drawn upon the particular circumstances of the north-western part of the Empire or, to a lesser extent, syntheses of evidence from across the Roman Empire. Given the great longevity of the Hispanic provinces and the range of cultural variation within them it is important to develop an appropriate definition of Romanization. In the first instance it is important to think of cultural change in the context of the broader incorporation of subject peoples into the Roman Empire. Some of the above definitions are too narrow and focus solely upon observed changes in material culture – the most immediately relevant to the archaeologist. Romanization is surely a greater process, which embraces techniques of subjugation, accommodation and settlement, the development of systematic economic exploitation and the imposition of Roman law. Cultural change *per se* took place within, and was part of, this. It involved the spread of Latin and the development of distinctive attitudes to urbanism, personal identities, dress, eating habits, religious practice and artistic representation tempered by extant regional traditions. However, it was never static and was in a constant state of change as the political tone of the Empire was transformed, firstly from Republic to Empire and subsequently from one imperial dynasty to the next.

An instinctive reaction to all this would be to follow in the sense of Sir Ronald Syme's comment and to desist from using the word 'Romanization' at all. Indeed some scholars (viz. Woolf in this volume) have begun to explore alternative perspectives for explaining cultural transition. However, given that the word is firmly rooted in the lexicon of many European languages, this seems unrealistic. The challenge must surely be to ensure that people recognize that this is a subjective and value-laden term whose definition will vary from one person to the next, and that its use should always be qualified. This said, it becomes important to define the position of this paper before moving on to look at its implication for the iberian peninsula. I understand the Romanization of material culture to have been a symbiotic but unequal process of cultural exchange. It hinged upon unequal relationships between a dominant imperial power and its subject communities which, writ large across the Empire as a whole, fuelled a dynamic cultural continuum and the emergence of regional provincial Roman cultures. In towns dominated by Roman citizens (provincial capitals and *coloniae*), interrelated suites of buildings, statues and inscriptions were symbols of Roman power which were deployed as public acts of loyalty to the Emperor and State by elites as a means of self-empowerment. They were also the physical manifestation of the repeated social actions which helped to define what it was to be Roman both at Rome and in the provinces. At the same time, however, they could only be "read" by those elites who shared Rome's view of the world and understood its grammar of symbolic representation (Woolf 1999: 238–49 for the link between culture and imperial power), thereby creating a gulf between them and the unprivileged "others". In the majority of towns (municipia and the civitates), however, these symbols were set up in the context of local competitive strategies in a more haphazard fashion. It is tempting to suggest that this represented little more than a straightforward emulation of established practice in Roman towns, which reproduced the gulf between the elites and others across the provinces. However, it is also possible that the resultant Hispano-Roman urban landscapes could really only be "read" satisfactorily by those who were well versed in regional cultural traditions as well as Roman cultural symbolism. The picture is further complicated by the fact that the character and meanings of 'official' Roman art and architecture, and other aspects of Roman material culture, were continually being re-negotiated in the course of the imperial period. They were the product of ideological transformation under Augustus and were transformed as Rome chose to define its present by re-interpreting its past (thus, see Elsner 1998, particularly 2–14).

In the provinces, therefore, Roman material culture would have been subject to a complex range of "readings" by different social groups. It would also have been constantly re-defined in a continuing dialectical relationship between the centre and the provinces. This generated a tension within the provincial communities as there was an increasing degree of cultural and, ultimately political, convergence amongst town-based elites and, at the same time, a sense of difference and dependance amongst the rest of the population.

Writ large this would have generated a complex and structured cultural landscape across the provinces.

Towards a General Model of Romanization in the Hispaniae

The Pre-Roman Communities

Lip-service is often paid to the range of cultural variation in the Iberian peninsula prior to the arrival of the Romans in 218 BC. The writings of Livy, Polybius and Strabo are all scrutinized and the point is made that Rome encountered a disparate range of peoples during the conquest of the Iberian peninsula. To accept this at face value, however, is to fall into the trap of seeing the late Pre-Roman Iron-Age peoples from the Graeco-Roman perspective as different, to some degree primitive and very often warlike (generally, see Gómez Espelosín *et al.* 1995) and that, ultimately, these traits either impeded or facilitated the progress of Roman armies and the Roman way of life across the peninsula. The archaeological reality, however, suggests that peoples of the south and east coast of Iberia had been influenced to some extent by broader cultural and political developments current elsewhere in the western Mediterranean, such as orientalization, urbanization on the Phoenician and Greek model and the spread of writing. The key issue, surely, is to establish how far the social systems encountered by Rome at the time of conquest lent themselves to the development of the urban networks that were fundamental to Rome's success in controlling provincial communities. A range of strongly differentiated political, social and cultural regions had developed in Iberia over the previous 600 years or so. Some of these were alien to Rome's earlier experiences in Italy and Sicily, although the strategies of accommodation which were worked out with the peoples of Iberia played a crucial role in their Romanization and gave rise to the distinctive character of the Hispanic provinces.

Archaeological research in recent years has done much to characterize the major cultural groupings that had developed prior to the later third century BC and to wean scholars off an unhealthy dependence upon the largely retrospective writings of the classical sources (Almagro Gorbea and Ruiz Zapatero 1993 for a good recent analysis). Sustained contact with the Phoenicians, Greeks and, later, Carthaginians in south and north-eastern Spain, together with distinctive underlying later Bronze Age traditions had given rise to one of the best known of the pre-Roman peoples of Iberia: the Iberian peoples of southern Spain and the Mediterranean coast. By the fifth century BC they had come to share a number of broad cultural characteristics and came to be known as Iberians by the Greeks. However, within this broad grouping, there was significant variation which cannot readily be equated to the individual Iberian peoples mentioned by the Classical sources. Western Andalucía, eastern Andalucía, south-eastern Spain, eastern Spain between the Segura and the Ebro, the lower Ebro valley, the northeast coastal Spain and the northeastern interior can all be distinguished from one another in terms of their settlement patterns, social organization, religious practices and artistic traditions (Ruiz and Molinos 1993 for a summary of evidence). The unequal survival of archaeological evidence makes it unwise to be too dogmatic, but it does seem that a range of competing archaic states had developed in the south and south-east by the sixth/fifth centuries BC (Ruiz 1996), while a less centralized network had emerged further north and in the lower

Ebro valley. It is possible to speak of towns throughout the iberian region at this stage, although there was substantial variation in their character, density and relationship to their surrounding countrysides. How far these towns were political centres in the Greek or Etruscan tradition is very much open to question and it is perhaps unwise to rely too heavily upon comments by the later, Roman, written sources like Livy. The other well-known people of the Iberia, the Celtiberians, are best known from accounts by the Classical sources (see most recently Burillo 1998). They inhabited lands immediately to the south of the middle Ebro, extending as far south as the headwaters of the Duero and the Tagus. The name 'celtiberians' was first mentioned by name by Livy in the context of events in 218 BC and has a complex range of political and ethnic meanings (Burillo 1998, 14–64). At the very least, it is clear that it refers to a range of peoples who had developed some kind of urban-based organizational system by the fourth century BC. It also hints at complex cultural relationships with the Iberians to the east and peoples ultimately of "celtic" extraction in the north and centre of the peninsula, which are also borne out by careful readings of the archaeological evidence (see, for example, Ruiz Zapatero 1996). There was a similar kind of cultural relationship between the peoples of the Spanish southern Meseta, with cultural influences from the Iberians to the east (Blasco Bosqued 1993: 292–5) and Tartessos and the later Iron-Age peoples of southern Spain playing an important role.

The cultural development of the Iberians was the result of interaction between existing late Bronze-Age traditions and both direct and indirect influences of the Greeks and Phoenicians (viz. Rouillard 1991 for example), with prestige goods economies playing a key role. By contrast, the Celtiberians were of indigenous Urnfield background, who drew some cultural inspiration from Greek influences transmitted indirectly through the medium of the Iberians to the east and, to some extent, celtic influences to the north (see Burillo 1987 and Ruiz Zapatero 1996). In a sense, therefore, the development of both 'peoples' could be partially ascribed to the pan-Mediterranean cultural convergence that became increasingly manifest from the sixth and fifth centuries BC onwards, and which gathered pace with the spread of broader Greek and Hellenistic cultural traits, and ultimately ideas, between the fifth and third centuries BC (see for example Rouillard 1991: 318–60; see also Curti in this volume). This ensured that unlike the situations that Rome had encountered in Italy, Sicily and Sardinia, in south and eastern Iberia Rome came into contact with peoples whose urban traditions were varying interpretations of Phoenician and, particularly, Greek ideas.

Phoenician influence from the 8th century BC has also been used to help explain the ultimate emergence large centralized settlements in southern, and to a lesser extent, central Portugal (Hipólito Correia 1995) and Spanish Extremadura (Celestino Pérez, Enríquez Navascués and Rodríguez Díaz 1993: 315–20). A settlement system dependant upon a trading relationship between coastal and inland settlements gave way to a distinct situation from the fifth century BC onwards. A series of smaller, fortified, sites – *castros* – came to form a hierrarchical network of settlements by the fourth century BC in southern Portugal.

By contrast, the development of the peoples of the northern Meseta and north-western Spain and northern and central Portugal responded less to Mediterranean influences and adhered more to a persistence of regional late Bronze Age traditions and a range of ill-defined celtic influences (generally, see Fernández-Posse 1998: 141–234). Throughout this area the late Bronze and early Iron Age populations were focused upon small hilltop settlements, or *castros*. In the northern Meseta these had largely given way to the emergence of ranked societies organized around a number of dominant settlements akin to the *oppida* of central Europe and a range of lesser lowland settlements (Ruiz Zapatero and Alvarez Sanchis 1995) between the fourth and late third centuries BC. In the mountainous regions to the north and west, however, the *castros* remained the predominant form of settlement, in many cases until the middle of the first century AD, and only started to give way to the larger *citania* settlements in the last two centuries BC (Martins 1996). This transition may perhaps be explained by increasingly intensive agricultural exploitation in the region rather than influences from further east. The Graeco-Roman urban model was largely alien to all these regions.

By the time of the arrival of Rome in Iberia in the late third century BC, therefore, the peoples of Iberia were organized in a number of different ways. Those bordering the Mediterranean had evolved stratified social hierarchies, some of whose urban centres were akin to those in other parts of the western Mediterranean. Within these, elite status was maintained by means of a range of strategies. Access to key natural resources, and the careful manipulation of prestigious imports would have undoubtedly played a significant role. The organizing principles of peoples away from the Mediterranean was distinct and large centralizing settlements only began to develop gradually. In both regions, however, and particularly in the latter, one should not ignore the importance to elites of large numbers of clients and conspicuous activities which would have further exalted the personal charisma of leaders, such as warfare, and the building of defences and other major communal projects. This is clearest in the commentaries of Rome's war against Carthage in Mediterranean Spain, and during the Celtiberian, and Sertorian wars in peninsular Iberia, by writers such as Livy, Appian, Polybius and Plutarch.

Roman Influence under the Republic
The conquest of Iberia and the absorption of its peoples into the Roman Empire was a sustained process (recently summarized in Richardson 1996: 41–126). It began at a time when Rome was struggling with Carthage for dominance in the western Mediterranean (218 BC) and was concluded when Roman power encompassed much of western Europe (19 BC). During this two hundred year period, Rome had been transformed from a powerful city-state into a structured imperial system. For Iberia, therefore, the Republican period was largely a time of confrontation, but also one during which Rome began to experiment with ways of subjecting conquered and allied peoples to her overall control. At the same time it should be emphasized that this was not a one-way process. Rome was dealing with peoples not territories and all her strategies were to some extent tempered by the responses of the native communities.

The overwhelming impression provided by the written sources is that Republican Iberia was the scene of almost continued warfare, highlighted by the better documented wars – either of conquest (Celtiberian and Lusitanian wars) or as struggles for personal supremacy (Sertorian and Civil wars). However, it is important to temper this and not exaggerate the impact of war upon the peoples of Iberia (Alcock 1993: 8–24 for a comparative study). One suspects that in comparison to the overall size of native populations the numbers of peoples involved in the conflicts were comparatively small. Moreover, the often harsh geography and great expanse of the country would have muted the direct impact of warfare and populations that were often quite dispersed.

Nevertheless, whatever its impact upon the settled peoples of Iberia, warfare was without doubt an instrument of domination by Rome during the Republic. For much of the last two centuries BC, Rome was more concerned about the control of conquered and adjacent peoples rather than the development of a smooth-running administrative system. This much is borne out by the very nature of the provinces. As Richardson (1986) has argued, the creation of Hispania Citerior and Ulterior in 197 BC did not represent the creation of two well-defined territorial units, so much as the assignation of notional areas of responsibility (*provinciae*) to two specially created empowered (*imperium*) magistrates. Moreover, it is probable that in general the Roman provinces were not perceived as distinct territories until at least the early first century BC, and more probably the administrative reforms of Augustus (Nicolet 1991: 189–207).

Fundamental to any understanding of the way in which Rome controlled provincial communities is the role of the city-state. Rome, which itself had become a city-state by the sixth century BC (Cornell 1996: 81–118), had developed a durable power-base by means of a unique confederation of Latin and Etruscan city-states between the fifth and third centuries BC. Similarly, the control of her earliest *provinciae* in Sicily and Sardinia/Corsica were largely structured around city-state organizations (see, for example Wilson 1990: 18–21: see also Van Dommelen in this volume). It is probable, however, that by the late third century BC, only communities in south and eastern Iberia were organized in a broadly similar manner (see, for example, Ruiz Rodriguez 1997: 67–9; Santos Velasco 1994: 89–119). Notwithstanding this, Rome's only conceivable strategy at this stage was to treat communities as city-states as far as possible (Knapp 1977: 37–57) – irrespective of whether or not they actually were – probably in an attempt to build-up the kind of confederate network to which she had become accustomed in Italy.

In practice this was only partially successful. The fractured pre-Roman geopolitical landscape meant that there was no single dominant native centre that Rome could use as a power-base in the peninsula. Thus, Roman power in Hispania Citerior was centred at two towns. In the south, Carthago Nova was the natural centre from which to coordinate the economic exploitation of the peninsula (most recently Ramallo Asensio 1989: 43–62), on account of its important metal resources, natural harbour and geographical position. The lack of a major port close to the mouth of the Ebro which could serve as a key strategic centre for coordinating the supply of troops for the conquest of Celtiberia during the second century BC, led to the rapid development of Tarraco as a strategic base in northern Citerior (recent summaries in Alföldy 1991: 27–33 and Aquilué *et al.* 1991: 13–19). Despite claims to the contrary, it seems unlikely that either of these were provincial capitals to the mid first century BC (*pace* Ruiz de Arbulo 1992: 115–30). Provincial capital is a term which should be approached with care and is perhaps more appropriate to the period following the Augustan provincial re-organization. Instead, they should perhaps be regarded as complementary economic and military centres through which Rome articulated her strategies of domination. In Ulterior, the resources and position of Corduba made this a convenient focus for both economic and strategic roles (Stylow 1990; id. 1993; Ventura *et al.* 1998).

There is little evidence that Rome imposed a new city-state system as such, which would have enabled her to "manage" settled communities in Iberia. Apart from Carthago Nova, Corduba and Tarraco, the only other known Roman foundations in Iberia prior to the middle first century were Italica (205 BC; Keay 1997), the *colonia latina* of Carteia (171 BC: Roldán Gómez *et al*. 1998: 169–93) and the *coloniae* of Metellinum and Norba Caesarine (Cáceres) (70s BC) in Ulterior, Valentia (138 BC: Ribera 1998) and the Roman town of Emporiae (c.100 BC) in Citerior (Mar and Ruiz de Arbulo 1993: 203–66). These were all too distant from one another to have functioned effectively as a network, while their inhabitants would have been in an absolute minority amongst the native communities in each region. In addition to these there were also a handful of Roman "sponsored" towns in Ulterior (Iliturgis) and Citerior (Gracchuris and Pompaelo), as well as sites with Latin names whose status and character remain unknown (Knapp cit). The peninsula as a whole only began to move towards the 'reality' of a network of autonomous city-states with the grants of municipal status made by Caesar, Augustus and the Flavians. How far the inhabitants of these towns were entirely of Roman or Italic origin is open to question. The literary and archaeological evidence points to the presence of Italians and Roman citizens being present in *conventus civium romanorum* at major towns like Tarraco and Carthago Nova from the first century BC (Marin Díaz 1988: 88–93). The literary sources alone suggest Italic veterans for Italica, a mixture of Italic veterans and natives for Corduba and people of mixed latin and native descent for Carteia, but are not clear about the origin of the original settlers at Valentia (Peña 1984). Otherwise one could only expect the sporadic granting of Roman Citizenship to natives prior to the mid first century BC.

In the absence of a network of autonomous city-states in Iberia, Rome dealt with many of the pre-existing native communities as if they had been city-states. A dialogue was established with native elites and patron-client relationships, which were crucial to Rome's control of native populations, and which rapidly developed between successive Roman generals and leading elites (discussed in Keay 1995, 293, and 300). Contingent upon this, the status and relationship of each community to Rome was carefully expressed in Roman legal terms, being defined variously as allied, free or tributary (Knapp cit.). The language used was similar to that applied to communities in Italy and other parts of the Roman west. However, this should not blind us to the reality that the political organization of native communities differed from one region to another: thus the archaic states of south and east Spain were probably closer to the reality of city-states in Italy, than the settled communities of Celtiberia and central Spain. At the same time, the geo-political geometry of local and regional settlement systems also underwent a gradual transformation, with communities responding to Roman authority and demands in different ways. Surveys have revealed the abandonment of sites and the transformation of settlement systems in the south, east and centre in the course of the last two centuries BC (for example, Ruiz Rodríguez 1987; Keay 1991: 127–40; Burillo 1991; Sacristán de Lama *et al*. 1995). This was part of a process, in which certain key centres that best served Rome's interests came to be enhanced at the expense of others.

The cooperation of key native elites was central to this strategy. Roman governors and generals needed to harness this through the fostering of patron-client relationships in their favour, tempered with the ever-present threat of force. Their existence is implicit in many of the recorded dealings between Iberians, Celtiberians and Romans during the Republican period, and which are conventionally expressed in terms of "*fides iberica*" and "*devotio iberica*" (Etienne 1958: 75–80). One assumes that they were promoted by granting certain privileges which visibly enhanced the status of native elites, such as access to architects and new architectural concepts, prestigious goods and a range of services and privileges.

As a result, Rome was able to retain control over the peoples of Iberia and to ensure the successful exploitation of their rich metal and agricultural resources. Some form of systematic taxation had been imposed by the 170s BC (Richardson 1976), while the silver mines of south-eastern and south Spain began to exploited systematically from the middle and late second century respectively (Domergue 1990: 178–96). The impact of this taxation amongst the subject communities of northern Citerior can perhaps be gauged by the spread of local silver and bronze coins from the middle of the second century BC onwards (Crawford 1985: 90–102), and the increasingly large-scale appearance of Roman silver coinage from the later the second century BC (Chaves 1996: 525–600). The situation in Ulterior is less well understood (Keay 1996: 155–60; Chaves 1998: 167–9), although some kind of accommodation between native bronze and imported Roman silver developed in the course of the later second and earlier first century BC.

All of the aforementioned changes could be defined as Romanization, since they were symptomatic of native communities being drawn into an increasingly close economic and political relationship with Rome. When thinking about the cultural changes that may have been taking place at this time, matters become more complex. If one assumes that this took place as the direct result of Romans and Italians settling in Iberia, it is perhaps worth reflecting upon how many – if any at all- prior to the mid first century BC would have been themselves "culturally Romanized". In many parts of central and southern Italy, Italic language and traditions persisted until very late, in some cases into the first century AD (viz most recently Terrenato 1998). It can also be argued that given Rome's love-hate relationship with Hellenistic culture during the third and second centuries BC (see for example Gruen 1992: 1–5; 84–130), her material culture was not easily distinguishable from that of the broader Hellenistic cultural koiné of the Mediterranean of which Iberia had become a part. Rome had not yet developed an ideology of Empire that would lend itself readily to being expressed by a standardized visual language of cultural symbols: that was a process that began during the Augustan age. Consequently, it is not clear that there was an all-embracing system of Roman values which native communities could readily perceive or emulate.

However, it would be absurd to argue that Roman, Italic and Hellenistic forms were absent from Republican Iberia. Recent archaeological research has begun to show Roman and Italic influences on different aspects of the daily life of communities, predominately in eastern Spain and the lower valley Ebro. The great influx of Greco-Italic, Dressel I wine amphorae and Italic Black Gloss pottery from central and southern Italy during the mid to later second century BC onwards to native sites along the eastern coast of Citerior (generally, see Molina Vidal 1997: 203–9; more specifically, see Carreté *et al.* 1985: 257–59; 276–77) is surely indicative of changes in their eating habits. By contrast, these imports tend to be much rarer at sites in Ulterior (for example, see Vaquerizo 1990: 113–32; for Córdoba, see Ventura 1996: the high volume of black gloss here may be exceptional). Roman or Italic house types, and occasionally bath-buildings and temples have begun to be recognized from the end of the second century BC onwards. There are not only examples at the Roman towns of Carthago Nova (Ramallo 1989), Corduba (Ventura *et al.* 1996: 88–93), Tarraco (Aquilué *et al.* 1991) and Valentia (Marín, Matamoros de Villa and Ribera 1991), but also at such native centres such as Azaila (Beltrán Lloris 1976), Contrebia Belaisca (Beltrán Martínez and Beltrán Lloris 1989) and La Caridad de Caminreal (Vicente *et al.* 1986) in the lower Ebro valley. An Italic-style extra-mural sanctuary of earlier (?) second century BC date has been located at La Encarnación de Caravaca in south-eastern Spain (Ramallo 1992). Analyses of the distribution and content of Iberian and early Latin inscriptions points to the spread of Roman ways of conceptualizing business and the gradual spread of Latin in the course of the second and first centuries BC (de Hoz 1995). It has also been suggested that the distribution of Roman Republican family names on early imperial inscriptions (Dyson 1980–1981) reflects the unofficial practice of Romans allowing native clients to use their names. By contrast to all of this, Italic influences are largely absent from southern and central Spain.

These new fashions were not adopted *systematically* in non-Roman centres. This is probably because there was no readily identifiable system of Roman cultural values at this time and that they were anyway closely linked to the Roman concept of town which did not manifest itself until the mid first century BC onwards. Instead they were adopted piecemeal and deployed in the cultural context of the users, raising the possibility that rather than being part of a Romanizing process this was part of an ongoing process of iberization or celtiberization. The case of La Caridad de Caminreal is a good example. Here, an Italic style house was built in a newly planned Celtiberian settlement in the early first century BC: one of its rooms was decorated by an *opus signinum* mosaic decorated with a standard geometric design but with an inscription in Celtiberian at its centre (Vicente *et al.* 1986; de Hoz 1995: 73–4). Thus, the architect Likinete – which be a celtiberization of the latin name Licinius – designed a house in the Italic style, even though the owner of the house chose to record this in celtiberian rather than latin. By contrast, at Illici (La Alcudia de Elche), an italic-style mosaic mentions three Iberian names in latin script.

Why native elites in certain parts of Iberia should have chosen to adopt certain aspects of Italic and Roman material culture at all is not clear. In the first instance, it should be stated that this was not a new phenomenon. In the seventh· sixth and fifth centuries BC, for example, natives elites in parts of south and eastern Spain had imported relatively small quantities of pottery and metalwork as well as adopting aspects of Greek architectural and sculptural style (evident, for example, in the 'heroic' sculptural groups from Porcuna and El Pajarillo: Negueruela 1990; Molinos *et al.* 1998: 323–47) – the so-called *orientalizing* process. This was similar to the Republican situation in so far as these items were adopted piecemeal, rather than necessarily being part of the wholesale deployment of a Greek or Phoenician value system. It differs in that the nature of the Roman presence in Iberia was distinct to that of the Greeks and Phoenicians: it was a structured, if somewhat rudimentary, system of exploitation.

The most straightforward explanation would be that as in the pre-Roman period, elites traded agricultural surplus or access to precious metal sources in exchange for the kinds of goods discussed above. Presumably, the motivation for this would have been the social distance and kudos gained from a monopoly over their supply. In this way, elites in Citerior, and to a lesser extent in Ulterior, would have chosen to drink Italian wine or build Italic-style houses as a way of reinforcing their position at the top of the social hierarchy. Another possibility is that access to these goods and ideas was facilitated by Rome as a means of retaining native loyalties in the context of the crucial patron-client relationships which underwrote the success of Roman control in the peninsula. By implication, therefore, the choice of a particular community to reject italic house-plans, concrete floors with mosaic decoration, the use of iberian and celtiberian names or scripts, or the import of italic wine and tablewares may have been a way of offering a subtle form of resistance to the cultural otherness represented by Rome (similar arguments are proposed for Sardinia by Van Dommelen in this volume; generally, see Webster 1996 on post-colonial perspectives on the Roman Empire).

Roman Influence under the Empire

For Hispania, as indeed other provinces in the western Empire, the period between the mid first century BC and the late first century AD saw more sustained cultural change than over the previous 150 years. In attempting to explain why this should have happened, it is worth remembering that it was not simply a case of native communities becoming more Roman. It was part of a more a complex series of cultural relationships in which the distinction between Roman and native became blurred, and Roman cultural symbols were deployed in a number of ways in a range of regional contexts.

This process was essentially a by-product of the changing nature of the Empire to which the communities of Iberia belonged. Ancient literature, histories, art and architecture make it clear that a new self-confident ideology of Empire had begun to emerge at Rome in the course of the second century BC. Hellenistic cultural forms were increasingly appropriated to express Roman dominance in the Mediterranean and specifically Roman material culture (Gruen 1992: 131–82). This development was symptomatic of the breakdown of the Republican system of government and the emergence of the imperial monarchy. It achieved its maturity with the Hellenistic-Roman cultural synthesis that was achieved under Augustus. His reign saw the emergence of a standardized visual language of Empire at Rome (Zanker 1990; Galinsky 1996: 332–75; Woolf this volume), which then evolved into a distinctively Roman imperial culture in the course of the first century AD. Central to this development was the way in which Rome defined herself as the centre of power by re-defining and re-expressing her relationship to subject peoples (Nicolet 1991: 95–122; 149–69). This necessarily involved changes in the character of the provinces themselves. They ceased to be the areas of magisterial responsibility that they had been under the Republic and developed into more geographically circumscribed communities whose subject relationship to Rome was explicit and were governed on a more systematic basis.

The conclusion of the Cantabrian Wars in 19 BC saw the end of nearly 200 years of sustained warfare in Iberia and precipitated a gradual re-definition of Roman power. This first becomes evident when the scope of Hispania Ulterior was reduced: western Iberia was assigned to the newly created *provincia* of Lusitania between 16 and 13 BC. Later, between 7 and 2 BC, Ulterior lost south-eastern Iberia to Tarraconensis, while

Citerior gained north-western Spain and northern Portugal (generally, see Mackie 1983: 16–17). The enlarged Hispania Citerior Tarraconensis was administered by the Emperor and his delegates, on account of its metal resources and military garrison, while Hispania Ulterior Baetica was managed by representatives of the Senate. Supra-provincial affairs, such as the collation of taxes and the administration of justice, were focused at leading provincial cities, or capitals, where the governor and procurator resided. In the case of the older provinces, these were sited at the key Republican centres of Corduba (Knapp 1983: 52), Tarraco and, for a short while, Carthago Nova (Alföldy 1991: 55–9). In the recently created province of Lusitania, a newly founded colonia (Emerita) was assigned this role (Richardson 1996a). Regional matters were coordinated through the creation of assize districts (conventus) in the course of the first century AD (for *conventus* see Mackie 1983: 8–11).

Re-definition of the provinces in this way marked the beginning of a new era during which Roman power in Iberia ceased to be manifested through continuous warfare and was instead articulated through a more integrated system of political control. Moreover, the focus of Roman attitudes towards the peninsula was increasingly directed towards ensuring the long-term Roman hegemony and developing a more systematic exploitation of its economic resources. Fundamental to the success of this was the conversion of subject peoples into autonomous communities by an extension of the city-state system throughout the peninsula (generally, see Abascal and Espinosa 1989; Le Roux 1996). This had made little progress under the Republic. However, from the mid first century BC onwards, a mixture of political expediency and regional geo-political considerations gave rise to the gradual municipalization of much of the peninsula. Caesar and Augustus began the process in two complementary ways. On the one hand, they settled Roman citizens at a number of newly created coloniae in Ulterior and, to a lesser extent, Lusitania and Citerior. On the other, they granted municipal status to a number of pre-existing native communities in Ulterior and, to a lesser extent, Citerior. This practice was continued very occasionally by Tiberius, Claudius and Galba but was only completed by the grant of *ius latii* to all free communities in the Iberian peninsula by Vespasian (assorted papers in Ortiz de Urbina and Santos 1996 discuss the most recent evidence).

The effect of all of these changes to create a new geo-political landscape in the Hispaniae, in which Roman interests were promoted through a hierarchy of Roman towns focused upon key centres of power structured by major routeways, such as the via Augusta (Castellví, Comps, Kotarba and Pezin 1997; Sillières 1991). This might suggest that cultural and geographical variation across the peninsula had been suppressed. However, this impression is misleading. Firstly, only a minority of towns within all three provinces were ever privileged with a grant of municipal status; Coloniae were even rarer. Secondly, the density of autonomous communities varied from one province to the next and was undoubtedly affected by the pre-disposition of different cultural regions to the Roman urban way of life. Thus, towns in Baetica, particularly along the Guadalquivir valley were very dense (see, for example Ponsich 1974, 1979, 1987, 1991) and differed considerably from densities in east (TIR K/J-31), central (TIR K-30) Tarraconensis and Lusitania (TIR J-29). At the same time, in those parts of the peninsula, such as north-west Tarraconensis (TIR K-29), where the Graeco-Roman concept of town was completely alien to the indigenous settlement tradition and where some municipalities without urban centres were created by Rome. Consequently, although the first century AD saw the spread of a largely urban system across the peninsula, there is little doubt that the political, social and economic roles of individual towns would have varied considerably from one region to another.

It seems clear, therefore, that regionalism thus lay close to the surface in this emergent network of autonomous cities. Consequently, social and political cohesion must have been of the utmost importance to the integrity of the provinces. Whether or not this was ever perceived of as an issue in antiquity, it is the contention of this paper that it was achieved to some degree though the development of a nexus between the new imperial ideology and an emergent Roman imperial culture (Woolf 1995). At Rome, the two were mutually supportive. The development of a standardized artistic language through the deployment of new architectural and artistic styles has been interpreted as the visible face of a new imperial ideology, which played an important role in legitimising the Augustan and Julio-Claudian monarchy to the Senatorial aristocracy in the City (Zanker 1990; 167–238). The adoption of key building and sculptural types, given cohesion by key epigraphic texts, therefore, implied at least an outward acceptance of imperial values in the Capital and some of the key towns in Italy (Zanker 1990: 297–333). Open promotion of these was an important public index of personal loyalty to the Emperor and State. In Italy, this was integral to the development of imperial cults at towns, until both imperial culture and cults to the Emperor, his family and predecessors formed mutually supporting systems promoting political loyalty to the Emperor and State. In other words, their many cultural and ritual practices were of key importance in the signalling of "belonging" to the Empire achieved by Roman religion across the Empire (Beard, North and Price 1998: 318).

How far this is true of the provinces is open to dispute. In the case of Iberia, both elements are present. In the first instance, cults to the Emperor developed from the Augustan period onwards. Following an early spontaneous gesture under Augustus in 27 BC, permission for a temple to the divus Augustus at Tarraco was granted in AD 15 (most recently Fishwick 1999). Municipal and other cults were established at other towns in Hispania subsequently, while under the Flavians, a provincial cult was established at each of the provincial capitals, Tarraco, Emerita Augustus (Mérida) and Corduba (Fishwick 1994–5). These developments were paralleled by the gradual transformation of urban centres. Recent research has revealed the extent to which new imperial architectural styles were rapidly adopted at Tarraco, Corduba and Emerita, as well as coloniae, municipia and other unprivileged towns across the provinces between the later first century BC and the middle/later first century AD (Trillmich and Zanker 1990; synthesized in Keay 1995 and with more recent evidence in Jiménez Salvador 1998). This process began under Augustus, with evidence for the appearance of new building styles at towns throughout all three provinces. However, the emergence of well-defined urban types with parallels to buildings in Rome and Italy does not really achieve maturity until the Claudian and Flavian periods (Baetican evidence summarized by Léon & Rodríguez Oliva 1993 and, more recently, Keay 1998a). Many of the buildings at the heart of these new urban enterprises were in some way involved in rituals connected with Emperor worship (TED'A 1989: 182–91, Fishwick 1994, Keay 1996a and Ruiz de Arbulo 1998: 41–8 for Tarraco; Stylow 1990: 271–82 and Trillmich 1996: 186–8 for Corduba; Trillmich 1996, Nogales

1996 and Fishwick 1996 for Emerita). However, this should not be taken to suggest that
the monumentalization of town centres is to be explained by this alone, because other
factors such as personal benefactions and civic pride were also involved (see for example
Melchor Gil 1994: 151–84; see however Mackie 1990 for a cautionary note). Nevertheless,
construction of many public buildings was often part of the creation of politico-religious
environments in which 'belonging' to the Empire and public participation in events
connected with well-being of the Emperor and Empire would have been acted out; this
wholesale transformation of city centres has been attested in Asia Minor (Price 1984:
133–67). Inscriptions would have played a key role in this, being an essential complement
of the monumentalized city centres (Woolf 1996; Mayer 1999) directly invoking the
Emperor and associated gods, the imperial house and public acts by members of urban
elites. In the older centres of Roman power in the Hispaniae, this was particularly true
for Augustus and members of the Julio Claudian House (Abascal 1996).

At this superficial level, therefore, it would be easy to say that a range of Roman and
native communities across the Hispaniae were acculturated with the wholesale adoption
of imperial cultural symbols and rituals in the course of the first century AD. In the
provincial capitals and the coloniae, Roman citizens would have deployed them in such
a way that they successfully reproduced the Roman way of life in a provincial context and
at the same time openly advertised their loyalty to the Emperor and State. This would
have been underscored by the fact that when deployed together in an urban context they
functioned as a "grammar" which could only be understood by those that shared Rome's
view of the world, namely the elites. A similar situation could be inferred for certain
municipalities, where their deployment would have been a far more effective means of
self-empowerment than it had been under the Republic. Here, as during the Republic,
patron-client relationships between well-connected Romans at Rome, the colonies and
the provincial capitals, and provincial elites would have continued to have acted as a key
conduit for the diffusion of new ideas and access to key materials.

But how far is it possible to say that all communities, urban and otherwise, in the
Hispaniae deployed Roman cultural symbols because they wanted to become Roman ? In
theory at least, openly adopting a suite of Roman public buildings, inscriptions and
regulatory laws in the name of Emperor and State would have been a very positive means
of enhancing personal status through the open advertisement of *romanitas* and loyalty to
the Emperor and State. In practice, however, it is unlikely that all communities would
have reacted to Roman power and culture in the same way. Prior to the later first century
AD, at least, their ethnic mix is likely to have been quite varied. Roman citizens originating
from Rome or Italy would probably have still been comparatively rare – particularly away
from the Mediterranean coast and the major colonies – although this is often hard to
glean from the epigraphic evidence. At the same time, it seems very likely that there was
a strong degree of social and ethnic continuity amongst regional and local communities,
particularly those in the interior (see, for example, González Rodríguez 1986).
Consequently, perception of, and aquiescence in, Rome and Roman cultural values will
have varied from one region to another. These, in turn, would have been tempered by
differing degrees of wealth, status, and connections to powerful patrons at Rome.
Consequently, while it would be all to easy to suggest that the appearance of Roman
architecture, inscriptions, sculpture, pottery etc on native sites was part of a process of

straightforward cultural integration, or Romanization, one should perhaps anticipate a more complex series of choices taking place.

The use of Roman cultural symbols in their broader social, cultural and ethnic contexts points, therefore, to the development of a range of overlapping and interlocking Hispano-Roman cultures. While the adoption of Roman buildings, inscriptions, names, eating habits etc may have been inspired by prototypes in the *coloniae*, provincial capitals and Rome itself, it does not necessarily follow that the communities in which they appear shared the same Roman social, religious or cultural values. It is important instead to look beyond the occurrence of individual cultural symbols, to note the broader cultural context in which they were deployed. Thus, while Latin was used by the communities of north-western Tarraconensis quite soon after their conquest, it is important to note that it was relatively rare outside the newly established towns of Asturica, Lucus and Bracara Augusta prior to the later first century AD (Pereira Menaut 1995). On the other hand, however, indigenous communities in north and central Tarraconensis used it to denote the continued existence of *gentilitates* and *castella*; in other words, they used a Roman medium of communication to advertise the continuity of pre-Roman social groupings.

In contrast to the older-established traditions of towns along the Mediterranean coast and in southern Spain, it seems likely that many of these new ideas would have been diffused by social networks that persisted well into the imperial period. Moreover, they would also have been used in the context of the ongoing cultural context of each community. Unless we are to posit the large-scale colonization of all Roman towns in Iberia by Romans or Italians, the contrasting ethnic and cultural backgrounds at these centres may have ensured that at each Roman cultural forms were perceived and used in a range of different ways. For example, the towns of Baelo (Bolonia: Sillières 1995), Termes (Tiermes: Argente Oliver *et al.* 1985), Valeria (Valera de Arriba: Fuentes 1987) and Segobriga (Cabeza del Griego: Almagro Basch 1975; more recently Almagro Gorbea and Lorrio 1989) all constructed suites of monumental Roman public buildings in the course of the first century AD. However, their cultural backgrounds were sufficiently distinct to suggest that for each, the perception of what was the best exemplar of "Roman" was different. Consequently, to concentrate upon trying to guage how far the rock-cut Celtiberian town of Termes may have measured up to a neighbouring colonia, such as Clunia (recent work summarized in Palol 1991), as a sophisticated Roman urban community is to miss the point. It is perhaps more productive to reflect upon how far it might have been a considered *interpretation* of Clunia's Roman style buildings and urban way of life, tempered by local perceptions of what was considered most typically Roman, passive resistance to some concepts or simply preferred choice. Consequently, the presence and absence of individual Roman building types at a town like Termes is important. However, it is even more relevant to establish how they were actually used and what their role was in the town as a whole. Was the so-called forum at the site actually used in the same way as that recently discovered at Caesaraugusta (Nuñez and Hernández 1998) ? Was the use of the lavishly decorated rock-cut peristyle-houses structured in the same way as those at the colonia ? Just because Roman style buildings are present, does not necessarily mean that they would have been used in the way they would have been in Rome or a provincial colonia. Individual buildings need to be analyzed in the context their of urban landscapes.

Another complementary approach would be to analyze material culture in the context of individual buildings. For example, it would be profitable to establish contexts in which imported Roman finewares, amphora-borne foodstuffs, jewellery, inscriptions and sculptures appear at a range of towns across Baetica, Tarraconensis and Lusitania. This would provide us with a means of characterising the ways in which Roman material culture were used to structure the way in which built environments were used and, by implication, to understand variations in social and cultural behaviour. Recent work of this kind, albeit at sites of Republican date, has been undertaken at the indigenous sites of Castellones de Ceal (Jaén; Mayoral Herrera 1996) in southern Spain and at La Caridad de Caminreal in the lower Ebro valley (Vicente, Punter, Escriche & Herce 1991).

In time, the aggregate impact of the changing nature of Roman imperial culture and native perceptions of it, gave rise to distinctive Hispano-Roman cultural groupings across Baetica, Tarraconensis and Lusitania. These still need to be properly defined by distinguishing regions where there were distinctive uses of Roman cultural ideas. At one level some of these can be readily defined. The social groupings of the *gentilitates* and *castella* in north-western Tarraconensis and northern Lusitania is an obvious example (Albertos Firmat 1975; Pereira Menaut 1982; Santos Yanguas 1985; González Rodriguez 1997), side by side with the persistance of *castro* type settlements, like Santa Tegra (A Guarda, Pontevedra) well into the imperial period (de la Peña Santos 1999). Another might be the principal areas of distribution of the products of *terra sigillata hispanica* producers in Tarraconensis and Baetica (for a recent summary, see Roca Roumens & Fernández García 1999). The area of influence of epigraphically attested deities, such as Ataecina in southern Lusitania, might be another (Blázquez 1975: 93, 167 and 39–42). Another approach would be to analyze the anatomy of epigraphic usage in key regions of the Hispaniae (see, for example the papers by Mayer, Abascal, Beltrán Lloris, Untermann, Velaza, Stylow, Salinas de Frias and Pereira Menaut in Beltrán Lloris 1995). Beyond this it would be interesting to establish how far areas of overlapping cultural difference were related to late iron age groupings and to establish what, if any, relationship these bore to the boundaries of conventus and province.

Conclusion

In a sense, this paper is a reaction to established views about the character of the Roman presence in Iberia and its broader impact upon the political, social and cultural lives of its inhabitants. In particular, it attempts to take the first steps towards deconstructing some of the certainties that have grown-up in recent years and to highlight the potential of the archaeology in a heavily text-based debate. Given the richness of both sources of evidence and the recent advances in interpretational theories, Iberia is ideal for a fundmental reappraisal of the whole question of cultural integration in the western Roman Empire.

There is little doubt that the presence of Rome in Iberia brought about a profound transformation in the political, social, economic and cultural life of its inhabitants (recently explored by Le Roux 1995). It had been a long process, inextricably linked to the changing nature of the Empire itself, beginning in the late third century BC and achieving some degree of internal consistency by the late first century AD. While it would be foolish to deny the importance of direct Italian, and later Roman, influence in this process, it has been the central tenet of this paper to argue that it was largely an internally driven process. In other words, Romans and Italians had very little direct agency for most of the cultural changes observable in native urban communities. It is of key importance to recognize the crucial relationship between Roman culture of the imperial period and Imperial power, both at a provincial and at a local level. Deployment of Roman cultural symbols "took off" from the Augustan period onwards, in the context of the progressive municipalization of the provinces, empowering those local elites who chose to adopt outward signs of the Roman way of life in their own communities.

At one level this contributed to political and social cohesion in the Hispaniae. Elites at the provincial capitals, coloniae and some of the older municipia undoubtedly shared Roman social, cultural and political values and probably thought of themselves as Roman. At another level, however, there was a surface tension of aquiescence in Roman rule as the elites of newer municipia and the civitates channelled their energies into the wholesale transformation of their towns or the adoption of individual Roman symbols as a way of expressing purely local concerns. Insofar as these communities had been inevitably drawn into a close economic and political relationship to Rome, it is possible to speak of Romanization. In cultural terms, however, the label is clearly inadequate, in that it emphasizes similarities at the expense of differences, and creates too straightforward an opposition between native and Roman. Prior to the middle of the first century AD at least, it might not be venturing too far to speak in terms of an *interpretatio iberica* in which the elites of many Hispano-Roman communities drew upon local and regional traditions when developing the cultural environment in which they lived. One of the key questions, therefore, that needs to be asked is not how far was Iberia "Romanized" by this time. Instead, one should seek to establish the extent to which late iron age ethnic or regional identities persisted during this transitional phase of cultural integration and the ways in which their use of Roman cultural symbols interacted with that of those who shared Rome's view of the world. It is only by doing this that it will be possible to gain a better understanding of the social, political and religious geographies of later the first and second century AD in the Hispaniae.

References

Abascal, J. M. 1996. Programas epigráficas augusteos. *Anales de Arqueología Cordobesa* 7: 45–82.
Abascal, J. M. and Espinosa, U. 1989. *La ciudad hispano-romana. Privilegio y poder.* Logroño.
Alarcão, J. de 1995. *O domínio romano em Portugal.* Publicacões Europa-America: Lisboa.
Albertos Firmat, M. L. 1975. Organizaciones suprafamiliares en la Hispania Antigua. *Studia Archaeologica* 37, Valladolid.
Alcock, S. 1993. *Graecia Capta. The Landscapes of Roman Greece.* CUP: Cambridge.
Alföldy, G. 1991. *Tarraco. Forum 8.* Tarragona.
Almagro Basch, M. 1975. *Segóbriga. Guía del conjunto.* Ministerio de Cultura: Madrid.
Almagro Gorbea, M. Lorrio, A. 1989. *Segóbriga III. La muralla norte y la puerta principal. Campañas de 1986–87. Arqueología Conquense IX.* Cuenca.
Almagro Gorbea, M. and Álvarez Martínez, J. M. 1998. *Hispania. El legado de Roma.* Ministerio de Cultura: Madrid.

Almagro Gorbea, M. and Ruiz Zapatero, G. 1993. Palaeoetnología de la Península Ibérica. Reflexiones y perspectivas de futuro. In A. Almagro-Gorbea, G. Ruiz Zapatero (eds.) *Palaeoetnología de la Península Ibérica. Complutum 2–3*, pp. 469–99.

Aquilué, X., Mar, R., Nolla, J. M., Ruiz de Arbulo, J. and Sanmartí, E. 1984. *El forum romà d'Empúries (Excavacions de l'any 1982)*. Diputació de Barcelona: Barcelona.

Aquilué, X., Dupré, X., Massó, J. and Ruiz de Arbulo, J. 1991. *Tarraco. Guía Arqueológica*. El Mèdol: Tarragona.

Argente Oliver, L. *et al*. 1985. *Tiermes. Guía del yacimiento aqueológico*. Ministerio de Cultura: Madrid.

Barrett, J. 1997. Romanization: a critical comment. In D. Mattingly (ed.) *Dialogues in Roman Imperialism. Journal of Roman Archaeology Supplementary Series, no.23*. JRA: Portsmouth, R.I., pp. 51–64.

Beltrán Lloris, F. (ed.) 1995. *Roma y el nacimiento de la cultura epigráfica en occident*. Institución Fernando el Católico: Zaragoza.

Beltrán Lloris, M. 1976. *Arqueología e Historia de las ciudades antiguas del Cabezo de Alcalá. Azaila,* Zaragoza.

Beltrán Martínez, A. and Beltrán Lloris, M. 1989. Hipótesis sobre la función del gran edificio de adobe de Contrebia Belaisca. In *XIX Congreso Nacional de Arqueología*. Zaragoza, pp. 353–9.

Bendala, M., Fernández Ochea, C., Fuentes Domínguez, A. and Abad Casal, L. 1988. Aproximación al urbanismo prerromano y a los fenomenos de transición y de potenciación tras la conquista. In AAVV *Los asentamientos ibéricos ante la romanización*. Ministerio de Cultura: Madrid, pp. 121–140.

Bendala, M. 1998. La génesis de la estructura urbana en la España antigua. *Cuadernos de Prehistoria y Arqueología de la Universidad Autónoma de Madrid* 16: 127–47.

Blagg, T. and Millett, M. (eds.) 1990. *The Early Roman Empire in the West*. Oxbow: Oxford.

Blasco Bisqued, Ma. C. 1993. Etnogénesis de la Meseta Sur. In M. Almagro-Gorbea, G. Ruiz Zapatero (eds.) *Palaeoetnología de la Península Ibérica. Complutum 2–3*, pp. 281–97.

Blázquez, J. M. 1975. *Diccionario de las religiones prerromanas de Hispania*. Madrid.

Blázquez, J. M., Montenegro, A., Roldán, J. M., Mangas, J., Teja, R., Sayas, J. J., García Iglesias, L. and Arce, J. 1978. *Historia de España antigua. II. Hispania romana*. Catedra: Madrid.

Blázquez, J. M. and Alvar, J. 1996. *La romanización en occidente*. Actas Editorial: Madrid.

Binford, L. 1972. *An Archaeological Perspective*. Seminar Press: London.

Brunt, P. A. 1971. *Italian Manpower, 225 BC–AD 14*. Oxford University Press: Oxford.

Burillo Mozota, F. 1991. The Evolution of Iberian and Roman Towns in the Middle Ebro Valley. In G. Barker, J. Lloyd (eds.) *Roman Landscapes. Archaeological Survey in the Mediterranean Region. Archaeological Monographs of The British School at Rome* 2. British School at Rome: London, pp. 37–46.

Burillo Mozota, F. 1987. Sobre el orígen de los celtíberos. In F. Burillo (ed.) *I Symposium sobre los Celtíberos*. Institución Fernando el Católico: Zaragoza, pp. 75–93.

Burillo Mozota, F. 1998. *Los Celtíberos. Etnias y estados*. Crítica: Barcelona.

Carreté, J. M., Keay, S. and Millett, M. 1995. *A Roman Provincial Capital and its Hinterland. The Survey of the Territory of Tarragona, Spain, 1985–1990. Journal of Roman Archaeology Supplementary Series 15*. Journal of Roman Archaeology: Michigan.

Castellví, G., Comps, J. -P., Kotarba, J. and Pezin, A. 1997. *Voies romaines du Rhône à l'Ebre: via Domitia et Via Augusta. Documents d'Archéologie Francaise 61*. Maison de les Sciences de l'Homme: Paris.

Celestino, S., Enríquez, J. J. and Rodríguez Díaz, A. 1993. Palaeoetnología del área Extremeña. In M. Almagro-Gorbea, G. Ruiz Zapatero (eds.) *Palaeoetnología de la península ibérica. Complutum 2–3*. Madrid, pp. 311–27.

Chaves, F. 1996. *Los tesoros en el sur de Hispania*. Caja del Monte de Piedad de Sevilla: Seville.

Chaves, F. 1998. Iberian and early Roman coinage of Hispania Ulterior Baetica. In Keay 1998, pp. 147–70.

Cornell, T. 1996. *The Beginnings of Rome: Italy and Rome from the Bronze Age to the Punic Wars* (c.1000–264 BC). Routledge: London

Crawford, M. 1985. *Coinage and Money under the Roman Republic.* Methuen: London.

Cunliffe, B. and Keay, S. (eds.) 1995. *Social Complexity and the Development of Towns in Iberia. From the Copper Age to the Second Century AD. Proceedings of the British Academy 86.* OUP: Oxford.

Curchin, L. 1991. *Roman Spain: Conquest and Assimilation.* Routledge: London.

De Francisco Martín, J. 1989. *Conquista y romanización de Lusitania.* Universidad de Salamanca: Salamanca.

De Hoz, J. 1995. Escrituras en contacto: ibérica y latina. In Beltrán Lloris 1995, pp. 57–84.

Díaz Andreu, M. and Keay, S. (eds.) 1996. *The Archaeology of Iberia. The Dynamics of Change.* Routledge: London.

Domergue, C. 1990. *Les mines de la péninsule ibérique sans l'antiquité romaine.* Boccard: Paris.

Dyson, S. 1980–1981. The Distribution of Roman republican Family Names in the Iberian Peninsula. *Ancient Society* 11/12: 258–99.

Dyson, S. 1993. From New to New Age Archaeology: Archaeological theory and Classical Archaeology-A 1990s perspective. *American Journal of Archaeology* 97: 195–206.

Edmonson, J. C. 1990. Romanization and the Urban Development in Lusitania. In Blagg and Millett, pp. 151–78.

Elsner, J. 1998. *Imperial Rome and Christian Triumph. The Art of the Roman Empire* AD 100–450. Oxford: OUP.

Etienne, R. 1958. *La Culte Impérial dans la péninsule ibérique d'Auguste a Dioclétien.* Paris.

Fernández Posse, Ma. D. 1998. *La investigación protohistórica en la Meseta y Galicia.* Síntesis: Madrid.

Fishwick, D. 1991. *The Imperial Cult in the Latin West,* 2 vols. Brill: Leiden.

Fishwick, D. 1994. Four Temples at Tarraco. In A. Small (ed.*) Subject and Ruler: the cult of the ruling power in classical Antiquity. Journal of Roman Archaeology Supplementary Series 17.* Michigan: Journal of Roman Archaeology, pp. 165–84.

Fishwick, D. 1994–5. Provincial Forum and municipal forum: fiction or fact? *Anas* 7–8: 169–86.

Fishwick, D. 1999. The 'Temple of Augustus' at Tarraco. *Latomus.* 58.1: 121–38.

Fuentes, A. 1987. Avance del foro de Valeria (Cuenca). In C. Aranegui (ed.) *Los Foros de las provincias occidentales.* Ministerio de Cultura: Madrid, pp. 69–72.

Galinsky, K. 1996. *Augustan Culture.* Princeton University Press: Princeton.

Giddens, A. 1984. *The Constitution of Society.* Polity Press: Cambridge.

Gómez Espelosín, F. J., Pérez Largacha, A. and Vallejo Girvés, M. 1995. *La imagen de España en la antigüedad clásica.* Madrid.

González Rodríguez, Ma. Cr. 1986. *Las unidades organizativas indígenas del área indoeuropea de Hispania. Anejos de Veleia II.* Vitoria.

González Román, C. 1981. *Imperialismo y romanización en la Provincia Hispania Ulterior.* Universidad de Granada: Granada.

Gruen, E. 1992. *Culture and Identity in Republican Rome.* Duckworth: London.

Hanson, W. 1997. Forces of Change and Methods of Control. In D. Mattingly (ed.) *Dialogues in Roman Imperialism. Journal of Roman Archaeology Supplementary Series .23.* Portsmouth, R.I., pp. 67–80.

Hidalgo, M. J., Pérez, D. and Gervás, M. (eds.) 1998. *"Romanización" y "reconquista" en la península ibérica: nuevas perspectivas.* Universidad de Salamanca: Salamanca.

Hill, J. D. 1997. The end of One Kind of Body and the Beginning of Another Kind of Body? Toilet Instruments and Romanization. In A. Gwilt, C. Haselgrove (eds.) *Reconstructing Iron Age Societies.* Oxbow: Oxford, pp. 96–107.

Hipólito Correia, V. 1995. The Iron Age in South and Central Portugal and the Emergence of Urban Centres. In Cunliffe and Keay 1995, pp. 237–62.

Jiménez Salvador, J. 1998. La multiplicación de plazas públicas en la ciudad hispanorromana. *Empúries* 51: 11–30.

Jundi, S. and Hill, J. D. 1998. Brooches and Identities in First Century AD Britain: more than meets the eye? In C. Forcey, J. Hawthorne, R. Witcher (eds.) *TRAC 97. Proceedings of the Seventh Annual Theoretical Roman Archaeology Conference*. Oxbow: Oxford, pp. 125–37.

Jones, S. 1997. *The archaeology of Ethnicity. Constructing Identities in the Past and Present*. Routledge: London.

Keay, S. J. 1988. *Roman Spain*. British Museum Press: London.

Keay, S. 1991. Processes in the development of the coastal communities of Hispania Citerior in the Republican Period. In Blagg and Millett 1990, pp. 120–150.

Keay, S. J. 1995. Innovation and adaptation: The Contribution of Rome to Urbanism in Iberia. In Cunliffe and Keay 1995, pp. 291–337.

Keay, S. 1996. La romanización en el sur y el levante de España hasta la época de Augusto. In. Blázquez and Alvar 1996, pp. 147–77.

Keay, S. 1996a. Urban transformation and cultural change. In Diaz-Andreu and Keay 1996, pp. 192–210.

Keay, S. 1997. Early Roman Italica and the romanization of western Baerica. In A. Caballos and P. León (eds.) *Itálica MMCC. Actas de las jornadas del 2.200 aniversario de la fundación de Itálica*. Consejería de Cultura: Seville, pp. 21–47.

Keay, S. (ed.) 1998. *The Archaeology of Early Roman Baetica. Journal of Roman Archaeology Supplementary Series No.29*. Journal of Roman Archaeology: Portsmouth R.I.

Keay, S. 1998a. The development of towns in early Roman Baetica. In Keay 1998, pp. 54–86.

Knapp, R. 1977. *Aspects of the Roman Experience in Iberia 206–100 BC*. Colegio Universitario de Alava/Departamento de Historia Antigua de la Universidad de Valladolid: Valladolid/Alava.

Knapp, R. 1983. *Roman Córdoba*. University of California Press: Berkeley.

Le Roux, P. 1995. *Romains d'Espagne. Cités et politique dans les provinces. IIe siècle av. J. -C. – IIIe siècle ap. J. -C*. Armand Colin: Paris.

León, P. (ed.) 1996. *Colonia Patricia Corduba. Una reflexión arqueológica*. Consejería de Cultura: Seville.

Léon, P. and Rodríguez Oliva, P. 1993. La ciudad hispanorromana en Andalucía. In M. Bendala (ed.) *La ciudad hispanorromana*. Ministerio de Cultura: Barcelona.

Laurence, R. 1994. *Roman Pompeii: Space and Society*. Routledge: London.

Mackie, N. 1983. *Local Administration in Roman Spain A.D. 14–212. British Archaeological Reports International Series 17*. British Archaeological Reports: Oxford.

Mackie 1990. Urban munificence and the growth of urban consciousness in Roman Spain. In Blagg and Millett 1990, pp. 179–92.

Mangas Manjarres, J. *et al.*, 1982. *España Romana (218 a. de J.C. – 414 de J.C.). Volumen II. La sociedad, el derecho, la cultura. Historia de España fundada por R. Menéndez Pidal Tomo II*. Espasa Calpe: Madrid.

Mar, R., Ruiz de Arbulo, J. 1993. *Ampurias Romana*. Ausa: Sabadell.

Marin Díaz, Ma. A., 1988. *Emigración, colonización y municipalización en la Hispania republicana*. Universidad de Granada: Granada.

Marín, C., Matamoros de Villa, C. and Ribera, A. 1991. Restos de una vivienda de época trado-republicana (s. II-I a. J. C.) en Valentia: los hallazgos del palau de les corts valencianes. In M. Beltrán (ed.) *La casa hispanorromana*. Institución Fernando el Católico: Zaragoza, pp. 61–6.

Martins, M. 1996. The Dynamics of Change in Nortwest Portugal during the First Millennium BC. In Díaz Andreu and Keay 1990, pp. 143–57.

Mayer, M. 1989. Plinio el viejo y las ciudades de la Baetica. Aproximación a un estado actual del problema. In J. González (ed.) *Estudios sobre Urso. Colonia Iulia Genetiva.* Alfar: Seville, pp. 303–33.

Mayer, M. 1999. El paisaje epigráfico como elemento diferenciador entre las ciudades. Modelos y realizaciones locales. In J. González (ed.) *Ciudades Privilegiadas en el occidente romano.* Universidad de Sevilla: Seville, pp. 13–32.

Mayer, M., Nolla, J. M. and Pardo, J. 1998. *De les estructures indígenes à l'organització provincial romana de la Hispània Citerior. Ítaca. Anexos I.* Itaca: Barcelona.

Mayoral Herrera, V. 1996. El hábitat ibérico tardío de Castellones de Ceal: organización del espacio y estructura socio-económica. *Complutum* 7: 225–46.

Melchor Gil, E. 1994. *El mecenazgo cívico en la Bética.* Universidad de Córdoba: Córdoba.

Metzler, J., Millett, M., Roymans, N. and Slofstra, J. (eds.) 1995. *Integration in the Early Roman West.* Musée d'Histoire et d'Art: Luxembourg.

Millett, M. 1991. *The Romanization of Britain.* CUP: Cambridge.

Molina Vidal, J. 1997. *La dinámica comercial romana entre Italia e Hispania Citerior.* Universidad de Alicante: Alicante.

Molinos Molinos, M., Chapa Brunet, T., Ruiz Rodríguez, A., Pereira Sieso, J., Rísquez Cuenca, C., Madrigal Belinchón, A., Esteban Marfil, Á., Mayoral Herrera, V. and Llorente López, M. 1998. *El santuario heroico "El Pajarillo".* Univeridad de Jaén: Jaén.

Mommsen, T. 1909. *The Provinces of the Roman Empire from Caesar to Diocletian,* London.

Negueruela, I. 1990. *Los monumentos escultóricos ibéricos del Cerrillo Blanco de Porcuna (Jaén).* Ministerio de Cultura: Madrid.

Nicolet, C. 1991. *Space, Geography and Politics in the Roman Empire.* University of Michigan Press: Ann Arbor.

Nogales, T. 1996. Programas iconográficas del foro de Mérida: el templo de Diana, In *Actes. II Reunió sobre escultura romana a Hispania.* Museu Nacional Arqueològic de Tarragona: Tarragona, pp. 115–34.

Nuñez, J. and Hernández, J. A. 1998. Nuevos datos para el conocimiento del foro de Caesaraugusta. *Empúries* 51: 93–104.

Ortiz de Urbina, E. and Santos, J. 1996. *Teoría y práctica del ordenamiento municipal en Hispania.* Instituto de Ciencias de la Antigüedad Aintzinate-Zientzien Instituta: Vitoria/Gasteiz.

Palol, P. de 1991. *Clunia 0. Studia Varia Cluniensia.* Junta de Castilla y León: Burgos.

Peña, M. J. 1984. Apuntes y observaciones sobre las primeras fundaciones romanas en Hispania. *Estudios de la Antigüedad I.* Univeritat Autònoma de Barcelona: Barcelona, 49–85.

Peña Santos, de la 1999. Santa Tegra (A Guarda, Pontevedra): Un ejemplo del urbanismo castrexo-romano del convento bracarense.' In A. Rodríguez Colmenero (ed.) *Los orígenes de la ciudad en el noroeste hispánico. Actas del Congreso Internacional. Lugo 15–18 de Mayo 1996* (2 vols). Diputación Provincial de Lugo: Lugo, pp. 693–714.

Pereira Menaut, G. 1982. Los castella y las comunidades de Gallaecia. *Zephyrus* 34–5: 249–68.

Pereira Menaut, G. 1988. Cambios estructurales versus romanización convencional. La transformación del paisaje político en el norte de Hispania. In J. Arce, J. González (eds.) *Estudios sobre la Tabula Siarensis en su contexto histórico. Anejos de Archivo Español de Arqueología.* Consejo Superior de Investigaciones Científicas: Madrid, pp. 249–59.

Pereira Menaut, G. 1995. Epigrafía política y primeras culturas epigráficas en el noroeste de la península ibérica. In Beltrán Lloris 1995, pp. 293–326.

Pons, J. 1994. *Territori i societat romana a Catalunya. Dels inicis al Baix Imperi.* Barcelona.

Ponsich, M. 1974. *Implantation rurale antique sur le bas-Guadalquivir I.* De Boccard: Paris..

Ponsich, M. 1979. *Implantation rurale antique sur le bas-Guadalquivir II*. De Boccard: Paris.

Ponsich, M. 1987. *Implantation rurale antique sur le bas-Guadalquivir III*. De Boccard: Paris.

Ponsich, M. 1991. *Implantation rurale antique sur le bas-Guadalquivir IV*. De Boccard: Paris.

Price, S. 1984. *Rituals and Power. The Roman Imperial Cult in Asia Minor*. Cambridge: CUP: Cambridge.

Ramallo Asensio, S. 1989. *La ciudad de Carthago Nova: La documentación arqueológica*. Universidad de Murcia: Murcia.

Ramallo Asensio, S. 1992. Un santuario de época tardo-republicana en La Encarnación, Caravaca, Murcia. *Cuadernos de Arquitectura romana Vol. I. Templos romanos de Hispania*. Universidad de Murcia: Murcia, pp. 39–65.

Ribera, A. 1998. *La fundació de València a l'època romanorepublicana (segles II-I a. de C.)*. Estudios Universitaris: Valencia.

Ribera, A. and Calvo, M. 1995. La primera evidencia arqueológica de la destrucción de Valentia por Pompeyo. *Journal of Roman Archaeology* 8: 19–40.

Richardson, J. 1986. *Hispaniae. Spain and the Development of Roman Imperialism, 218–82 BC*. CUP: Cambridge.

Richardson, J. 1996. *The Romans in Spain*. Blackwell: Oxford

Richardson, J. 1996a. Conquest and Colonies in Lusitania in the Late Republic and Early Empire. In E. Ortiz de Urbina, J. Santos (eds.) *Teoría y páctica del ordenamiento municipal en Hispania. Revisiones de Historia Antigua II,* Editorial Universidad del País Vasco: Vitoria/Gasteiz, pp. 53–61.

Roca Roumens, M. and Fernández García, M. I. 1999. *Terra Sigillata Hispánica. Centros de fabricación y producciones altoimperiales*. Universidad de Jaén/Universidad de Málaga: Málaga.

Roldán Gómez, L., Bendala, M., Blánquez, J. and Martínez, S. 1998. *Carteia*. Consejería de Cultura: Seville.

Rostovsteff, M. 1926.*The Social and Economic History of the Roman Empire*. OUP: Oxford.

Rouillard, P. 1991. *Les grécs et la péninsule ibérique du viiie au ive siècle avant Jésus-Christ*. De Boccard: Paris.

Ruiz de Arbulo, J. 1998, Tarraco. Escenario del poder, administración y justicia en una capital provincial romana (s. II aC – II dC). *Empúries* 51: 31–61.

Ruiz Rodríguez, A. 1987. Ciudad y territorio en el problamiento ibérico del Alto Guadalquivir. In AAVV *Asentamientos Ibéricos ante la romanización*. Ministerio de Cultura: Madrid, pp. 9–21.

Ruiz Rodríguez, A. 1996. Desarrollo y consolidación de la ideología aristocrática entre los iberos del sur. In R. Olmos Romera, and J. A. Santos Velasco (eds.) *Iconografía ibérica. Iconografía italíca. Propuestas de interpretación y lectura. Coloquio Internacional*. Universidad Autònoma de Madrid: Madrid, pp. 61–71.

Ruiz Rodríguez, A. and Molinos Molinos, M. 1992. *Los Iberos. Análisis arqueológico de un proceso histórico*. Crítica: Barcelona.

Ruiz de Arbulo, J. 1992. Tarraco, Carthago Nova y el problema de la capitalidad en la Hispania Citeripor republicana. In X. Dupré I Raventós (ed.) *Miscel.lània Arqueològica a Josep M. Recasens*. El Mèdol: Tarragona, pp. 115–30.

Ruiz Zapatero, G. 1996. Migration revisted. Urnfields in Iberia. In Díaz Andreu and Keay 1996, pp. 158–74.

Ruiz Zapatero, G. and Alvarez-Sanchis, J. 1995. Las Cogotas: Oppida and the Roots of Urbanism in the Spanish Meseta. In Cunliffe and Keay 1995, pp. 209–35.

Sacristán de Lama, J. D., San Miguel Maté, L. C., Barrio Martín, J. and Celis Sánchez, J. 1995. El poblamiento de época celtibérica en la cuenca media del Duero. In F. Burillo (ed.) *Poblamiento Celtibérico. III Simposio sobre los Celtíberos*. Institución Fernando el Católico: Zaragoza, pp. 337–67.

Salinas de Frías, M. 1986. *Conquista y romanización de Celtiberia*. Museo Numantino: Soria.

Santos Velasco, J. A. 1994. *Cambios sociales y culturales en época ibérica: el caso del sureste*, Colección CRAN Estudios: Madrid.

Santos Yanguas, J. 1985. *Comunidades indígenas y administración romana en el noroeste hispánico.* Bilbao.

Santos Yanguas, N. 1994. *La romanización de Asturias.* Ediciones ISTMO: Madrid.

Sillières, P. 1991. *Les voies de communication de l'Hispanie meridionale.* De Boccard: Paris.

Sillières, P. 1995. *Baelo Claudia. Une cité romaine de Bétique.* Casa de Velázquez: Madrid.

Stylow, A. 1990. Apuntes sobre el urbanismo de la Corduba romano. In Trillmich and Zanker, pp. 259–82.

Stylow, A. 1993. De Corduba a Colonia Patricia. La fundación de la Corduba romana. In León 1993, pp. 77–85.

Stylow, A. *et al.* 1998. *Corpus Inscriptionum Latinarum. Volumen Secundum. Inscriptiones Hispaniae Latinae Editio Altera. Pars V. Conventus Astigitanus (CIL II²/5).* De Gruyter: Berlin.

Syme, Sir R. 1983. Rome and the Nations, in R. Syme (ed.) *Roman Papers IV.* OUP: Oxford, pp. 62–93.

TED'A 1989, El foro provincial de Tarraco, un complejo arquitectónico de época flavia. *Archivo Español de Arqueología 62:* 141–91.

Terrenato, N. 1998. *Tam Firmum Municipium:* The Romanization of Volaterrae and its Cultural Implications. *Journal of Roman Studies* 88: 94–114.

TIR J-29= Alarcão, J. de, Álvarez Martínez, J. M., Cepas Palanca, A. and Corzo Sánchez, R. 1995. *Unión Academica Internacional. Tabula Imperii Romani. Hoja J-29: Lisboa. Emerita – Svallabis – Pax Iulia – Gades.* Ministerio de Cultura: Madrid.

TIR K-30= Fatás Cabeza, G., Caballero Zoreda, L., García Moreno, L. and Cepas Palanca, A. 1993. *Unión Academica Internacional. Tabula Imperii Romani. Hoja K-30: Madrid. Caesaraugusta – Clunia.* Ministerio de Cultura: Madrid.

TIR K-29= Balil Illana, A., Pereira Menaut, G. and Sánchez Palencia, J. 1991. *Unión Academica Internacional. Tabula Imperii Romani. Hoja K-29: Porto. Conimbriga – Bracara – Lucus – Asturica.* Madrid: Ministerio de Cultura: Madrid.

TIR KJ-31= Guitart Durán, J., Fatás, G. and Cepas, A. 1997. *Unión Academica Internacional. Tabula Imperii Romani. Hoja K/J-31: Pyrénées orientales-Baleares Tarraco-Baliares.* Ministerio de Cultura: Madrid.

Tranoy, A. 1981. *La Galice Romaine.* De Boccard: Paris.

Trillmich, W. and Zanker, P. (eds.) 1990. *Stadtbild und ideologie. Die monumentalisierung hispanischer Städte zwischen Republik und Kaiserzeit.* Bayerische Akademie der Wissenschaften: München.

Trillmich, W. 1996. Los tres foros de Augusta Emerita y el caso de Corduba. In León 1996, pp. 175–93.

Vaquerizo, D. 1990. *El Yacimiento ibérico del Cerro de la Cruz.* Córdoba: Diputación Provincial de Cultura.

Ventura, A. 1996. El origen de la Córdoba romana a travès del estudio de las cerámicas de barniz negro. In León 1996, pp. 49–62.

Ventura, A., Bermúdez, J. M., León, P., López, I., Márquez, C. and Ventura, J. 1996. Análisis arqueológico de la Córdoba romana: Resultados e hipótesis de la investigación. In León 1996, pp. 87–118.

Ventura, A., León, P. and Márquez, C. 1998. Roman Cordoba in the light of recent archaeological research. In Keay 1998, pp. 87–107.

Vicente, J. D., Punter, Ma. P., Escriche, C. and Herce, A. I. 1986. *La ciudad celtibérica de "la Caridad" (Caminreal, Teruel).* Teruel.

Vicente, J., Punter, Ma, P., Escriche, J. and Herce, A. I. 1991. La Caridad (Caminreal, Teruel). In M. Beltran (ed.) *La casa hispanorromana.* Zaragoza: Institución Fernando el Católico, pp. 81–129.

Webster, J. 1996. Roman Imperialism and the 'post imperial age'. In J. Webster, and H. Cooper (eds.) *Roman Imperialism. Post-Colonial Perspectives*. University of Leicester Press: Leicester, pp. 1–17.

Whittaker, C. R. 1995. Intergation of the Early Roman West: The Example of Africa. In Metzler *et al.*, pp. 19–32.

Wilson, R. 1990. *Sicily under the Roman Empire. The archaeology of a Roman province, 36BC–AD 535*. Aris Phillips: Warminster.

Woolf, G. 1995. The Formation of Roman Provincial Cultures. In Metzler *et al.*, pp. 9–18.

Woolf, G. 1999. *Becoming Roman. The Origins of Provincial Civilization in Gaul*. CUP: Cambridge.

Woolf, G. 1996. Monumental Writing and the Expansion of Roman Society in the Early Empire. *Journal of Roman Studies* 86: 22–39.

Zanker, P. 1990. *The Power of Images in the Age of Augustus*. University of Michigan Press: Michigan.

Chapter 13

Conquest and Romanization of the upper Guadalquivir valley

Marcelo Castro López and Luis Gutiérrez Soler

Introduction

This study analyzes archaeological evidence for the Romanization of the upper Guadalquivir valley. This key region, which corresponds to the present-day province of Jaén (Andalucía, Spain), straddled the boundaries of the Roman provinces of Baetica and Tarraconensis. Our research attempts to understand developments following the Roman conquest of this region, by focusing upon two neighbouring territories. The results highlight apparent contradictions and divergences in the archaeological record for the region as a whole (Castro 1993; Gutiérrez 1998). In particular, it analyzes the archaeological evidence from the two contrasting *oppida* of Giribaile and Atalayuelas, of which the former represents a break with earlier settlement patterns, while the latter points to their continuation. It is suggested that these differences can be explained by Rome's adaptation of a particular strategy of domination and exploitation to the distinctive conditions of the region, as well as by its development of administrative policies through time (Castro 1989). Previous research has already underlined the distinctive organization of the Sierra Morena mining district, the occupation of new land in the San Juan river valley (Castro *et al.* 1993), in the foundation of colonies under Augustus and in the appearance of the first terra sigillata production centres (Roca 1976; Sotomayor 1977; Fernández García 1998). Such diversity in the techniques of the economic exploitation of the region demands an overall historical framework of interpretation to explain the Romanization of the region between the Roman conquest and the concession of *ius Latii* to communities in the region by the Emperor Vespasian (Pliny, N H 3.30), between AD 70 and 74 (according to Segura 1988; Cortijo 1993: 201).

Geographical Location

The study area is situated in the modern province of Jaén, in upper Andalucía (fig. 13.1). It has a distinctive topography on account of the river Guadalquivir which rises in the Sierra de Cazorla in the east of the province. This has created the Great Central, or Baetic, Depression which widens out as the river makes its way westwards. In the upper reaches of the river, the landscape of the valley is determined by the confluence of two very different morphogenetic units. To the north, lies the Sierra Morena, which belongs to the underlying ancient massif of the Iberian Peninsula, while to lay the newer relief of the Subbética range. Both of these mountain ranges formed a depression, or central

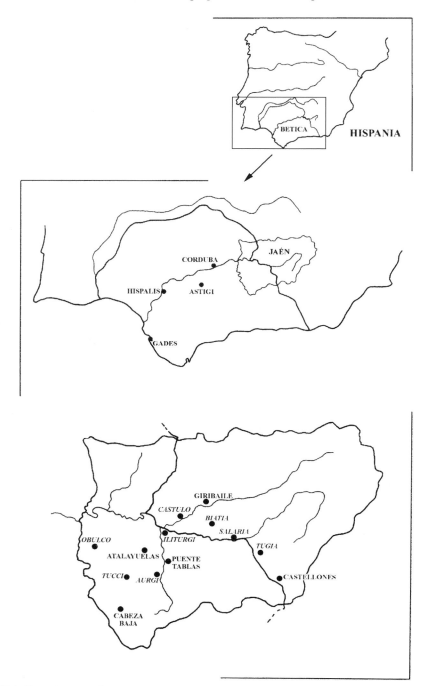

Figure 13.1: Location map showing the position of Baetica in Hispania (upper), the position of the modern province of Jaén in Baetica (middle), and the archaeological sites mentioned in the text (lower)

basin, within which lay much of the agricultural resources of the upper Guadalquivir valley (fig. 13.2).

In the centre of this basin stands "La Loma de Úbeda" (the Hillock of Úbeda), which separates the course of the Guadalquivir from one of its main tributaries, the Guadalimar. One of the survey projects which forms the subject of this paper, that focusing upon the *oppidum* of Giribaile and the middle valley of the river Guadalimar (Royo *et al.* 1995; Gutiérrez *et al.* 1995), lay in this region. Between the Guadalquivir and the southern mountain rages (Subbética range) in the western area of the upper valley, lay a flat area of cultivable land, known as the Campiña de Jaén. This was the site of the second survey project, which focused upon the Roman landscape around the settlement of Atalayuelas.

Research into the Roman period
Archaeological research in Jaén has concentrated upon the study of Iberian settlement patterns, particularly those centred in the campiña de Jaén. These have suggested that a cereal economy was based on the existence of a network of *oppida* (Ruiz and Molinos

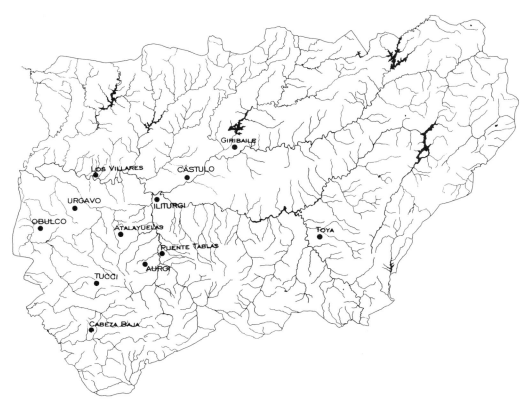

Figure 13.2: Location map showing the location of archaeological sites mentioned in the text in the context of the hydrological scheme of the Guadalquivir in the province of Jaén

1993), which articulated the control of political and economic territories in the region. There is little doubt that the best-known and most productive contribution in this field has been the systematic excavation of the *oppidum* of Plaza de Armas de Puente Tablas (Ruiz and Molinos 1987). With this model as a point of reference, an alternative pattern of settlement has been proposed for the easternmost area of Jaén province. This was centred upon an analysis of the Guadalquivir basin, and revealed alignments of *oppida* following the direction of the rivers.

Analyses of the landscape are our principal source of information about the process of Romanization in the upper Guadalquivir valley. For some scholars, this represented a continuity of the iberian pattern until at least the Republican period, to the point that the period between the end of the Second Punic War and the reign of Augustus has been labelled as the "late Iberian horizon" (Bendala 1981; Ruiz Rodríguez *et al.* 1985). Aside from landscape studies, however, there are other important sources of archaeological data which can contribute to this debate. In the last few years, there has been a great increase in urban archaeology in the city of Jaén, the site of ancient Aurgi. This has uncovered much evidence for the presence of peasant rural sites involved in irrigated agriculture (Hornos *et al.* 1998) during the early empire. This can be paralleled by the recent discovery of similar settlements on the industrial estate of Martos, the ancient Colonia Augusta Gemella Tucci (Serrano *et al.* 1997) and elsewhere in the upper Guadalquivir region. In addition, there have also been important new results from excavations at ancient Cástulo (Linares) and Obulco (Porcuna).

Romanization and Urban Development
Traditional studies have reduced the study of towns to a simple architectural entity emerging from native communities in response to stimuli of Roman civilization (Fernández Castro 1982; Arteaga and Blech 1987). Consequently, it has been assumed that this culture was little more than a facade and that it was both hierarchical and the result of cultural impulses emanating from Rome alone. These assumptions have underpinned a persistent view of the Roman period in Iberia which is still maintained in some quarters. This sees the need to isolate agents of Romanization and recognizes differing degrees of maturity, in an almost biological explanation of cultural change.

The line of argument that Romanization was an undeniable and inevitable evolutionary process is still sustained by many scholars, and only a few suggest that it may have been a contradictory or unequal process (see Keay, this volume, for Hispania in general). This was supported by the established historical picture. Traditional historiography (Cortadella 1988) has established an impenetrable net of arguments and facts. More recently, however, the position has changed somewhat, with the admission that certain issues, such as the motivation of Roman expansion or seeing Romanization as simply a cultural phenomenon, being dropped (González 1981). Consequently, the archaeological evidence has been interpreted to suggest that native communities underwent the same kind of linear evolution, with no room for any alternative hypotheses. This is supported by the continued appearance of some distinctive elements of the material culture of the pre-Roman communities in contexts dating to the Roman period. Other important evidence, however, is omitted since it is considered to be residual and, therefore, best considered in the pre-Roman context.

When materialist and other approaches have approached Romanization from the social and economic perspective, there has been a genuine attempt to provide alternative explanations. However, the perspective adopted has been one which sees the Iberian Peninsula as a socially backward periphery (Barbero and Vigil 1974), and in which the south is understood to have undergone a rapid process of Romanization. This view is furthered by assumptions that have been made about the awareness that local communities may have had about city-based organization prior to the arrival of Rome in the region (Cortijo 1993; León and Rodríguez Oliva 1993). In any event, the traditional view that Romanization was the consequence of Roman military and political activity still dominates. As a result, the cultural aspect of the Romanization of indigenous communities has been reduced to such superficial aspects as the Latin language, the recruitment of natives into the Roman army, the adoption of certain classes of Roman style pottery (Roca 1976) or the adoption of well-defined architectural types (Arteaga and Blech 1987)

It has been stated that the introduction of the Roman town was inextricably linked with the imposition of a way of production. In effect, from the traditional standpoint which has emphasized the inter-dependence of the economy and political institutions of the city, this means that the political-institutional determines, and is part of, social and economic transformation (González 1981: 96). Consequently, once the constitution and new political framework of a city is known, then we are in a position to understand how the means of production were transformed. Our perspective is to look at this from the other way round. Namely, that one can only be sure that a new political order has been established if the means of production have been transformed.

In fact, Romanization cannot be understood without reference to the imposition of the social and economic organization as represented by the Roman town. Yet, the Roman Republic was not interested in the indiscriminate promotion of urban institutions (Gros 1988), nor had the development of their own native communities necessarily resulted in the constitution of Roman towns (Ruiz 1987). The introduction of the Roman town would thus have been the result of contradictory interaction among different interest groups. On the one hand, there were those involved in the political and social strategies who would have retained local power after the Roman conquest, while on the other there were those who came directly from Rome and were able to play a leading role in provincial politics.

In contrast to the more traditional and generalist approach to Romanization, ours attempts to recognize the historical nature of the process. Consequently, if the town is understood to be an immediate consequence of the Roman conquest, it is not surprising that it has been often been seen as a catalyst in the political, social and economic transformation of native peoples, or Romanization. In this scenario, the town almost behaved as an independent entity, hastening the crisis of native social relationships brought about through the extension of Roman concepts property and possession (González 1981). In time, this would lead inexorably to the establishment of the slave mode of production in the agricultural economy which, in turn developed within a framework of growing crop specialization and an increase in regional market exchange (Funari 1986).

If Roman towns had not developed within the context of the social and political transformation of the native communities, they would have been little more than an empty archaeological setting (Gros 1988). The key to understanding their role does not lie in any single morphological or juridical definition, but rather in analysing their spatial organization and the way in which it reproduced the new Roman urban society. The form that this took cannot be reduced simply to their orthogonal layout or the sanctity imposed by their walled enclosures – since these have both been attested on indigenous sites long before the Roman conquest (Ruiz and Molinos 1987; Castro *et al.* 1989; Cunliffe and Fernández 1990). The most obvious contrast between Roman towns and the *oppida* which preceded them, lies in the way in which former projected itself upon its surrounding territory. The physical presence of the town cannot be divorced from its role in structuring the administrative and economic management of the surrounding population or, indeed, their agricultural exploitation.

Finally, it must be emphasized that the immediate cause of this new agrarian way of production is to be explained by a change in the way that the Roman State administered its conquered territories. They came to be governed through municipalities, which were able to regulate a steady source of income from agrarian production and also to bring about an increase in profits. This transformation came about under the Flavians with the concession of *ius Latii* to settled communities in the province and represent a significant change in the politics of Roman political administration. However, it also raises important questions at the local level of our research. What implications did it have for the landscapes in Jaén province and how far did it represent a break from the pre-Roman situation?

Conquest and Romanization
If we restrict the focus of the Romanization debate to the establishment of Roman towns and their territories, it should be stated that it was initially strictly limited to the colonial settlements of the early Imperial period, like the Colonia Salaria (Úbeda) and the Colonia Augusta Gemella Tucci, and only became generalized with the municipalization of the Flavian period. However, some changes clearly did begin to take place amongst the native communities of the Guadalquivir valley prior to the early imperial period and even though they do not fall within the concept of Romanization as we have defined it here, should be explained.

For example, the territory of the *oppidum* of Giribaile provides an example of the traumatic consequences that the Roman conquest had for some native communities (Gutiérrez 1998). By contrast, that of the *oppidum* of Atalayuelas illustrates the way in which the military and political organization of the region under the Republic ensured the fossilization of the pre-existing territorial order (Castro and Choclán 1988; Ruiz *et al.* 1992). Between these two extremes are a range of other post-conquest situations elsewhere in the upper Guadalquivir valley. Thus, some Iberian *oppida*, such as the Plaza de Armas de Puente Tablas (Ruiz and Molinos 1987) were simply abandoned after the conquest, whereas others, such as the Cabeza Baja de Encina Hermosa in Castillo de Locubín (Castro *et al.* 1993), were completely rebuilt. These contrasting responses to the Roman conquest, and indeed others at the key native centres of Castulo and Obulco, should perhaps warn us against searching for a common Roman policy against native communities in the region, in the aftermath of the Second Punic War. The same is true for the subsequent early imperial period. The politics of the colonial foundations of Salaria and Augusta Gemella Tucci in the present-day province of Jaén, or the establishment of the first production centres of *terra sigillata hispanica*, such as at Los Villares de Andújar (Roca 1976), in the Tiberian and Claudian periods shows that Romanization can be manifested in many different ways. Moreover, analysis of the recent archaeological evidence for the Roman conquest and subsequent Romanization makes it clear that there were a variety of different 'responses' and that a single cause of explanation is not sufficient.

The Roman Conquest

The Roman conquest of the Iberian Peninsula can be understood as an indirect consequence of conflicts between Rome and Carthage that had begun towards the middle of the third century BC. While military activity was clearly key to Rome's ultimate success, it should be remembered that diplomatic activity was also important (Roldán 1989). In other words, both the Carthaginians and the Romans searched for an understanding with local communities. Consequently, warfare seemed to occur in the context of a fragile network of alliances, the continuity of which was dependant upon the success or failure of the Romans or Carthaginians. After the disembarcation of Cnaeus Cornelius Scipio at Empúries in 218 BC, the Romans consolidated their positions to the north of the river Ebro before reaching the upper Guadalquivir valley at around 215 BC. In this same year, the Romans ratified a pact with Iliturgi (Cerro Máquiz, near Mengíbar) and shortly afterwards enlisted the support of Cástulo and were able to win battles at Biguerra and Auringis. This first stage in the Roman occupation of the region ended with the disaster of the year 211 BC, when the region was again seized by the Carthaginian army and the Romans withdrew to the north of the river Ebro.

The final stages of Rome's conflict with Carthage in Iberia began with the arrival of Scipio Africanus. In 209 BC he re-established Roman control over the upper Guadalquivir valley, after defeating Hasdrubal at the battle of Baecula (Livy 28.13). The Romans subsequently sacked Orongis (possibly a mistranslation of Auringis) and then directed their attention to the conquest of the middle and lower Guadalquivir valley. However, Roman domination of the upper valley was not completed until 206 BC. It was in this year that Scipio Africanus destroyed Iliturgi and Roman diplomacy brought about the surrender of the Punic garrison at Cástulo after signing a pact with a representative of the town's aristocracy (Cerdubeles; Livy 28.19). This, therefore, was the way that Roman control of the upper Guadalquivir was achieved during the last years of the third century BC, even though continued military operations and diplomacy were needed to sustain it for the greater part of the following century. In the meantime, however, the systematic exploitation of the conquered native communities had begun.

Friends and Allies

The payment of tribute to the Roman State and their agents by provincials, necessarily required the co-operation of the local aristocracy, who gained the gratitude of Rome as a result. This may sometimes have been made explicit in the granting Roman citizenship to certain individuals. This meant that pre-existing systems of production and taxation were essentially compatible with the mechanisms of the Roman administrative system and, therefore, must have been largely retained. In this way, the development of the native aristocracy under Roman domination was linked to their role in being subordinate to the broader interests of Rome (Ruiz *et al.* 1992). In economic terms, this would have involved managing key stockpiles in the region. In political terms, it meant that key features of native society at the end of the third century BC would have become fossilized, with crucial social relationships being underpinned by a combination of taxation and military control.

The spoils of war were the main economic "fruits" of the military occuption of the region, and may well have accounted for an important part of Roman activity during the Second Punic War and the subsequent years of military control in the region. Moreover, this kind of intervention was to have a small influence throughout the second century BC, while the social and political conditions that would sustain a more regular and systematic exploitation were being established. Key members of the regional native aristocracy, the *regulus* and *princeps*, would have acted as interlocutors between Rome and the indigenous communities and would have to have been created *ex novo* (Ruiz *et al.* 1992). This arrangement would have ensured the continued pre-eminence of the *oppida* in the region during the Roman period, in terms of its role as a fortified centre for the residence of elites and the surrounding population engaged in a range of non-agricultural activities.

The colonization of the upper Guadalquivir valley during the Republican period can be viewed from the perspective of a double strategy of Roman exploitation. The abandonment or destruction of some *oppida* would establish the scope of the military exploitation of the region, whereas the continuation of others suggests that some kind of regular taxation was introduced immediately after the conquest. It seems likely that the latter would have involved the active participation of the native aristocracy, which implies that they were to some degree integrated into the new order established by the conquerors. The imposition of regular taxation had repercussions on certain settlements only, such as Giribaile, in whose territory a dispersed model of colonization was developed. Elsewhere, on the other hand, local communities occupied stretches of land which hitherto had been neglected; the San Juan river valley is one example. Furthermore, other areas which had been affected by military action at an early stage of the conquest were also reorganized. While these developments clearly represent change, it is difficult to support the idea that these territories were immediately Romanized with the development of a Roman civic system, since native elites remained at their head of their social hierarchies with Roman approval (Ruiz 1989).

The oppidum *and the territory of Giribaile*

Location and Background

Systematic surface survey in the region of the *oppidum* of Giribaile in the middle Guadalimar valley (Gutiérrez *et al.* 1995; Royo *et al.* 1995), allows us to develop a model of Romanization for the initial years of the Roman occupation in the innermost lands of the upper Guadalquivir. The survey defined a succession of archaeological horizons in the middle course of the Guadalimar dating to between the first half of the fourth century BC (the foundation date of Giribaile), and the first century AD (the first distribution of land to Roman citizens). This long timescale from the Iberian to the early imperial periods was important in providing the necessary chronological perspective in understanding the development of settlement patterns in the region.

Republican Occupation

The survey has revealed a dispersed settlement pattern consisting of approximately one hundred new sites located on flat ground in the Guadalimar valley (fig. 13.3). Many were located on the first river terrace, and yielded materials dateable to the second century BC. The detailed analysis of the sites by means of transects suggested revealed a fairly standardized ceramic assemblage, which included amphorae. Distribution of the sites, however, suggests that only the best quality agricultural lands were occupied and that, prior to the imposition of a Roman centuriated landscape, this was a largely agrarian mode of exploitation. Only a few sites were located to near rich silver seams or seem to have taken advantage of them to complement their agricultural economies.

It seems that this new pattern of exploitation, which probably began immediately after the conclusion of the Second Punic War, can be understood as a response to the introduction of Roman power at Cástulo, a short distance to the north. The appearance of rural settlements around Giribaile is perhaps to be explained by the need of the community to pay taxes to Rome. Achieving this, however, could only be managed by

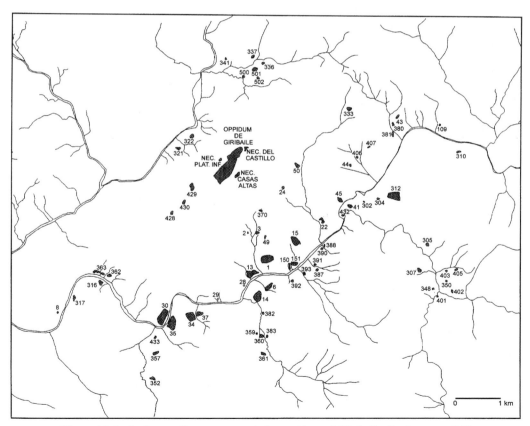

Figure 13.3: Settlement Patterns around the oppidum of Giribaile (2nd century BC)

breaking with more traditional means of exploitation. A proportion of the population would have left the security of the *oppida*'s fortifications and been settled directly on the land so that it could be worked more intensively and generate the necessary surplus. In this way, the community was effectively paying tribute in return for being able to continue being ruled by its own elite. In some senses, therefore, the advent of the Roman period represented a rupture with the preceding period. At the same time, however, there were important elements of continuity. For example, Rome was clearly respecting pre-existing social links between *oppida*, which had been articulated through the practice known as *fides iberica* (Rodríguez 1948). Moreover, throughout the period, traditional burial places are maintained and there is no evidence for cemeteries in the valley. However, it should be noted that transformations in the landscape similar to those taking place at Giribaile were comparatively rare elsewhere in the upper Guadalquivir valley, and have only been attested at sites like Toya in the easternmost part of Jaén province (Ruiz and Molinos 1996).

Territorial Reorganization during the Sertorian Period
This model of settlement had a relatively brief duration. Recent work has revealed that many sites were abandoned in the first half of the first century BC, while Giribaile itself was violently destroyed and later replaced by La Monaria, a fortified lowland settlement (Royo *et al.* 1997). In addition, two towers were constructed as part of a strategy to control the main route of communication running through the Guadalimar valley. At the same time, metalworking refuse at some sites attests to the continued exploitation of some of the richer metal seams in the region. This is part of a large-scale reorganization of settlement in the region, which involved the re-commencement of mining in the Sierra Morena, on the north side of the Guadalquivir valley, which began towards the end of the second century BC (Domergue 1987). Sites like El Centenillo, Los Escoriales, Palazuelos and Salas de Galiarda were major fortified mining settlements involved in this activity.

However, this new phase of economic exploitation in the valley enjoyed an even briefer period of life than its predecessor. It seems to have come to a violent end, with traces of burning being found at the great majority of settlements, such as Castellones de Céal (Chapa *et al.* 1998). The discovery of coin hoards in the region also points to general instability in the region, which may perhaps be explained as the result of factional struggles during the Civil War of the middle first century BC (García 1991).

The Flavian Period
The archaeological record in the region is now silent until the middle of the first century AD. At some time around this date, however, there is evidence that the territory previously belonging to Giribaile was centuriated. Clearly this belonged to a new settlement focus, and it seems likely that this would have been the Flavian municipality of Baesucci, possibly to be identified with present day Vilches (González and Mangas 1991). The associated patterning of rural settlement was very clearly different from that of the preceding periods. It suggests that the land was subdivided into regular lots, each of which corresponded to divisions of *centuria*, which would then have been distributed to settlers at Baesucci as private property.

The oppidum *and the territory of Atalayuelas*

Historical Antecedents and Territorial Definition

Research in this part of Jaén province has attempted to reconstruct the agricultural landscape of a small town between the first and second centuries AD. It lies to the south-west of Giribaile and the Guadalimar valley, in what was the easternmost limit of the province of Baetica. Its focus is the *oppidum* of Atalayuelas (Fuerte del Rey, Jaén), a settlement which was occupied between the Copper Age and the middle of the second century AD.

During the early Imperial period, this was a relatively small site which covered between five and seven hectares. The absence of monumental architecture and epigraphic evidence for possible municipal status initially suggested that it may have been a village (*vicus*) that might have been dependant upon the Flavian municipality of Aurgi (Jaén), a short distance to the south. Recent archaeological research, however, suggests that this view should be revised – or at least qualified. The regularity of the settlement pattern, as well as the discovery of commemorative inscriptions during the 1987 excavations at Atalayuelas (Castro *et al.* 1989), suggests that the settlement was in fact a town and possibly yet another Flavian municipality. At present, however, no further corroborative epigraphic evidence has come to light in recently published compilations (González and Mangas 1991), while the inscription from the 1987 excavation is at most, little more than suggestive.

The *oppidum* of Atalayuelas was probably established in around the seventh or sixth century BC. The boundaries of its territory can be traced with some confidence and seem to have followed the line of secondary water courses, usually streams of the third and fourth order, which only coincided with the interfluvial line in areas close to the river headwaters. During the late Iberian period and prior to the Roman conquest in the late third century BC, the *oppidum* raised a number of towers (*turres*) to watch over this territory. These were rectangular in plan and constructed from large blocks of stone. They were established at regular distances of between one and two km to form a fairly impenetrable system of control, similar to that at nearby *oppida*. Early research has suggested that amongst other purposes, these towers served to defend the territory (Fortier and Bernier 1970; Ruíz Rodríguez *et al.* 1983; Ruíz Rodríguez *et al.* 1985; Cortijo 1985), even though it is not clear how this defence would have been articulated. However they may have functioned, it is clear that nearly all these towers continued to be used into the Roman period, providing a fairly clear impression of the limits of the territory of the Roman town of Atalyuelas.

Survey work has shown that before the Roman conquest of the campiña de Jaén, the landscape in which Atalayuelas lies, Iberian *oppida* were distributed fairly regularly. The first Roman intervention in the region, which was intended to strengthen military control of the region and establish the regular taxation of conquered communities, led to the abandonment of some *oppida*. This has been verified by excavations at the Plaza de Armas de Puente Tablas (Ruiz and Molinos 1987) and is suggested by surface survey at other sites, such as the Cerro Villargordo and Torrejón (Ruíz *et al.* 1992). However, most settlements, such as Atalayuelas, continued to be occupied. Later, after the conclusion of the Cantabrian Wars in the later first century BC, a contingent of legionary veterans was settled on the site of an Iberian *oppidum* to found the Colonia Augusta Gemella Tucci (Serrano 1987). This coincided with the appearance of rural settlements, that was almost unique in the region. It was a dramatic innovation because hitherto there were no small permanent settlements in the upper Guadalquivir valley. Even though little is known about farming in the Iberian period, it seems that exploitation of the land was managed directly from the *oppida*, and may have been organized on a collective basis.

Indeed, it is not until the late first century AD that one sees a similar process happening elsewhere in the region and seems to have coincided with the promotion of native communities to municipal status. This coincided with important changes in the character of the *oppida* themselves. There is evidence for the advent of true urban-style planning and the private ownership if land, which gave rise to a distinctive agrarian landscape.

The Agrarian Landscape in the Flavian Period
Analysis of the survey evidence suggested that archaeological sites tended to concentrate in the southern area of the territory of Atalayuelas. The reason for this was not immediately apparent. However, given that the settlement might have been a Flavian municipality, it seemed possible that it reflects the way in which the land around it may have been assigned and distributed. In an attempt to verify this hypothesis, the distribution of rural sites were analyzed to establish whether or not they suggested possible Roman land divisions, rather than adducing the rural settlements to confirm the existence of pre-determined land-divisions. As it happens, analyses of aerial photographs and 1:10,000 maps did suggest the existence of reticulate divisions of the landscapes. By themselves alone they do not prove that the landscape was regularly subdivided. However, when taken in conjunction with the survey, they do suggest the existence of a Roman system of land-division.

Consequently, there does seem to have been some kind land division in the territory of Atalayuelas in the late first century AD. A synthesis of the consecutive steps which led to the configuration of this particular model of land-division was prepared (fig. 13.4). This is an attempt to rationalize the decisions that led to the division of the land, rather than a dissection of the sequence followed in their gestation. The divided lands form a compact block whose centre is situated at the highest point of the territory, and near the Roman town. From this point, the main axes of the land-division would have been made to coincide with the longer axes of the territory, which deviate approximately 15.3° in relation to the geographical north-south axis. The smallest unit of the division has been the square *centuria* of 706 m x 706m. A group of four *centuriae*, named *saltus* by the Roman surveyors (Ariño 1990), is formed by three assigned *centuriae* and one *centuria* free of occupation. The latter may have been exploited from the nearby assigned plots, possibly as common grazing land belonging to the local *saltus*. The best justification for the distribution of the settlements was the second division of the land inside the *centuria* boundaries, which should have consisted of its division into three lots or plots of the same size. The first of these was parallel to the *decumanus maximus* and occupied the northern third of the *centuria*, while the second and third plots were in the two remaining thirds and their main boundaries would have been transverse to the first. The assigned plot had a surface area of 16.6 hectares, while the overall group of arable lands and grazings that were created by this division covered an area of 3143 hectares, which is approximately half the territory of Atalayuelas.

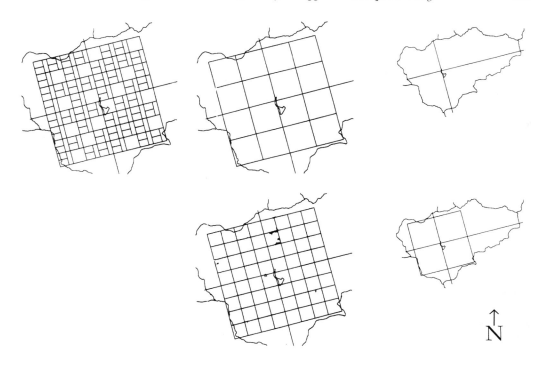

Figure 13.4: Centuriation in the territory of Atalayuelas

The remaining half of the territory of the town was organized in a different way. The land where the Iberian *turres* were sited, formed an almost continuous belt around the periphery of the territory, and was only interrupted at points where centuriated land lay adjacent to the borders of neighbouring territory. This unassigned land was used to support longer-term agricultural strategies. On the other hand, unassigned land lying away from the edges of the territory of Atalayuelas, particularly to the north, remained unoccupied. This was presumably given over to forests, which would have been developed on a collective basis.

One exception to this situation in the north consists of an important rural settlement which is located close to where the unoccupied land abutted assigned lands. Indeed, it is the only example from the territory of first and second century Atalayuelas of a settlement which may be identified as a Roman villa; all other rural sites are perhaps better identified as farms. This site, called Buenaharina, is located beneath the modern village of Fuerte del Rey and covers a slightly larger area than most Flavian sites recorded to date. The site has yielded columns, wallplaster, *tesserae* and other evidence which suggests that it boasted a magnificent residence, while the presence of large millstones and dolia indicates that it was also involved in large-scale agricultural production.

Conclusions

The traditional conception of Romanization in southern Hispania has been based on the idea of an early appearance of Roman towns. However, this does not help explain the pattern and development of rural settlement in the upper Guadalquivir during the Republican and early Imperial periods. Indeed, this part of Iberia is distinctive in that the territorial changes contingent upon the emergence of Roman towns do not appear until comparatively late. They either coincide with the first Augustan colonies or with the extension of municipal status to native communities under the Flavians. When the Roman town eventually appears as an extended and generalized phenomenon of territorial organization, it would appear to have been based on an agrarian economy supported by a predominance of the small and medium peasant property-owners. This conclusion challenges the traditional conception of Baetica as a province where specialized agriculture and the slave mode of production enjoyed wide currency.

The late establishment of Roman towns in the upper Guadalquivir does not imply that the Roman conquest had no immediate consequences for native communities. Indeed, at least two alternative scenarios can be outlined: the appearance of new settlement patterns around *oppida* like Giribaile, and the continuity of the Iberian settlement pattern, as in the case of Atalayuelas. These different cases can be understood as symptomatic of the different responses to the presence of Rome that are conventionally labelled as "Romanization". Alternatively, they can be interpreted as Rome's adaptation of strategies of control and domination to the distinctive social and political conditions of each native community. This hypothesis seems to be the most reasonable approach to understanding the divergences found in the archaeological evidence, and is the main interpretative framework for our current research into the Romanization of the upper Guadalquivir.

References

Ariño, E. 1990. *Catastros Romanos en el Convento Jurídico Caesaraugustano. La Región Aragonesa.* Departament de Ciencias de la Antigüedad-Universidad de Zaragoza: Zaragoza.

Arteaga, O. and Blech, M., 1987. La romanización en las zonas de Porcuna y Mengibar (Jaén). In *AAVV Coloquio Los Asentamientos Ibéricos ante la Romanización.* Ministerio de Cultura-Casa de Velazquez: Madrid, pp. 89–101.

Barbero, A. and Vigil, M. 1974. *Sobre los Orígenes Sociales de la Reconquista.* Ariel: Barcelona.

Bendala, M. 1981. La etapa final de la cultura ibero-turdetana y el impacto romanizador. In *La Baja Época de la Cultura Ibérica*, Asociación Española de Amigos de la Arqueología: Madrid, pp. 30–48.

Castro, M. 1989. De César a Teodosio (49 a.C.–395 d.C.). In *Jaén*, tomo II. Editorial Andalucía: Granada, pp. 423–441.

Castro, M. 1993. Reconstruyendo un paisaje agrario: La campiña de Jaén en los siglos I-II. In *Actas de las III Jornadas Históricas del Alto Guadalquivir*, i.p.

Castro, M. and Choclán, C., 1988. La campiña del alto Guadalquivir en los siglo I-II d.C.: Asentamientos, estructura agraria y mercado. *Arqueología Espacial* 12: 205–221.

Castro, M., Hornos, F. and Choclán, C., 1993. Cabeza Baja de Encina Hermosa (Castillo de Locubín, Jaén): Una reflexión sobre el desarrollo del territorio ciudadano en la Campiña. In *Actas del I Coloquio de Historia Antigua de Andalucía.* Publicaciones del Monte de Piedad y Caja de Ahorros de Córdoba: Córdoba, pp. 451–467.

Castro, M., López, J., Zafra, N., Crespo, J. and Choclán, C. 1989.'Prospección con sondeo estratigráfico en el yacimiento de Atalayuelas, Fuerte del Rey (Jaén). *Anuario Arqueológico de Andalucía II/1987*. Consejería de Cultura y Medio Ambiente: Sevilla, pp. 207–215.

Chapa, T., Pereira, J., Madrigal, A. and Mayoral, V. 1998. *La Necrópolis Ibérica de Los Castellones de Céal (Hinojares, Jaén)*. Junta de Andalucía-Universidad de Jaén: Jaén.

Cortadella, J. 1988. M. Almagro Basch y la idea de la unidad de España. In *Studia Historica-H.ª Antigua*, vol. VI.

Cortijo, M. L. 1993. *La Administración Territorial de la Betica Romana*. Caja Provincial de Ahorros de Córdoba: Córdoba.

Cunliffe B. W. and Fernández, M. C. 1990. Torreparedones (Castro del Río-Baena, Córdoba). Informe preliminar. Campaña de 1987. Prospección arqueológica con sondeo estratigráfico. *Anuario Arqueológico de Andalucía II/1987*. Consejería de Cultura de la Junta de Andalucía: Sevilla, pp. 193–200.

Domergue, C. 1987. *Catalogue des Mines et des Fonderies Antiques de la Péninsule Ibérique*. Diffusion de Boccard: Madrid.

Fernández Castro, M. C. 1982. *Villas Romanas en España*. Ministerio de Cultura: Madrid.

Fernández García, M. ªI., 1998. *Terra Sigillata Hispánica. Estado Actual de la Investigación*. Universidad de Jaén: Jaén.

Fortea, J. and Bernier, J. 1970. *Recintos y Fortificaciones Ibéricos en la Bética*. Universidad de Salamanca: Salamanca.

Funari, P. P. A. 1986. As estrategias de exploraçao de recursos do Vale do Guadalquivir em época romana. *Revista Brasileira de História*.

García, F. 1991. *Quinto Sertorio. Roma*. Universidad de Granada: Granada.

González, C. 1981. *Imperialismo y Romanización en la Provincia Hispania Ulterior*. Universidad de Granada: Granada.

González, C. and Mangas, J. 1991. *Corpus de Inscripciones Latinas de Andalucía, volumen III: Jaén, tomo I*. Consejería de Cultura de la Junta de Andalucía: Sevilla.

Gros, P., 1988. L'età imperiale. In P. Gros and M. Torelli, *Storia dell'Urbanistica: Il mondo romano*. Laterza: Bari, pp. 165–426.

Gutiérrez, L. M., 1998. *El poblamiento ibérico en el curso medio del río Guadalimar*. Tesis doctoral. Microfichas, Servicio de Publicaciones de la Universidad de Jaén: Jaén.

Gutiérrez, L. M., Royo, M. A., Barba, V. and Bellón, J. P. 1995. Informe sobre la primera campaña de prospección superficial en el Guadalimar Medio-Hinterland de Cástulo. In *Anuario Arqueológico de Andalucía II/1992*. Consejería de Cultura y Medio Ambiente: Sevilla, pp. 249–256.

Hornos, F., Zafra, N. and Castro, M. 1998. La gestión de una zona arqueológica urbana: La experiencia de investigación arqueológica aplicada en Marroquíes Bajos (Jaén). *Boletín del Instituto Andaluz del Patrimonio Histórico* 22: 82–91.

León, P. and Rodríguez, P. 1993. La ciudad hispanorromana en Andalucía. In M. Bendala (ed.) *La ciudad hispanorromana*. Ministerio de Cultura: Madrid, pp. 13–53.

Roca, M. 1976. *Sigillata Hispánica producida en Andújar*. Instituto de Estudios Giennenses: Jaén.

Rodríguez, F. 1948. La fides ibérica. *Emérita* XIV.

Roldán, J. M. 1989. *La España Romana*, Historia 16: Madrid.

Royo, M. A., Gutiérrez, L. M., Bellón, J. P. and Barba, V. 1995. Prospección arqueológica superficial de urgencia en la Presa de Giribaile (Jaén). *Anuario Arqueológico de Andalucía III/1992*. Consejería de Cultura y Medio Ambiente: Sevilla, pp. 408–414.

Royo, M. A., Gutiérrez, L. M., Bellón, J. P. and Barba, V. 1997. Documentación gráfica del yacimiento romano de La Monaria. In *Anuario Arqueológico de Andalucía III/1993*. Consejería de Cultura y Medio Ambiente: Sevilla, pp. 386–390.

Ruiz, A. 1987. Ciudad y territorio en el poblamiento ibérico del Alto Guadalquivir. In *AAW Coloquio Los Asentamientos Ibéricos ante la Romanización*. Ministerio de Cultura-Casa de Velazquez: Madrid, pp. 9–21.

Ruiz, A. 1989. La Protohistoria: El 1.º milenio a.n.e. In *Jaén*, tomo II, Editorial Andalucía: Granada, pp. 401–422.

Ruiz, A., Castro, M. and Choclán, C., 1992. Aurgi-Tucci: La formación de la ciudad romana en la campiña de Jaén. *Dialoghi di Archeologia.* 3.ª Serie, 1–2: 211–229.

Ruiz, A. and Molinos, M. 1987. Excavación arqueológica sistemática en Puente Tablas (Jaén). *Anuario Arqueológico de Andalucía II/1986*. Consejería de Cultura y Medio Ambiente: Sevilla, pp. 401–407.

Ruiz, A. and Molinos, M. 1993. *Los iberos. Análisis arqueológico de un proceso histórico*. Crítica: Barcelona.

Ruiz, A. and Molinos, M. 1996. Desde los cazadores-recolectores a los agricultores. In *Historia de Jaén y su provincia*. Ideal: Granada.

Ruiz, A., Molinos, M., Hornos, F. and Choclán, C. 1985. El poblamiento ibérico en el Alto Guadalquivir. In *Iberos. Actas de las I Jornadas sobre el Mundo Ibérico*. Ayuntamiento de Jaén-Junta de Andalucía: Jaén, pp. 239–256.

Ruiz, A., Molinos, M., López, J., Crespo, J. M., Choclán, C. and Hornos, F. 1983. El horizonte ibérico antiguo del Cerro de la Coronilla (Cazalilla, Jaén). Cortes A y F. *Cuadernos de Prehistoria de la Universidad de Granada* 8: 251–299.

Segura, M. L. 1988. *La ciudad Ibero-romana de Igabrum (Cabra, Córdoba)*. Diputación de Córdoba: Córdoba.

Serrano, J. L., Zafra, J., Sánchez, M. C. and Chica, M. P. 1997. Intervención arqueológica de urgencia en el polideportivo de Martós (Jaén) y terrenos aledaños-1993. *Anuario Arqueológico de Andalucía II/1993*. Consejería de Cultura: Sevilla, pp. 367–374.

Serrano, J. M. 1987. *La Colonia Romana de Tucci*. Asociación Artística Cultural Tucci: Jaén.

Sotomayor, M. 1977. Marcas y estilos en la Sigillata decorada de Andújar, Instituto de Estudios Giennenses, Jaén.

Chapter 14

Leptis Magna. The Romanization of a major African city through burial evidence

Sergio Fontana

Introduction

In a major African city like Leptis Magna, the cultural changes induced by Romanization can be investigated through a variety of archaeological and historical sources. This paper will deal with the evidence concerning the funerary realm, in the context of a comparison with the urban evidence. The archaeological, epigraphic and osteological evidence from the city's cemeteries can become a valuable tool to understand the complexity of the cultural changes and persistencies in action at Leptis in the first centuries of the Empire. The burials illustrate the forms of individual and community self-representation, but at the same time they provide a glimpse of death as a private event, experienced within the family and its traditional structures.

The political Romanization of Leptis, an important centre of Punic culture and language, began with the defeat of Pompey's partisans at Thapsos in 46 BC (Dio 45.9.4–5; Caes. *B. Af.* 79.1–88). At that point, the city, because of the support given to Juba II and Sextus Pompeius, became part of the Roman provincial system and was condemned by Caesar to pay tribute in oil (Caes. *B. Af.* 97.3). In the preceding decades Leptis had maintained its independence, despite becoming part, ever since the Second Punic War, of the periphery of the Numidian kingdom (Pol. 31.21; Di Vita 1982: 516–518). The process of political incorporation by Rome continued with the grant of municipal status by Vespasian (Di Vita Evrard 1984), then of colonial status around 110 AD (Gascou 1972: 75–80). This institutional evolution can be considered complete with the concession of *ius Italicum* (*Dig. L.* 15.8.11) during the reign of Septimius Severus. In the late second century AD, the urbanized area extended over 150 hectares with an estimated population of about 50,000 (Di Vita Evrard 1993: 295–297). At this stage, Leptis was, after Carthage, the largest and most populated city in Africa Proconsularis.

Ever since the Augustan era the interaction between Roman authority and local elites is attested by an early adoption of the imperial cult (Di Vita 1982: 551–553, 558–560) as well as the public munificence on the part of prominent citizens. The latter courted both local approval and the favour of the emperors, in honour of whom monuments were erected. Local elites, who were not yet Roman citizens, adopted Latin elements in their names, imitating Roman nomenclature (Birley 1988: 4; Torelli 1973: 400–403; Benabou 1976: 513–516). This is the case of *Annobal Tapapius Rufus*, who in 8 BC financed the construction of a *macellum* (IPT 21=IRT 319) and, ten years later, the Theatre (IPT

16=IRT 321–322–323). A similar instance is that of *Iddibal Caphada Aemilius*, who in AD 12 dedicated the Chalcidicum (IRT 324) and whose extant togate portrait demonstrates the impact of Roman styles on self-representation.

In the age of Vespasian, with the concession of *ius Latii*, local magistrates acquired Roman citizenship, later granted to all of Leptis under Trajan. The eponymous Punic office of the sufetate is maintained after the city is governed as a *municipium*. However, such pre-Roman institutions disappear completely with the creation of the colony. Already in the Trajanic period, some local families probably reached senatorial status, and Septimius' rise to imperial power in AD 193 represents the climax of the process of assimilation by Rome.

In evaluating Romanization at Leptis we must keep in mind that we cannot speak of a process of acculturation arising from direct contact between diverse ethnic groups. The city never experienced an influx of Italian colonists and A. R. Birley's onomastic analysis shows a marginal presence of immigrants. The Italian component seems to be limited to three family groups: the banker *Titus Herennius* (Cic. II Verr. 5.155); the *Perpernae*, of evident Etruscan origin; the *Fulvii Lepcitani* (Birley 1988: 3–5). In this respect, Leptis is atypical in comparison to other African cities and ultimately to the entire Western Empire. In contemporary perceptions, the autochthonous Berber-Libyan element was perfectly integrated with the Punic one. The ethnic denomination *Libyophoenices* is attested by Strabo to refer to the inhabitants of the Tripolitanian coast (Strab. 17.3.19; Mattingly 1995: 25–29). In Sallust's treatment of the Phoenician foundation of the city, the 'Sidonian' language was modified by fusion with local populations (*Bel. Iug.* 78).

Both Leptis' institutional history and its civic building activity suggest that Romanization was an uninterrupted process sustained by the desire for integration into the wider sphere of the Roman Empire. Public architecture in the city was indeed inspired by Roman models both in terms of styles and of monument typology. While certainly true, this is only part of the story. To examine in depth the processes of cultural change and persistence we must also take into account the funerary evidence, integrating the study of public displays with that of more private behaviours, such as those concerning death.

The tombs

The burial evidence allows an evaluation of cultural changes induced by Romanization from various points of view. We can in this way investigate the forms of interaction with outsiders as well as the image presented by the community of itself and the deceased through inscription and architecture. In addition, the burials may allow us to reconstruct social and familial structures. Finally, funerary practices throw light on ideological and religious conceptions of death.

Our knowledge of the city's cemeteries has been greatly expanded in recent years. For the Punic period, the evidence is still limited to the old excavations of the necropolis under the theatre, which includes several tombs datable between the sixth and the second century BC (De Miro and Fiorentini 1974). In all likelihood, urban expansion under the Empire completely obliterated the Hellenistic burials. Beginning in the first century AD the cemeteries developed within a well-structured hinterland, whose arrangement matched the regular layout of the centre. The Imperial period cemeteries were primarily composed of mausolea, hypogean tombs and surface graveyards with single tombs. The mausolea were clearly the strongest form of self-representation and in some cases they served as markers for the underground structures. There are about 15 of them around Leptis, largely datable to the Early Empire (Romanelli 1925: 162–166; Fontana 1996). This monumental tomb-type had been adopted in Africa since the first half of the second century BC both by Numidian rulers and by the aristocracies of the Tripolitanian *emporia*, as is documented at Sabratha (Di Vita 1976; Coarelli and Thebért 1988; Rakob 1979). The typology of mausolea at Leptis shows Hellenistic architectonic and decorative elements, already present in pre-Roman Africa, combined with Italian traits. The reference to Roman models is evident in the mausoleum at Gasr Duirat, a three-storied structure culminating in a *tholos* similar to the mausoleum of the *Iulii* at Glanum (Romanelli 1925: 165–166; 1970: 273–274). The decoration of this monument, datable to the second century AD, had a cosmological programme with reliefs of the Seasons and the Zodiac. Above its entranceway, the *tabula ansata* inscribed in Latin (IRT 729) was surmounted a representation of the *capsa* (the container of law scrolls). The monument belonged to *C. Marius Boccius Zurgem*, a prominent local figure, who thus emphasized his status as a Roman magistrate. The representation of the *capsa* is a device that Italian municipal elites had used for the same purpose on their funerary monuments, since the first century BC.

The hinterland of Leptis at the time would not have seemed dissimilar to that of many other cities of the Empire. The roads leading into the city were flanked by tombs and inscriptions that, beginning in the second century AD, were almost always in Latin. What is anomalous, however, is the diffusion of hypogean tombs containing multiple burials. Underground burials were a trait peculiar to Punic funerary custom that persisted into the Roman era at Leptis and other Tripolitanian centres. In many other African cities, such as Carthage, underground shaft graves came to be abandoned during the late Hellenistic period, to be replaced by single surface burials. As we shall see, the use of hypogea survives at Leptis at least until the third century AD. This can probably be explained with reference to the continuity of familial and social structures between the Punic and Roman periods.

For the period under consideration, the first to third centuries AD, 42 hypogean tombs are known from an area of 3 kilometres around Leptis, and 24 from the ancient territory of the city. They contain about 700 burials, of which over 500 belong to the first group. Most of the burials are cremations within stone urns. Only occasionally are small amphorae or glass jars employed as containers for the ashes. Cremation is apparently the dominant practice at Leptis between the first and the end of the second centuries AD. The number of interments within the hypogea range from a few to several dozen. Over 130 cremations were found in a tomb excavated in 1976 in the western hinterland of the city. The tombs therefore were used over several generations, for many decades or even more than a century. The period of use of the tombs can be determined on the base of ceramic grave goods and coins.

The limestone urns used in the first century AD are generally boxes with pitched-roof lids secured by lead fasteners. Beginning in the late Flavian era, or at the start of the second century AD another more refined urn type appears: vase-shaped, made of limestone, but also marble and alabaster. Most of the burials continued, however, to employ simple boxes, which beginning in the early second century AD tend to be smaller and to have a sliding lid. About half of the stone urns (circa 200) have an inscription, generally limited to recording the name of the deceased. Both Latin and neo-Punic are used in most of these texts. On the older type of box urns the inscription mostly used neo-Punic letters, while on the vase-shaped urns and the later form of box urns, Latin letter forms are exclusively employed. These texts indicate that the deceased belonged to the highest social strata of Leptis.

The tomb at Gasr Gelda, in the south-east hinterland, belonged to a prominent family, the *Flavii*. They had probably obtained Roman citizenship during the African proconsulate of Vespasian, from whom they got their *gentilicium*, prior to the creation of the *municipium* (Di Vita-Evrard *et al.* 1996: 130–131). Of particular interest is the discovery in this tomb of the remains of folding iron chairs, perhaps indicating that some of the deceased had been magistrates, in line with the depiction of the *capsa* on the mausoleum at Gasr Duirat (Di Vita-Evrard *et al.* 1996: 119–120). Another tomb found in the western periphery near the old hospital of Khoms contained the burial of an individual of senatorial status. His ashes were placed in an alabaster urn inscribed with his initials followed by C(larissimus) V(ir). The hypogeal tombs, however, were not peculiar to the upper classes. Indeed, the large number of these tombs in itself suggests that middle class families also used this type of burial. Even some privileged slaves could afford a hypogeum, such as *Secundius*, accountant (*actor*) of *Q. Servilius Candidus*, a prominent local known from other Flavian and Hadrianic inscriptions. *Secundius* had himself buried in a vase-shaped urn with a Latin inscription, thus imitating in all ways the burial customs of the local elites (Di Vita Evrard 1996). The lowest levels of Leptis' society, the *humiliores*, the clients, the less fortunate slaves, were buried in surface graveyards, without funerary inscriptions. In these humble burials, the ashes were normally placed in reused amphorae. These graveyards are found in the vicinity of the hypogean tombs, suggesting a dependent relationship with the *gentes* buried in them (see the recent excavations in the western hinterland of Leptis; Fontana and Usai 1997).

Figure 14.1: Interior of a hypogeum at the time of its discovery (Wadi er-Rsaf, Leptis Magna: 1997 excavations)

The relationship between the funerary typology and social class is illustrated schematically in fig. 14.5. This hypothetical reconstruction is valid only for the first and second centuries AD. Beginning with the first half of the third century, with the abandonment of the majority of the hypogea, the evolution of elite tombs at Leptis becomes difficult to trace. In all likelihood single surface graves became increasingly common.

Inscriptions and languages

Having reviewed the volume of the burial evidence at Leptis Magna for the period of Romanization, it remains to be asked how becoming Roman affected funerary practices and processes of social and cultural change during the first centuries of the Empire. In particular, funerary inscriptions provide an exceptional record of a community dealing with Romanization. They document the linguistic transition from Punic to Latin, as well as the evolution of personal names from indigenous tradition to the *tria nomina* system. The epigraphic evidence can be profitably integrated with that of the city's public monuments. This shows how the use of Punic or Latin was often dependent upon the intended audience of the texts.

Latin appears in the public inscription of Leptis for the first time in the market inscription dated to 8 BC, whose text is repeated in Punic and Latin (IPT 21=IRT 319). Bilingualism becomes frequent in public epigraphy in the following decades: thus, the dedication of the theatre in 1–2 AD (IPT 16=IRT 321–322–323); in an inscription referring to work carried out in the Old Forum in 53–54 AD (IPT 26=IRT 338) and again in 61–62 AD (IPT 23, 28=IRT 341). The last known example of a bilingual inscription can be dated to the late Flavian era (IPT 27=IRT 318). In the second century, possibly as a result of the creation of the colony, Punic disappears altogether from the city's monuments.

Figure 14.2: Box-shaped limestone urn with neopunic inscription, from the tomb at Gasr Gelda

Concerning funerary inscriptions, a distinction needs to be drawn between texts placed on the exterior of the tomb and those placed within it. Occasionally, in the same monument Latin could be used on the outside, while Punic was used inside. A particularly clear example is the hypogeum tomb near Zliten, 15 km East of Leptis, where Latin is used for the altar that marks the tomb (IRT 852), while a Punic text written in Latin letters is scratched on the plaster of the underground funerary chamber. Both inscriptions name the same individual, *Q. Licinius Piso* (Bartoccini 1927: 233; Levi Della Vida 1963: 83–84; Garbini 1986: 73).

The chronology and diffusion of Latin in funerary contexts is quite different from that in public monuments. In funerary inscriptions visible from the outside, the use of Latin appears only sporadically beginning in the second half of the first century AD. The earliest preserved example is the inscription on a block, possibly from a mausoleum, recording the dedication of *Tapafius Diodorus Nizaz* (IRT 745). The latter was a member of the most important family in Leptis, but not yet a Roman citizen. On ash-urns, on the other hand, Latin begins to be used only in the first decades of the second century AD, and even then, not always consistently. A tomb found in 1994 near Uadi Rsaf contained an urn inscribed with neo-Punic characters, datable to after 128–132 AD on the basis of a Hadrianic coin inside it. The linguistic transition occasionally involves only the alphabet. In some cases, Punic kinship terms are transliterated with Latin characters, such as *byn* for *filius* and *asht* for *uxor*.

Figure 14.3: Vase-shaped urn with a latin inscription from the tomb at the Gasr Gelda

In addition to the aforementioned inscription from Zliten, there is a small group of Punic-Latin funerary texts at Leptis (IRT 826–827–828; Levi Della Vida 1963: 79–85; Garbini 1986). The use of Latin characters for Punic text seems limited, however, in and around Leptis proper, whereas it is much stronger inland and on the desert fringe. In rural areas the Latin alphabet long continued to be used to write Punic. As late as the fifth century AD, in the catacombs of Sirte, the formula *avo sanu* (equivalent to Latin *vixit annis*) recurs frequently (Bartoccini 1928–29: 187–200; IRT 855). The language spoken at home, according to several literary sources, remained predominantly Punic until the late imperial era (August. *Epist.* 66.2; 84.2; 108.14; 209.2; Benabou 1976: 483–487; Harris 1989: 170–180). The use of Punic also must have persisted even among elites, if Septimius Severus' sister had such difficulties speaking Latin (*vix latinae loquens*) that the emperor was embarrassed during her visit to Rome (HA *Severus* 15.7; *Epit. De Caes.* 20.8; Birley 1971: 106). Latin came to be increasingly more identified as the language of power and public self-representation, while Punic remained part of everyday life at Leptis. The funerary sphere proved to be much less receptive to Latin than most other walks of life.

Nomenclature followed an evolutionary path similar to that of language. We have already mentioned the paradigmatic example of two members of Leptis' elite in the Augustan era who Latinized their names. *Annobal Tapapius* added *-ius* to his Libyan family name, as well as the unequivocally Roman cognomen *Rufus*. *Iddibal Caphada*, on the other hand, adopted the *gentilicium Aemilius* as his cognomen. Later on, the municipal status allowed prominent local families to acquire easily Roman citizenship and thus standard Roman nomenclature. After the creation of the colony, this privilege was in theory extended to all free citizens of Leptis.

In contrast, only a few, about a tenth, of the inscriptions on urns from the hypogea show a fully Latinized naming system. With few exceptions, the inscriptions using the male *tria nomina* or the female *duo nomina* are in Latin characters and appear on vase-shaped urns. It is not a coincidence that this is the most expensive type of ash container used at Leptis. Occasionally the urns are made of alabaster and imported from Egypt and they influence the local productions in limestone and marble. The vase-shaped urns themselves are an indication of Roman influence, as they imitate a custom of the aristocracies of Rome (Di Vita-Evrard *et al.* 1996: 89–97). Thus, the highest level of emulation of Roman models in funerary practices is represented by both the choice of container and the use of the complete Latin name. However, even when the family had already received citizenship, most inscriptions only record a single onomastic element (Di Vita-Evrard *et al.* 1996: 130), most likely the name by which the deceased was known within the family. Women largely continued to use indigenous names, while men very frequently adopt Latin or Latinized names, beginning in the second half of the first century AD. Moreover, female burials with inscriptions are much less frequent, representing only less than a third of inscriptions from ash-urns. Such a disparity should be explained in the context of women's more private existence, making them less inclined to the adoption of Roman models.

Among above ground funerary monuments of the second century AD, the norm was the use of the entire Latin name. However, cognomina of indigenous origin appear more frequently in funerary context than in public ones, where prominent locals often display an irreproachable Roman name (eg *Q. Servilius Candidus, Ti. Plautus Lupus, Q. Marcius*

Rusonianus). M. Benabou (1976: 536) explains this phenomenon by correlating it with social class: the preservation of indigenous names would thus be peculiar to the lower classes. This interpretation was rightly questioned by G. Di Vita Evrard (1993: 299), who demonstrated that the context of the inscriptions, public or funerary, influenced the use of indigenous names. Probably the same individuals who in public used a completely Latinized name retained indigenous ones in funerary inscriptions.

We certainly cannot relegate to the lower classes the dedicator of the mausoleum of Gasr Duirat, *G. Marius Boccius Zurgem*. In this and in other examples, such as *Q. Domitius Camillus Nysim* (IRT 692); *Q. Caecilius Cerialis Phiscon* (IRT 673); *G. Calpurnius Tracachalus Dosiedes* (IRT 677), the indeclinable indigenous name becomes the fourth element appended to the Latin *cognomen*. It has been suggested that nomenclature at Leptis before the concession of Roman citizenship included *cognomina* of Libyan origin (Amadasi Guzzo 1986). This was atypical for Punic communities, where individuals were generally designated simply by name and patronymic.

These appended indigenous names, of mostly Libyan origin, can perhaps be interpreted as referring to local lineage groups. Although these names could be omitted in official contexts, they needed to be maintained in familial and funerary contexts, where they were considered essential for the individual and group identity. A certain example of a collective name is that of the family of the *Tapapii*, whose members dominated public life and civic commissions, between the Augustan and early Flavian era (Amadasi Guzzo 1983). No Roman *gentilicium* was added to this family's nomenclature and we do not

Figure 14.4: Representation in relief of a capsa *carved on a stone block from the mausoleum of Gasr Duirat*

know when and how this powerful family Latinized its name (Torelli 1973). In fact, we do not know how large this family was, but they probably were an expanded lineage group, similar to a clan. Every trace of them disappears after the Flavians: their importance might have declined, or they might have been split into several *gentes* after the concession of citizenship. Such a grant could have had a disruptive effect on traditional lineage groups, making them invisible in the city's public life. In the rural areas, and especially along the desert fringes, clans could preserve their original nature and continue to be fundamental elements in landholding patterns.

In some cases, the hypogea do refer to extended lineage groups. A tomb in the western hinterland of Leptis contained 139 cremations. Given the use of the tomb for approximately a century, a living community of about 30 can be estimated. The suggestion of a clan tomb is reinforced by the repetition of the same collective name in many of its Punic and Latin inscriptions. The continuation of collective tombs in the Roman period can be linked to the persistence of extended families, demonstrating that the social structures of the city underwent few changes during Romanization.

The burial rituals

Burial rituals can throw light on the processes of acculturation and cultural resistance at Leptis in the first centuries of the Empire. The diffusion of cremation during the first century BC is in line with similar developments in Italy and the western provinces. It would be tempting, therefore, to see this phenomenon in connection with the Roman conquest. If, however, the transition is examined in more detail, we can see a continuity of Punic traditions. Of particular significance is the practice of using amphorae, often painted with Punic religious symbols, for the non-human remains of the pyre, such as charcoals, the bed and the offerings. Such a practice is documented at Carthage in the archaic period and seems to be a characteristically Punic trait. This practice is attested at Leptis as late as the second century AD (Di Vita-Evrard *et al.* 1996: 125–129). A further confirmation of Punic influence is the use of box-shaped urns with pitched-roof lids, similar to those at Carthage. At the same time, from the second century AD onwards, prestige burials will have vase-shaped urns in the style of the ruling Roman class.

Another element of Leptis' funerary customs that may be traceable to the Punic tradition is the treatment of infant death. Very few infant burials have been found in hypogean tombs: among over a hundred individuals aged on the basis of skeletal remains only three or four cases were below ten years old. The scarcity of infant burials in the hypogea suggests that younger individuals were buried elsewhere, as attested by Punic tofets and infant cemeteries. There is no positive evidence for a tophet at Leptis, but one has been found farther inland at Msellata (Abd al-Rahman 1995). At this site, the pottery used to contain the remains of infants and lambs suggests a date in the first century AD. At Sabratha, the tophet found just outside the city continued to be used until the second century AD (Brecciaroli Taborelli 1979).

Burial evidence from Leptis illustrates the complexity of the Romanization process. While public behaviours rapidly conformed to the Roman model, funerary practices remained untouched in certain areas. Language and nomenclature record different levels of emulation, but above all different forms of self-representation, ranging from the private and oral context of family life, to the group visibility in the funerary sphere, all the way to self-representation as Roman citizens in public life. The process of Romanization also seems to affect only minimally women, relegated to a domestic life removed from power.

A possible key to conceptualizing the cultural processes in action at Leptis is the use of binary oppositions, such as high and low (also in the sense of above ground and underground), external and internal, public and private. High is represented by a hinterland with tombs structured in a similar way to many Roman cities, while low is the continuity of hypogeal tombs and of Punic burial customs. This is the context in which the variability in nomenclature can be understood: men appear oriented towards the public world and a quicker acculturation, while women remain almost completely outside the sphere of Latin and Romanization. At the same time the preservation of indigenous familial systems stands in contrast to the rapid assimilation process that characterizes public life. Leptis shows us an indigenous community in its development towards integration within the Roman Empire, an integration, however, that did not involve a radical transformation of social and ritual structures.

Acknowledgements

This paper is based on my doctoral dissertation (*Sepoltura e società nella Tripolitania Romana: le necropoli di Leptis Magna*, 1996), written at University of Pisa under the supervision of E. La Rocca. The evidence discussed in it is largely the result of work conducted by the

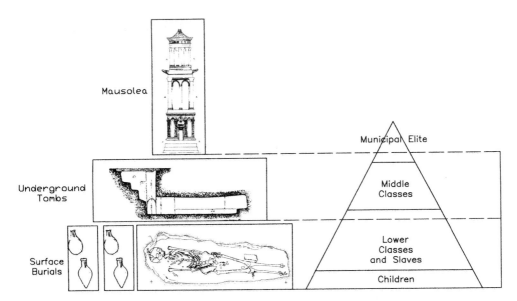

Figure 14.5: Society and burials at Leptis in the early empire: a schematic representation

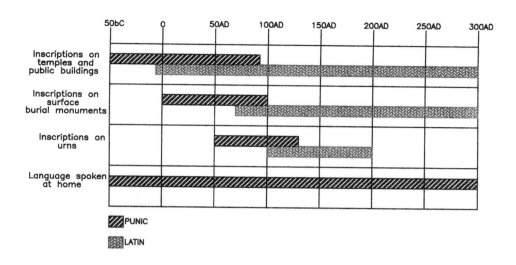

Figure 14.6: Punic and latin in diverse contexts of use at Leptis

Missione Archeologica in Libia of the University of Rome III, in collaboration with the Libyan Department of Antiquities. A comprehensive and interdisciplinary investigation of the burial evidence from Leptis is in progress, combined with the excavation of a large site in the western suburbs of the city (Musso *et al.* 1997). The project has profited from the contribution of many scholars: for epigraphy, G. Di Vita Evrard (CNRS, Paris); for numismatics, M. Munzi; for palaeo-anthropological studies, F. Mallegni (University of Pisa); for the study of ash-urns, L. Musso (University of Rome III).

References

Abd al-Rahman, A. S. 1995. Latest tomb findings at Leptis Magna and in the vicinity. *Libya Antiqua*, ns 1: 154–155.

Amadasi Guzzo, M. G. 1983. Una grande famiglia di Lepcis in rapporto con la ristrutturazione urbanistica della città (I sec.a.C.-I sec.d.C.). In *Architecture et Societè de l'archaisme grec à la fin de la republique romaine*, pp. 377–85.

Amadasi-Guzzo, M. G. 1986. L'onomastica nelle iscrizioni puniche tripolitane, *RSF* 14: 21–51.

Bartoccini, R. 1927. Rinvenimenti vari di interesse archeologico in Tripolitania. *Africa Italiana* 1: 213–248.

Bartoccini, R. 1928–29. Scavi e rinvenimenti in Tripolitania negli anni 1926–27. *Africa Italiana* 2: 77–110.

Benabou, M. 1976. *La résistance africaine a la romanisation*. Paris.

Birley, A. R. 1971. *The African Emperor Septimius Severus*. London.

Birley, A. R. 1988. Names at Leptis Magna. *LibStud* 19: 1–19.

Brecciaroli Taborelli, L. 1979. Il tofet neopunico di Sabratha. In *Atti del I Congr. Int. di Studi Fenici e Punici II*. Rome, pp. 54–545.

Coarelli, F. and Thébert, Y. 1988. Architecture funéraire et pouvoir réflexions sur l'hellenisme numide. *MEFRA* 100: 761–818.

De Miro, E. and Fiorentini, G. 1977. Leptis Magna. La necropoli greco-punica sotto il teatro, *Quaderni di Archeologia della Libia* 6: 5–75.

Di Vita, A. 1976. Il mausoleo punico-ellenistico B di Sabratha. *MDAI(R)* 83: 273–285.

Di Vita, A. 1982. Gli emporia di Tripolitania dall'età di Massinissa a Diocleziano: un profilo storico-istituzionale. In *Aufstieg und Niedergang der Romischen Welt*, 2, *Principat*, 2, pp. 515–592.

Di Vita Evrard, G. 1984. Municipium Flavium Lepcis Magna. *BCTH* ns. 17: 197–210.

Di Vita Evrard, G. 1993. Prosopographie et population: L'exemple d'une ville africaine, Lepcis Magna. In *Prosopographie und Socialgeschichte, Herausgegeben von Werner Eck*. Böhlau, pp. 293–314.

Di Vita Evrard, G. 1996. L'Epitaphe de Secundio et la Richesse des Servilii Lepcitains. *Libya antiqua* n.s. 2: 138–142.

Di Vita Evrard, G., Fontana, S., Mallegni, F., Munzi, M. and Musso, L. 1996. L'Ipogeo dei Flavi a Leptis Magna presso Gasr Gelda. *Libya Antiqua* n.s. 2: 85 -133.

Fontana, S. 1996. Le necropoli di Leptis Magna. *Libya antiqua* n.s. 2: 79–83.

Fontana, S. and Usai, L. 1997. L'area funeraria a ovest della villa. In Musso *et al.* 1997, pp. 278–284.

Garbini, G. 1986. *Venti anni di epigrafia punica nel Magreb (1965–1985)*. (Suppl. RSF 9) Roma.

Gascou, J. 1972. *La Politique municipale de l'empire romain en Afrique Preconsulaire de Trajan et Septime Sévère*. Paris.

Harris, W. V. 1989 *Ancient Literacy*. Cambridge Mass, London.

IPT =Amadasi Guzzo, M. G. and Levi Della Vida, G., 1987. *Iscrizioni puniche della Tripolitania*. (Monografie di Archeologia Libica 22) Roma.

IRT = Reynolds, J. M. and Ward Perkins, J. B., 1952. *The Inscriptions of Roman Tripolitania*. Rome.

Mattingly, D.J. 1995. *Tripolitania*. London.

Musso *et al.* 1997. Missione archeologica dell'Università Roma Tre a Leptis Magna. *Libya Antiqua*, n.s. 3: 257–294.

Romanelli, P. 1925. *Leptis Magna*. Roma.

Romanelli P. 1970. *Topografia e archeologia dell'Africa romana*. Torino.

Torelli, M. 1974. Per una storia della classe dirigente di Leptis Magna. *Rendiconti Accademia dei Lincei* ser.8, 28: 377–410.

Chapter 15

The Roman Cultural Revolution in Gaul

Greg Woolf

Evading Romanization

Early Roman Gaul experienced widespread cultural changes, changes typical of the transformations commonly termed Romanization (e.g. Brandt and Slofstra 1983; Barrett *et al.* 1989; Blagg and Millett 1990; Millett 1990, Wood and Queiroga 1992; Metzler *et al.* 1995; Cherry 1998). So, change was most intense around the turn of the millennium; the peculiarities of local societies affected how change happened and remained reflected in the new provincial cultures that emerged; so too local elites played a central role in these changes, and they enriched and empowered themselves in the process. New settlement patterns, new styles of monumentality and of mundane goods, along with new tastes and new forms of cult. The material conditions of Gallic life changed, and so too did the Gauls' conceptions of the world, as they became Romans (Woolf 1998).

Yet there are other ways – other than in terms of Romanization, that is – for us to understand all this. The terminology of Romanization has not been central to studies of the Roman east (cf. Woolf 1994), yet there too the same period is characterized by urbanization, changes in settlement patterns and the appearance of new monumental and religious forms, all orchestrated again largely by provincial elites (e.g. Price 1984; Bowman and Rathbone 1992, Alcock 1993; 1997). The essays in this present collection reveal similar processes underway in Italy too. All early imperial cultures were new and all also incorporated elements of the old. Likewise all were intensely local and also markedly Roman, in the sense that Roman power had largely determined what would be preserved, what introduced and the terms of their eventual cohabitation.

The realization that cultural change was ubiquitous within the empire has important consequences. Take, for instance, the attempts to 'measure' Romanization, endlessly criticized, yet endlessly repeated. Yet if everyone and everywhere was 'Romanized', the measuring exercise is futile, and all we have recovered are cultural differences between town and country, plain and mountain, army and civilian, between this locality and that. If Romanization is not seen as the (imperfect) dissemination or imitation of a static metropolitan culture, this recognition of cultural difference has to be made to serve other ends: such as asking which kinds of diversity are relics of earlier difference; which were actually produced by imperial rule (Woolf 1997); and which reflect the impact of external forces (cf. Reece 1990).

A second approach rendered obsolete is the explanation of change in terms of the acculturation of one people by another. If the cultures of Rome and of Italy were as new as those of Gaul, it makes little sense to explain provincial culture as a product of the interaction of two cultural entities. Leaving aside issues of misplaced concreteness – cultures have no agency and cannot be objectively defined or described, they have no objective existence except as the sum total of cultural actions, and so forth – in this case the cultural activity on all sides is far too complex to be adequately described even by variants of the model such as reverse-acculturation, two-way acculturation or complementary processes of Romanization and indigenization. There are other reasons too for abandoning the paradigm of 'Romanization' (Freeman 1993; Barrett 1997; Woolf 1998: 1–23). But this paper is not intended to reiterate those critiques. Instead, in the spirit of trying to establish common ground between provincial and Italian archaeology, it sets out to revisit the cultural transformation of Rome's Gallic provinces through an alternative problematic, one recently developed in discussions of the contemporaneous transformation of the cultural life of the city of Rome, the idea of a "Roman cultural revolution".

I should state clearly at the outset that this is by way of an experiment, an attempt to show how familiar phenomena might look when seen from a different perspective. Replacing "Romanization theory" with the notion of "cultural revolution" would have costs as well as advantages. Yet other problematics might be devised or, as the example of the eastern provinces shows, it would be perfectly possible to do without one (although that choice too would have costs). My choice of alternative perspective is not wholly arbitrary. The transformation of epic poetry, elite sexuality and urban space in the capital (to name just a few of the media affected), coincided *in time* very closely with the most dramatic cultural changes in the provinces. Southern Gaul came progressively under Roman dominance over the second century BC, and was a province well before the cultural revolution really got underway, but the cultural ramifications were very slight. The Caesarian conquest of the north in the 50's BC, however, coincided with the period when "the intellectualization of Rome runs parallel, by more than coincidence, with a transformation of the structures of its power and society" (Wallace-Hadrill 1988: 225). Cicero's philosophical works were produced in the late 50's and mid 40's BC. Varro's main works were published in the 40's and early 30's BC, but research presumably began earlier for the 41 books of *Roman Antiquities, Human and Divine*, that were published in 47 BC. Pompey's theatre was built in 55 BC, and the *Forum Iulium* dedicated in 46 BC. The chronological correlation between this frenetic cultural activity and the period of most rapid imperial expansion is not a coincidence, and both were linked with the series of personal hegemonies – the domination of Pompey, the first triumvirate, the dictatorship of Caesar – which culminated in the principate. During the same period the first really dramatic signs of cultural change appeared in southern Gaul, too, and indeed in most provinces (Woolf 1995).

Without question some connections existed – beyond rough contemporaneity – between the metropolitan cultural revolution and the origins of provincial Roman civilizations. Common to both, for example, was the centrality given to imperial images. Some monumental forms – the arch for instance – became suddenly popular in both spheres. More mundanely, Campanian ware and late La Tène finewares were alike swept away by *terra sigillata*. Those changes in material culture have often been interpreted as signs that elites of the period, provincial, Italian and metropolitan alike, were especially interested in public display and self-representation of various kinds, shared a concern to define as well as assert their Roman identity, and were energetic in trying to use these changes to strengthen and entrench their social power. For all these reasons, and as a complement to the Romanization of Rome (Terrenato, this volume), it seems worthwhile to approach the creation of Gallo-Roman civilization in terms of a provincial cultural revolution.

The Roman Cultural Revolution

The term "Roman cultural revolution" was first coined by Andrew Wallace-Hadrill in a review discussion (1990) of Paul Zanker's (1988) influential study of the relationship between art and politics in Augustan Rome. Wallace-Hadrill has not used the phrase systematically in the series of studies he has undertaken of Hellenization in Rome (e.g. 1988; 1990; 1998), but it was recently adopted as the title for a collection of essays on the subject (Habinek and Schiesaro 1997) to which he contributed the lead essay (Wallace-Hadrill 1997). It is used here as a convenient shorthand for a set of currently popular arguments about the transformation of metropolitan Roman culture around the turn of the millennium. As yet there is only a limited consensus about the causation of these changes. One area of particular disagreement concerns the extent to which this cultural revolution was driven by political change, as opposed to simply encompassing changes in political culture (such as the naturalization at Rome of an autocratic style). While some represent these developments as promoted or even co-ordinated by Augustus, others see his regime as capitalizing on a cultural revolution already underway in the previous generation (see Purcell 1990, on Nicolet 1988). Naturally there are a number of nuanced variants available. What is not disputed, however, is the range of the changes concerned: archaeologists like Zanker, historians like Wallace-Hadrill and philologists like Karl Galinsky (1996) all agree that none of their disciplines can offer an adequate account of the phenomenon on its own.

The Roman cultural revolution may also be thought of as the formative period of the "high" culture of the early empire (Rawson 1985). During it were created the literary, intellectual, aesthetic and monumental styles against which much of the cultural activity of the next three hundred years had repeatedly to define itself, whether by imitation or variation, by elaboration, subversion or outright rejection. Epic poetry and the imperial *fora* provide two examples. Latin epics of various sorts had been composed since the third century BC, but it was the epic composed by Virgil under Augustan patronage that came to be seen as the authoritative definition of the genre: the epics composed in the first century AD by Lucan, Statius, Silius, Valerius and others all looked back to Virgil's work as the model to imitate and depart from (Hardie 1993). As for the imperial *fora*, the city of Rome had been organized for centuries around a series of irregularly shaped public spaces – the *forum Romanum*, the *forum Boarium* and the *Campus Martius* being the most important – used for a range of political, ritual and commercial activities. All these spaces contained and were flanked by free-standing monumental structures of various ages and various kinds, temples, basilicas and statues being the most common. At the end of the Republic, two new public spaces were created, the *forum Iulium* and then the *forum Augustum*, which consisted of piazzas dedicated to mainly ceremonial use. Each was enclosed on all sides by porticoes and focused on a single temple, facing a main entrance, and each was planned in some detail as an architectural ensemble (Zanker 1988). Many of these features were anticipated in the slightly earlier Theatre of Pompey, and indeed by individual features of earlier public spaces, but it was these two Augustan monumental complexes that set the pattern for creating public spaces both in Rome, where several later emperors created their own imperial *fora*, and in many provincial metropoleis (Walker 1997).

A further approach to the Roman cultural revolution emphasizes it as a key episode in Rome's long encounter with Hellenism, a crucial moment of appropriation of and emancipation from Greek models. So Latin epic was created first through translating, and then through adapting Greek models. Virgil's epic challenged not only his Latin predecessors like Ennius and their Hellenistic Greek contemporaries, but also Homer whose two epics enjoyed unparalleled prestige in Roman as well as Greek culture. Deliberately like and deliberately unlike the Homeric model, Virgil's *Aeneid* succeeded to the extent that later Latin epic poets return to Homer mainly through Virgil's reading of him. Likewise, the new public spaces of late Republican and Augustan Rome may have been modelled on those of Hellenistic capitals like Pergamon and Alexandria, but they then became archetypes for new public spaces, not just in the Latin west but also in the Greek East.

Arguably this intense reflection on and departure from Greek models was just one facet of a wider Roman preoccupation with tradition and innovation. The same issues were being fought out over religious change (North 1976), over philosophy (Beard 1986), over consumption, and in many other areas of Roman life. Besides, the relevance of tradition to any society undergoing rapid change is well known (Hobsbawm and Ranger 1983), and Romans display all the usual cultural manoeuvring of such situations. New traditions were invented (e.g. Hardie 1997) while old ones were documented and "revived" (Wallace-Hadrill 1988). *Mos maiorum*, the "customs of our ancestors", became a political slogan; a contested centre of social debate (Wallace-Hadrill 1997); and a disciplinary discourse through which change might be policed and legitimated (Edwards 1993). And because Roman society was perhaps a little unusual in the extent to which membership was defined in terms of *mos* (meaning tradition, morality and culture) this was also a period when discussions of literature, sexuality, cuisine, religion, ethics, architecture and a dozen other subjects tended to circle around what it meant to be Roman.

Knowledge and Authority in early Roman Gaul

It is time to ask how the Gauls might have participated in this sort of cultural revolution. Wallace-Hadrill offers a starting point, when he writes (1997: 12), in relation to late Republican intellectual preoccupation with ancestral customs, law, temporal systems and the Latin language, that "what seems to us in retrospect an inevitable adoption of superior civilization and rationality also involves a redefinition of authority: a collapse of the authority of the traditional Republican ruling class; a shift in the control of knowledge from social leaders to academic experts; and an appropriation of that authority by Augustus." Cultural change in the western provinces too has sometimes been seen as "an inevitable adoption of superior civilization". Equally the early Roman period in most provinces was marked by significant shifts in authority.

For the Gauls, the most obvious area in which to consider power/knowledge is religion. Recent work has shown how important religion was as a focus of debates about change in late Republican Rome (e.g. Beard 1986; 1989; Gordon 1990a). The political dominance of the *nobiles* may well have depended largely on their monopoly of religious authority (North 1989: 155–6), but over the last century of the Republic this authority was undermined by elections to major priesthoods, by new interest in Greek philosophy and 'foreign' cults, and finally by the emperors' remodelling of the ritual space of the city, of the religious calendar and of Roman priestly colleges. The appearance in Rome, Italy and the provinces of the various ritual and representational traditions that modern scholars group together as 'imperial cult' was only the most prominent feature of these shifts in religious authority and belief (Beard, North and Price 1998: 168–9).

Much less is known of La Tène cosmologies. Little relevant written and iconographic evidence has survived from late prehistory and it is difficult to interpret, while Gallo-Roman elites did little to preserve their ancestral culture. But if there was no Gallo-Roman Varro, the same was not true in the late Iron Age when religious knowledge and religious power did intersect in the persons of the Druids. A great deal is uncertain about these figures, but it is clear that although they were probably drawn from the same social strata as the military and political leaders of Gallic communities, and although some individual political leaders may have been Druids, in general they formed a distinct specialized priestly group. More importantly, they possessed significant social authority, connected in many ancient sources with the prestige they acquired from their possession of arcane knowledge acquired through long education (Piggott 1968). Caesar describes them as having a supra-tribal organization and being influential enough to negotiate peaces between states. Classical testimony represents Druids either as uncivilized, especially because of their alleged involvement in human sacrifice, or else praises them as natural philosophers, wise men at the edge of the world who taught the transmigration of souls, but all agreed that the Druids represented a combination of knowledge and power distinct from that of pagan Roman priests.

Like other priesthoods of un-classical type elsewhere in the empire (Gordon 1990b), Druids were first sidelined and then suppressed in the early imperial period (Woolf 1998: 220–222), and new priests of a more conventional Roman type appeared, drawn from the political elite. Most categories of Roman priests combined ritual functions, such as presiding over public animal sacrifices at altars set up before temples containing cult-statues, with the role of religious expert. Collectively colleges of priests ruled on matters of ritual and had oversight over the use of sacred space of various kinds, while some priests had particular functions that required a special knowledge, for instance of divination (Beard 1990). Little is known of the extent to which Gallo-Roman priests were expected to have such expertise, but they tended to have titles modelled on Roman priesthoods and to perform similar ritual functions, while religious authority in provincial *municipia* and *coloniae* was managed much as in Rome. The establishment of a colony or a *municipium* required the civic authorities to establish the priesthoods and cults of the city, and to fix a religious calendar for the city's cults (Scheid 1991). Subsequent management of the community's cults – such as decisions over the introduction of new deities, the control of sanctuaries, the management of temples, adjudications of disputes involving priesthoods and the like – were from then on the responsibility of the council of *decuriones*. As in Rome, a monopoly of religious authority may have gone some way towards entrenching the power of the new elites that emerge in Gaul in this period. At the very least, these priesthoods provided a powerful medium to express status within these communities and beyond them. The culmination of a municipal career and the most prominent item on most career inscriptions from the Three Gauls was the priesthood of the imperial cult within the city. The most successful Gallic nobles competed for the annual priesthood of Rome and Augustus at the Altar of Lyon (Drinkwater 1979). Provincial priests of Rome and Augustus celebrated their election with games, held at their own expense, and presided over the provincial council.

The creation of new priesthoods and new cults into Gaul entailed the creation of new kinds of knowledge. Likewise, the re-ordering of Gallic religion involved the effective abolition of an entire sacrificial and ritual tradition and the naturalization of a new one. The very designing of new cults involved formal acts of syncretism, that in some cases evidently were taken on expert religious advice (Scheid 1991). What deity should each local god be syncretized with, and how ought he or she to be portrayed? The management of a new calendar was no trivial task. When should each god be worshipped and with what rites? Which imperial festivals needed to be celebrated? When was the *Saturnalia*? Some Gauls, perhaps rather later, went to some trouble to design authentically Gallic calendars of their own (Duval 1986). The very conduct and terminology of Roman ritual was complex. What was a *suovetaurilia*? What remedy was required if a sacrificial animal had seemed unwilling to be killed? And then there were the less public ritual technologies to be acquired: Gauls were quick learners when in came to classical ways of cursing.

Part of this knowledge might be learned, rather as Gallo-Roman potters learned how to make kilns capable of firing at high temperatures, and the sons of Gallic chiefs learned Latin rhetoric. But some kinds of religious knowledge had to be created within Roman Gaul. The representation of the gods provides a good example. Iron age religion was not wholly aniconic, but the introduction of Roman media of representation forced Gauls to decide how to portray their own gods, so they could set up cult statues in the new temples and offer images of the gods to redeemed their vows to them. General conventions had to be agreed, such as how to deal with gods traditionally imagined in the form of animals, and particular iconographic schemes had to be devised to represent gods like Sucellus. Syncretistic acts of this kind may be compared to the efforts of Cicero and other Roman intellectuals to domesticate Greek philosophy (Beard 1986), and also to the ways in which Etruscan religious knowledge was recast and harnessed to new ends in the same period (Terrenato 1998: 110–12). It is not just in humbler, cheaper imagery that the Gallo-Roman gods retained some non-Roman features. Whether by making divine epithets out of indigenous gods or by providing new images of gods with 'visual epithets' – a wheel for a Jupiter, a horse for an Epona – the syncretizers made certain to signal that they were adapting, rather than adopting Roman gods. New knowledge and new authority was formulated in the Gauls' own Roman cultural revolution.

Foreign Bodies

So far, so good. But there are obvious objections to this line of argument, or at least to this procedure. Little is known of intellectual life in Gaul before the late third century AD, by which point Gallo-Roman authors described their past in purely Roman terms, often demonstrably on the basis of having read the Latin classics. Indeed, pre-Roman traditions seems to have been forgotten as deliberately in the early Roman West as they were remembered in the Roman East (Woolf 1996). Fascinating as this phenomenon is, it imposes severe limits on the extent to which approaches developed to deal with Latin literary culture may be applied in Gaul. Less serious is the objection that any approach to cultural change that begins from intellectual life is elitist. Certainly the main actors in the processes discussed above were all members of various elites, but these elites made use of their social power to construct the physical and imaginative environments within which other Gallo-Romans were compelled to live. It made a real difference to Gauls that as a result of the Roman cultural revolution, religious authority was handed over to the political elites who also now, as Roman citizens, had title under Roman law to most of the landed wealth of their communities, and that the public cults in which they participated now included worship of Rome and of the emperors. Nevertheless, it still seems worth pursuing the idea of a Gallo-Roman cultural revolution through other, more mundane, media.

Several possibilities suggest themselves. The creation of *terra sigillata*, also new, also derived from eastern models before going on to influence them, also if not Roman then certainly Italian in origin, might be brought into relation with what Virgil did to epic and Augustus to public space in Rome. *Terra sigillata* is also a fruitful medium for the exploration of the Gallo-Roman contribution to the new cultures of the Roman empire. The development of specifically Gallo-Roman iconography and forms, under the control of Gallic potters, has already made it a good field in which to explore the appropriation of Roman culture (Vickers 1994; Woolf 1998: 181–93). The new forms also reflect new ways of choosing, preparing and most of all of consuming food (Meadows 1994). Along with the evidence of transporter amphoras, and of the *triclinia* of Gallo-Roman domus and villas, the elaborate table services show Gauls had learned new ways of eating at least on semi-public occasions. Individual dishes and cups hint at quite major changes in Gallo-Roman constructions of the self. Finally, the decoration of the more elaborate pieces of *terra sigillata* communicates new ways of thinking about myth, about the natural world and about public and private leisure. Creativity at this level reveals wide sectors of Gallo-Roman societies participating in the development and sharing of new kinds of knowledge of the world and of themselves (Woolf 1998: 187–205).

But rather than repeat myself on the subject of *sigillata*, I have chosen as my second example of the Roman cultural revolution in Gaul, the transformation of Gallic bodies. The history of the body has received less attention from students of the early Roman empire than it has from historians of classical Greece or early Christianity, but new notions of the body were certainly involved in the Roman cultural revolution in a number of ways. Ciceronian invective shows how dress had become highly politicized, and how same-sex relations of certain kinds moved from being stigmatized to becoming accepted and even fashionable in some circles. Habinek (1997) has even written of "the invention of sexuality" as a component of this process: whether or not that formulation is accepted, it is certainly true that a discourse of sexuality becomes more differentiated in this period. These changes are not just reflected in erotic poetry, but also appear in visual media from wall-paintings to (again) *terra sigillata*. Various sciences of the body also became better known in Rome, not just medicine and hairdressing, but also physiognomics (the art of deducing a person's true nature from his or her face) and rhetoric, since instruction in speaking included instruction in deportment and in gesture. This last art, at least, was widely taught in Gaul.

The Gallo-Roman body was a privileged site of cultural conflict. On some of the trophies and monumental arches set up in Gaul in the early first century, sharp contrasts are drawn between the appearances of barbarian Gauls and those of Romans (Silberberg-Pierce 1986; Walter 1993; Küpper-Böhm 1996). Civilization is shown to involve the removal of moustaches and a closer cropping of hair, together with a more restrained body language. Naturally these monuments drew on representational stereotypes and many were set up by generals or colonial founders and authorities who considered themselves to be Romans as opposed to Gauls. Yet the honorific images commissioned by Gallo-Roman aristocrats themselves show that they too chose to be portrayed according to those canons, and had thus internalized these idealizations of the body and perhaps expected some other members of their communities to share them. The busts and statues of these grandees present the modern observer with an impression of uniformity. The gaze of the statue, the way the limbs are held either close to the body or in a restrained gesticulation as if in mid-speech (or more rarely in mid-sacrifice); the *toga*, the quintessential Roman formal costume, often linked to citizenship or office; and the hairstyles – often conforming to current metropolitan styles – all conjure up a sense of *decorum*, dignity and cultural conformity.

This was no mere representational conceit: some Gallo-Roman bodies really looked at least a bit like that. The development of specialized toilet instruments for the grooming of some bodies is known from the late iron age, but much greater quantities of these objects – tweezers and probes, razors and nail cleaners and so on – have been recovered from early Roman sites. The evidence has been best examined for Britain (Hill 1997) but similar material is known throughout Gaul. Dress codes changed too. Gallo-Roman men did not display their wealth and status by wearing elaborate jewellery as their fathers and grand fathers had done (Johns 1996). Representations modelled ideal faces, bodies and hairstyles: as usual, ideals attracted even when they were not completely achieved. Educational systems too disciplined the movement and posture of the Gallo-Roman body. The classical literature read in Gallo-Roman schools put a high premium on correct posture and dress (Kremer 1994: 20–30), as do the surviving rhetorical manuals. Presumably the most cosmopolitan Gauls were indistinguishable from (other) Romans. Indeed the savage attacks made on the body language, appearance and speech of the sophist Favorinus of Arles by his Greek rival the physiognomist Polemon, were not aimed at exposing his barbarism, but – tacitly conceding his mastery of civilized speech and gesture – were directed at his sexual ambivalence (Gleason 1995).

One final indication of the development of new attitudes to the body in Roman Gaul, is provided by the efforts and money expended by some Gauls on providing the bath-complexes without which proper Roman bodies could not be properly maintained. The remains of baths, fountains and the aqueducts built primarily to serve them, are so numerous in Gaul that Albert Grenier devoted one of the four volumes of his (1931–60) *Manuel d'Archéologie Gallo-Romaine* to "monuments des eaux". The chronology of aqueduct building is notoriously difficult to establish (Wilson 1996: 12–18) but it seems the first dated baths in Gaul are those constructed at Glanum and Vaison at the turn of the millennium (Goudineau 1980: 285). By the mid-second century AD all major Gallic cities were surrounded by networks of aqueducts, and some major bath houses are known, the largest being the Barbarathermen at Trier (Grewe 1988; Nielsen 1990). The longest aqueduct known is that of Köln (around 95 kilometres); but Lyon had eventually four, totalling well over 150 kilometres; and Vienne had a network of ten. The cost of introducing this new regime of bodily hygiene into Gaul was considerable. Not only were aqueducts and bath-houses expensive to construct and maintain, the baths also consumed great quantities of olive oil, all of which had to be imported into non-Mediterranean Gaul, and fuel, presumably required in even greater quantities in the north. But the price was evidently worth paying to enable cultivated Gauls to cultivate their bodies, to bathe and exercise with their equally cultivated friends, to shave and oil themselves before dinner and in short to adopt the rhythms of a Roman day, dividing business from pleasure with elaborate rituals of self-fashioning (Yegül 1992: 30–43). It was not merely rich and urban bodies that were so cared for. Baths are common in the secondary towns of Gaul, private baths were constructed on some villas, and most sanctuaries had baths at which the worshippers might purify themselves before sacrifice and the ritual dinner that followed.

Was the re-fashioning of Gallo-Roman bodies really creative in the same way as was the invention of Gallo-Roman ritual and religious imagery? The knowledge required was considerable but most of it was learned rather than created in Gaul, and Gallo-Roman physiques cannot easily be distinguished from Roman ones. Perhaps the idea of a cultural revolution works less well for bodies than the idea of a deep penetration of alien social practices and cultural models into Gallic society (Goudineau 1980: 282–94)? But while it is true that new styles of deportment and hygiene were neither created nor significantly modified in Gaul, the same might be said of Rome itself at least as far as bathing is concerned. The new kinds of self-care that became so widespread in the early empire drew on many sources – gymnasial culture, Greek bathing, technical inventions like the hypocaust – but none of them were native to Rome, nor were they first combined there as far as we can tell. Evidence for the hypocaust and the replacement of individual bathing with communal bathing and the alternation of baths of different temperatures appears in the late second and early first centuries BC in several areas of central Italy and the Greek east. Examples from the Vesuvian cities are the best documented, although most recent work is cautious about seeing Campania as a single place of origin. The first huge recreational public bath complex constructed in the capital was that built by Agrippa around 20 BC. This component of the cultural revolution evidently did not start in Rome, even if it was Roman enthusiasm that facilitated its spread throughout much of the empire, and imperial resources that funded the most splendid installations. A comparison might be made with *sigillata*. Neither its main models were located in Rome nor was it created there, yet it undoubtedly emerged as part of the same set of cultural transformations as those included within the cultural revolution. Gauls played more of a role in the development of *sigillata* than of ideas of the body, but less of a role than in creating Gallo-Roman cults. Rome itself evidently participated to a variable degree in driving and controlling some aspects of the cultural revolution of the late first century BC.

Implications

What has been gained by looking early Roman Gaul in terms of a cultural revolution rather than Romanization? One immediate gain of any new approach to an old problem is that it enables one to evade old stalemates and impasses in debate, and this has been the case here. For a start, the issue of agency (Romanization from above versus self-Romanization) seems less central when the debate is not set in terms of 'Romans' interacting with 'natives'. The cultural revolution problematic allows us to see how authority was granted in Rome, Italy and Gaul alike to those who succeeded in dominating cultural production. Equally the arguments over continuity versus change appear no longer as a Gallic or provincial problem, but instead as a local case of a dilemma faced by all participants in the cultural revolution, how to reconcile tradition with innovation and how to manage change in areas of culture that are central to collective identity. More tentatively, an approach of this sort maybe allows archaeologists and historians to make more out of the differences they notice from one area to another. Differentiating the products of local cultural revolutions may have more potential for future analysis than simply ranking areas in terms of how Romanized they are. Finally, the shift in perspective allows new and rich bodies of evidence to be brought into the discussion, raising in the process new questions and possibilities for research.

Caution might, however, be advisable before embracing these ideas as a panacea. The shortcomings of Romanization have become clear only after many studies employing it and after much historiographical and theoretical debate. The Roman cultural revolution is a newer idea and, as noted already, not yet fully worked out. To the (largely unexpressed) disagreements over how it is to be related to political change might be added a lack of consensus over the linked issue of the chronological period to which it should be applied. Moreover, it has so far been applied to only a limited range of material, even the issues it tackles – time, tradition, space, sexuality and so on – are big ones. Those looking for an alternative to Romanization ought to be aware that the term cultural revolution was in part designed as an alternative to other kinds of revolution (Habinek and Schiesaro 1997: xv–xvi), as a new way of writing the fall of the Roman Republic and the Augustan coup without relegating culture to propaganda. It may well turn out to be more of a provisional tactic than a paradigm shift.

So much for what the idea of a cultural revolution has to offer provincial archaeologists. Does the discussion of the case of Gaul have anything to offer those who study the cultural revolution in the metropolis? I suggest it might help in at least three ways.

First, seeing the cultural revolution in wider perspective raises questions about the precise roles played by the city of Rome and its local-cum-imperial elite in the creation of early imperial culture. Rome and its environs provided a key site for the creation of some new cultural forms. Roman philosophy, for instance, was developed in and about the metropolis in debates among Roman intellectuals familiar with both Roman tradition and also the writings and lectures of Hellenistic philosophers (cf. Beard 1986; Sedley

1997). Much the same might be said of most literary activity in the period, and of the development of law. The most expensive new cultural projects, like *fora*, were naturally piloted in Rome. On the other hand, it does not follow that Rome was the birthplace of *every* component of the cultural revolution. The discussion of bathing and *terra sigillata* has already brought that out, to say nothing of the creation of Gallo-Roman religion. Likewise, Ward-Perkins (1970) long ago showed the links between various Italian regional styles of architecture and the neighbouring provinces. Viticulture seems to have passed via Marseilles into Gaul where new techniques and grapes were developed in precisely the same period as they were in Italy (Purcell 1985: 18–19). Put bluntly, how *Roman* was the Roman cultural revolution?

Second, the involvement of the west in the process might be seen as one means by which Romans succeeded in challenging Greek cultural hegemony. As Wallace-Hadrill (1997, 22) put it "[Augustus] wanted a universalizing culture, not local knowledge, to define his empire and a new sense of being Roman". From at least the age of Cicero, Romans described their culture in terms of *humanitas* (civilization; Woolf 1998: 54–60; The Latin word *romanitas*, although often used in the modern literature, is first attested in Tertullian's *de Pallio* 4.1.1, an oration delivered in early third century AD Carthage, in a context in which both Roman and Greek cultures are represented as parochial and temporary orders compared to the truly universalising value-system offered by Christianity). If we ask, how could Romans plausibly represent their culture as more than just the local customs and habits of one city state on the fringe of the Hellenistic world, one part of the answer might be that their *mores* (culture, traditions, values) came to be shared by half the empire. The involvement of western 'barbarians' made possible a civilizing process, in the course of which Roman culture might be elevated to the status of Civilization.

Finally, attention to the cultural revolution in the west relativizes the significance of Rome's encounter with Hellenism. Seen from Gaul, that latest phase of "Hellenization" seems just one manifestation of the Romans' linked preoccupations with reconciling tradition to innovation, and with defining what it was to be Roman. Recently several of those working on Hellenism in Rome have showed how Romans partly constructed themselves as not-Greek, while incorporating some deliberately undigested Greek culture into their new "universal" civilization (e.g. Beard 1994; Wallace-Hadrill 1998). Various metaphors have been suggested: Feeney (1998: 25–28) writes of "a Greek province of the brain" while Wallace-Hadrill (1988: 227–8) compares "Roman intellectual civilization" to a new university in which Roman power has staffed some faculties entirely with Greeks, but taken over others for themselves. What I am suggesting is that the Roman brain also had within it an un-barbarian province, and that Roman power also maintained the prestige of its academy by restricting tenure to only some of Rome's subjects. *Not* borrowing from the barbarians, in other words, said as much about Romans as the fact that they did borrow (selectively) from Greek culture. Engagement with the west may have taken a different form to engagement with the Greek world, but Roman culture, as created in that cultural revolution, was defined in relation to both.

Acknowledgements

I am very grateful to the audience at Ravenna and to the editors for comments on earlier drafts of this paper. Responsibility of all errors remains my own.

References

Alcock, S. E. 1993. *Graecia Capta. The Landscapes of Roman Greece*. Cambridge.

Alcock, S. (ed.) 1997. *The Early Roman Empire in the East*. Oxford.

Barrett, J. C., Fitzpatrick, A. P. and Macinnes, L. (eds.) 1989. *Barbarians and Romans in North-West Europe from the Later Republic to late Antiquity*. British Archaeological Reports International Series 471, Oxford.

Barrett, J. C. 1997. Romanization: a critical comment. In D. Mattingly (ed.) *Dialogues in Roman Imperialism. Power, discourse and discrepant experience in the Roman Empire, Journal of Roman Archaeology* supplement 23, Portsmouth, RI, pp. 51–64.

Beard, M. 1986. Cicero and divination: the formation of a Latin discourse. *Journal of Roman Studies* 76: 33–46.

Beard, M. 1989. Acca Larentia gains a son: myths and priesthood at Rome. In M.M.Mackensie and C. Roueché (eds.) *Images of Authority. Papers presented to Joyce Reynolds on the occasion of her 70th birthday* (Cambridge Philological Society supplement 16) pp. 41–61.

Beard, M. 1990. Priesthood in the Roman Republic. In M. Beard and J. North (eds.) *Pagan Priests. Religion and Power in the Ancient World*. London, pp. 19–48

Beard, M. 1994. The Roman and the foreign: the cult of the "Great Mother" in imperial Rome. In N. Thomas and C. Humphrey (eds.) *Shamanism, History and the State*. Ann Arbor, pp. 164–90.

Beard, M., Price, S. and North, J. 1998. *Religions of Rome I. A History*. Cambridge.

Blagg, T. F. C. and Millett, M. (eds.) 1990. *The Early Roman Empire in the West*. Oxford.

Bowman, A. K. and Rathbone, D. W. 1992. Cities and administration in Roman Egypt. *Journal of Roman Studies* 82: 107–27.

Brandt, R. and Slofstra, J. (eds.) 1983. *Roman and Native in the Low Countries. Spheres of interaction*, British Archaeological Reports International Series 184, Oxford.

Cherry, D. 1998. *Frontier and society in Roman North Africa*. Oxford.

Drinkwater, J. F. 1979. A note on local careers in the three Gauls under the early empire. *Britannia* 10: 89–100.

Duval, P. -M. 1986. *Receuil des Inscriptions Gauloises III: Les Calendriers (Coligny, Villards d'Héria)*. (*Gallia* supplément 45) Paris.

Edwards, C. 1993. *The Politics of Immorality in Ancient Rome*. Cambridge.

Feeney, D. 1998. *Literature and religion at Rome. Culture, contexts and beliefs*. Cambridge.

Freeman, P. W. M. 1993. 'Romanisation' and Roman material culture. *Journal of Roman Archaeology* 6: 438–45.

Galinsky, K. 1996. *Augustan Culture. an interpretive introduction*. Princeton.

Gleason, M. W. 1995. *Making men. Sophists and self-presentation in ancient Rome*. Princeton.

Gordon, R. 1990a. From Republic to Principate: religion, priesthood and ideology. In M. Beard and J. North (eds.) *Pagan Priests. Religion and Power in the Ancient World*. London, pp. 179–98.

Gordon, R. 1990b. Religion in the Roman empire: the civic compromise and its limits. In M. Beard and J. North (eds.) *Pagan Priests. Religion and Power in the Ancient World*. London, pp. 235–55.

Goudineau, C. 1980. Les villes de la paix romaine. In G. Duby (ed.) *L'Histoire de la France Urbaine. I La ville antique*. Paris, pp. 237–391.

Grenier, A. 1931–60. *Manuel d'Archéologie Gallo-Romaine.* Paris.

Grewe, K. 1988. Wasserleitungen nördlich der Alpen. In *Die Wasserversorgung antike Städte: Geschichte der Wasserversorgungen* 3. Mainz am Rhein, pp. 45–97.

Habinek, T. 1997. The invention of sexuality in the world-city of Rome. In T. Habinek and A. Schiesaro (eds.) *The Roman Cultural Revolution,* Cambridge, pp. 23–43.

Habinek, T. and Schiesaro, A. (eds.) 1997. *The Roman Cultural Revolution.* Cambridge.

Hardie, P. 1993. *The Epic Successors of Virgil. A study in the dynamics of a tradition.* Cambridge.

Hardie, P. 1997. Questions of authority: the invention of tradition in Ovid Metamorphoses 15. In T. Habinek and A. Schiesaro (eds.) *The Roman Cultural Revolution.* Cambridge, pp. 182–198.

Hill, J. D. 1997. 'The end of one kind of body and the beginning of another kind of body'? Toilet instruments and 'Romanization'. In A. Gwilt and C. Haselgrove (eds.) *Reconstructing Iron Age Societies.* Oxbow: Oxford, pp. 96–107.

Hobsbawm, E. and Ranger, T. (eds.) 1983. *The Invention of Tradition.* Cambridge.

Johns, C. 1996. *The Jewellery of Roman Britain. Celtic and classical traditions.* London.

Kremer, B. 1994. *Das Bild der Kelten bis in augusteische Zeit: Studien zur Instrumentalisierung eines antiken Feindbildes bei griechischen und römischen Autoren.* (Historia Einzelschriften 88) Stuttgart.

Küpper-Böhm, A. 1996. *Die römischen Bogenmonumente der Gallia Narbonensis in ihrem urbanen Kontext.* (Kölner Studien zur Archäologie der römischen Provinzen 3) Espelkamp.

Meadows, K. 1994. You are what you eat. Diet, identity and Romanization. In S. Cottam, D. Dungworth, S. Scott and J. Taylor (eds.) *TRAC 94. Proceedings of the Fourth Annual Theoretical Roman Archaeology Conference Durham 1994.* Oxford, pp. 132–40.

Metzler, J., Millett, M., Roymans, N. and Slofstra J. (eds.) 1995. *Integration in the Early Roman West. The role of culture and ideology.* (Dossiers d'Archéologie du Musée National d'Histoire et d'Art 4) Luxembourg.

Millett, M. 1990. *The Romanization of Britain. An essay in archaeological interpretation.* Cambridge.

Nicolet, C. 1988. *L'Inventaire du Monde. Géographie et Politique aux Origines de l'Empire Romain.* Paris [translated into English in 1991 as: *Geography, Space and Politics in the Early Roman Empire,* Ann Arbor].

Nielsen I. 1990. *Thermae et Balnea. The architecture and cultural history of Roman Baths.* Aarhus.

North, J. A. 1976. Conservatism and change in Roman Religion. *Papers of the British School at Rome* 44: 1–12.

North, J. A. 1989. The Roman Counter-revolution. *Journal of Roman Studies* 79: 151–56.

Piggott, S. 1968. *The Druids.* London.

Price, S. R. F. 1984. *Rituals and Power: the Roman imperial cult in Asia Minor.* Cambridge.

Purcell, N. 1985. Wine and wealth in ancient Italy. *Journal of Roman Studies* 75: 1–19.

Purcell, N. 1990. Maps, lists, money, order and power. *Journal of Roman Studies* 80: 178–82.

Rawson, E. 1985. *Intellectual Life in the Late Roman Republic.* London.

Reece, R. 1990. Romanization: a point of view. In T. F. C. Blagg and M. Millett (eds.) *The Early Roman Empire in the West.* Oxford, pp. 30–34.

Scheid, J. 1991. Sanctuaires et territoire dans la Colonia Augusta Treverorum. In J.-L. Brunaux (ed.) *Les sanctuaires celtiques et le monde méditerranéen.* (Dossiers de Protohistoire 3) Paris, pp. 42–57.

Sedley, D. 1997. The ethics of Brutus and Cassius. *Journal of Roman Studies* 87: 41–53.

Silberberg-Pierce, S. 1986. The many faces of the Pax Augusta: images of war and peace in Rome and Gallia Narbonensis. *Art History* 9: 306–24.

Terrenato, N. 1998. *Tam Firmum Municipium:* the Romanization of Volaterrae and its cultural implications. *Journal of Roman Studies* 88: 94–114.

Vickers, M. 1994. Nabataea, India, Gaul and Carthage: reflections on Hellenistic and Roman gold vessels and red-gloss pottery. *American Journal of Archaeology* 98: pp. 231–48.

Wallace-Hadrill, A. 1988. Greek Knowledge, Roman Power. *Classical Philology* 83: 224–233.

Wallace-Hadrill, A. 1989. Rome's cultural revolution. *Journal of Roman Studies* 79: 157–64.

Wallace-Hadrill, A. 1990. Roman arches and Greek honours: the language of power at Rome. *Proceedings of the Cambridge Philological Society* 36: 143–181.

Wallace-Hadrill, A. 1997. *Mutatio morum*: the idea of a cultural revolution. In T. Habinek and A. Schiesaro (eds.) *The Roman Cultural Revolution*. Cambridge, pp. 3–22.

Wallace-Hadrill, A. 1998. To be Roman, Go Greek. Thoughts on hellenization at Rome. In M. Austin, J. Harries and C. Smith (eds.) *Modus Operandi. Essays in honour of Geoffrey Rickman, Bulletin of the Institute of Classical Studies* (supplement 71) London, pp. 79–91.

Walker, S. 1997. Athens under Augustus. In M. C. Hoff and S. I. Rotroff (eds.) *The Romanization of Athens,*.Oxbow: Oxford, pp. 67–80.

Walter, H. 1993. *Les Barbares d'Occident romain*. (Annales Littéraires de l'Université de Besançon 494) Paris.

Ward-Perkins, J. B. 1970. From Republic to Empire: reflections on the early imperial provincial architecture of the Roman West. *Journal of Roman Studies* 60: 1–19.

Wilson, R. J. A 1996. Recent studies on Roman aqueducts and water supply. *Journal of Roman Archaeology* 6: 5–29.

Wood, M. and Queiroga, F. (eds.) 1992. *Current Research on the Romanization of the Western Provinces*, British Archaeological Reports International Series 575, Oxford.

Woolf, G. D. 1994. Becoming Roman, Staying Greek: Culture, Identity and the Civilizing Process in the Roman East. *Proceedings of the Cambridge Philological Society* 40: 116–43.

Woolf, G. D. 1995. The Formation of Roman Provincial Cultures. In J. Metzler, M. Millett, J. Slofstra and N. Roymans (eds.) *Integration in the Early Roman West. The role of culture and ideology*. Dossiers d'Archéologie du Musée National d'Histoire et d'Art 4, Luxembourg, pp. 9–18.

Woolf, G. D. 1996. The uses of forgetfulness in Roman Gaul. In H.-J.Gehrke and A. Möller (eds.) *Vergangenheit und Lebenswelt. Soziale Kommunikation, Traditionsbildung und historisches Bewußtsein*, ScriptOralia 90, Tübingen, pp. 361–81.

Woolf, G. D.1997. Beyond Romans and natives. *World Archaeology* 28: 339–50.

Woolf, G. D. 1998. *Becoming Roman. The origins of provincial civilization in Gaul*. Cambridge.

Yegül, F. 1992. *Baths and bathing in classical antiquity*. Cambridge, Mass.

Zanker, P. 1988. *The Power of Images in the age of Augustus*. Ann Arbor [German original published in 1987 as*: Augustus und die Macht der Bilder*. Munich].

Chapter 16

'Romanization' and the peoples of Britain

Simon James

Introduction

There are many significant resonances in current thinking between the cases of Roman Italy and Roman Britain, and the ways in which elements, at least, of their respective scholarly communities currently envisage the incorporation of their homelands into the Roman world. (For the nature and development of Romano-British studies, see Frere 1987, Salway 1981, and especially Millett 1990; see also Freeman 1997). Specifically, I have chosen to respond to the formulation presented here by Terrenato, which I seen as the most radically new and fruitful of the various interpretations which have come out of Italian scholarship in recent decades (for a summary, see Terrenato 1998b, 20–3; 1998c).

In his introduction to the Italian section of the present volume, Terrenato effectively presents a new, integrated model for the creation of Roman Italy. This emphasizes elite interaction and negotiation in explaining the mechanics of the entry of communities into the nascent empire – processes which I shall call 'incorporation events' (a neutral expression covering all the more loaded terms like 'conquest', 'annexation', 'federation' etc.). Equally, it presents the convergence of elite culture and values as central in explaining the durability and longevity of the Roman world which, paradoxically, is now seen to be regionally far more diverse than hitherto appreciated. These views, illustrated in his case study from Etruria (1998a) and in the present volume, are in many respects closely paralleled among British scholars looking at the Roman episode in their own country (notably, Millett 1990; some are also applying similar ideas to other provinces, e.g. Gaul: Woolf 1998). However, Terrenato's particular emphasis on 'elite negotiation' in the unification of Italy is a perspective I wish to explore for understanding the creation of Roman Britain.

There are two distinct but related issues to examine here:

- In explaining the establishment of Roman power and the course of cultural change in the western empire, how valid is the now widely-shared emphasis on two-way, if asymmetric, interaction between Roman and indigenous social elites as a (and perhaps the) fundamental factor?
- Is cultural change still best conceptualized as a process of 'Romanization'? Or is the concept too laden with the historical baggage of discredited assumptions to be of any specific value beyond Terrenato's minimal, 'weak' definition: 'a convenient

denomination covering the events involved in the creation of a new and unified political entity, disclaiming any assumption concerning the occurrence or the directionality of acculturation between Romans and non Romans' (Keay & Terrenato, this volume: i)? In Britain, a number of scholars are questioning the entire Romanization paradigm (e.g. Hingley 1996).

Comparisons of Roman archaeology in Italy and Britain

General parallels between the Italian and British cases are to be found in the organization of academic research, and the consequences of the drawing of inter-disciplinary boundaries, barriers often hindering the kind of holistic approach which Terrenato's formulation demands: considering Rome and her neighbours jointly. Britain, like Italy, exhibits a deep disciplinary division between prehistorians and Romanists (see Williams, this volume). Whereas British prehistorians have long drawn on anthropology, sociology and philosophy, developing processual and post-processual approaches, cultural-historical methods predominated in Romano-British studies until very recent times. In Britain, as in continental countries (Terrenato, this volume: 1), explanations of the expansion of Roman power traditionally focused on the unique qualities of Rome, not least due to overt or subliminal nationalist or imperialist identification with an idealized Roman past (Freeman 1997).

The last decade, especially, has seen major advances in the theoretical basis of Roman archaeology in Britain, manifested in the establishment of the annual university-based Theoretical Roman Archaeology Conference (TRAC), and in many session of the new biennial Roman Archaeology Conference (RAC) under the auspices of the Society for the Promotion of Roman Studies (the ninth TRAC and third RAC were held jointly in Durham in April 1999; a volume of papers is published following each TRAC, the most recent being Fincham *et al.* 2000). Yet despite increasing convergence of philosophy and methodology, there is still insufficient interaction between prehistorians and Romanists in Britain. This is partly due to deeply-felt emotional barriers: classically-trained scholars find the technical discourse of many prehistorians impenetrable, alienating and pretentious, while a prominent British Iron Age specialist recently said to me, 'I *hate* the Romans', and was less than half-joking. Such emotive reactions can be a powerful force constraining the course of research (James 1993b).

Moves by some scholars in both Italy and Britain to broaden the explanatory framework beyond traditional emphases on military power or economic processes, to include at least elements of the non-Roman peoples as key players in processes of incorporation and integration, have been broadly simultaneous, yet largely parallel and independent. However, both draw on theoretical developments in Anglo-American anthropology and prehistoric archaeology (for an accessible survey of major theoretical trends, see Johnson 1999). In the UK, the decisive shift was marked by Millett's *Romanization of Britain* (1990), the key synthetic text of the 1990s, which made indigenous elites central actors in the establishment of Roman provincial civilization. Henig (1998), and Creighton (2000, 2001) have gone further, in explaining the origins of the Roman province in terms of elite interaction and negotiation mechanisms similar to Terrenato's conception. Recently, more direct cross-fertilization has begun, as exemplified by the present volume.

Such convergent developments are partly due to similar discoveries from similar methodological approaches, not least in exploring rural settlement evidence; field survey has revolutionized our understanding of both countries, and much of that carried out in Italy has been of British execution or inspiration. Both Italy and Britain have seen the discovery of diverse pre-Roman and Roman cultural patterns in varied landscapes, less uniform than the former concentration on urban-biased evidence had suggested (e.g. Taylor 2001).

With regard to the picture from archaeology, of course there are also fundamental differences, not least in the nature of the data itself. Much of Britain was never annexed, while the province produces patterns of archaeological data very different from those typical of Italy: many traditional markers of Romanized life (towns, villas) are far sparser, while the quantity and – according to traditional judgements – the quality of material culture seem poorer. *Britannia* also lacks anything like the scale of epigraphic and prosopographic data seen in Italy. Consequently, effort has been concentrated where the data is rich, not least on rural settlement archaeology, so that in these aspects Iron Age and Roman Britain are currently better known than much of modern Italy, as Williams notes for Cisalpina (this volume). Nevertheless, the similarities in thinking remain compelling. In Britain, as in Italy, it is now clear that the development of Britain under Roman domination owed far more to indigenous traditions than traditional models of conquest and unidirectional acculturative Romanization would allow.

Prelude to incorporation: the Late Pre-Roman Iron Age in Britain

British scholarly treatment of Roman Britain long paralleled the tendency noted by Terrenato (this volume, Introduction) for earlier Italian historiography of Roman Italy, in playing down pre-existing regional identities. Despite the plethora of named peoples in classical texts, indigenous populations were treated as essentially all the same, as 'Ancient Britons', or 'Celts', 'tribal' distinctions being implicitly regarded as superficial. Only recently has reconceptualization of 'the Britons' begun.

Britain in the Iron Age (from around the seventh century BC) is no longer seen as part of a basically uniform 'Celtic' world. The traditional model of waves of continental La Tène Celtic invaders has been generally abandoned as a nineteenth century theory now discredited by rich archaeological testimony and more sophisticated theoretical frameworks (Gwilt and Haselgrove 1997; Hill 1995; James and Rigby 1997; James 1998; 1999a). Of course there are important similarities with the continent, including shared La Tène art and, later, southern Britain was deeply influenced by developments in Gaul. However, these relatively limited connections are best explained in terms of long-established contact and resultant cultural convergence between diverse indigenous societies rooted in local Late Bronze Age cultures.

Britain was a geographical unit, but not a uniform cultural or ethnic entity. It was home to a multiplicity of social formations, highly diverse in lifestyle, economy, material culture and social organization (Cunliffe 1991). The cultural map of the island was arguably as complex and dynamic as that of Italy before the rise of Rome, although it is unclear whether there was a similar degree of linguistic variation and self-defined 'ethnic' difference (Jones 1997). In the later Iron Age there is evidence for nascent, limited, regional cohesiveness between groups (see below), but not of much sense of overarching 'Britishness', as shown by the piecemeal pattern of polity-by-polity partial Roman annexation.

Societies in Britain also followed divergent trajectories of development. Like Italy, much of the island's topography tended to isolate populations; for most, life was small-scale and very local. Inter-group communications were at least as much outwards, across the seas, as overland across difficult terrain. Western and Northern societies were linked by the coastal routes from Atlantic Scotland to Biscay, while eastern and southern lowland regions looked across the Channel.

During the late pre-Roman Iron Age (hereafter LPRIA, c. 120 BC to AD 43), particularly in the 'Lowland Zone' of southern and eastern Britain, many polities underwent profound change in material culture and ways of life, with great expansion in the number of rural settlements, and innovations ranging from new crops and more intensive farming regimes to the introduction of regional coinages. New attitudes to the body and identity are reflected in, for examples, elaboration of brooches and the appearance of toilet instruments (Hill 1997), and new burial rites. All this was intimately bound up with substantial population growth, increasing specialization and social differentiation, culminating in the appearance of very rich individual interments (e.g. Colchester, Lexden: Foster 1986; Crummy 1997b: 22–5; Colchester, Stanway: Crummy 1997a; 1997b: 23, 26–7; Verulamium, Folly Lane: Niblett 1999). These correlate with nascent aristocracies and the dynasts named in the Classical sources and on coins. The decades preceding the Claudian intervention also saw the appearance of major new sites, '*oppida*', broadly analogous to the continental centres known by the same name (Woolf 1993a). Shaping these innovations were more intensive contacts with the peoples of Gaul, who were taking such developments farther and faster than the polities of southern Britain.

By the last century BC Lowland Britain formed one end of a band stretching across Europe north of the Alps which, while in growing contact with Rome, was not merely under the influence of the Classical world; the process of accelerating regional change it exhibited arose from internal dynamics, and was underway before major contact with the Roman Mediterranean began. It drew on the Mediterranean as a useful source of goods and ideas for which it was developing internal needs (James 1993a: 120–1). In large parts of lowland Britain, as in Italy, a major degree of cultural and political convergence between societies preceded and facilitated Roman annexation (as Haselgrove has suggested for Belgic Gaul, 1990: 45–6).

Older ideas about large-scale migration from Gaul have fallen out of favour, due to evidence of strong local continuity and lack of identifiable material correlates for major intrusions. Small-scale, and especially elite movements best explain the meagre and contradictory literary tradition. Caesar claimed the inhabitants of Britain were mostly indigenous with some coastal immigration and settlement (*BG* 5.12; 5.14), while Diodorus Siculus described them as autochthonous (5.21). Strabo makes no statement about their origins, while Tacitus speculates about their possible origins purely on the basis of alleged similarities with other peoples (*Ag.* 11). Nevertheless, Gaulish cultural influence in LPRIA lowland Britain was very marked, perhaps representing Gallic cultural and even political hegemony, 'Gallicization' on the analogy of the acculturative notion of Romanization, and as a precedent for it. However, as with 'Romanization', the very construction of a term like 'Gallicization' implies a predominately one-way flow, situating southern Britain as essentially peripheral to and dependent on continental developments (James and Rigby 1997: 72). While in many respects the island was indeed the recipient of continental innovations, there is good reason to see cross-Channel processes as developing into a truly bidirectional interchange, although the cultural relationship may have remained asymmetric. It might be better construed as slightly belated participation of the nearer British polities in a zone of cultural convergence among transalpine societies already broadly similar. Caesar's account suggests that there were significant British cultural and political 'invisible exports', such as Druidism and mercenary manpower (Caesar *BG* 6.13; 4.20), while in terms of dynastic politics, the Channel lands constituted a true interaction zone (see below).

Southern Britain's convergent relations with the continent form a precedent and unwitting preparation for incorporation into the Roman world; or, to reject 'Romanocentrism', the imperial episode may be seen from an insular perspective as constituting a development, albeit a redirection, of pre-existing processes. Most pertinent to the present discussion, it seems to me that there are striking and instructive parallels between this model of a zone of cultural convergence North of Alps which included Lowland Britain, and the model which Terrenato has synthesized for Italy before and during the rise of Rome.

This Italian model envisages two stages: first, before urbanization fully developed, powerful, deeply interconnected aristocracies established themselves; and later, broadly coincident with the 'Hellenistic' period, oligarchic city-states in Italy and beyond began to accrete into larger entities, and were then definitively united under Rome. Archaeologically, Italy attests a series of widespread phenomena, which express these cultural interactions. To (over)simplify, the 'Orientalising' and later 'Hellenising' and 'Hellenistic' tendencies in the archaeology appear to represent the interaction of powerful elites through an increasingly standardized, shared culture, which expressed their convergent interests and values. For such groups connections with their peers in neighbouring polities were as important as vertical links within their own, which as a whole often retained much of their traditional organization and culture throughout (Terrenato, this volume, Three cities; 1998a). Further, widespread expansion of rural settlement, which Terrenato links broadly with the 'Hellenistic' phase, represents a profound shift in life and economy which may have helped facilitate the spread of Roman power, rather than resulting from it (Terrenato: 63). A remarkably similar sequence of cultural development can be identified in the zone from the English Channel lands to the Alps, running parallel with, if slightly later than, these Mediterranean processes. Southern Britain, for example, also saw a dramatic intensification of agriculture and rise in the density of rural settlement, broadly synchronic with the appearance of increasingly hierarchical societies, controlled by powerful interacting elites by the time Rome appeared on the scene. Italy and much of the Mediterranean world on the one hand, and a swathe of Transalpine Europe reaching to southern Britain on the other, each constituted a zone of intimately 'networked', largely aristocratic polities, expanding in population and moving towards greater internal complexity, including state formation (although how far the northern zone was truly urbanizing is disputed: Woolf, 1993a).

There is reason to think that, as in Italy, interaction and convergence between elites, across polity and 'ethnic' boundaries, were central to the development of this Transalpine world. Such links provide a satisfying alternative explanation for the nature, and the remarkable geographical distribution, of La Tène artefacts during the Iron Age. The dissemination of La Tène art and material culture across much of Europe from the fifth century BC onwards can be seen as analogous to the 'Orientalising' and 'Hellenising' phases of Italy. La Tène art is largely to be found on personal items relating to martial and ritual display and consumption, which on this model represent the shared culture of emerging political and religious elites across a wide area of Europe; they were for mutually-intelligible symbolic displays of status within societies, and for exchanges which maintained kinship, alliance and clientage links between elites. They are not an indicator of common 'Celtic' ethnicity or mass migrations at all, any more than the widespread adoption of Hellenistic material culture in the Mediterranean beyond specifically Greek *poleis* is taken to represent uniform ethnicity of its users, let alone Greek 'invasions' (James 1999, 93).

Classical texts on southern Britain and Gaul clearly describe elite interactions closely similar to those attested in Archaic and Classical Italy, including cases of aristocratic migration (e.g. Commius, below), and examples of nobles whose personal ambitions disregarded 'ethnic' boundaries (e.g. Dumnorix of the Gallic Aedui: Caesar, *BG* 1.3–4; 1.9; 1.18; Orgetorix of the Helvetii: Caesar, *BG* 1.2–4). Elite power networks spanned the Channel, allowing the Gallic Atrebatic prince Commius to establish himself as a king in Britain in the Caesarian period (albeit probably with Roman support: Creighton 2000, 2001). A century later, the ability of the Catuvellaunian prince Caratacus to establish authority in Wales suggests the existence of elite networks across Britain (Tacitus, *Ann.* 12.33–6). If it is historical, the power of Diviciacus of the Suessiones on both sides of the Channel well before Caesar (*BG* 2.4) suggests these were not simply cases of new behaviour in the face of encroaching Roman power.

'Tribal' polities were also tending to accrete into larger associations exhibiting considerable asymmetries of power, under the hegemony of stronger peoples in Gaul such as the Arverni, Bituriges, and at the time of Caesar the Aedui and Sequani (Caesar, *BG* 6.11–12). The case of Diviciacus is an interesting indication that the Southern Britons, like the Gauls, were familiar with the idea of supra-group connections, even spanning the sea, before Caesar. Federation into larger groupings, voluntary or not, was thus thinkable in these areas *before* Rome arrived, as it was in much of Italy and the Aegean world while Rome was still just one city state; the various Italian leagues, the hegemonic empires of Athens and Sparta, and the territorial expansion of Macedon all reveal these tendencies.

Terrenato's formulation for Italy, then, also provides a valuable model for understanding many northern polities as far as southern Britain, their relations, and their compatibility with the growing Roman empire. Rome–or more precisely, Roman senatorial families, and later the Julio-Claudian house–was becoming directly linked into the northern elite network from the 120s BC, when friendly relations with the Aedui were instigated. From Caesar's time the Romans were dominant players.

The partial incorporation of Britain, 55 BC to the second century AD

Due to their own internal dynamics, then, LPRIA societies of lowland Britain and many adjacent regions were undergoing major changes, not least in scale of organization and social differentiation. These resulted in a network of polities, structurally similar in key respects to that of Roman Italy. Just as Rome proved to have qualities uniquely suited to exploiting this situation in Italy, so with relatively little adaptation she was able to work in much the same way in this northern zone as well, leading to the successful political assimilation of many transalpine societies. We might now reorient our perspective, drawing on the Italian model described above by Terrenato, and suggest that, as in Italy, in many polities as far as Britain, aristocratic regimes—or at least factions within nobilities—actively *sought* engagement with Rome.

I long envisaged the establishment of Roman power in southern Britain as an 'imperial confidence trick' or 'protection racket' which was half-blackmail, half-bribery, and in which local nobles were given some compensation for acquiescing. On this view, once direct military resistance proved futile, active belligerents capitulated, fled, or were liquidated, while other groups came to terms simply because they had no choice. This does not allow for the possibility that some aristocrats may have seen the arrival of the Romans as, on balance, a 'good thing' – at least for themselves, and perhaps paternalistically as good for their subordinate communities. For there is no evidence that Rome conquered certain British polities at all; their regimes may have been amenable to incorporation. This is not to deny that many others resisted, or even that the majority of the population would have preferred to stay out (see below). However, many British nobles may have found *rapprochement* much to their liking, as the better-documented cases of the Gallic Aedui or Remi suggest. I realize my own attitude resulted from assuming that the Romans were worldly military bullies, the Britons rural indigenes innocent of the realities of the wider world who would 'naturally' have preferred independence. This was clearly a colonialist hangover rooted ultimately in Tacitean-derived portrayals of poor, duped, savage yet innocent and noble Britons (e.g. Tac. *Ag.* 11, 13 and especially 21). Terrenato's model of elite negotiation is less asymmetric, and permits the indigenes involved often to have a more knowing and active role in incorporation.

In the limited documentary evidence for Britain, cases such as that of Verica (Cassius Dio, 60.19) are entirely consistent with the idea of elite-negotiated incorporation of polities. It now seems clear that much of southern Britain was effectively under Roman hegemony from Caesar's time, even if not directly controlled, and that the effects of this on at least some elite groups before 43 AD were far more profound that we had allowed for (Creighton 2000, 2001). We have been long aware of the connections of British princes and the imperial house, but usually emphasis has been on the Roman exploitation of the 'grievances' of individuals such as Verica as a pretext for *bellum iustum* (Whittaker 1996: 34); however, it now seems that members of British elites may have been far more cosmopolitan in terms not only of Gallo-Roman but of Italian-Roman society, politics and culture than we have usually allowed, even though we have long known some of them visited Rome itself and were in close contact with the emperor. They may be presumed to have been affected by the imperial ideological shifts which matured in the Augustan period (Woolf 1995; 1998). The Claudian incursion may therefore initially have been more the consolidation of long-established hegemonic power than a new military aggression (Henig 1998; Creighton 2000, 2001). The key role of client kingdoms in the early history of the Roman province, and particularly the eventual peaceful incorporation of the large southern state ruled by Cogidubnus, provide further testimony for successful elite negotiation.

Why might incorporation have seemed so attractive to some British nobles and dynasts? As in Italy, the promise of engagement and influence on a wider imperial stage, and potential access to greater wealth, are plausible aims; however, the very limited evidence for Britons embarking on careers in imperial service and politics suggests more local concerns were paramount. For Italy, it has been argued that a significant factor was security for nobles in societies where personal power was vital, and where peer-group conflict or unrest from below could bring disaster and exile to aristocratic families. Perceived disadvantages of Roman domination were evidently outweighed in the eyes of many by guarantees of support, sanctioned by law and backed if needed by the army. The attraction to established oligarchic families of such political stabilization is obvious; Roman rule guaranteed their own power at the local level, probably for the first time. It thereby secured, perhaps even fossilized, many aspects of the extant social order. It was much the same in Southern Britain and Gaul, where aristocratic or royal power was highly personal and dynastic ambitions were often demonstrably more important than local 'ethnic' ties, while any sense of 'national' identity was weakly developed. Gauls like Dumnorix and Diviciacus of the Aedui, and the Helvetian Orgetorix were happy to make private alliances outside their own peoples (*BG* 1.2–4), while regimes negotiated or intrigued with Germans (the Sequani: *BG* 1.31; 6.12) and Romans (the Aedui: *BG* 6.12). British dynasts like Adminius and Verica similarly treated with the imperial house for advantage in domestic politics and war. In Britain, among networked nobilities already accustomed to alliance and tributary relations spanning the Channel, the choice of overlord, familiar and nearby or distant, imperial and alien, evidently raised few 'patriotic' qualms.

It is clear enough that LPRIA British aristocrats would find attractions in access to Roman troops as a guarantee of their personal power. Indeed, the polities they sought to control appear to have been more unstable than the relatively settled mosaic of city-states which appeared in sixth century Italy. At least some British 'tribes' and 'petty kingdoms' may not have been self-aware 'ethnic' units at all, but personal fiefs welded by dynastic unions or carved out by conquest and tribute. Many appear to have been highly volatile, unstable superstructures only recently developing on top of the intense regionality of the British Iron Age; almost all the 'tribal' names recorded by Caesar (*BG* 5.20–1) vanished by the time of the Claudian intervention, just a century later.

Looking from Britain back to Italy, and generalising, we can now turn traditional views of Roman expansion on their head, and suggest that, as much as Rome *drove* into these regions for her own internal purposes, she was (increasingly willingly) *drawn* into areas with social formations of certain kinds, where her presence was felt more desirable than not by factions of the politically powerful. Such a view sees Roman expansion as built on a basic compatibility, and powerful resultant interaction, between the Roman system, and processes in nearby societies which were fundamentally autonomous in origin.

Romanization(s) and Britain

It can be argued, then, that the success of the Roman province of Southern Britain was for reasons similar to those responsible for the solidity of the Roman hold of Italy, namely the perception of shared interests between imperial power and local elites, and the widespread survival and continued resilience – even consolidation – of existing sociopolitical structures (even if these were reformulated through 'cultural bricolage': Terrenato 1998b). The lowland aristocracies of Britain were 'networked' into the empire through their long-standing ties of kinship, clientage and alliance with the Gallic nobility, and through these–and more directly through the personal links established with the Julio-Claudian house during Caesar's interventions–they were also connected into the Italian system (Creighton 2000, 2001).

As we have seen above, with regard to the elite convergence which constitutes the heart of this process, in many ways southern Britain was already engaged before the establishment of the province, and rapidly started to catch up with Gaul. It is especially noteworthy that some of the earliest developments, e.g. in urbanization, were made not in the Roman province *per se*, but in the southern client kingdom, at Silchester and at Chichester with its remarkable Italianate 'palace' at nearby Fishbourne (Cunliffe 1971; 1996).

In southern Britain, then, we see a pattern basically analogous to that of Italy. Analogous but not identical, following slightly different rules, with no great development of the epigraphic habit, its urbanization based more on collegiate effort than individual competitive euergetism and exhibiting more emphasis on religious than secular public buildings. Yet there were also far more fundamental divergences between the cases of Italy and Britain, for so far we have concentrated on only the southern (and especially the south-eastern) part of the island. Elsewhere, the situation was very different (Bevan 1999).

Perhaps the most profound contrast between Italy and Britain is that annexation of the latter was only partial; the process of territorial incorporation halted roughly halfway up the island, which thereafter retained a permanent internal military frontier and political divide, resulting in a pattern of responses to, and experiences of, Roman civilization across the island far more varied than that in the peninsula.

Late in the first century AD, major wars in other provinces meant that direct administration, which in the 80s had been extended north of the river Tay, contracted, and the army withdrew into northern England and the Borders. Much of Scotland remained thereafter beyond the direct reach of Rome, despite later campaigning. From Chester and York up to roughly the modern Scottish border, besides parts of Wales, the middle region of the island was henceforth permanently dominated by the Roman military.

Consequently, in a sense Britain contained a complete radial cross-section through the Roman world, from a fully integrated civil province in the south, to entirely 'free' *barbaricum* in the far north, with liminal zones between. The Romano-British case discussed above constituted just one of several regional patterns within the island. We can suggest the provisional definition of a number of zones which followed different historical trajectories:

1   the civil province, roughly equating to the 'Lowland Zone' of the South and East
2   the directly occupied and controlled military zone, comprising most of the 'Highland Zone' up to and beyond Hadrian's Wall, extending for periods up to the Forth-Clyde line

3   the '*Limesvorland*', i.e. nearby areas of *barbaricum* under military surveillance and in close contact with the Roman province and the imperial authorities
4   'Free' areas, less accessible to Roman intervention or interaction, such as the Caledonian Highlands and islands. Ireland might usefully be considered part of this zone.

'It appears clearly… that [while] the ruling elites of many urbanized communities play a major role in the process of expansion, … equivalents in less structured or non-sedentary ethnic groups, faced with the same prospect, often oppose a fierce fight.' (Terrenato, this volume, Introduction). These comments are relevant to the cases of Zones 3 and 4, outside the occasionally shifting bounds of the province. Like those of Samnium, Liguria, Gallia Cisalpina and Germany, the peoples of Upland Britain were evidently not amenable to incorporation. However, whether they were 'less structured', or elaborated on lines incompatible with Roman structures, is debatable. These societies either were not organized in the oligarchic manner required for successful interaction or, if they were, for some reason were not linked into the essential social networks which bound their peers inside the Roman empire. At least, they saw no advantage in *rapprochement* and integration, but chose resistance and independence (although the later appearance of larger 'barbarian' federations, such as the *Picti*, probably reflects long-term socio-political effects of contact with Rome). More detailed consideration of why these groups *actually* resisted incorporation is needed for a complete picture, and will throw light on why others co-operated, but space precludes further discussion here.

The territorial province of *Britannia* is conventionally considered to comprise two distinctly different regions: the self-governing *civitates* of the lowlands, the already-discussed heart of the civil province (Zone 1), and the military-dominated uplands (Zone 2). It has long been obvious that these regions exhibit very different patterns of development. It is argued here that they exhibit at least two contrasting types or mechanisms of 'Romanization', one of which does not correspond at all to the 'elite negotiation and convergence' model.

As we have seen the Italian-derived model works in Zone 1, the South, where the civil province broadly coincided with those lowland polities which had been part of the Transalpine elite network. But it works much less well for the North and West of the province. In Zone 2 there was no rush to urbanism. Civil towns are sparse and small (e.g. Brough, Aldborough), while in the countryside there are few 'villas'; the overwhelming majority of the orthogonal masonry rural residences regarded as villas in Britain are found in regions of the lowland zone. There is also relatively little evidence for Roman material culture reaching many of the plentiful indigenous-style rural settlements. All this is not just due to poorer agricultural potential or other such determinants; as in the South, many regions saw considerable settlement densities achieved by the Roman period. Much of the difference demands a cultural explanation.

It is clear that in Zone 2, the 'normal' model of integration through amenable factions of the indigenous elites did not occur to any great degree; the documentary and archaeological correlates for the usual pattern are meagre compared with the South. Was this because of basic social differences between the two regions, as postulated (but not proved) for Zones 3 and 4? Perhaps, in contrast with the lowland polities which underwent rapid and extensive change in interaction with Gaul, upland societies, while also changing, did not develop clearly-defined aristocracies—and so were less amenable to the elite interaction model. Or was the difference within the province actually a side-effect of Rome's failure to annexe the peoples of Scotland?

It has been suggested that the extent of underlying social differences between North and South may be exaggerated, and that at least some areas of the North had embarked on the 'normal' pattern of civil development; Millett argues that Stanwick and Traprain Law, for examples, show nascent centralization but did not grow into towns, the development of such centres being stunted by the unforeseen reappearance and permanent establishment of the army in Northern England and the Borders (Millett pers. comm.). Garrison commanders and other officers, as direct imperial agents, constituted a *de facto* power structure which undercut, and perhaps effectively replaced, indigenous elites. In my view, it is likely that the establishment among indigenous populations of the army – or, to see it from a social rather than institutional viewpoint, of substantial, relatively wealthy and self-contained communities of soldiers and their dependants (James 1999b: 23–4) – resulted not in the aborting of 'Romanization' *per se*, but in another *type* of 'Romanization' structured on principles entirely different from those shared in Southern Britain, Gaul and Italy.

In some ways, the overtly Roman archaeology of the military zone is actually more like that of Italy than is the civil province, for example in the extent of stone construction, and in the scale of use of epigraphy. This is because, to a far greater degree than the cities of the South, it was created by immigrant Roman citizens – some from Italy but mostly their provincial-born descendants – and by other provincials immersed in an overtly Roman military culture directly preserving Italian traditions. Regiments were also commanded by Italians and provincials of equestrian and senatorial rank with Roman elite values and education. However, these officers only spent relatively short periods in command and, to a large extent, were socially isolated by rank from their men. The permanent garrisons consisted overwhelmingly of long-term enlisted men of less exalted backgrounds who formed another peculiar Roman world of their own; this military culture was in origin a narrow, largely plebeian, and specialized aspect or version of Roman culture, and became increasingly distinctive. Soldiers looked to their *commilitones* in other frontier provinces, not to metropolitan or elite cultural values, in expressing an identity at once self-consciously Roman, yet also highly provincialized; that of the *milites*. I suggest that the soldiers constituted the heart of another mechanism of 'Romanization' in the provinces, distinct from and more plebeian than 'elite negotiation'-based processes, and more important in some permanent frontier zones. This will be discussed in more detail elsewhere (James 2001).

Britain 'became Roman', then, in more distinct ways than the elite negotiation/ convergence model allows, highlighting one limitation of the latter in explaining observed cultural change in the provinces. It seems to me that there are others at least as significant.

General reflections on the 'elite negotiation model'

Of course, as Terrenato would be the first to admit, any scheme such as the Italian elite negotiation model is only a partial and inevitably incomplete description of a process as prolonged, vast and complex as the formation of the Roman world. It may be as informative, and thought-provoking, to examine the places where it does not fit the evidence (as in northern parts of the British province), as those where it does; and even where the model appears to be valid and of great explanatory power, other aspects of the evidence may highlight its limitations, and perhaps provide pointers to how it may be built on. There follow some critical reflections from a British perspective on Roman studies, as well as in the light of Romano-British research in particular, on the value of the notion of elite negotiation.

The role of violence

Terrenato is unquestionably right to say that 'an interpretation based solely on army, taxation and coinage' is insufficient to explain what created and maintained the empire (Terrenato, this volume, Introduction); however, equally unsatisfactory is any interpretation which plays down the role of coercion too far. Despite his direct attempt to deal with critique focusing on this (*supra*), in my view the elite negotiation formulation continues to underplay the significance of violence, repressive or resistant, from the symbolic and implicit to the threatened and the lethal.

While the case for the profound importance of negotiation in the creation of the empire is well made, I believe it would be a mistake to base our 'default' reconstruction of the process on it, as a *replacement* for 'war, repression and struggle'. Rather, I think it may be argued that negotiation and repressive violence are two major factors – perhaps the two key factors – which almost always *both* operated simultaneously in shaping 'incorporation events'; we are simply arguing about their roles, and relative importance, in each unique case. For example, even in the obliteration of Veii – the archetypal case of Roman military ferocity against another polity – there are signs of the survival and incorporation of some prominent Veientine families into the Roman citizen body, representing some degree of 'negotiated' incorporation (Torelli 1982).

British cases show negotiation and violence both in action during the course of incorporation events. Roman dealings with the Iceni saw initially successful negotiation (Prasutagus as client king) followed by extreme violence (Prasutagus' widow Boudica as leader of a huge revolt which cost tens of thousands of lives: Tacitus, *Ann.* 14,31–8). The resistance of the Silures resulted in virtual genocide, if Tacitus is to be believed (Tacitus, *Ann.* 12,39). However, in both examples the Romans were ultimately successful in negotiating peaceful incorporation with (presumably) amenable indigenous factions; both peoples subsequently formed moderately successful and apparently stable civil communities within the province.

Coercion surely played a part even in many nominally peacefully-negotiated cases, in that elements in the society to be incorporated allied themselves with the imperial power, while others – the majority – were not consulted. Even if this was effected without recourse to formal warfare (such as an invasion to 'restore a rightful ruler' like Verica, the nominal *casus belli* for the Claudian expedition), nonetheless it surely still involved a great deal of non-martial violence, symbolic or actual, to enforce the 'new order' against dissident aristocratic factions or popular discontent. The difference is that the violence here is relabelled, as 'internal security measures' and 'judicial punishment' on one side, while on the other, instances of active resistance were (and are) portrayed as 'criminal activity' or 'brigandage' (for a critical view of the '*pax Romana*' see Woolf 1993b).

The over-concentration on elites

While, under the elite negotiation model, the ruling groups of the incorporated peoples become active agents in integration, such an approach all too easily leaves the mass of the population out of account, or at best includes them as a passive herd. An illustration of this tendency is to be found in Terrenato's introductory discussion of the case of Italy itself, where he ventures to suggest '... that the new federation existed only because the majority (although by no means the totality) of Italians were in favour or neutral about it.' (Terrenato, this volume, Introduction). Surely this ignores the probability that the majority of the people as a whole were not neutral but neutralized, disempowered, especially when, on this model, the elites – often only factional noble regimes – acquired access to 'federal security forces' (Roman troops) to suppress any dissent.

In the present volume Keay and Woolf, as well as Terrenato, also largely skirt around the role of the non-elite majority as, up to this point, I have myself. It seems to me that this tendency largely derives from the implicit assumption that it is what happens at the top of society, between the politically prominent, that should take priority in our understandings of past polities. These historically and archaeologically most visible groups, and the large-scale interactions and processes they were engaged in, are seen as more significant than action at the small-scale, local level, especially among the unprivileged.

This focus on aristocrats is partly justified, at least by Woolf for Gaul, through arguing that their agenda demanded and determined changes in the rest of society as well: 'Certainly the main actors in the processes discussed... were all members of various elites, but these elites made use of their social power to construct the physical and imaginative environments within which other Gallo-Romans were compelled to live' (Woolf, this volume: 179). Indeed, *in the processes discussed*, 'Romanization' or the 'Roman cultural revolution' really was about elite views and actions. But do these constitute a valid and adequate treatment of the nature and mechanisms of cultural change?

Especially for provincial elites, the changes brought about by incorporation into the empire were only partly about 'becoming Roman' *per se*. While they were accepting, internalising and helping to create a Roman-defined universe, precisely because this was to apply to everyone living under imperial power, it was *distinctions within* that Roman universe – those features which expressed their privileged standing in the new order – which were particularly important to them.

Through euergetistic provision of public buildings and staging of public events in cities, and taking on civic offices, local elites helped to create the physical environments and manifestations of the ideal Roman order. Through the creation and control of this cultural capital they actively helped to found and maintain a political order and ideological hegemony which guaranteed and validated their privileges. They established their credentials for membership of the homogenizing ruling strata of this Graeco-Roman world by enjoying the appropriate lifestyle and cultural trappings in town and country. It was acquisition of that quite exclusive knowledge of largely Greek arts and letters, and possession of those tastes and sensibilities that marked out the cultivated insiders – the quality of *humanitas* – which set elites apart from the common herd (Woolf 1998: 54–60). Thus aristocrats redefined, newly rationalized, 'naturalized' and reinforced existing social divides, expressing their distinction from their subordinates through new symbols of exclusion.

For while they themselves became Roman, so did others; and while possession of Roman-citizenship was long a significant privilege in the provinces, it was one shared with members of non-elite groups, ex-slaves and common soldiers, from Italy and soon from the provinces themselves. By 100 AD any time-expired Thracian, Iberian or Batavian auxiliary became a Roman citizen, with minimal exposure to the original Italian cultural matrix of 'Roman-ness'. To be Roman was formally a legal status, not an ethnic or even necessarily a cultural identity; one could be legally Roman, without assimilating traditional Roman *mores*, as the examples of Arminius (Vell. 2.118) and St. Paul (*Acts* 22–28) make abundantly clear. To be Roman in a Roman world was desirable, then, and initially a considerable privilege, but for aristocrats it was not enough on its own; one also had to express one's superiority within that universe.

Indeed, 'Roman-ness' was curiously little emphasized in the documentary record. It is surely highly significant that there was no term to describe any such concept in republican or early imperial Latin; the word '*romanitas*', much bandied around in the secondary literature today but never properly defined, is not attested until around AD 200 (Tertullian, *de Pallio*, 4: thanks to Louise Revell, pers. comm., for highlighting this important point; see Woolf, this volume, for more detailed discussion). '*Romanitas*' is essentially a modern conceptual fiction, projecting anachronistic nationalist notions of a shared, class-transcendent community identity into a past where they hardly existed.

Many of the cultural and political changes we have described as manifesting 'Romanization', then, were indeed about elite power, distinction, and exclusivity within a universe presented as Roman defined, and Roman-dominated. They were intended to situate and confine the bulk of the population within Rome's universal hegemony, but to *exclude* most (poorer citizens, provincials and slaves) from its inner circle – those who possessed *humanitas*. Yet even in their own terms, the elite formed only part of the Roman universe. While the masses, urban or rural, free or servile, were not conceptualized as active participants in its building, they were nonetheless also part of that world.

In our elite-focused models of cultural change under Rome, we have essentially adopted the Roman elite perspective, and largely ignore any other factors – or actors. Such an approach effectively denies agency to anyone outside the elite. Others are represented as passively receptive, and are not considered as actively contributing to the changes under discussion (although Terrenato, in presenting the process of elite negotiation as partly about securing aristocracies from the threat of subordinate resistance, implicitly admits an active, non-consensual role for others). This conception reflects shortcomings common in 'systemic' approaches, which often treat human agency inadequately, not least in over-focusing on the roles of elites in oiling the wheels of social development while showing much less interest in subordinate groups. They also tend to minimize the role and significance of conflict in their concentration on larger-scale processes (Johnson 1999: 76, 78, 82–4; see above).

Cultural change among the bulk of provincial populations is largely conceived as emulative, or the result of 'trickle-down' and passive acceptance; but was it? If we accept that the societies under discussion were typically hierarchical (generally demonstrable in Italy, and consistent with the evidence for many regions as far as southern Britain), wider knowledge of such societies suggests we must include subordinate 'sub-cultures' too, as active – if relatively constrained – participants in determining the course of overall cultural change. In thought and deed, no society is entirely governed by the hegemonic agenda of the dominant. For, even in hierarchical, deference societies, people of the 'lower orders' are rarely, if ever, docile automata but are significant, at least partially autonomous agents with their own views of the world. To some degree they resist and constrain, as well as facilitate, the actions of their 'betters'.

In eighteenth-century England, for example, the social order was regulated through deference to church and crown preached from pulpits which formed the ideological rationale for acquiescence to the *status quo*. Yet the masses made themselves felt, especially in London; the period was marked by fear of the mob, and frequent rioting. However, rioting actually followed quite strict, if of course unwritten and unarticulated rules, implicitly understood by all (Porter 1990: 100–105). It was tacitly tolerated to a degree (indeed, it could not be prevented), and it acted as a safety-valve; it never developed into revolution. The social system allowed for, and was partially constrained by, a significant degree of dissent and resistance from the poor. The influence of subordinate groups, and the constraints they could place on the actions of elites, are likewise seen in the history of Rome itself, from the struggle of patricians and plebeians in the early republic, to the role of mobs and of semi-private legions drawn from the urban proletariat in the clash of *'optimates'* and *'populares'* in the last century BC. To be sure, the power of the masses was channelled by nobles in these cases, but that power was a real and terrifying factor in metropolitan Roman life; it helped precipitate the collapse of the senatorial oligarchy and the establishment of imperial rule. Autonomous action of non-elite groups only occasionally appears in the aristocratic classical literature on the provinces, and then in cases where it exceeded tolerable bounds, as in the rural disturbances of the *bagaudae* in third-century Gaul (which Drinkwater argues reflect local disruption of established hierarchical social relations: 1989: 198–9). However, beyond these extreme manifestations, and perhaps far more significant for models of social change, we must recognize that in the Roman world even the poorest and slaves were able routinely to exercise control over some aspects of their own lives, and were active decision-makers, even if their knowledge and power were far more circumscribed than those of elites.

Further, most of the daily transactions of living were conducted between themselves, according to their own values, with little or no regard to their superiors (see next section). To pursue the analogy of eighteenth-century England (where aristocrats often consciously modelled themselves on republican or imperial Roman figures), E. P. Thompson has pointed out that when strongly hierarchical societies are truly viewed from the 'bottom up', what was happening at the big house was of little interest to, and little seen by, the mass of the people, who pursued their own ways (Thompson 1978: 135–6). The same argument applies to Roman villas.

Ordinary people also made decisions in routine negotiation of their reciprocal duties and responsibilities with their superiors – almost always a genuinely two-way relationship, even if highly asymmetric. They conducted these dealings according to local agendas, within the framework of local society, according to (perhaps long-established) local relations of power, which might involve conflict as much as reciprocity. While Terrenato has usefully pointed out that paternalism and the sense of security given by traditional hierarchical structures could have a positive value to subordinates, particularly in time of intensive change, e.g. through patrons protecting dependants from external threats

(Terrenato 1998a: 108–10), we must be also wary of adopting too rosy a view of conservative paternalist societies (Thompson 1978: 135–6).

The recent incorporation of provincial elites as active agents in models of the creation of the Roman world, then, does not *remove* the boundary between the active and powerful and the supposedly passively-receptive dominated; it simply shifts it, from the interface between the Roman empire and 'native' societies, to the divide between the culturally-convergent Italian and provincial elites, and the mass of the population. This hardly constitutes a 'bottom-up' view to contrast with the top-down, centre-outwards conceptions of the Roman world which prevailed in the past (*pace* Keay, this volume). In class-divided societies like those of the Roman world (Giddens 1984: 182–4), active negotiation and conflict between classes, as well as between elites, is an important area to be examined, yet one still largely omitted from current elite-focused models of the empire. It is important to seek a truly holistic view of the societies in question, not least by including truly 'bottom upwards' perspectives (see below).

The range of processes effecting cultural change in the Roman world
While the notion of a widespread convergence of the nature of polities and of elites on a common Graeco-Roman culture has great utility, any general model of cultural change must take into account other important modes and levels of interaction, and also the question of regional variation and diversity within and between component societies, the depths of which are proving even greater than we suspected. If we are to test, refine or replace our current approaches, of course we have to explore the nature of this complexity. In particular, it may be useful to distinguish between mechanisms of integration which were radial/centripetal (between the imperial regime and metropolitan 'core', and provincial societies), and complex patterns of cultural change and convergence between the many components of the empire which constituted more of a network.

Imperial cult and ideology, and convergence between Italian and provincial elites, were not the only radial mechanism of cultural transmission. For example, we have also looked at non-elite 'Roman-ness' moving 'radially' to frontier provinces like Britain through the 'migration' of ordinary soldiers, establishing a more plebeian Roman cultural tradition around the frontiers. This military-based 'expatriate Roman-ness', largely cut off from the original Italian cultural matrix, and permanently established among many other cultural groupings from which it increasingly replenished its ranks, developed along lines very different from Italy or trans-provincial elite culture (see above).

Conversely, some cultural traits which became universal in the later empire, such as male dress conventions, moved 'centripetally' from origins both provincial/peripheral and 'lowly'. By the fourth century AD, long breeches, long-sleeved tunics and cloaks were widely worn by males across the Roman empire, but in the first century such an ensemble had been confined to northern provincials and 'barbarians'. Yet, particularly via recruitment of such men into the armies, this style of dress spread through the ranks and across the empire; by AD 200 the dress even of legionaries was overwhelmingly of this provincial and 'barbarian' type, and largely 'de-Italianized' (James 1999b: 21–3). From the soldiers it spread to their *commilito* the emperor himself, and so to the rest of the imperial service and outwards into the wider imperial elite.

Non-elite inter-polity connections, constituting more of a network directly interlinking provincial societies, may also have been much more influential in shaping Roman provincial civilization than is usually allowed, for example via direct inter-provincial contacts through movements of the 'lowly', such as traders, transport-workers, slaves, provincial military recruits and soldiers' families following the standards. These contacts may have resulted in the direct movement between provinces of artefacts, and the direct transmission of practices, beliefs and even entire mentalities which may have had little or nothing to do with 'Roman-ness' beyond being situated temporally and spatially within the ambit of imperial power. One material correlate reflecting such links is the new eastern Mediterranean technology of glass-blowing, which spread as far as London through imperial trade-routes, but was not especially Roman in any other sense. Provincial land transportation technology, especially vehicle designs and equestrian equipment such as saddles, was largely of Gallic and other 'barbarian' origin (Greene 1992: 104; Connolly and Van Driel-Murray 1991). The movement of many religious beliefs and practices, most famously the spread of Christianity, provides further examples of the potentially profound impact of non-elite, interprovincial cultural exchanges and changes shaping the Roman world.

Finally, and far from least, we must not underestimate the importance of very small-scale, short-range processes, for the lives of millions consisted primarily of the daily reproduction and development of local social relations with little or no reference to 'Rome'. For local life was not lived primarily in terms of a Roman : native political, cultural or ethnic dichotomy, but through long-established local frameworks of domination and differential access to resources through class/rank/status distinctions. At the quotidian level, it was perhaps mostly about gender relations, age sets, and religion.

Consequently, how far are changes such as the widespread appearance of *terra sigillata* on Gallic or British rural sites (Woolf 1998: 181–93), for example, about 'becoming Roman', about accepting or acquiescing, or even resisting or subverting Roman ideological hegemony? All these alternatives constitute action in terms of Rome and its culture; but what if some groups were ignoring 'Rome' or 'Roman-ness' as irrelevant? What if they were actively seizing opportunities presented by the unification of the Roman world, and the development of trade and industry, to appropriate new ceramics and other traits (which *we* regard as 'Roman') for entirely different cultural agendas and usages? These may have been about continuity and development of traditional local social relations, or creation of new ones. How meaningful would it then be to discuss this in terms of 'becoming Roman', or 'Romanization', or 'resistance'?

After all, it is now well established that the cultural meanings of artefacts are not fixed as implied by the notion of acculturation (i.e. a 'Roman' pot somehow 'contained Romanness', and its presence on a site can be used as testimony for 'Romanization'); their meanings are infinitely mutable and context-dependent. A contemporary example, from a radio report I recently heard on BBC Radio 4's *Correspondent* programme, makes this point well. After the USA attacked alleged terrorist bases in Afghanistan with cruise-missiles in August 1998, a BBC journalist attended an anti-American rally in Pakistan, where militant Moslems called for holy war and vengeance. American culture and values are clearly anathema to such groups, whose activities represent 'cultural resistance' in a very overt form. Afterwards, while interviewing the clerics who organized the demonstration, the reporter was offered Coca-Cola for refreshment. If some day archaeologists find the bottle or the can from which he was served, they might infer 'Americanization'. Yet in reality the symbolic cultural meaning of the drink was changed totally by its context; it was more important that it was a refreshing, non-alcoholic beverage than that it was a (supposedly) universal symbol of Americanness – a quality simply ignored in this specific context. Its offering was about *local* cultural traditions – Islamic dietary rules and the importance of hospitality – not wider cultural or political identities.

This has major implications for the interpretation of finds of *terra sigillata* vessels and those other portable objects which constitute the archaeological basis for discussion of the 'Romanization' of non-elite, especially rural populations. In the Roman provincial context, the presence of 'Roman' artefacts *may* indicate adoption of 'Romanness' by the user, especially if used in Roman ways; in the case of the elite, we often have enough contextual evidence to support this interpretation. But we do not know this for most of those outside the elite, and it is invalid to assume it. In southern Britain in the first century AD for example, an Atrebatic noble may have acquired *terra sigillata* vessels because they were used by Romans with whom he was increasingly seeking to identify himself – and perhaps also because they were fashionable among his peer-group and his Gallic kinsfolk; here, the contextual meaning of the pottery would indeed relate to 'becoming Roman'. However, the main symbolic meaning of similar vessels recovered from ordinary farmsteads nearby may have been that 'we serve beer in the same pots the local lord drinks wine from', perhaps representing emulation, or 'trickle down' Romanization; but equally it may reflect resistance to the establishment of class distinctions. Yet they may also represent an entirely local, plebeian tradition of peer-competition in hospitality, exploiting the increased accessibility of novel goods, rather than 'Romanness' in any sense whatsoever. (This is, in a way, the mirror of Terrenato's concept of Romanization as 'cultural bricolage': 1998b; here 'Roman' artefacts are co-opted and perhaps refunctionalized for entirely different, local purposes.)

To properly understand the evidence for the mosaic of local and regional social formations which made up the empire, and the true diversity of human experience within them, we need both to broaden our aims, and to sharpen the focus: broaden in the sense of expanding our view to include non-elites in the picture, as well as elites and the imperial regime; and sharpen in the sense of a finer resolution in the scale of research.

It is not new to suggest that we need better detailed treatments of specific regions, to comprehend local diversity and variation which represents cultural processes in action among small groups of people, detail rendered invisible by provincial-scale analysis (e.g. Haselgrove 1990: 46); Terrenato argues for the central importance of these (1998a: 94, 99, 114), and his Volaterrae work provides a fine example (this volume, Three cities; Terrenato 1998a). However, these must pay greater attention to the local life of non-elites at the site and locale level, and the dynamics of *all* interactions between elements of the social hierarchy. We must get away from the *prior* assumption of the existence, and overriding significance, of named ethnic units, or binary cultural oppositions (especially 'Roman : native'), or the centrality of elite life, as virtually the only determinants of cultural change. As Sîan Jones has argued through the example of a Romano-British regional study, we need instead to consider the evidence in local terms, as a test, and not simply an illustration, of such pre-determined categories and expectations (Jones 1997: 129–35). Since so much of the surviving archaeology, particularly from rural sites, relates to the daily domestic activities of subordinate groups, the potential exists to develop this truly bottom-up perspective on the Roman world. I anticipate that radically different models of cultural change will emerge from such local studies, particularly for the permanent frontier zones where many frontier communities interacted as much with those beyond the *limites* as with the interior of the empire. Our views of the 'core' provinces will probably also be radically modified by the shifted perspective.

Conclusion: characterizing cultural change in the Roman world

Much current work in Italy, Britain and elsewhere, has to a degree 'de-centred' metropolitan Roman civilization by incorporating native elites as actors in creating the Roman world. This constitutes a major conceptual advance, an exciting change bursting with new interpretative possibilities. Yet it remains an incomplete revolution. Even though diversity and local, indigenous continuity become ever-more apparent features of the provinces, those elements attesting convergence on a shared Roman elite culture and civilization – if no longer on a discredited Italocentric 'Platonic ideal' of Romanness – remain the dominant subject-matter. Still too concentrated on the traditional foci of public, state and aristocratic cultural correlates, most accounts tend to assume that the actions of social elites constitute the only real game in town; all else is secondary or peripheral. It seems that we, like many of our ancestors, are still grappling with the hegemony of the Roman imperial world view, which re-established itself over our own culture during the Renaissance, and remains dominant in most discourse on the Roman empire.

If we seek a truly holistic conception of cultural change in the Roman world, we must stop over-privileging the role of elites in our narratives to the exclusion of virtually all else; instead we must contextualize it as a part – a profoundly important one, but still only a part – of a wider picture, one which accounts not only for the convergence, but also the sustained diversity of life in the Roman provinces. We must explore the probability that much cultural change occurred for reasons unconnected with elite negotiation with Roman power, at local scales, and along dimensions of identity other than 'Romanness' and its reified 'native' opposites: it was shaped by traditional social hierarchies, gender and age distinctions, religious affiliations, etc.

In an effort to ensure the most comprehensive representation of society, it may be useful to consider the evidence for Roman provincial culture in terms of a hierarchy of interacting scales or perhaps *aspects* which, at least in Italy and the civil provinces (patterning in frontier regions may have been substantially different), may have consisted of:

- 'state culture', comprising the occasional imperial presence, and its permanent representative manifestations, in the provinces, such as imperial governors and office-holders, their retinues, actions, and any associated material culture, monuments and dedicated spaces, not least the military as an institution, and its installations (e.g. the Cripplegate fort in London).
- 'public culture', consisting of political and religious institutions at the provincial and *civitas* level, and the built environments to house them (e.g. imperial cult centres, city forum complexes). These were created across the provinces by the imperial regime

and the regional elites to express and manifest imperial hegemony. 'Public culture' tended to be highly homogeneous.
- 'elite culture', manifesting the convergent nature, values and life-styles of the privileged classes, through prestige artefacts, privately-owned but semi-public built spaces (town houses, villas), and associated display and behaviour. 'Elite culture' was also highly homogeneous, and self-consciously Graeco-Roman.
- 'mass culture(s)', reflecting much more regionally diverse popular traditions, especially outside urban contexts. This remained much more heterogeneous, with convergence long confined to limited areas, e.g. in adoption of small artefacts and other consumer goods ('industrially made' ceramics, glassware and metalwork), and even these may have been ascribed local meanings far more diverse than those attached to elite material culture. These meanings may often have had little or nothing to do with Roman, or Graeco-Roman, values or identities.

While we may be able to conceptualize some trends and processes of cultural change as 'Romanization', 'cultural bricolage', and indeed 'provincialization' or 'indigenization', as Woolf (this volume) argues, the development of the empire is far too complex usefully to characterize in terms of these, or even simple combinations of them. Given this complexity, is there still a place for the term, and concept, of 'Romanization'? Long establishment and widespread usage are insufficient reasons for retaining a term or paradigm, if it is seriously compromised. For example, the internationally-established cultural label 'Celtic' has been generally abandoned in British Iron Age archaeology for just such reasons (James 1999a).

Undoubtedly the empire did 'become Roman' at a broad level: as it became articulated by a shared, avowedly Roman public culture and consciously Graeco-Roman elite culture, which depended on the umbrella of Roman political and military power, this world was outwardly the *Roman* empire. No advocate of underlying 'imperial federalism' is going so far as to claim this was a Jeffersonian 'United City-States', a relatively egalitarian constitutional form which certain Hellenistic polities like the Aetolian league had approached (Walbank 1992: 152–4). The term 'Romanization' will continue to be useful in at least this broad, 'weak' sense.

In any case, despite the assaults on it, Romanization is so deep-rooted a paradigm that it is hard to envisage its displacement as the dominant discourse any time soon, and its various versions retain many powerful advocates, as is evident in this volume and elsewhere (including 'strong' Romanization, i.e. as deliberate policy: e.g. Hanson 1997). And as yet we have no fully-developed alternatives. Those who criticize it do not agree on what might replace it, and indeed may feel no need to do so; after all, it may simply be impossible to devise a model of cultural change in the Roman world at once simple enough to hold in mind and to discuss clearly, yet adequately reflecting the diversity of human experience in provincial societies. In any case, any particular terminology, while it defines concepts, clarifies and enables thought, also constrains thinking, and may render alternatives invisible and inaccessible – as, I would argue, 'Romanization' discourse often has. Consequently multiple paradigms and competing viewpoints, rather than any new orthodoxy, may provide the best potential for progress, as Terrenato suggests (this volume, Introduction).

Just as this is an exciting time in Italian archaeology, so it is the most dynamic episode in British Roman studies since Haverfield. As we approach the centenary of his successful establishment in Britain of the concept of Romanization (Haverfield 1906), new interactions with other traditions, not least current Italian work, bode well for research on the Roman world. Many archaeologists in Britain and Italy share much in common in their recent disciplinary history and in their shared situation in contemporary Europe, yet they also have differing experiences and perspectives to contribute; Britain, notably, as part of the 'Anglo-Saxon' academic world, has major developments in post-colonial and multi-cultural theory to offer. We are entering the twenty-first century with a stimulating range of theoretical positions to explore.

Acknowledgements

I would like to thank Simon Keay and Nicola Terrenato for inviting me to contribute to the volume, and also to apologize to them for the delay in finalising this paper. One important and very unfair advantage of submitting one's text late is the possibility of seeing others' contributions – notably those of Keay, Terrenato and Woolf – in time to incorporate responses and amendments, when they do not have the reciprocal opportunity. Simon Keay additionally provided invaluable feedback and critique on earlier drafts. Thanks also to Louise Revell for information.

Ancient sources

Acts of the Apostles
Caesar, *Commentaries* (*de Bello Gallico*)
Cassius Dio, *Roman History*
Diodorus Siculus, *History*
Strabo, *Geography*
Tacitus, *Agricola*
Tacitus, *Annals*
Tertullian, *de Pallio*
Velleius Paterculus, *Roman History*

References

Bevan, W. (ed.) 1999. *Northern Exposure: interpretative devolution and the Iron Ages in Britain*. Leicester Archaeology Monographs No. 4. Leicester.
Connolly, P. and Van Driel-Murray, C. 1991. The Roman Cavalry Saddle. *Britannia* 22: 33–50.
Creighton, J. 2000. *Coins and Power in late Iron Age Britain*. Cambridge.
Creighton, J. 2001. The Iron Age – Roman Transition, in James and Millett 2001, 4–11.
Crummy, P. 1997a. Colchester: The Stanway burials. *Current Archaeology* 159: 96–101.
Crummy, P. 1997b. *City of Victory: the story of Colchester–Britain's first Roman town*. Colchester.
Cunliffe, B. 1971. *Excavations at Fishbourne, 1961–1969*. London.
Cunliffe, B. 1991. *Iron Age Communities in Britain*. London and New York (3rd. edn).
Cunliffe, B. 1996. *Excavations at Fishbourne 1969–1988*. Chichester Excavations Vol. IX. Chichester.

Drinkwater, J. 1989. Patronage in Roman Gaul and the problem of the Bagaudae. In A. Wallace-Hadrill (ed.) *Patronage in Ancient Society*. London and New York, pp. 189–203.

Fincham, G., Harrison, G., Rodgers Holland, R. and Revell, L. (eds.) 2000. *TRAC 99. Proceedings of the Ninth Theoretical Roman Archaeology Conference*. Oxford.

Foster, J. 1986. *The Lexden Tumulus: a re-appraisal of an Iron Age burial from Colchester, Essex*. British Archaeological Reports No. 156. Oxford.

Freeman, P. 1997. Mommsen to Haverfield: the origins of studies of Romanization in late 19th-c. Britain. In D. Mattingly (ed.) *Dialogues in Roman Imperialism*. (Journal of Roman Archaeology Supplementary Series No. 23). Portsmouth R.I., pp. 27–50

Frere, S. S. 1987 *Britannia* (3rd edn.). London and New York.

Giddens, A. 1984. *The Constitution of Society*. Cambridge.

Greene, K. 1992. How was technology transferred in the western provinces? In M. Wood and F. Quieroga (eds.) *Current research on the Romanization of the western provinces*, British Archaeological Reports International Series 575, Oxford, pp. 101–5.

Gwilt, A. and Haselgrove, C. C. (eds.) 1997. *Reconstructing Iron Age societies*. Oxford.

Hanson, W. S. 1997. Forces of change and methods of control. In D. Mattingly (ed.) *Dialogues in Roman Imperialism*, Journal of Roman Archaeology Supplementary Series No. 23. Portsmouth R.I., pp. 67–80.

Haselgrove, C. C. 1990. Belgic Gaul: some archaeological perspectives. In T. Blagg, and M. Millett (eds.) *The Early Roman Empire in the West*. Oxford, pp. 45–71.

Haverfield, F. J, 1906. *The Romanization of Roman Britain* (reprinted from the *Proceedings of the British Academy*, vol. 2), London.

Henig, M. 1998. Togidubnus and the Roman liberation. *British Archaeology*, No. 37, September 1998: 8–9.

Hill, J. D. 1995. The Pre-Roman Iron Age in Britain and Ireland (ca. 800 B.C. to A.D. 100): An Overview. *Journal of World Prehistory* 9.1: 47–98.

Hill, J. D. 1997. The end of one kind of body and the begionning of another kind of body? Toilet instruments and "Romanization". In Gwilt and Haselgrove 1997, pp. 96–107.

Hingley, R. 1996. The "legacy" of Rome: the rise, decline and fall of the theory of Romanization. In J. Webster and N. Cooper (eds.) 1996. *Roman imperialism: post-colonial perspectives*. Leicester Archaeology Monographs 3, Leicester, pp. 35–48.

James, S. T. 1993a. *Exploring the World of the Celts,* London (= *The World of the Celts,* New York).

James, S. T. 1993b. How was it for you? Personal psychology and the perception of the past. *Archaeological Review from Cambridge* 12.2: 87–100.

James, S. T. 1998. Celts, politics and motivation in archaeology. *Antiquity* 72: 200–9.

James, S. T. 1999a. *The Atlantic Celts*, London and Madison.

James, S. T. 1999b. The community of the soldiers: a major identity and centre of power in the Roman empire. In P. Baker *et al.* 1999, pp. 14–25.

James, S. T. 2001. Soldiers and civilians: identity and interaction in Roman Britain. In James and Millett forthcoming.

James, S. T. and Millett, M. J. (eds.) 2001. *Britons and Romans: advancing an archaeological agenda*. York.

James, S. T., Rigby, V. 1997. *Britain and the Celtic Iron Age*. London.

Johnson, M. 1999. *Archaeological Theory: An Introduction*. Oxford and Malden.

Jones, S. 1997. *The Archaeology of Ethnicity: Constructing identities in the past and present*. London and New York

Millett, M. 1990. *The Romanization of Britain*. Cambridge.

Niblett, R. 1999. *Folly Lane*. (Britannia Monograph 14) London.

Porter, R. 1990. *English society in the eighteenth century*. London (rev. ed.).

Salway, P. 1981. *Roman Britain*. Oxford.

Taylor, J. 2001. Rural Society in Roman Britain. In James and Millett 2001, 46–59.

Terrenato, N. 1998a. *Tam firmum municipium*: the Romanization of *Volaterrae* and its cultural implications. *Journal of Roman Studies* 88: 94–114.

Terrenato, N. 1998b. The Romanization of Italy: global acculturation or cultural bricolage? In C. Forcey, J. Hawthorne, and R. Witcher (eds.) *TRAC 97: Proceedings of the Seventh Annual Theoretical Roman Archaeology Conference, Nottingham 1997*. Oxford, pp. 20–27.

Terrenato, N. 1998c. Fra tradizione e trend. L'ultimo ventennio (1975–1997). In M. Barbanera, *L'archeologia degli italiani*. Roma, pp. 175–192.

Thompson, E. P. 1978. Eighteenth century English society; class struggle without class? *Social History* 3: 135–6.

Torelli, M. 1982. Ascesa al Senato e rapporti con i territori d'origine. Italia: Regio VII (Etruria). In S. Panciera (ed.) *Epigrafia e ordine senatorio*. Edizioni di storia e letteratura: Rome, 4–5, pp. 275–299.

Walbank, F. 1992. *The Hellenistic World*. London (amended).

Whittaker, C. R. 1996. Where are the frontiers now? In D. L. Kennedy (ed.) *The Roman Army in the East*. (Journal of Roman Archaeology Supplementary Series No. 18), pp. 25–41

Woolf, G. 1993a. Rethinking the Oppida. *Oxford Journal of Archaeology* 12(2): 223–33.

Woolf, G. 1993b The Roman Peace. In J. Rich and G. Shipley (eds.) *War and Society in the Roman World*, 171–94. London.

Woolf, G. 1995. The formation of Roman provincial cultures. In J. Metzler, M. Millett, N. Roymans and J. Slofstra (eds.) *Integration in the Early Roman West. The role of Culture and Ideology*. Luxembourg, pp. 9–18.

Woolf, G. 1998. *Becoming Roman: the origins of provincial civilization in Gaul*. Cambridge.

Chapter 17

The Romanization of Diet in the Western Empire: Comparative archaeozoological studies

Anthony King

Mammal bones from excavations are the data source used in this paper to explore the notion of Romanization in the western parts of the Roman empire. A simple definition of Romanization is used here as a working hypothesis: that there was a dominant diet originating in Rome itself that was imposed on or taken up by provincial societies. An ancillary hypothesis is that agents of the Roman state, principally the army, also had dietary patterns that were imposed on or copied by the peoples of the provinces.

The comparative analysis of mammal bones from archaeological faunal assemblages has only developed significantly since the 1970s, and is therefore relatively new in terms of yielding useful results. Faunal assemblages can be used for inter-site comparisons (with the caveat that the counting methods in each sample have to be similar), and are capable of giving numerical results that can be used for statistical analysis. For the discussion that follows, the assemblages used are all counted in roughly the same way, using the number of species-identified fragments (including teeth) from the three major food species, cattle, sheep (and goats) and pigs. The sites used are also functionally similar, in that they are settlement zones, not ritual or burial sites. In general, bones from settlement zones are taphonomically the remains of food preparation and consumption, but more rarely can also be interpreted as the debris from craft or industrial production. Where possible, overtly industrial sites have not been included. Assemblage size is also important, since small assemblages (i.e. under c. 200/300 fragments identified to species) can be very variable and are usually discounted, unless they are from an uncommon site category or from a region with few animal bone reports.

In this way, it is possible to put together a sample for study that compares taphonomically similar groups of bones, in order to explore the extent of variation between the assemblages, on a regional, chronological and a site category basis. The samples are obtained primarily from bibliographic research, but also from unpublished reports and archives. For the purposes of this study, the regions used are in effect the larger provincial groupings, e.g. Gaul, Spain, North Africa, and the site categories are generalized divisions into urban, secondary urban (vici and small towns), military, villa and other rural sites. The basic working assumptions are (a) that the variation is caused primarily by differences in diet, (b) that the samples therefore reveal dietary changes over time, between regions and between site categories, (c) that social status affects dietary patterns by site category, and (d) that development of diet can be detected through diachronic changes in the assemblages, both regionally and by site category.

The data used for this paper is published elsewhere (King 1999a), and forms part of a research project on animal bone assemblages from the Roman empire. This paper concentrates on the regions of the western empire, in relation to the data from Italy.

Italy

A clear pattern exists in the data of very high pig percentages in western central Italy during the period late first century BC to third/fourth century AD (fig. 17.1). The area covered includes Etruria, Latium and Campania and such sites as Rome (Barker 1982), Ostia (IPU 1968–77), Pompeii (King n.d.; Jashemski 1979), Naples (King 1994), Settefinestre (King 1985) and Monte Gelato (King 1997). It was not always the case that western central Italy had a dietary pattern of this sort. Greek, Etruscan and other pre-Roman sites in Italy, including many from Etruria and Campania, tend to have significantly fewer pig bones, having more sheep/goat and cattle instead. Many display roughly equal percentages of the main food-providing domesticates, which in practice meant a meat diet that was more reliant on beef than other meats. The high pork pattern, therefore,

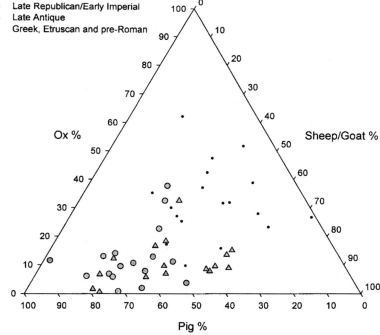

Figure 17.1: Italy, triangular graph showing relative percentages of cattle, sheep/goat and pig bones from assemblages in western/central Italy of late republican to late imperial date. Greek, Etruscan and pre-Roman assemblages from peninsular Italy are also shown. Data from King 1999a, Appendix, Table A

was a feature of the diet that emerged in the late Republic. The chronological parameters
are clearest in the Bay of Naples area (fig. 17.2), where prior to the first century BC, a
cattle-dominant pattern was in place, to be replaced in the imperial period by the high pig
pattern, and from the late Roman period, a sheep and goat-dominant pattern. It is likely,
from available data, that Latium saw the emergence of a pig-dominant pattern earlier
than Campania; in the third-second centuries BC.

If we turn to an individual site, an interesting differentiation can be seen at Settefinestre
villa, where intra-site analysis indicates that the higher status parts of the site had a higher
pig percentage than the zones interpreted as being occupied by lower status inhabitants,
such as the slaves (fig. 17.3; King 1988a: 52–53). This appears to show that pork,
particularly cuts of young pork and suckling pig, was considered to be a desirable and
high-status dietary element. Villas such as Settefinestre were production sites, supplying
the urban centres with pork and other meats, so that it is not surprising that a
correspondence can be seen between the producer and consumer sites in terms of
assemblage statistics. Rome, Ostia and the other towns tended to have pork-rich meat
diets, presumably as a result of cultural preference, and were able to obtain supplies from
the villas, which in turn were able to raise the animals in a fairly intensive manner (King
1985: 299). This is an idealized model, that presupposes a relatively perfect market
mechanism for satisfying demand, but nevertheless, appears to be appropriate for
interpreting this type of slowly-changing dietary pattern.

The pork-rich diet seems from the data presented above to be the dietary pattern that
was normal and desirable in the region around Rome itself. As such, it is the 'Roman'

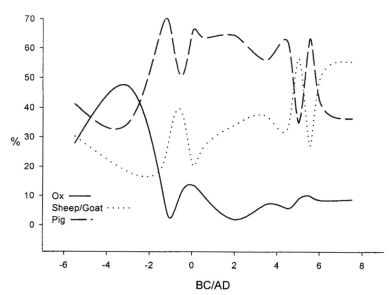

*Figure 17.2: Chronological graph of animal bone percentages from assemblages in the Bay of Naples area.
Data from King 1994, Tab. 51*

dietary pattern in the late republic and early to middle empire. The obvious question therefore arises; was this pattern exported as a 'Romanization' of the diet in other regions of the western provinces?

Spain

Spain has only recently started have faunal remains reported on regularly for Roman sites, and so the sample is not large (fig. 17.4). The sites include the towns of Munigua (Boessneck and Driesch 1980), Tarragona (Miró i Miró 1989), Tiermes (Miguel and Morales 1984), Celti (King 2000), and the villas of Vilauba (King 1988b) and Arellana (Mariezkurrena and Altuna 1994). Several of the sites are in Baetica, where it is possible to detect a trend of increasing pig percentages in the early imperial period, rising to 40% or more, before declining again in the late Roman period. However, it is important to note that we do not see the classic 'Roman' pattern being established, since cattle percentages are generally higher, for instance, and there are other smaller variations in the dietary pattern. Elsewhere in Spain, the evidence is not enough to suggest trends, but there does appear to be regional patterns within the peninsula. It seems best to suggest that local patterns persist that become modified as a result of the introduction of 'Roman' ideas of diet, but which are never entirely supplanted.

North Africa

There are, at present, very few assemblages from the North African provinces. Most date

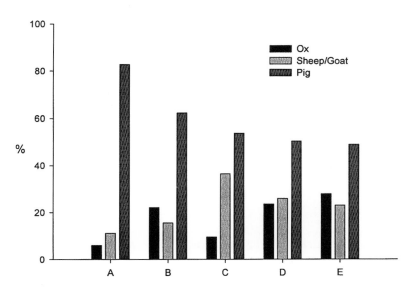

*Figure 17.3: Intra-site variation in the composition of the animal bone assemblage at Settefinestre villa, phase II (early imperial). A, central living area (*pars urbana*); B, entrance courtyard; C, turreted garden; D, granary; E, new slaves' quarters. Data from King 1985, fig. 187 and King 1988a, 53*

from the late Roman period or later (King 1990: 253), leaving only Cherchel (Clark 1993) and some of the Libyan Valley Survey sites (Clark 1986) to provide data pertinent to Romanization. The Libyan sites all present a markedly sheep/goat dominated pattern that in fact persists throughout the imperial period and into the Byzantine era (e.g. at Leptis Magna: Siracusano 1994). It seems likely that Romanization had little influence on a strong indigenous dietary culture, that was reinforced by environmental determinants acting against the extensive rearing of cattle and pigs.

In the Maghreb, Cherchel presents a different picture, with cattle bones predominant in the Juban to early imperial assemblage (phase 2: Clark 1993), followed by sheep/goat and pig. Pig, too, is much more common than on the Libyan sites. By the late Roman period, sheep and goats are dominant, pig almost as common, but cattle markedly less so, as noted on sites such as Cherchel, Sétif (King 1990) and Carthage (Reese 1977; 1981; Schwartz 1984). There are significant changes, therefore, but at a later period than might reasonably be expected to be the outcome of Romanization of the diet. More data are needed from sites dating to the late republic and early empire in order to pursue hypotheses concerning the Romanization of the diet in this region.

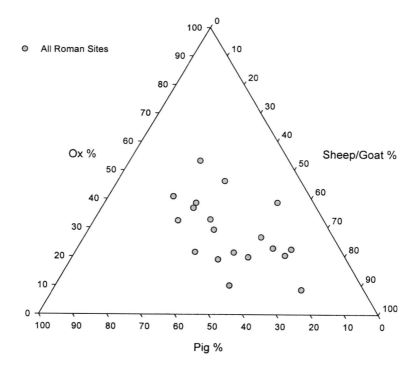

Figure 17.4: Spain, triangular graph showing relative percentages of cattle, sheep/goat and pig bones. Data from King 1999a, Appendix, Table B. See also King 2000, Fig. 6.3

Gallia Narbonensis

Another Mediterranean area of interest is the Provincia (Gallia Narbonensis), especially to the east of the river Rhône (fig. 17.5). Analyses from Massalia (Jourdan 1976) and other urban and rural sites (Leguilloux 1989; Columeau 1991; 1993) show a pattern of very high sheep and goat percentages. A strongly regional dietary pattern seems to be established here, which displays little of the 'Roman' pattern, and appears to refer back to local and Greek influences from the second half of the first millennium BC. It is interesting in this respect that Greek assemblages in the Aegean, of both the Roman period and earlier, are often sheep/goat dominant (Reese 1987; King 1999a: 184). Presumably, it is a process of Hellenization rather than Romanization that is paramount in the diet of this region, which appears to last right through the Roman period.

Not all the sites in Provence display the high sheep/goat pattern, however. An interesting exception to the main grouping is a series of urban assemblages with high pig percentages. They all come from Fréjus (Columeau 1991: 69–74) except for one group with pig bones as high as 82% from Aix-en-Provence (Leguilloux 1997). Both these towns were Roman colonies, and may well have had a significant population of Italian or

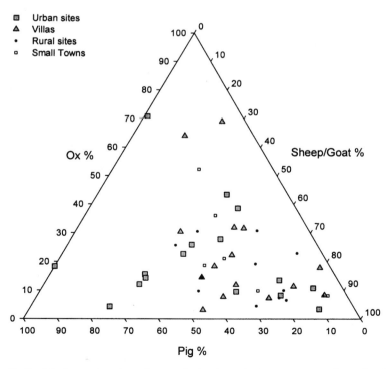

Figure 17.5: Gallia Narbonensis, triangular graph showing relative percentages of cattle, sheep/goat and pig bones. Data from King 1999a, Appendix, Table C; King 1984, Table 4B

Roman descent, especially in the case of the military base at Fréjus. This probably accounts for the 'Roman' pattern at these sites, very similar to the norm for western central Italy. Several Iron Age *oppida* and Roman-period rural sites also have a pattern with relatively high percentages of pig bones (only a little less than sheep/goat percentages), and a reasonable representation of cattle bones, too (Leguilloux 1989; Lepetz 1996: 122, 124). This is also a regional dietary pattern, not dissimilar to northern Italy and the rest of Gaul (Lepetz 1996: 124), which may represent those sites where the influence of Hellenization was less.

The Three Gauls and Germany

Further north, the situation is different again. In Gaul and Upper Germany, a pattern of high cattle and high pig percentages was prevalent, that can be traced back to the Middle-Late Iron Age (Meniel 1987; Lepetz 1996). Gaul had its own tradition of pig rearing and consumption, going back to the Iron Age, and referred to by ancient writers such as Strabo (4.4.3). The Three Gauls (fig. 17.6) tend to have relatively high percentages of pig bones, higher than in Provence but not at the very high levels seen in Italy. Aquitania

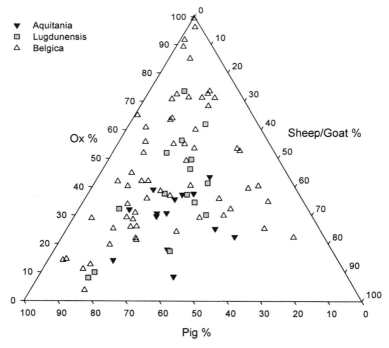

Figure 17.6: Three Gauls, triangular graph showing relative percentages of cattle, sheep/goat and pig bones. Data from King 1999a, Appendix, Table D; King 1984, Tables 4A-B; King forthcoming b, Table 1B

displays the largest average total of pig percentages in the three provinces. Towns are also significant in this respect, and it seems that urban communities had a meat diet of pork and beef, with relatively little dependence on mutton or goat meat. Lugdunensis tends to have a slightly higher percentage of cattle bones and fewer sheep/goat bones than Aquitania. Belgica also has a relatively high percentage of cattle, and indeed is notable for having a number of assemblages with 65% or more cattle bones, clearly indicating a beef-dominated meat diet. Germany, Raetia and Noricum (fig. 17.7) have generally the same pattern as the Three Gauls, forming with them a large zone north and west of the Alps that was beef and (to a lesser extent) pork dominated. However, beef was more common on sites in Germany, particularly in Germania Inferior and the lower Rhineland. In this area, there are many sites of all categories with 60% or more cattle bones. There seem to be strongly established regional characteristics, which at first sight display little 'Roman' influence.

However, some individual sites yield additional information of relevance. Dangstetten (Uerpmann 1977) and Zurzach (Morel 1994), two Augustan military establishments, have the high-pork 'Roman' pattern, probably as a result of the Italian origins of many of the troops on these sites. It is interesting that the contemporary vicus at Zurzach has

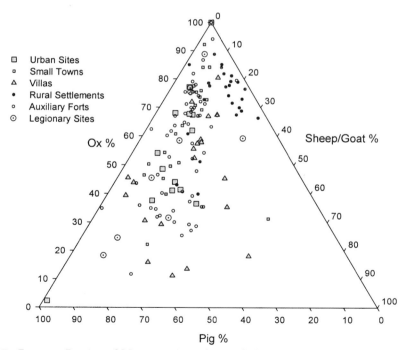

Figure 17.7: Germany, Raetia and Noricum, triangular graph showing relative percentages of cattle, sheep/ goat and pig bones. Data from King 1999a, Appendix, Table F; King 1984, Tables 3-4; King forthcoming b, Tables 1A-B

a different, more beef dominated diet, reflecting the different social composition of its inhabitants. In addition, the pig percentage at Zurzach fort declines over time to approach that of the vicus, apparently reflecting a convergence in the diet. Nijmegen also has an Augustan deposit with a 'Roman' style high pig pattern (Thijssen 1977), and a legionary canabae with higher percentages of cattle bones; but there are also many other deposits from the same period or just after from this site that have cattle as the most common species (Lauwerier 1988), so the picture here is not so clear-cut. There are also some villas with a high pig percentage, Dietikon (Fischer and Ebnöther 1995) and early-second century Bondorf (Kokabi *et al.* 1994), showing a clear preference for a pork-rich diet. Interestingly, Dangstetten, Zurzach, Dietikon and Bondorf are all in the south-west Germany and eastern Switzerland region, possibly indicating a sub-region that favoured high levels of pork consumption on higher status sites.

Britain

This region of the empire has many faunal remains assemblages (fig. 17.8). It is possible to show that the Gallic-German pattern, probably already established as the military dietary pattern (see below), became the standard for dietary change in the new province

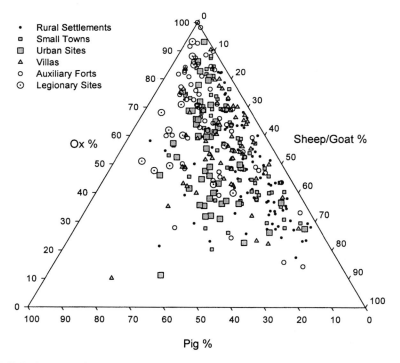

Figure 17.8: Britain, triangular graph showing relative percentages of cattle, sheep/goat and pig bones. Data from King 1999a, Appendix, Table E; King 1984, Tables 1-2.; King 1999b, Table 1C

(King 1978; 1984; forthcoming b). The indigenous dietary pattern in the Late Iron Age is largely one of high sheep percentages (Hambleton 1999). In the Roman period there is a change, evidenced by a gradient towards higher average cattle and pig percentages that goes in the sequence; rural settlements, villas, secondary urban centres, urban sites, military sites, legionary sites (King 1984: 189–90). This appears to show that the urban, military and legionary sites set a dietary pattern, presumably derived from Gaul and Germany, that was emulated by social groups seeking to become more Romanized. This was a process that achieved some success by the late Roman period, since the high cattle/high pig pattern eventually comes to dominate all site types by the late Roman period (King 1984: 193–4). However, there was always a residual dietary pattern that looked back to the pre-Roman high sheep assemblages. Many rural settlements (i.e. non-villas) retained this pattern to some degree, and it is interesting to note that in the post-Roman period, there was ultimately (but not immediately) a more general reversion to high sheep/goat percentages in bone assemblages (King 1978). In this respect, Romanization was not complete, and as in other provinces, regional patterns were able to retain a significant hold on the diet.

As in the case of Germany, there is an individual site that is worthy of mention: Fishbourne, a large and exceptional Mediterranean-style villa, which is one of the only

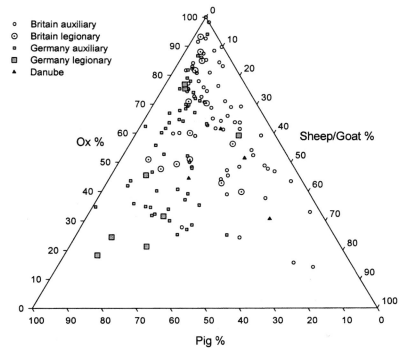

Figure 17.9: Military sites in Britain, Germany and Danube region: triangular graph showing relative percentages of cattle, sheep/goat and pig bones. Data from King 1999a, Appendix, Tables D-F; King 1984, Tables 1 and 3; King 1999b, Table1

British sites to display the high pig 'Roman' pattern (Grant 1971). This seems to indicate that the inhabitants of this imported villa-type emulated the dietary styles of the Mediterranean as well.

Military Diet

The influence of the army is an important element in any discussion of Romanization of the provinces. As far as diet is concerned, it seems clear that the classic 'Roman' pattern was the exception rather than the rule on military sites (fig. 17.9), and that the Gallic-German pattern was in fact the standard for a military style of diet (King 1984: 198; King 1999b). There is a good degree of conformity in the military dietary pattern, running across the provinces of Britain, Germany and Raetia. The meat diet was largely of beef, averaging 45–65% on most sites, but with an emphasis on pork consumption in the German establishments and on mutton consumption on British sites, particularly auxiliary forts and their vici. This demonstrates the residual component of pre-existing indigenous diet as a factor in military food supply. For the most part, however, the army, particularly the legions, would have been able to operate a command economy, and exercise dietary preferences without the constraints that applied to those living nearer to subsistence level. Legionary assemblages have higher percentages of pig bones than their auxiliary counterparts, presumably because pork consumption was regarded as being of higher status. Indeed, some Augustan legionary sites in Germany (see above) have a western central Italian style of assemblage, probably reflecting the geographical origin of the troops stationed there. The issues connected with the nature of military food supply are discussed in more detail in King (1999b).

Conclusion

When we consider the western provinces as a whole, the dominant characteristic is one of dietary regions that roughly correspond to provinces, but also to climatic and topographic zones (fig. 17.10). This is not to say that patterns were environmentally determined, however, since cultural processes also had an influence on these patterns. Cultural influence appears to take two forms; emanating from western-central Italy on the one hand, and from the army on the other. The 'Roman' high pig pattern of western central Italy was probably a high-status diet that brought about an elevation in pork (especially young pork) consumption. In some regions, such as southern Spain, perhaps parts of Gaul, and perhaps parts of Italy itself (although data are lacking), this was probably a significant influence, but in the north-west provinces only sites of strong Mediterranean orientation (singled out above) display the 'Roman' pattern.

The pork-rich 'Roman' diet was, in fact, an exceptional pattern within the Empire as a whole. It was a wealthy diet that probably relied on the flow of produce to Rome in the form of taxes and the *annona* for its existence. Basic foodstuffs were as likely to have been imported as home-produced, and were probably low in price because of the economic effect of the *annona*. This would have opened the way for the high pig percentage meat diet to have become not just a high-status preserve, but to have achieved widespread currency amongst the regional population as a whole. It was a diet that was difficult to export because the peculiar socio-economic circumstances of Rome and its hinterland were not reproduced elsewhere, except perhaps in microcosm at certain Roman colonies, such as Fréjus, and other high-status, highly 'Roman' sites.

The other form of cultural influence on the diet was a 'military' pattern originating in the army stationed north of the Alps during the first century AD, and reflecting the origins of the majority of troops in Germany, Gaul, northern Italy, northern Spain, etc. This pattern became the main dietary influence in provinces such as Britain, and was much more significant there than the 'Roman' pattern. Thus, for many regions of the western provinces we cannot refer to a common Italian origin for the Romanization of the diet. In Britain, for instance, it is preferable to refer to the 'Gallicization' or 'Germanization' of the diet, with the Roman army as the apparent catalyst for dietary change.

In terms of diet, therefore, the effect of the Italian core was very weak on the distant peripheral provinces. Regional patterns retained their strength, and cultural dietary influences also flowed between provinces that had significant personnel movement

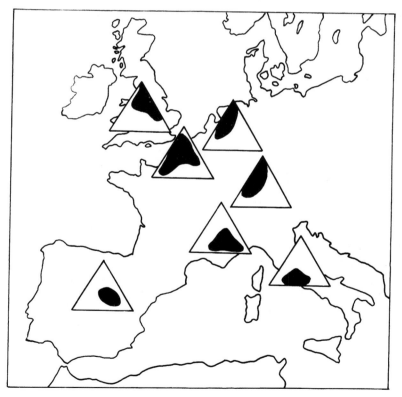

Figure 17.10: Western Europe and North Africa, showing summary triangular graphs for Roman imperial assemblages. The orientation and data for the graphs are the same as for Figs 17.1 and 4-9

between them. We cannot conclude that Romanization of diet was a uniform cultural process throughout the western provinces. Even if other aspects of culture became markedly Roman in style, regional identity within a loosely drawn Roman koiné seems to be the most appropriate way to characterize the diet of the western provinces.

References

Barker, G. 1982. The animal bones. In D. Whitehouse *et al.* The Schola Praeconum I: the coins, pottery, lamps and fauna. *Papers of the British School at Rome* 50: 81–91.

Boessneck, J. and Driesch, A. von den 1980. Knochenfunde aus dem römischen Munigus (Mulva), Sierra Morena. *Studien über die frühe Tierknochenfunde von der Iberischen Halbinsel* 7: 160–85.

Carandini, A. (ed.) 1985. *Settefinestre. Una Villa schiavistica nell'Etruria romana*. Panini: Modena.

Clark, G. 1986. ULVS XIV: archaeozoological evidence for stock-raising and stock-management in the pre-desert. *Libyan Studies* 17: 49–64.

Clark, G. 1993. The faunal remains. In N. Benseddik and T. Potter (eds.) *Fouilles du Forum de Cherchel 1977–1981* (Bull. Arch. Algérienne Supp. 6), Algiers, pp. 159–95.

Columeau, P. 1991. *L'Animal pour Homme. Recherches sur l'alimentation carnée dans le sud de la France du Néolithique au Moyen-Age d'après les vestiges osseux. I, le monde rural* (Travaux du Centre Camille Jullian 9), Aix.

Columeau, P. 1993. Le revitaillement en viande, la chasse et l'élevage sur les rives de l'étang de Berre. In P. Leveau and M. Provansal (eds.), *Archéologie et Environnment de la Sainte Victoire aux Alpilles*. Paris: CNRS, pp. 301–14.

Fischer, M. and Ebnöther, C. 1995. Tierknochen. In C. Ebnöther, *Der römische Gutshof in Dietikon* (Monog. Kantonsarch. Zürich), Zurich, pp. 254–63.

Hambleton, E. 1999. *Animal Husbandry Regimes in Iron Age Britain* (BAR 282), Oxford.

Grant, A. 1971. The Animal Bones. In B. Cunliffe (ed.) *Excavations at Fishbourne, 1961–9. Vol. II, the finds*. London, pp. 377–88.

IPU (Istituto di Paleontologia Umana) 1968–77. Reperti osteologici e malacologici. In A. Carandini, *et al.*, *Ostia I-IV* Studi Miscellanei 13, 122–4; pp. 16, 158; 21, 649–50; 23, 275, 393–4.

Jashemski, W. F. 1979. *The Gardens of Pompeii, Herculaneum and the Villas destroyed by Vesuvius*. New Rochelle.

Jourdan, L. 1976. *La Faune du Site gallo-romain et paléo-chrétien de la Bourse (Marseille)*. Paris.

King, A. C. 1978. A comparative survey of bone assemblages from Roman sites in Britain. *Bull. Inst. Archaeol. London* 15: 207–32.

King, A. C. 1984. Animal bones and the dietary identity of military and civilian groups in Roman Britain, Germany and Gaul. In T. Blagg and A. King (eds.) *Military and Civilian in Roman Britain*, British Archaeological Reports, pp. 187–217.

King, A. C. 1985. I resti animali; i mammiferi, i rettili e gli anfibi. In A. Carandini (ed.) *Settefinestre. Una villa schiavistica nell'Etruria romana*. Modena: Panini, III, pp. 278–300.

King, A. C. 1988a. Villas and animal bones. In K. Branigan and D. Miles (eds.) *The Economies of Romano-British Villas*, University of Sheffield, pp. 51–9.

King, A. C. 1988b. Estudi de les restes faunístiques. In A. Roure i Bonaventura *et al. La Villa Romana de Vilauba (Camós)*, Centre d'Investigacions Arqueològiques de Girona, pp. 95–6.

King, A. C. 1990. Animal bones. In E. Fentress (ed.) *Fouilles de Sétif 1977–1984* (Bull. Arch. Algérienne Supp. 5), Algiers, pp. 247–58.

King, A. C. 1994. Mammiferi. In P. Arthur (ed.) *Il Complesso Archeologico di Carminiello ai Mannesi, Napoli (scavi 1983–1984)*. Universita di Lecce, pp. 367–406.

King, A. C. 1997. Mammal, reptile and amphibian bones. In T. W. Potter and A. C. King (eds.) *Excavations at the Mola di Monte Gelato. A Roman and Medieval Settlement in South Etruria.* London: British School at Rome Archaeological Monograph 11, pp. 383–403.

King, A. C. 1999a. Diet in the Roman world: a regional inter-site comparison of the mammal bones. *Journal of Roman Archaeology* 12: 168–202.

King, A. C. 1999b. Animals and the Roman Army: the evidence of animal bones. In A. Goldsworthy and I. Haynes (eds.) *The Roman Army as a Community.* Portsmouth, RI: Journal of Roman Archaeology Suppl. 34, pp. 139–50.

King, A. C. 2000. The Animal Bones. In S. Keay *et al. Celti (Penaflor): the archaeology of a Hispano-Roman town in Baetica, Survey and Excavations 1987–1992.* Oxford: Univ. Southampton Dept. Archaeology Monog. 2, pp. 113–21, 235–40.

King, A. C. n.d. Mammal bones from the 'impianta elletrica' excavations at Pompeii, 1980–81. Unpublished bone report for P. Arthur, Naples. (Interim report on http://www.barnarch.u-net.com/pompeii.html

Kokabi, M., Amberger, G. and Wahl, J. 1994. Die Knochenfunde aus der Villa Rustica von Bondorf. In Gaubatz-Settler, A., *Die Villa Rustica von Bondorf.* Stuttgart, pp. 285–335.

Lauwerier, R. C. 1988. *Animals in Roman Times in the Dutch Eastern River Area* (Ned. Oudheden 12), Amersfoort.

Leguilloux, M. 1989. La faune des villae gallo-romaines dans le Var: aspects économiques et sociaux. *Revue Archéologique de Narbonnaise* 22: 311–22.

Leguilloux, M. 1997. A propos de la charcuterie en Gaule romaine: un exemple à Aix-en-Provence (ZAC Sextius-Mirabeau). *Gallia* 54: 239–59.

Lepetz, S. 1996. *L'Animal dans la Société gallo-romaine de la France du Nord* (Rev. Archéol. Picardie No Spécial 12), Amiens.

Mariezkurrena, K. and Altuna, J. 1994. Arqueozoologia de la villa romana del Alto de la Cárcel, Arellano (Navarra). *Trabajos de Arqueologia Navarra* 11: 109–25.

Méniel, P. 1987. *Chasse et Elevage chez les Gaulois.* Paris.

Miguel, J. de and Morales, A. 1984. Informe sobre los restos faunisticos recuperados en la excavacion de la Muralla de Tiermes. In J. L. Argente, *et al.* Tiermes II: campañas de 1979 y 1980. *Excavaciones Arquelogicas en España* 128: 292–309.

Miró i Miró, J. M. 1989. La fauna. In X. Dupré i Raventos, *et al. Un Abocador del Siglo V d.c. en el Fòrum Provincial de Tàrraco* (Memories d'Excavacio 2), Tarragona, pp. 403–14.

Morel, P. 1994. Die Tierknochenfunde aus dem Vicus und den Kastellen. In R. Hänggi *et al. Die frühen römischen Kastelle und der Kastell-Vicus von Tenedo Zurzach* (Veröff. Gesell. Pro Vindonissa 11), Brugg, pp. 395–410.

Reese, D. 1977. Faunal remains (osteological and marine forms) 1975–76. In J. Humphrey (ed.) *Excavations at Carthage 1976 conducted by the University of Michigan.* Ann Arbor, III, pp. 131–66.

Reese, D. 1981. Faunal remains from three cisterns (1977.1, 1977.2 and 1977.3). In J. Humphrey (ed.) *Excavations at Carthage 1977 conducted by the University of Michigan.* Ann Arbor. VI, pp. 191–258.

Reese, D. 1987. A bone assemblage from Corinth of the second century after Christ. *Hesperia* 56: 255–74.

Schwartz, J. H. 1984. The (primarily) mammalian fauna. In H. Hurst and S. Roskams (eds.) *The Avenue du President Habib Bourguiba, Salaambo: the site and finds other than pottery* (Excavations at Carthage: the British Mission, vol. 1,1), Sheffield, pp. 229–50.

Thijssen, J. R. 1977. Zoologica. In J. Bogaers and J. Haalebos (eds.) Opgravingen in de romeinse legioensvestingen te Nijmegen II. *Oudheidkundige Mededeelingen* 58: 73–157.

Uerpmann, H. 1977. Schlacterie-Technik und Fleischversorgung im römischen Militärlager von Dangstetten (Landkreis Waldshut). In *Festschrift Elisabeth Schmid* (Regio Basiliensis 18/1), Basel, pp. 261–72.

PART 3
DISCUSSION

Chapter 18

Vulgar Romanization and the Dominance of Elites

Susan E. Alcock

I admit that I have come to detest the word 'Romanization' – largely, no doubt, thanks to over-exposure to still ongoing debates about just what this means. For a long time these were healthy and helpful discussions – much bad baggage was thrown overboard and many problems newly appreciated in their full complexity (Freeman 1993; Mattingly 1997; Webster and Cooper 1996; Woolf 1992). But the danger today lies in how easy it is to fall into increasingly familiar paths of argumentation: just how much central authority does the term inevitably convey, do you capitalize the 'R' in Romanization, do we have to begin every article reviewing and defining what *we* mean by the term, lest others criticize or misunderstand? What this obsession too often prevents are other, fresher ways of talking about what happens to people when they engage in various forms of imperial interaction and the repercussions of empire. The quality of work on the material play of culture contact in other time periods and other parts of the world (e.g. Cusick 1998; Rogers 1990) reinforces my sense that to remain at a terminological or definitional level of discourse is not the way to encourage innovations in, or respect for, Roman archaeology.

By no means, however, does this book fall into that trap; it is no exercise in beating a dead horse. It is true that, working through these papers, readers may be struck by a very marked care with vocabulary. Definitions, redefinitions, critiques of definitions and counter-critiques abound, not least of 'Romanization' – that 'ugly and vulgar' term (in Ronald Syme's eyes at least, as quoted in Keay, this volume). Yet each essay advances or extends the discussion in some specific fashion, and the volume as a whole clearly tries to focus its attention on future directions, not past battles. In just the papers for this section, for example, we see authors paying more careful attention to particular regions, aiming to free them from the tyranny of text-based interpretations (Keay; Lopez and Soler); they employ and assess Terrenato's provocative model of elite negotiation and convergence in a non-Italian context (James); they explore the dissonance between choices in public display and more private, individual and family decision-making in the mortuary sphere (Fontana); they road-test a potential new paradigm of 'cultural revolution' (Woolf). All the authors are sensitive to language, and explicit about their intentions and goals, and the result is an impressively high-minded group of essays.

Perhaps the most unexceptionable *general* contribution made by the volume lies in its encouragement of comparative perspectives, notably by bringing Italy into discussions of imperial expansion and control. The peninsula's very status as 'heartland', as a supposedly undifferentiated 'core', long made it seem somewhat irrelevant to analyses of the provincial 'periphery'. Many of us thus comfortably assumed we could safely ignore Italy. That comfortable conceit is now exploded. Recent work, including the papers in this volume, reveals an Italian landscape as variable in treatment and in response to incorporation as any province, with the advantage – as Terrenato points out in his introduction – of possessing good textual accounts with which to monitor events and processes. This comparative exploration of Italy and the west is extremely stimulating (as the papers by James and Woolf particularly reveal, if in very different ways), and sustains an ongoing argument that studying different portions of the Roman empire side-by-side (and not necessarily in large, predictable blocks such as east versus west) should become a major research agenda for Roman archaeologists (see, for example, Alcock and Millett, in Alcock 1997).

Apart from encouraging comparative studies, where I believe this book makes perhaps its biggest and most original contribution is with its treatment of elites, particularly Terrenato's elite negotiation/convergence model (this volume; see also Terrenato 1998). I predict this model will prove influential in future, and hence requires some critical examination now. To summarize, Terrenato argues for the central and continuing role of local elites, for how negotiated relationships, largely positive, with their Roman equivalents shaped the course of regional or community incorporation, and for how a growing convergence of elite culture and values (both Roman and local) helps to explain the longevity of imperial hegemony. It is – in this framework – the elites who very much make things happen, who make things tick within the empire.

The elite negotiation/convergence model is both argued and critiqued within this volume. To a great extent, these criticisms prove more a matter of emphasis and nuance, rather than of outright rejection of the model as a whole. Several authors in the book (Curti, James, Williams) are concerned about the model's relative silence on the subject of violence or repression, when sometimes the Roman do send in the Marines! If one isn't careful, rather overly cheerful scenarios can be envisioned, with elites doing deals with their Roman peers and doing good to the less fortunate below. Room must be allowed either for areas where the model doesn't work (as explored by James, this volume, in northern Britain) or for greater tension among the supposedly more or less passive, neutral underclass. Curti (this volume) remarks that recent scholarly emphasis on 'negotiation, debate and cultural interaction' is something of a sanitization of the past, a politically correct scholarly response to the pressures of our age. I actually worry more that such conceptions may, in the wrong hands, be employed as highly justificatory, highly conservative, and highly elitist formulations: with the Romans now acquiring their empire in fit of absent-minded amiability.

This leads directly to another principal, and closely related, concern – the deliberate emphasis on elite behavior and decision-making, inevitably at the expense of the *hoi polloi*, the less empowered of society. To a certain extent, this has been a general trend in recent literature on Romanization, for example in Greg Woolf's excellent work. Close attention and great stress is laid on issues such as rhetorical education, literary styles, elite culture and bodily practice, and so on: all building to the notion of a 'Roman cultural revolution' (1999; this volume).

Such emphases and investigations are completely justified, but surely they must also be recognized as providing only a portion of the total picture. Woolf remarks: 'Certainly the main actors in the processes discussed... were all members of various elites, but these elites made use of their social power to construct the physical and imaginative environments within which other Gallo-Romans were compelled to live' (p. 179). On one level, it is difficult to quarrel with that statement. On another, it may be begging, or bypassing, other ways of seeing. Interest in elite responses and adaptation to Rome, and how they use such relations to maintain their social position, is quite different from interest in how *all* people within a region, or within a community, reacted to and were transformed by the direct or indirect interventions of Rome. James too is concerned about this potential occlusion of the non-elite, addressing it squarely and, in my opinion, rightly:

> ... The recent incorporation of provincial elites as active agents in the creation of the Roman world... does not *remove* the boundary between the active and powerful and the supposedly passively-receptive dominated; it simply moves it, from the interface between the Roman empire and 'native' societies, to the divide between the culturally convergent provincial elites and the mass of the provincial population... (this volume, p. 202).

The question thus becomes how best to trace the reactions and attitudes of those provincial masses. Or, to put it another way, perhaps we have to think more carefully about just who is 'becoming Roman' and just how we can tell. The silence of the silent majority, of the non-elite, cannot be confused with either their consent, or their unimportance.

Again, these comments are intended as more a matter of nuancing than rejecting the overall model. It would be impossible to deny that local elites – their activities, their priorities – were the imperial fulcrum, the point around which so much else of the dance of empire revolved. It would be foolish to advocate neglect of this group as we move forward in the study of local processes within imperial systems. In fact, we should probably bend still more attention to 'getting inside' this particular body. Often we refer to 'the elite' or 'the local elite' – and leave it at that. As archaeologists, we too seldom confront how such elites are created or altered over time, their private versus public presentation, their gender distinctions (issues touched on here by Fontana and Benelli). The possibility of internal factions must also be allowed: surely 'the elite' was rarely a unified force. The archaeology of factions and factional competition has been explored in the New World; it is a promising category for analysis for Roman archaeologists to consider (Brumfiel and Fox 1994).

Finally, we must extend a point touched on by Terrenato in his introduction. He notes the astonishing variety of responses to Romanization observed across ethnic groups, social classes, gender differences and 'within the same person in different conjunctures of his or her life' (p. 1). In recent work on cultural identity and social memory in the Roman east, it has been argued that the new political and social order in which the Greeks found themselves – with new tensions between imperial, regional and local loyalties – led to greater mobility in individual identities and attitudes (Alcock, in press; cf. Smith 1998; Woolf 1994). People could 'shift' in self-perception and self-representation, depending on their specific contingent need and social context. Surely western elites would similarly follow such a polyphonic course, leaving 'elite behavior' an actually rather open-ended and fluid category. This is not, of course, the place to expand on these arguments in detail. The essential point is that we cannot allow 'elites' to become our new silver bullets, our new quick-fix panacea for all our provincial questions; nor can we leave 'elite' as a kind of uninvestigated, unquestioned, automatic category. That is not, of course, what is happening in this volume, which explores new territory and suggests new approaches in a provocative and useful fashion. As we all know, however, it is what people *do* with what we write that must above all be feared. Forewarned is forearmed, as we think about our next steps in studying vulgar Romanization.

References

Alcock, S. E. (ed.) 1997. *The Early Roman Empire in the East*. Oxbow: Oxford.

Alcock, S. E. (in press). The reconfiguration of memory in the eastern Roman empire. In S. E. Alcock, T. D'Altroy, K. Morrison and C. Sinopoli, (eds.), *Empires: Perspectives from Archaeology and History*. CUP: Cambridge.

Brumfiel, E. and J. W. Fox. (eds.) 1994. *Factional Competition and Political Development in the New World*. CUP: Cambridge.

Cusick, J. G. (ed.) 1998. *Studies in Culture Contact: Interaction, Culture Change, and Archaeology* (Occasional Paper No. 25, Center for Archaeological Investigations).Carbondale: Illinois.

Freeman, P. 1993. 'Romanization' and Roman material culture. *Journal of Roman Archaeology* 6: 438–45.

Mattingly, D. (ed.) 1997. *Dialogues in Roman Imperialism: Power, Discourse and Discrepant Experience* JRA: Portsmouth, R.I.

Rogers, D. 1990. *Objects of Change: The Archaeology and History of Arikara Contact with Europeans*. Washington, D.C.

Smith, R. R. R. 1998. Cultural choice and political identity in honorific portrait statues in the Greek east in the second century A.D. *Journal of Roman Studies* 88: 56–93.

Terrenato, N. 1998. *Tam firmum municipium*: the Romanization of Volaterrae and its cultural implications. *Journal of Roman Studies* 88: 94–114.

Webster, J. and N. Cooper (eds.) 1996. *Roman Imperialism: Post-Colonial Perspectives* (Leicester Archaeology Monographs No. 3). Leicester: University of Leicester Press.

Woolf, G. 1992. The unity and diversity of Romanization. *Journal of Roman Archaeology* 5: 349–52.

Woolf, G. 1994. Becoming Roman, staying Greek: culture, identity and the civilizing process in the Roman east. *Proceedings of the Cambridge Philosophical Society* 40: 116–43.

Woolf, G. 1999. *Becoming Roman: The Origins of Provincial Civilization in Gaul*. CUP: Cambridge.

Chapter 19

Reflections on a one day conference "Italy and the West: Comparative Issues in Romanization"

Jean Andreau

A debate on the central theme of this book was organized at the École des Hautes Études en Sciences Sociales in Paris on the 29th May 2000 by Jean Andreau (EHESS), Claudia Moatti (Université de Paris 8, Institut Universitaire de France) and Jean-Pierre Vallat (Université de Paris 13). It began with two presentations by S. Keay and N. Terrenato, who outlined the objectives of their book and the main ideas that it puts forward. This was followed by interventions on different aspects of the book by a number of historians and archaeologists. Two of them were not specialists in antiquity and thus introduced a comparative dimension into the discussion: S. Gruzinski (EHESS) for the history of Latin America down to the present-day, and B. Lelouche (Université de Paris 8) as a specialist in the Medieval Ottoman Empire. If we are to understand the logic of this book and this debate, we should begin with the notion of *romanitas*? What does it mean to be Roman? This is not easy to answer, particularly for the Republican period, since from its origins, the unity represented by Rome was composed of several cultural strands and, in terms of modes of thought and ways of life, underwent major transformations (J. -M. David). There was no single Roman unity that was perpetuated through the centuries unchanged. It is perhaps slightly better to define a model of 'romanness' for the imperial period (P. Le Roux), although it should not be forgotten that if 'Romanization' did exist, then it first prevailed upon Italy, whose relative unity was the end result of long processes of evolution. One of the original contributions of this book has been to study the Romanization of Italy and the western provinces together.

The contributors to the debate shared the feeling of the editors of the book that the word Romanization should not be completely abandoned. However, when it is used, its scope and meaning should be properly defined. By comparison, through explaining the different meanings of the word "Ottomanisation", B. Lelouch has shown the complexity of Romanization. The resistance studied by M. Bénabou in north Africa is another interesting avenue of research to pursue, since it allows us to appreciate what N. Wachtel has called the "vision of the conquered"; it suggests that we should lend more attention to the evidence of autochthonous communities. Unfortunately, this kind of information is not very abundant for the Roman period. However, archaeology does enrich it considerably while at the same time providing very striking examples of Romanization: we can cite the evolution of construction techniques, of habitats, monuments to the dead, etc. (O. Buschenschutz, A. -M. Adam). Native cultures are, of course, manifold as the book makes clear, particularly in the case of Sardinia presented by P. Van Dommelen: here Punic influences themselves became an expression of native communities.

The dating difficulties that confront the archaeologist sometimes make the problem more complex, above all if they do not allow the conclusions derived from available evidence to conform to ancient texts, or the interpretation which is often ascribed to them. O. de Cazanove showed that in southern Italy, certain structures and developments are dated to either the late 4th, the 3rd or even the 2nd centuries BC, something that clearly transforms the significance, notably in terms of "Romanization", of influences of natives, Greeks or Romans. There is a kind of logic in the archaeological evidence that is not shared by either texts or inscriptions. One must follow the logic of the material that one studies as far as possible. However, a rapprochement between different kinds of data is absolutely indispensable, provided that it does not happen too early in the process of analysis; indeed, it can be left until very late, provided it does take place!

"Romanization" is used in a double sense; there is also the influence of the vanquished on their conquerors; that is another one of the important ideas running through the book. However, we must not forget that Romanization is an expression of domination. Both parties were not equal partners. One must be careful to avoid an excessively consensual and idyllic vision of the conquest. Its evolution and chronology varies from one region to the next. Should we limit ourselves to the west? Can this traditional divide between east and west be justified? This is the question that S. Alcock has rightly posed. The evolution also changes from one region to the next. Linguistic Romanization is not the same as that of law, construction techniques, diet or municipal institutions (which probably happened more rapidly than the others). These diverse sectors need to be considered separately and their chronologies should be addressed. The army is a powerful agent of Romanization, cultural métissage, as well as of social promotion (M. Christol). Slavery and emancipation constituted another tool of Romanization, and their effects were probably quicker and more profound than those influences prevailing upon native communities. Unfortunately, the book has neglected to deal with these issues.

One is led to distinguish between the centre (Rome, and later Italy) and the periphery, or peripheries. For North Africa, above all the Mauretanias, R. Rebuffat has suggested that three zones should be distinguished: the civic zone, which was already urbanised and settled before the Roman conquest; the zone of the *gentes* (whose chiefs are romanized); the remainder, composed of unromanized peoples. The first two of these three zones probably corresponded to the two types of countryside that Ph. Leveau distnguished in the territory of Caesaraea. It must be emphasised that, following the authors in this book, Romanization more frequently begins before the conquest.

The book places a lot of emphasis upon the role of indigenous elites in the cultural metissage, and it was often an issue during the debate. S. Gruzinski spoke of the situations in colonial and post-colonial Latin America, to which Spain hardly sent a single soldier, and where domination was only possible through negotiation with the elites. The idea of negotiation with the elites is very suggestive for the Roman world, if one uses the word "negotiation" in its broader sense and if one remembers that Rome had legions at its disposal and did not hesitate to use them, even if this varied from one period to another, and from one region to the next. Moreover, were these elites the same throughout the Empire and through time? Certain texts (for example, Apuleius or Dion of Prusa) suggest that, in spite of their power and wealth, they were often subject to strong social control by their dependant populations.

This day of discussion was ample testimony to the richness and originality of this book, which makes us think again about what is conventionally labelled as "Romanization".